SEVEN SEAS ENTERTAINMENT PRESENTS

story and art by MINTAROU

TRANSLATION
Elina Ishikawa

ADAPTATION
Betsy Aoki

LETTERING AND RETOUCH
Ray Steeves

COVER DESIGN
Nicky Lim

PROOFREADER
Shanti Whitesides
Holly Kolodziejczak

ASSISTANT EDITOR
Jenn Grunigen

PRODUCTION ASSISTANT
CK Russell

PRODUCTION MANAGER
Lissa Pattillo

EDITOR-IN-CHIEF
Adam Arnold

PUBLISHER
Jason DeAngelis

DNA WA OSHIETE KURENAI VOL. 1
© Mintarou 2016
All rights reserved.
First published in Japan in 2016 by Kodansha Ltd., Tokyo.
Publication rights for this English edition arranged through Kodansha Ltd., Tokyo.

Seven Seas books may be purchased in bulk for promotional, educational, or business use. Please contact your local bookseller or the Macmillan Corporate and Premium Sales Department at 1-800-221-7945, extension 5442, or by e-mail at MacmillanSpecialMarkets@macmillan.com.

Seven Seas and the Seven Seas logo are trademarks of Seven Seas Entertainment, LLC. All rights reserved.

ISBN: 978-1-626927-61-2

Printed in Canada

First Printing: March 2018

10 9 8 7 6 5 4 3 2 1

FOLLOW US ONLINE: *www.sevenseasentertainment.com*

READING DIRECTIONS

This book reads from *right to left*, Japanese style. If this is your first time reading manga, you start reading from the top right panel on each page and take it from there. If you get lost, just follow the numbered diagram here. It may seem backwards at first, but you'll get the hang of it! Have fun!!

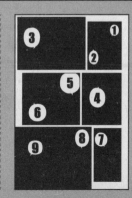

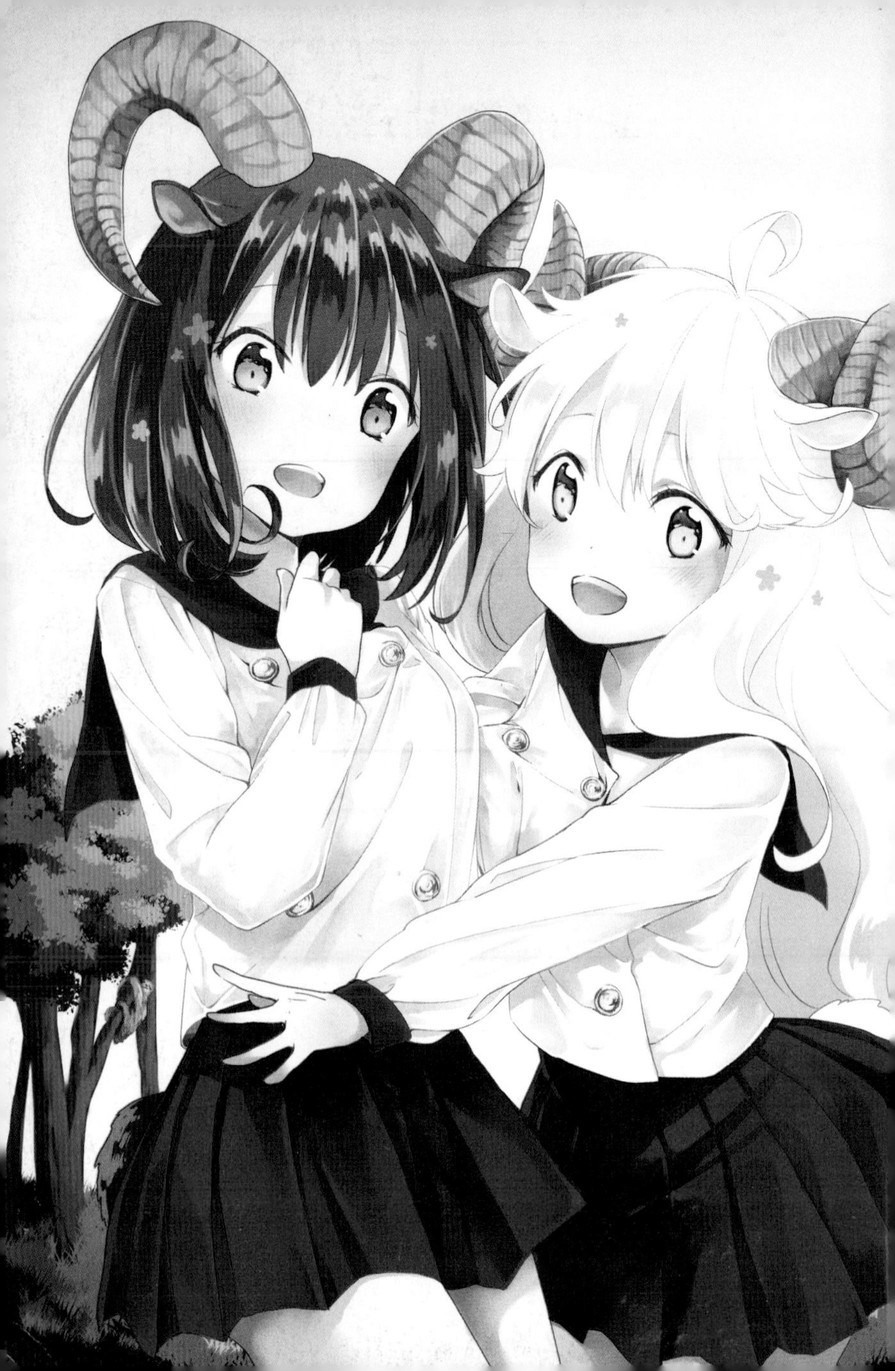

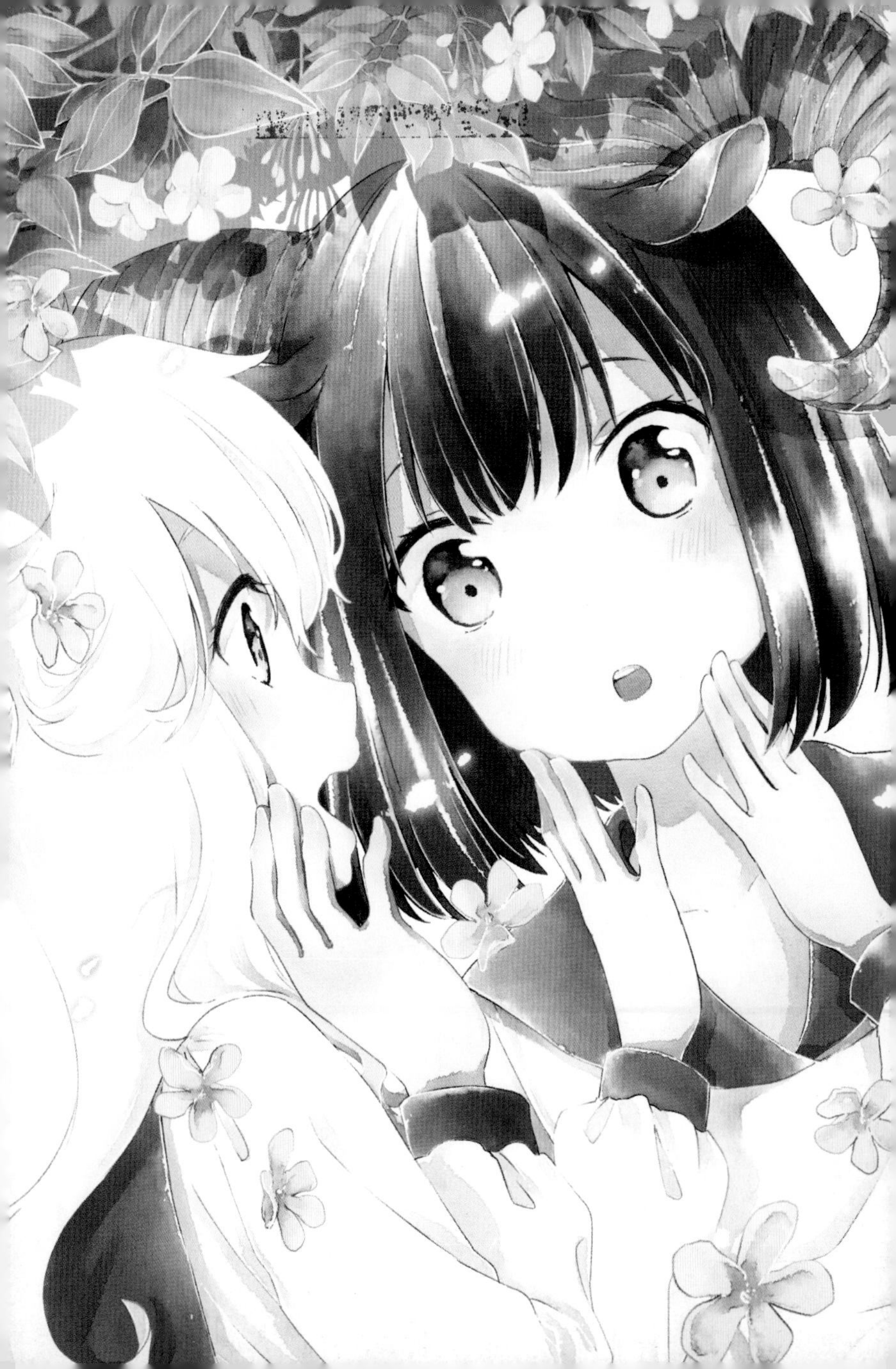

MAY 2018

DNA Doesn't Tell Us

VOL. 1

Bighorn Sheep

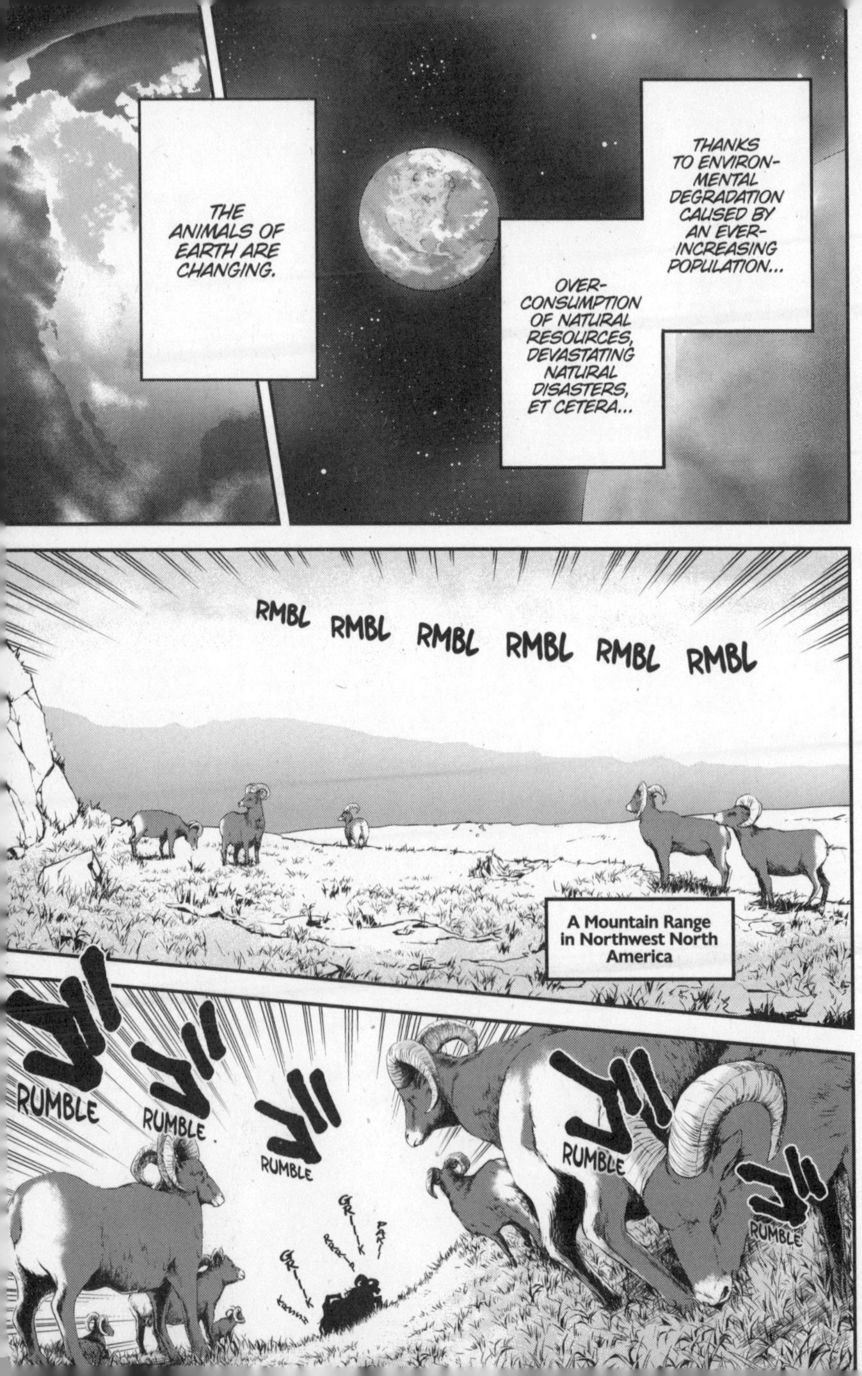
THANKS TO ENVIRON-MENTAL DEGRADATION CAUSED BY AN EVER-INCREASING POPULATION...
OVER-CONSUMPTION OF NATURAL RESOURCES, DEVASTATING NATURAL DISASTERS, ET CETERA...
THE ANIMALS OF EARTH ARE CHANGING.
RMBL RMBL RMBL RMBL RMBL RMBL
A Mountain Range in Northwest North America
RUMBLE
RUMBLE
RUMBLE
RUMBLE
RUMBLE

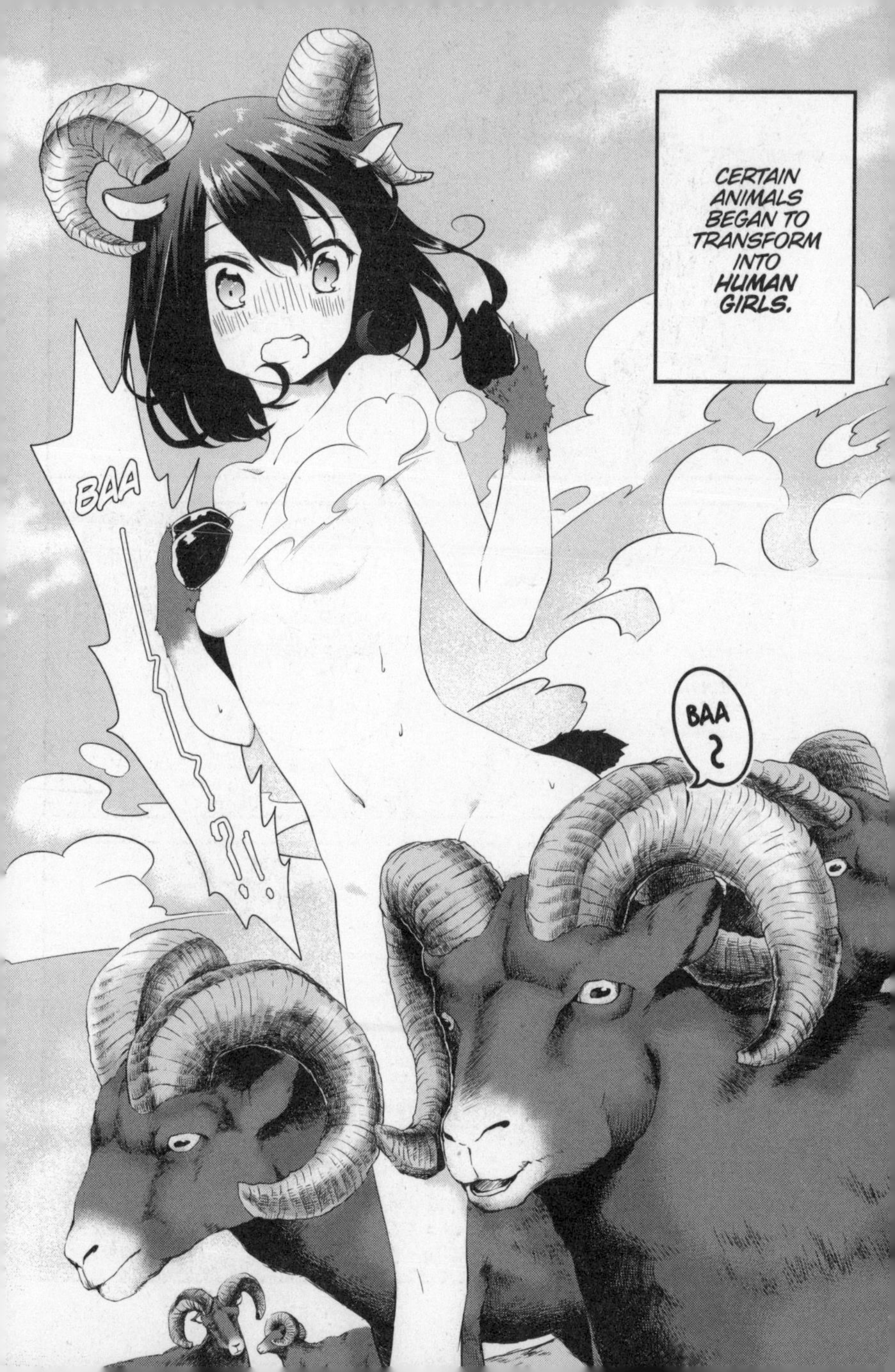
CERTAIN ANIMALS BEGAN TO TRANSFORM INTO HUMAN GIRLS.
BAA
?!!
BAA~

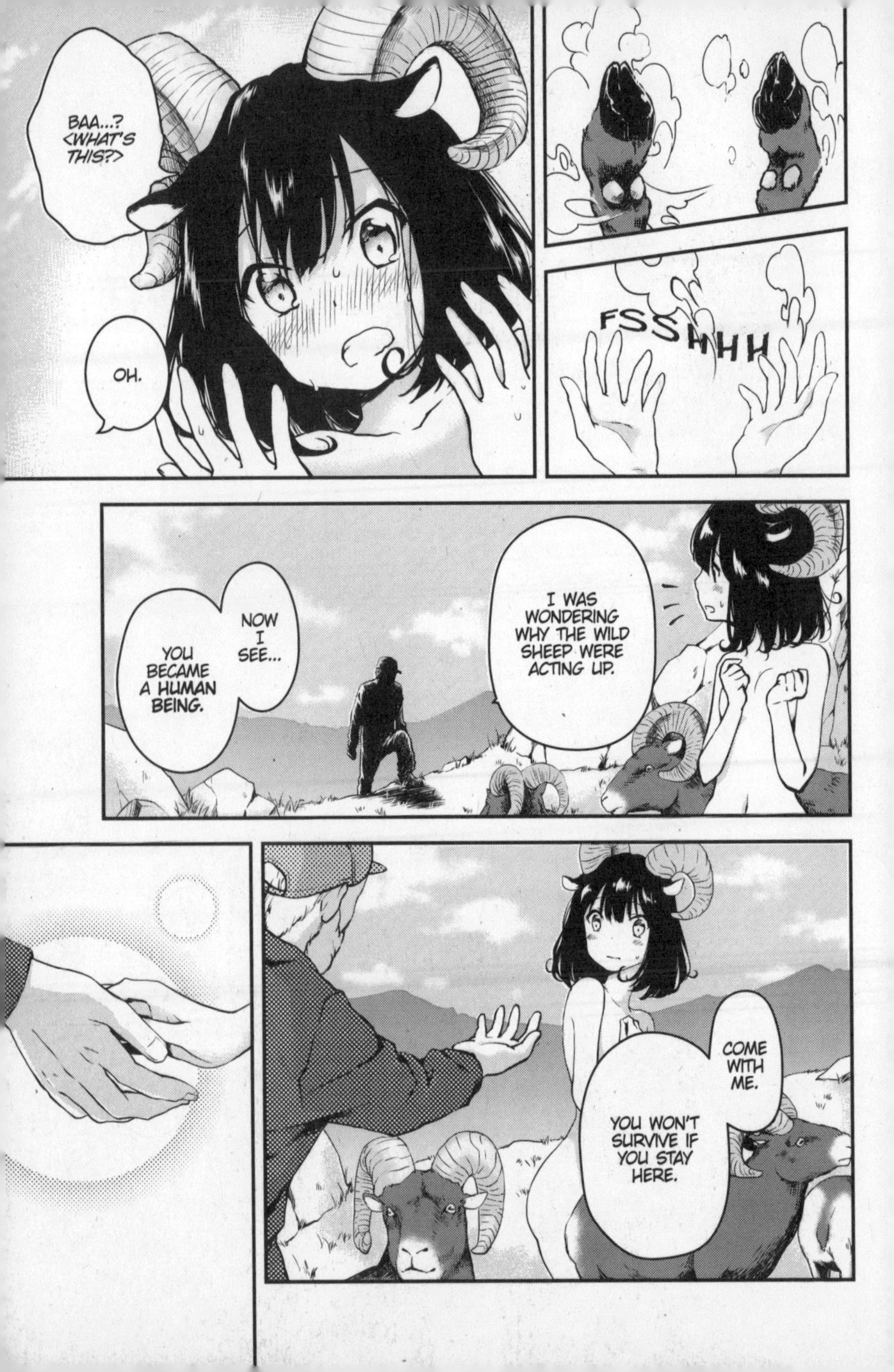
FSSHHH
BAA...? <WHAT'S THIS?>
OH.
I WAS WONDERING WHY THE WILD SHEEP WERE ACTING UP.
NOW I SEE...
YOU BECAME A HUMAN BEING.
COME WITH ME.
YOU WON'T SURVIVE IF YOU STAY HERE.

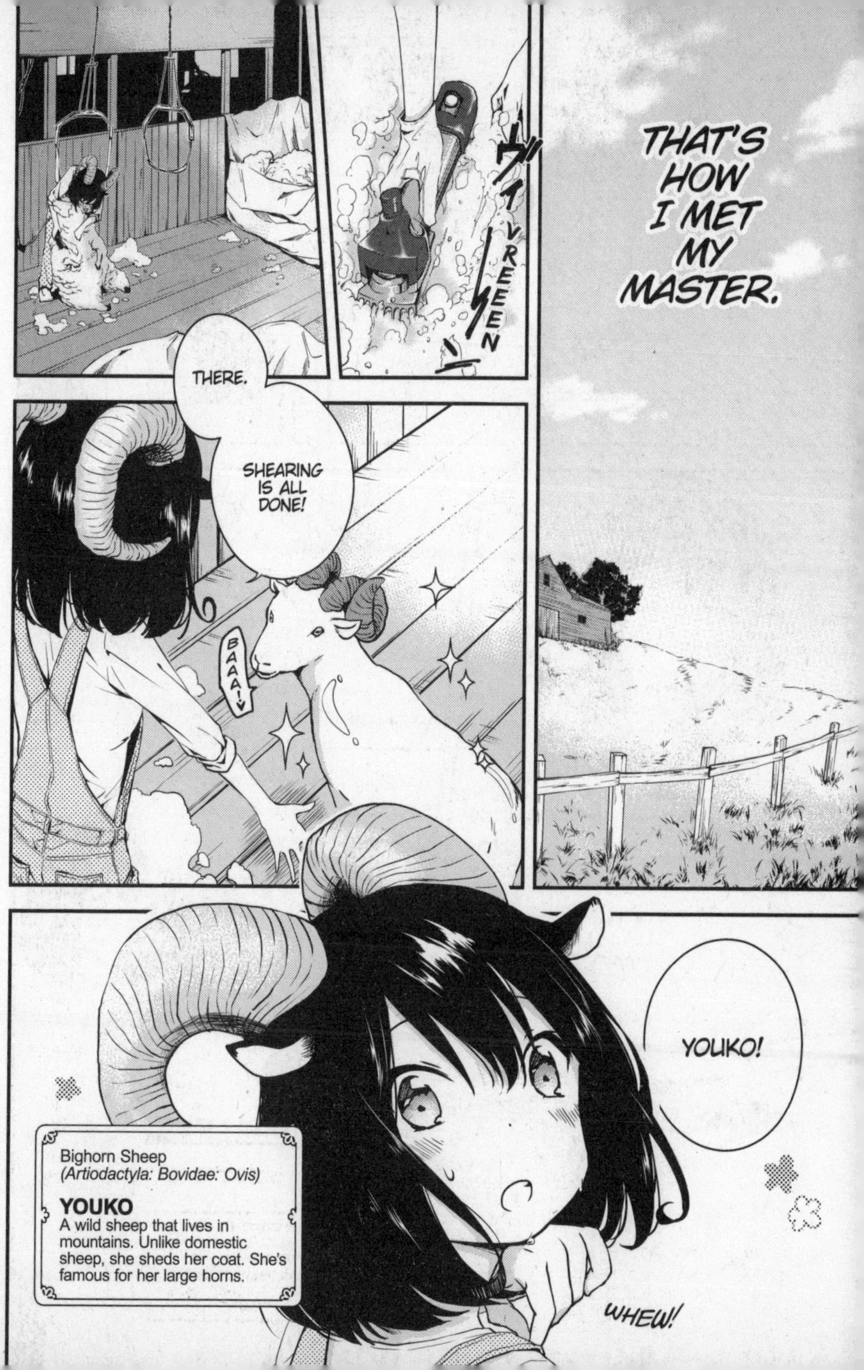
THAT'S HOW I MET MY MASTER.
VREEEN
THERE.
SHEARING IS ALL DONE!
BAAA!♥
YOUKO!
Bighorn Sheep
(Artiodactyla: Bovidae: Ovis)
YOUKO
A wild sheep that lives in mountains. Unlike domestic sheep, she sheds her coat. She's famous for her large horns.
WHEW!

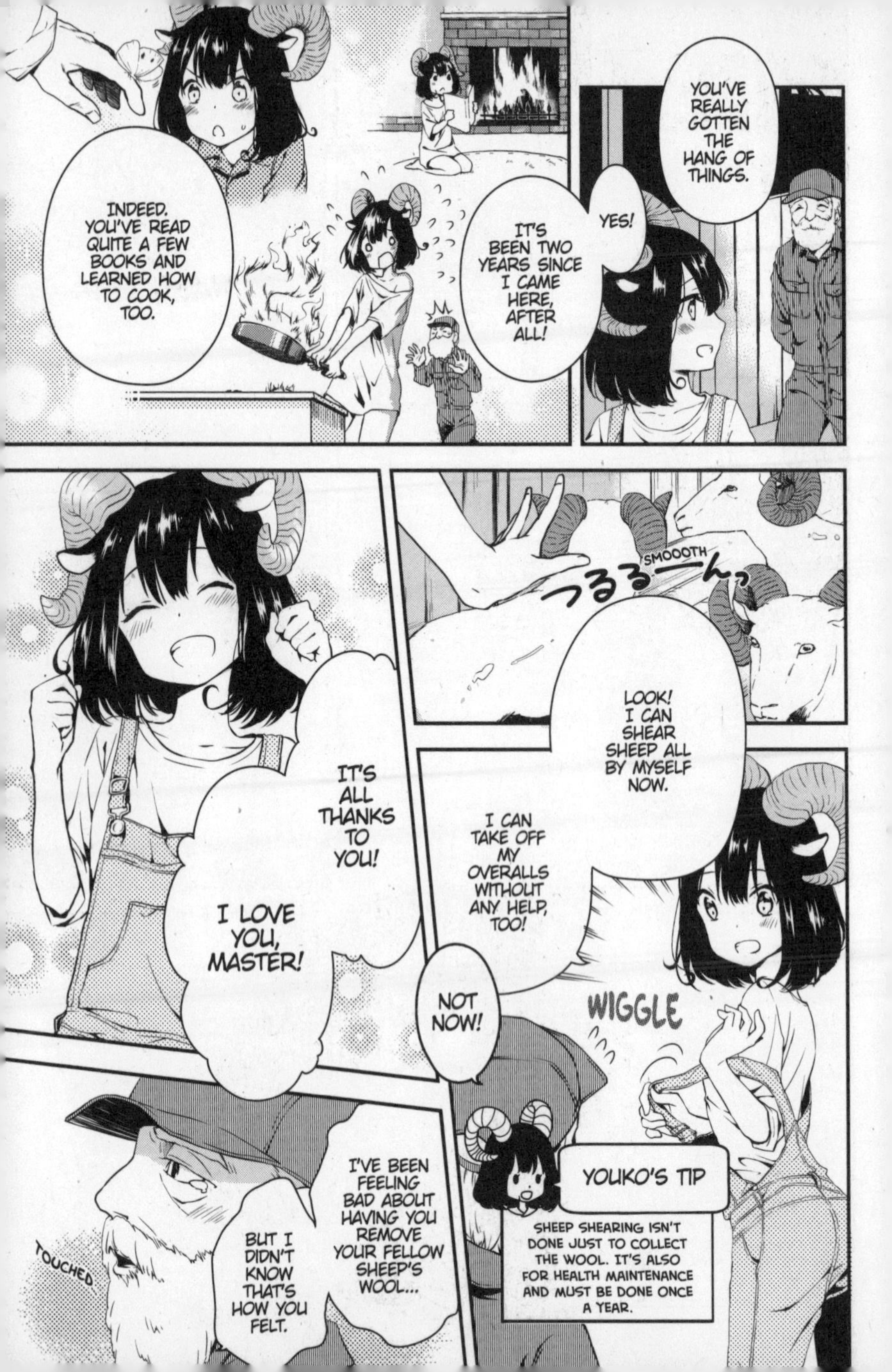

YOU'VE REALLY GOTTEN THE HANG OF THINGS.
YES!
IT'S BEEN TWO YEARS SINCE I CAME HERE, AFTER ALL!
INDEED. YOU'VE READ QUITE A FEW BOOKS AND LEARNED HOW TO COOK, TOO.
SMOOOTH
つるるーんっ
LOOK! I CAN SHEAR SHEEP ALL BY MYSELF NOW.
I CAN TAKE OFF MY OVERALLS WITHOUT ANY HELP, TOO!
WIGGLE
NOT NOW!
YOUKO'S TIP
SHEEP SHEARING ISN'T DONE JUST TO COLLECT THE WOOL. IT'S ALSO FOR HEALTH MAINTENANCE AND MUST BE DONE ONCE A YEAR.
IT'S ALL THANKS TO YOU!
I LOVE YOU, MASTER!
I'VE BEEN FEELING BAD ABOUT HAVING YOU REMOVE YOUR FELLOW SHEEP'S WOOL...
BUT I DIDN'T KNOW THAT'S HOW YOU FELT.
TOUCHED.

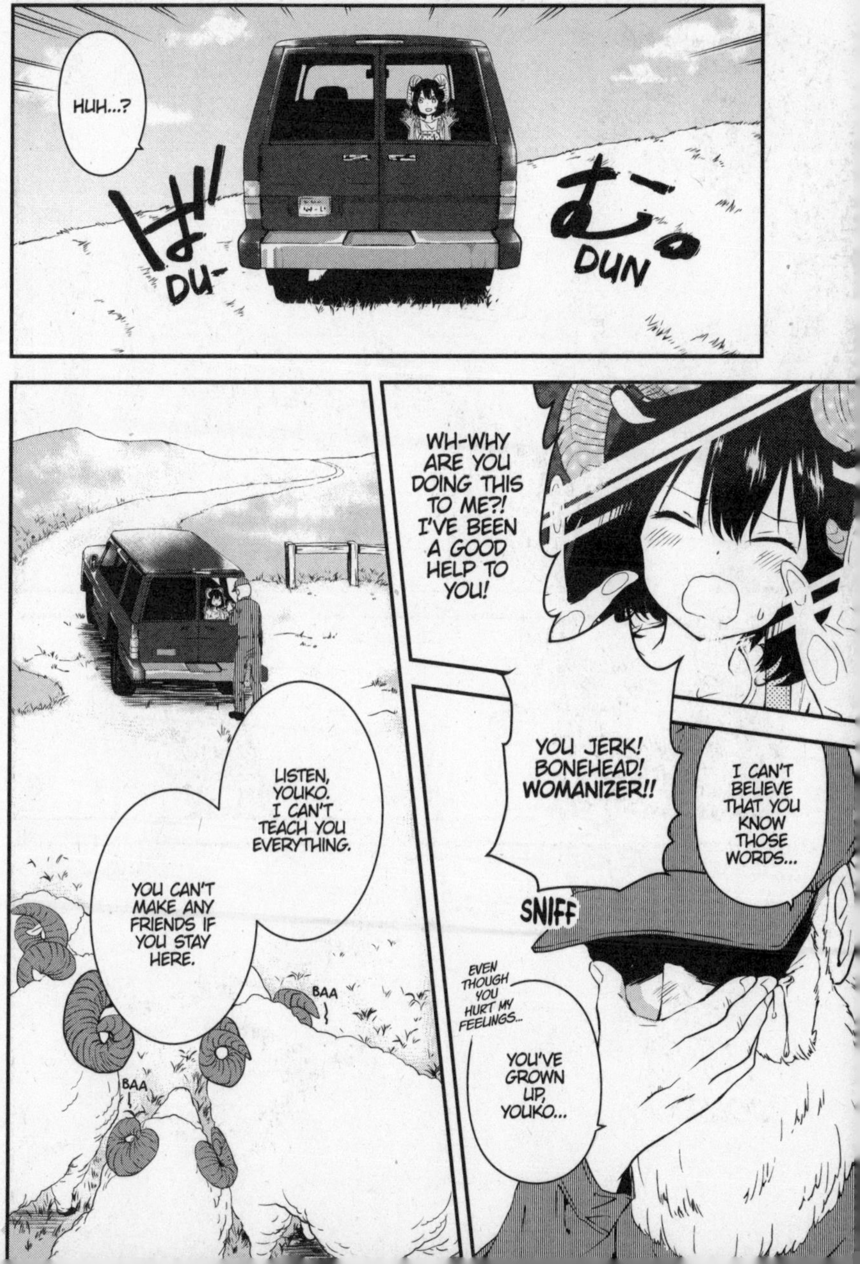
HUH...?
ば
DU-
む。
DUN
WH-WHY ARE YOU DOING THIS TO ME?! I'VE BEEN A GOOD HELP TO YOU!
YOU JERK! BONEHEAD! WOMANIZER!!
I CAN'T BELIEVE THAT YOU KNOW THOSE WORDS...
SNIFF
EVEN THOUGH YOU HURT MY FEELINGS...
YOU'VE GROWN UP, YOUKO...
LISTEN, YOUKO. I CAN'T TEACH YOU EVERYTHING.
YOU CAN'T MAKE ANY FRIENDS IF YOU STAY HERE.
BAA
BAA

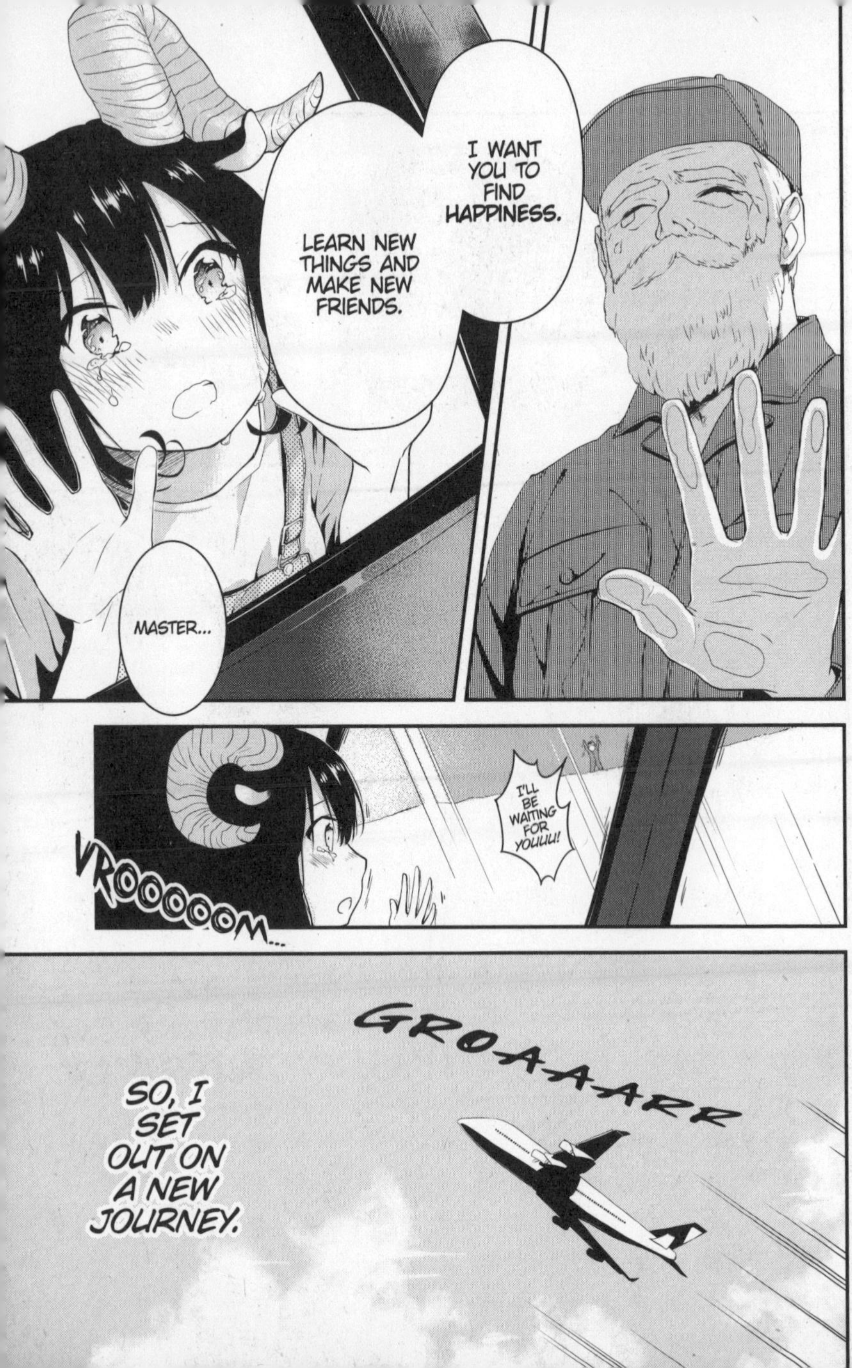
I WANT YOU TO FIND HAPPINESS.
LEARN NEW THINGS AND MAKE NEW FRIENDS.
MASTER...
I'LL BE WAITING FOR YOUUU!
VROOOOOOM...
GROAAAARR
SO, I SET OUT ON A NEW JOURNEY.

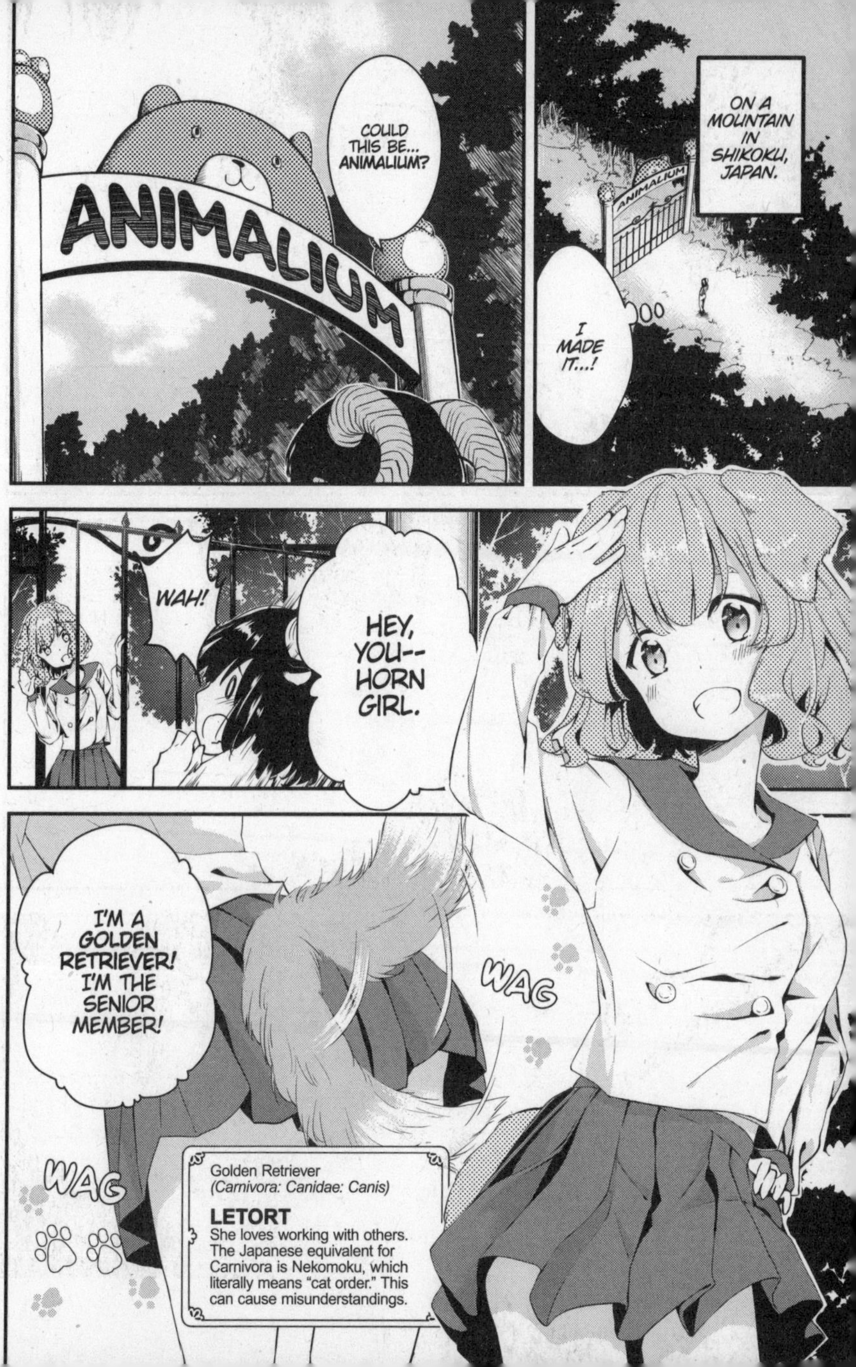
ON A MOUNTAIN IN SHIKOKU, JAPAN.
ANIMALIUM
I MADE IT...!
COULD THIS BE... ANIMALIUM?
ANIMALIUM
HEY, YOU-- HORN GIRL.
WAH!
I'M A GOLDEN RETRIEVER! I'M THE SENIOR MEMBER!
WAG
WAG
Golden Retriever
(Carnivora: Canidae: Canis)
LETORT
She loves working with others. The Japanese equivalent for Carnivora is Nekomoku, which literally means "cat order." This can cause misunderstandings.

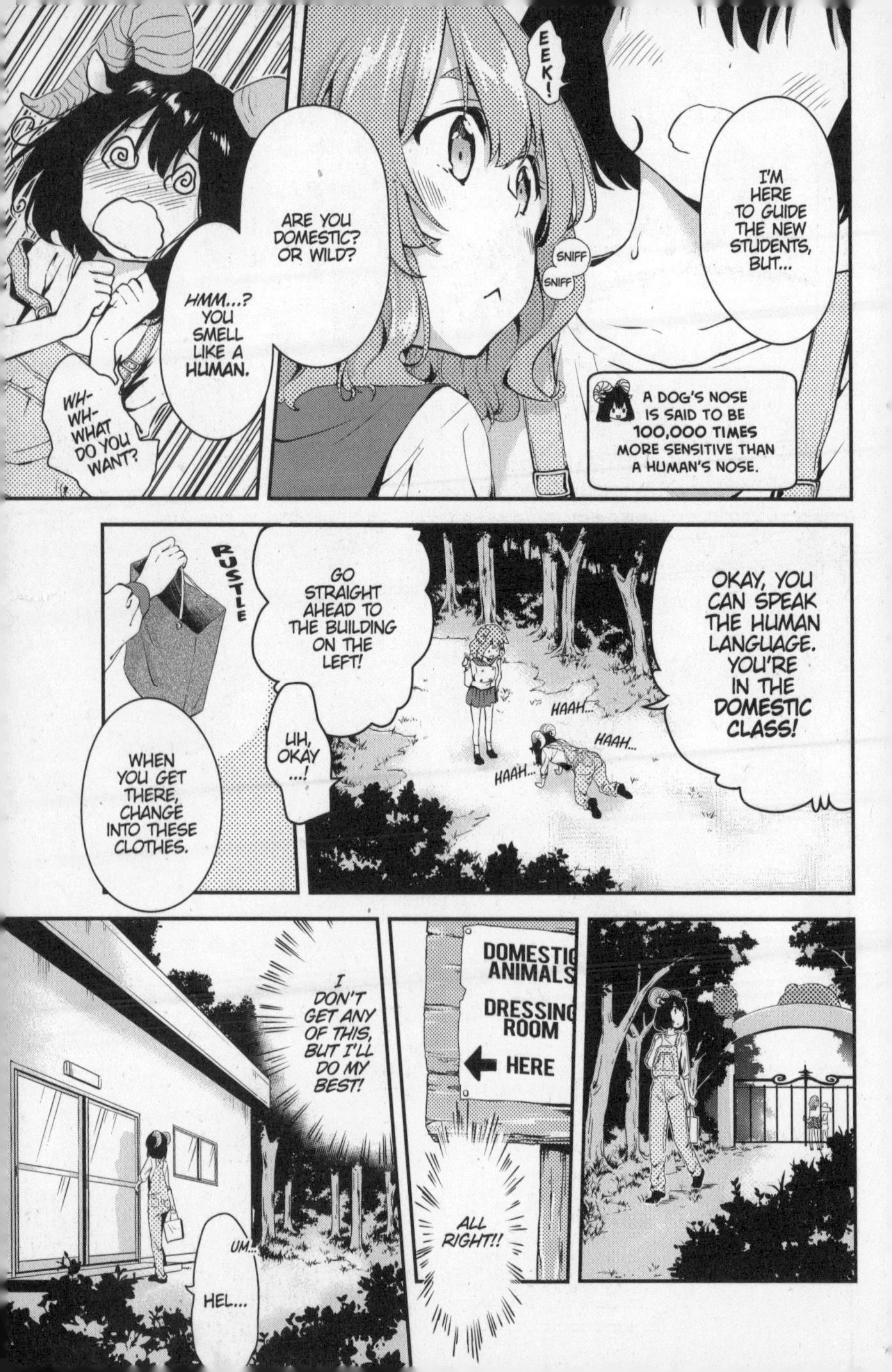
EEK!
I'M HERE TO GUIDE THE NEW STUDENTS, BUT...
SNIFF
SNIFF
ARE YOU DOMESTIC? OR WILD?
HMM...? YOU SMELL LIKE A HUMAN.
A DOG'S NOSE IS SAID TO BE 100,000 TIMES MORE SENSITIVE THAN A HUMAN'S NOSE.
WH-WH-WHAT DO YOU WANT?
OKAY, YOU CAN SPEAK THE HUMAN LANGUAGE. YOU'RE IN THE DOMESTIC CLASS!
HAAH...
HAAH...
HAAH...
GO STRAIGHT AHEAD TO THE BUILDING ON THE LEFT!
UH, OKAY...!
RUSTLE
WHEN YOU GET THERE, CHANGE INTO THESE CLOTHES.
DOMESTIC ANIMALS
DRESSING ROOM
HERE
ALL RIGHT!!
I DON'T GET ANY OF THIS, BUT I'LL DO MY BEST!
UM...
HEL...

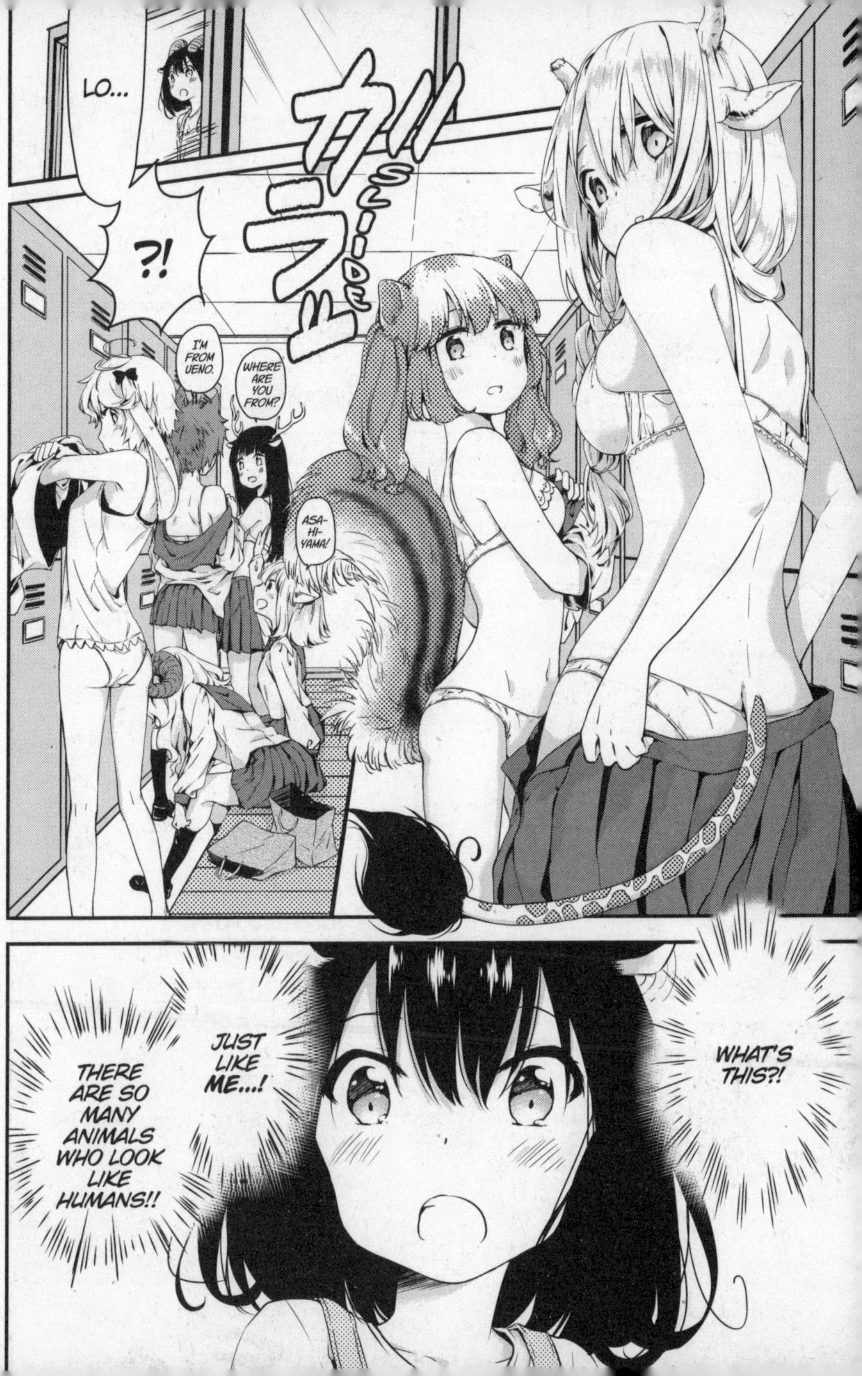
SLIIIDE
LO...
?!
WHERE ARE YOU FROM?
I'M FROM UENO.
ASA-HI-YAMA!
WHAT'S THIS?!
JUST LIKE ME...!
THERE ARE SO MANY ANIMALS WHO LOOK LIKE HUMANS!!

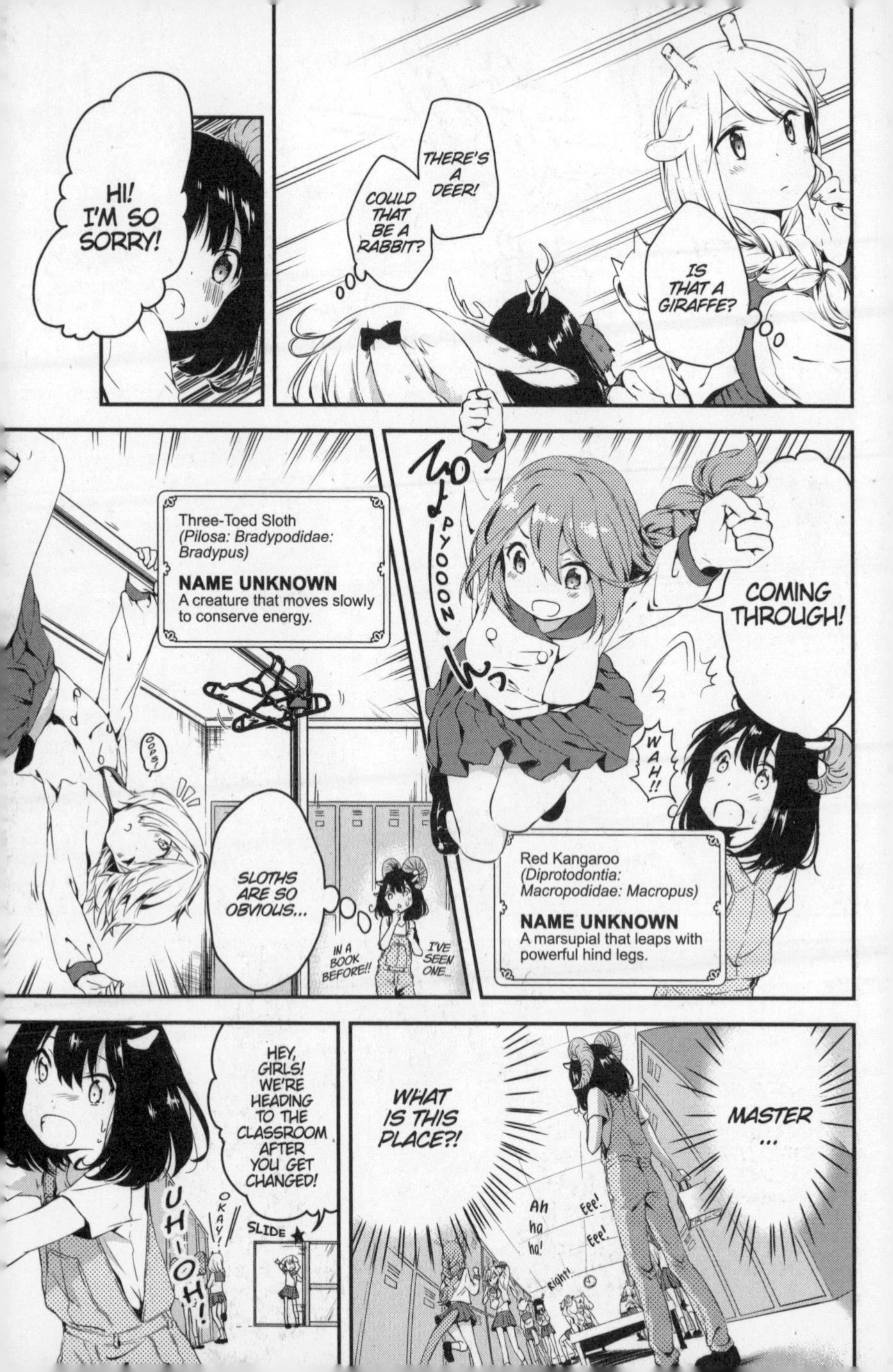
IS THAT A GIRAFFE?
THERE'S A DEER!
COULD THAT BE A RABBIT?
HI! I'M SO SORRY!
PYOOON
COMING THROUGH!
WAH!!
Red Kangaroo
(Diprotodontia: Macropodidae: Macropus)
NAME UNKNOWN
A marsupial that leaps with powerful hind legs.
Three-Toed Sloth
(Pilosa: Bradypodidae: Bradypus)
NAME UNKNOWN
A creature that moves slowly to conserve energy.
OOPS!
SLOTHS ARE SO OBVIOUS...
I'VE SEEN ONE...
IN A BOOK BEFORE!!
MASTER ...
WHAT IS THIS PLACE?!
Eee! Eee!
Ah ha ha!
Right!
HEY, GIRLS! WE'RE HEADING TO THE CLASSROOM AFTER YOU GET CHANGED!
OKAY!
SLIDE
UH-OH!

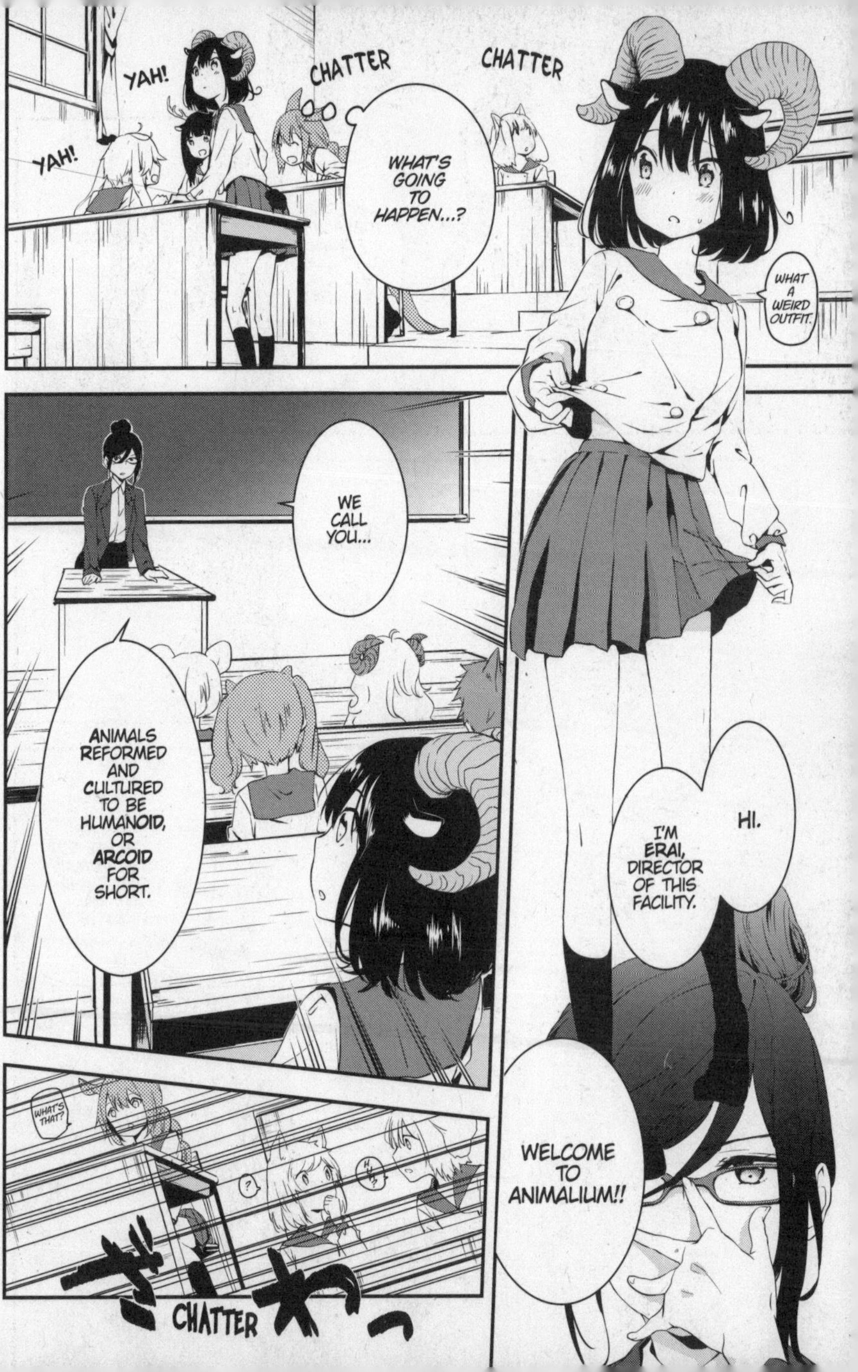

CHATTER
WHAT A WEIRD OUTFIT.
HI.
I'M ERAI, DIRECTOR OF THIS FACILITY.
WELCOME TO ANIMALIUM!!
CHATTER
YAH!
YAH!
WHAT'S GOING TO HAPPEN...?
WE CALL YOU...
ANIMALS REFORMED AND CULTURED TO BE HUMANOID, OR ARCOID FOR SHORT.
WHAT'S THAT?
HUH?
?
CHATTER

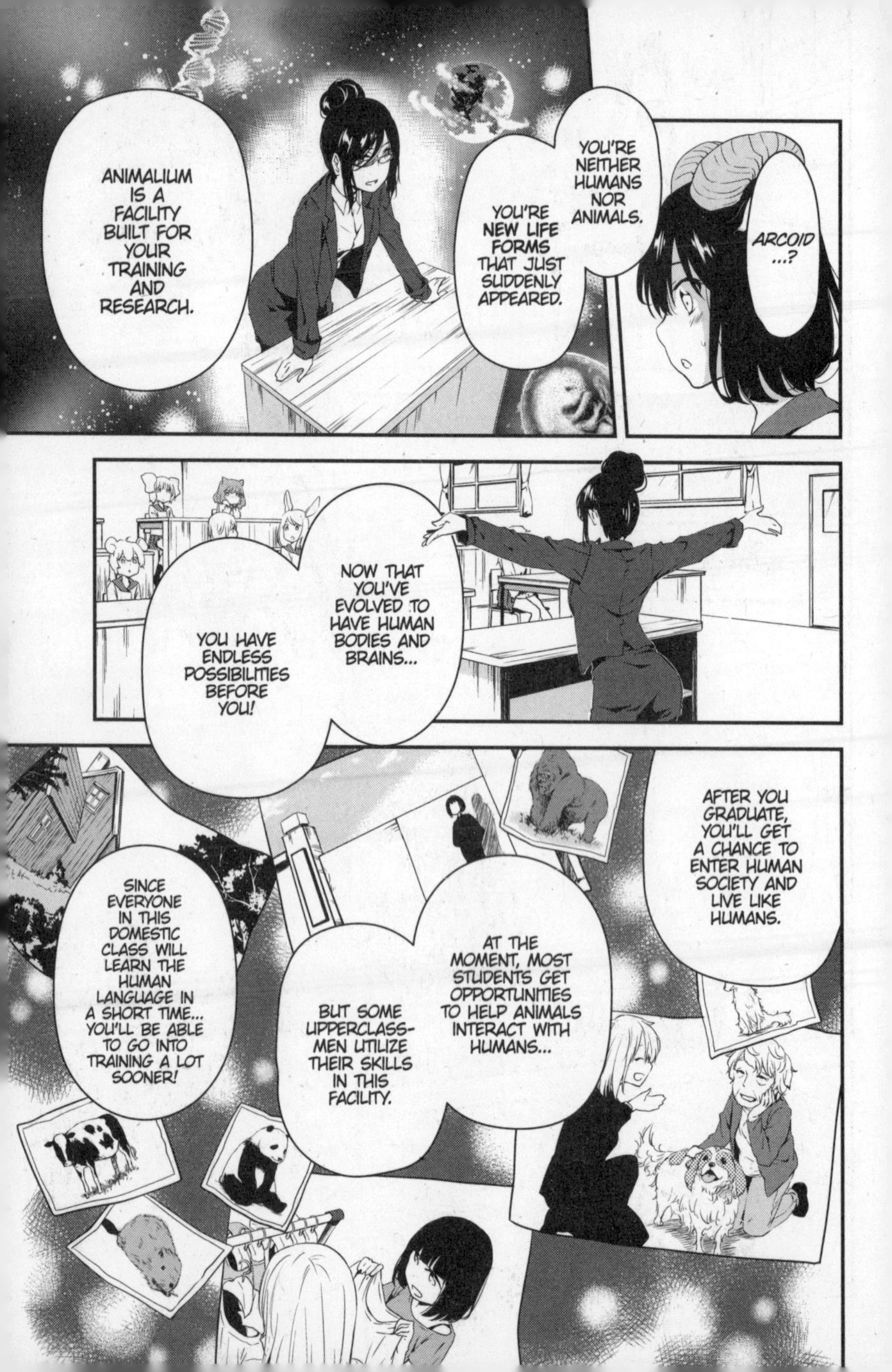
ARCOID ...?
YOU'RE NEITHER HUMANS NOR ANIMALS.
YOU'RE NEW LIFE FORMS THAT JUST SUDDENLY APPEARED.
ANIMALIUM IS A FACILITY BUILT FOR YOUR TRAINING AND RESEARCH.
NOW THAT YOU'VE EVOLVED TO HAVE HUMAN BODIES AND BRAINS...
YOU HAVE ENDLESS POSSIBILITIES BEFORE YOU!
AFTER YOU GRADUATE, YOU'LL GET A CHANCE TO ENTER HUMAN SOCIETY AND LIVE LIKE HUMANS.
AT THE MOMENT, MOST STUDENTS GET OPPORTUNITIES TO HELP ANIMALS INTERACT WITH HUMANS...
BUT SOME UPPERCLASSMEN UTILIZE THEIR SKILLS IN THIS FACILITY.
SINCE EVERYONE IN THIS DOMESTIC CLASS WILL LEARN THE HUMAN LANGUAGE IN A SHORT TIME... YOU'LL BE ABLE TO GO INTO TRAINING A LOT SOONER!

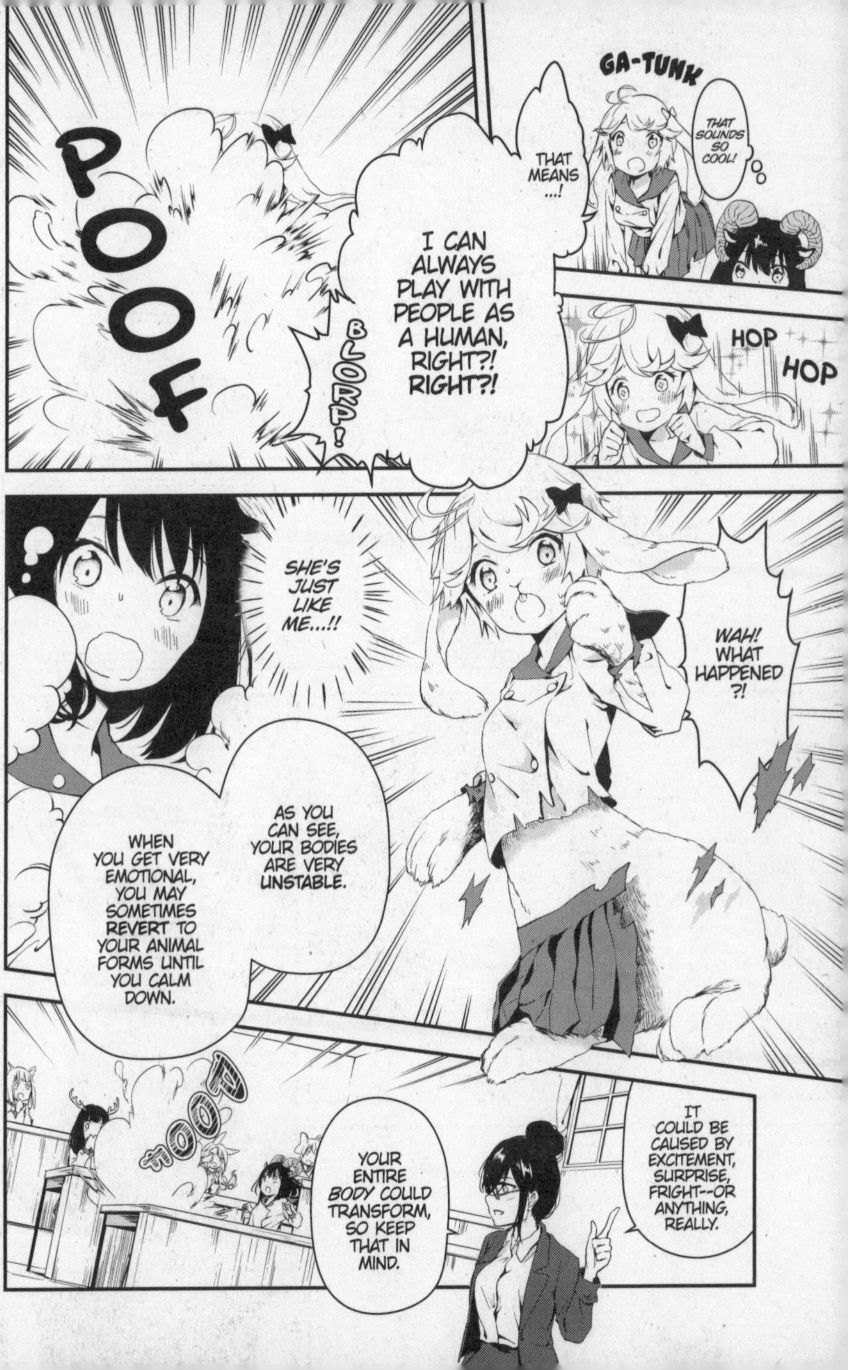
GA-TUNK
THAT MEANS ...!
THAT SOUNDS SO COOL!
HOP HOP
I CAN ALWAYS PLAY WITH PEOPLE AS A HUMAN, RIGHT?! RIGHT?!
BLORP!
POOF
WAH! WHAT HAPPENED ?!
SHE'S JUST LIKE ME...!!
AS YOU CAN SEE, YOUR BODIES ARE VERY UNSTABLE.
WHEN YOU GET VERY EMOTIONAL, YOU MAY SOMETIMES REVERT TO YOUR ANIMAL FORMS UNTIL YOU CALM DOWN.
IT COULD BE CAUSED BY EXCITEMENT, SURPRISE, FRIGHT--OR ANYTHING, REALLY.
YOUR ENTIRE BODY COULD TRANSFORM, SO KEEP THAT IN MIND.
POOF

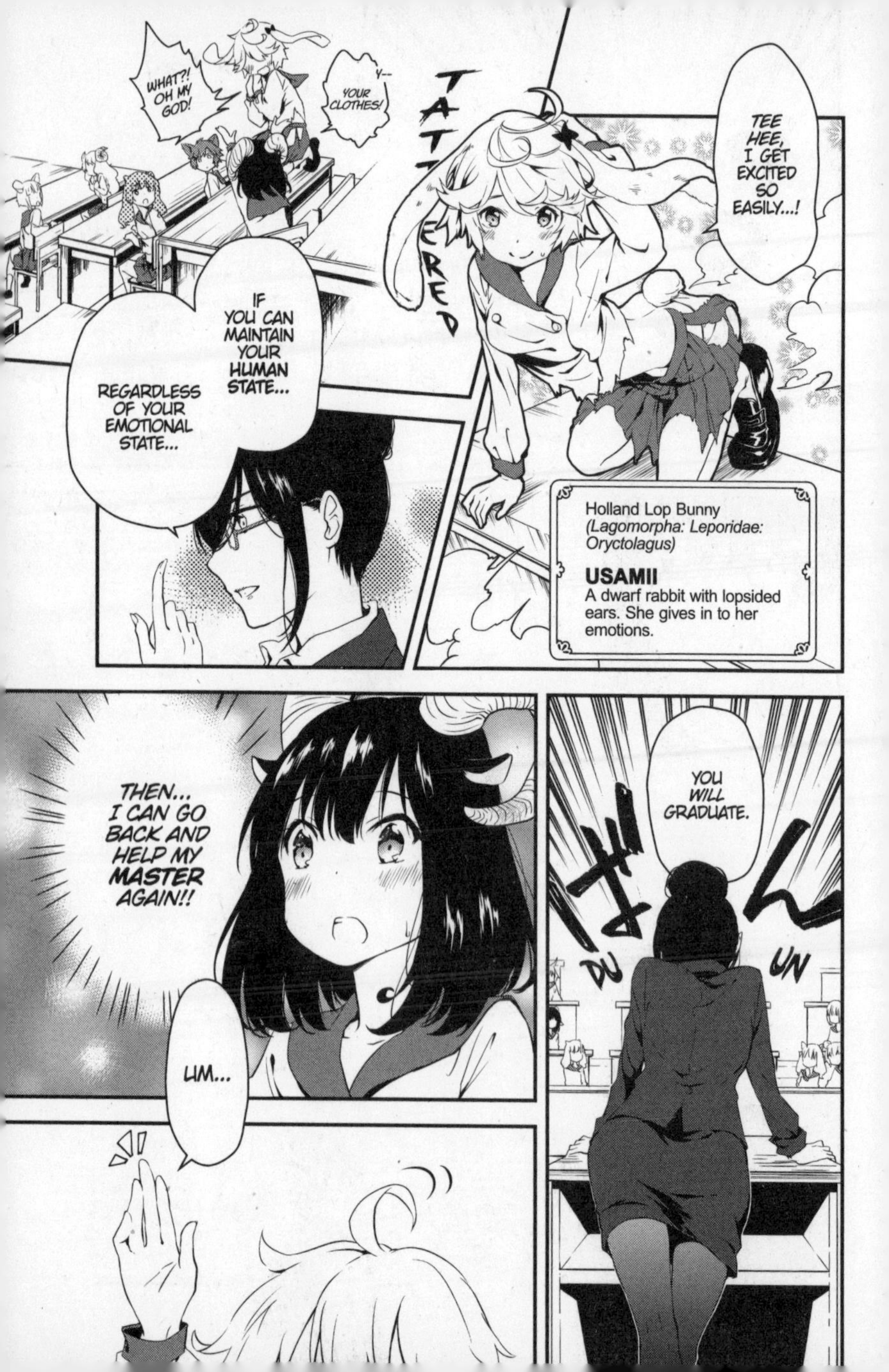
TEE HEE, I GET EXCITED SO EASILY...!
TATTERED
Holland Lop Bunny (Lagomorpha: Leporidae: Oryctolagus)
USAMII
A dwarf rabbit with lopsided ears. She gives in to her emotions.
Y-- YOUR CLOTHES!
WHAT?! OH MY GOD!
IF YOU CAN MAINTAIN YOUR HUMAN STATE...
REGARDLESS OF YOUR EMOTIONAL STATE...
YOU WILL GRADUATE.
DU
UN
THEN... I CAN GO BACK AND HELP MY MASTER AGAIN!!
UM...

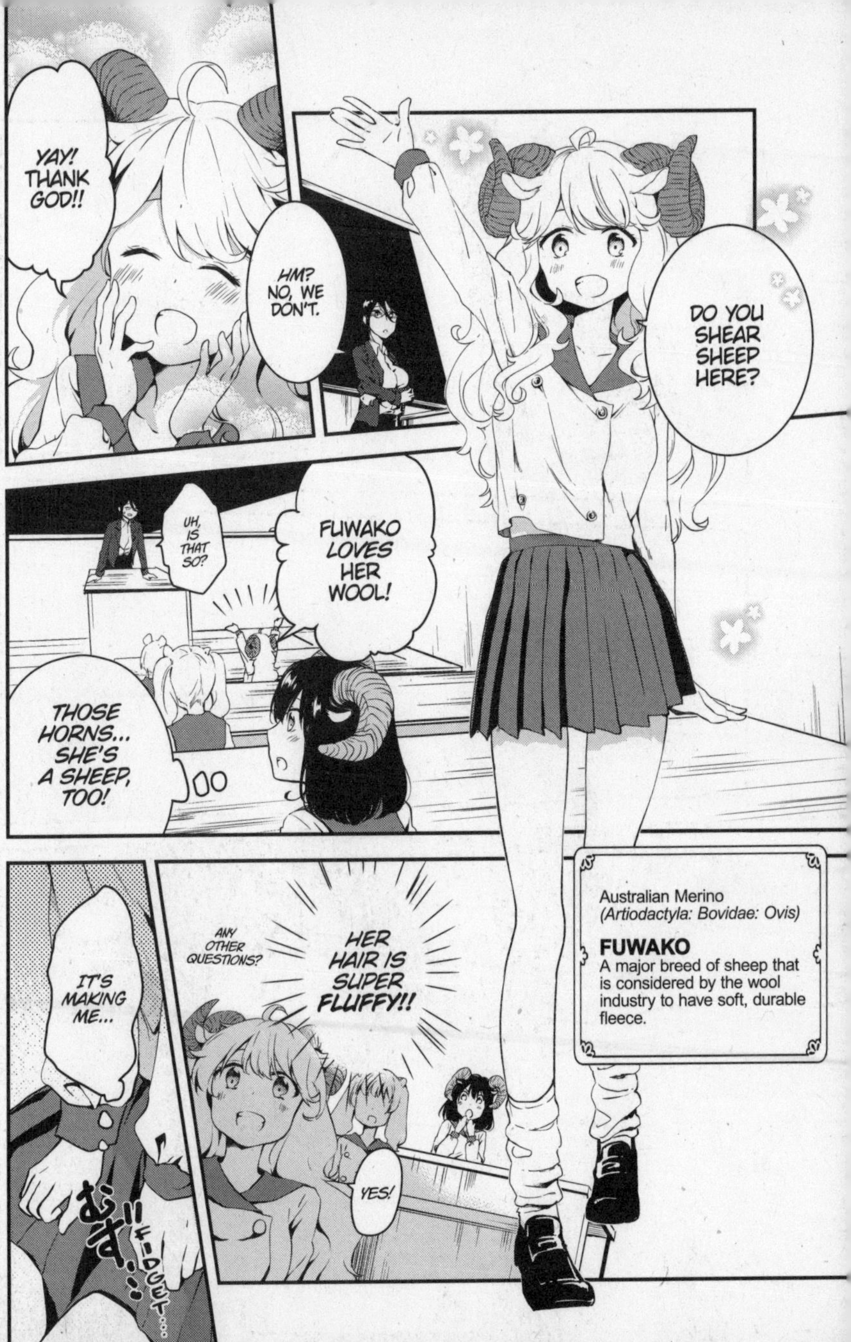
DO YOU SHEAR SHEEP HERE?
HM? NO, WE DON'T.
YAY! THANK GOD!!
FUWAKO LOVES HER WOOL!
UH, IS THAT SO?
THOSE HORNS... SHE'S A SHEEP, TOO!
Australian Merino
(Artiodactyla: Bovidae: Ovis)
FUWAKO
A major breed of sheep that is considered by the wool industry to have soft, durable fleece.
HER HAIR IS SUPER FLUFFY!!
ANY OTHER QUESTIONS?
YES!
IT'S MAKING ME...
FIDGET...

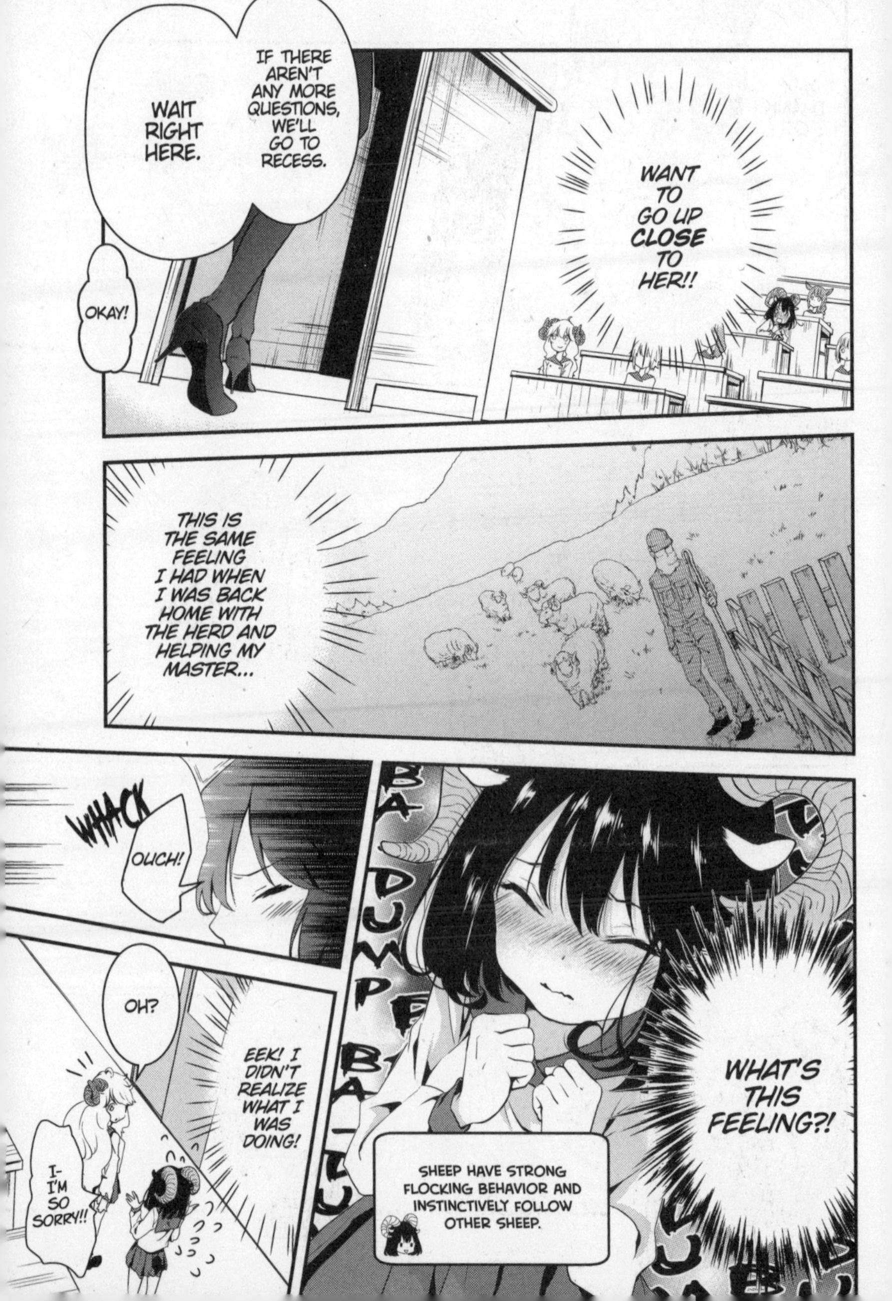
IF THERE AREN'T ANY MORE QUESTIONS, WE'LL GO TO RECESS.
WAIT RIGHT HERE.
OKAY!
WANT TO GO UP CLOSE TO HER!!
THIS IS THE SAME FEELING I HAD WHEN I WAS BACK HOME WITH THE HERD AND HELPING MY MASTER...
BADUMP
WHAT'S THIS FEELING?!
SHEEP HAVE STRONG FLOCKING BEHAVIOR AND INSTINCTIVELY FOLLOW OTHER SHEEP.
WHACK
OUCH!
OH?
EEK! I DIDN'T REALIZE WHAT I WAS DOING!
I-I'M SO SORRY!!

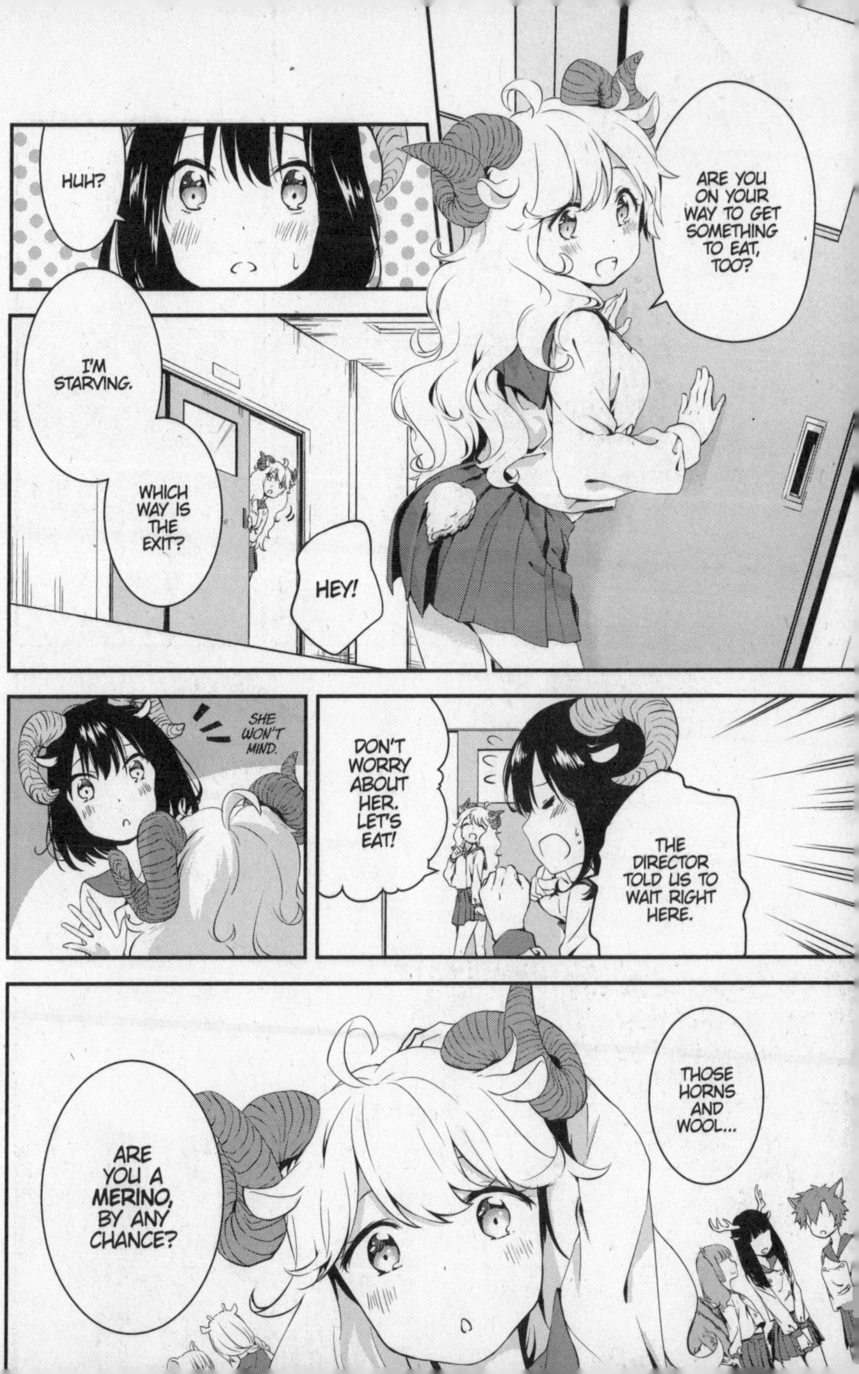
ARE YOU ON YOUR WAY TO GET SOMETHING TO EAT, TOO?
HUH?
I'M STARVING.
WHICH WAY IS THE EXIT?
HEY!
THE DIRECTOR TOLD US TO WAIT RIGHT HERE.
DON'T WORRY ABOUT HER. LET'S EAT!
SHE WON'T MIND.
THOSE HORNS AND WOOL...
ARE YOU A MERINO, BY ANY CHANCE?

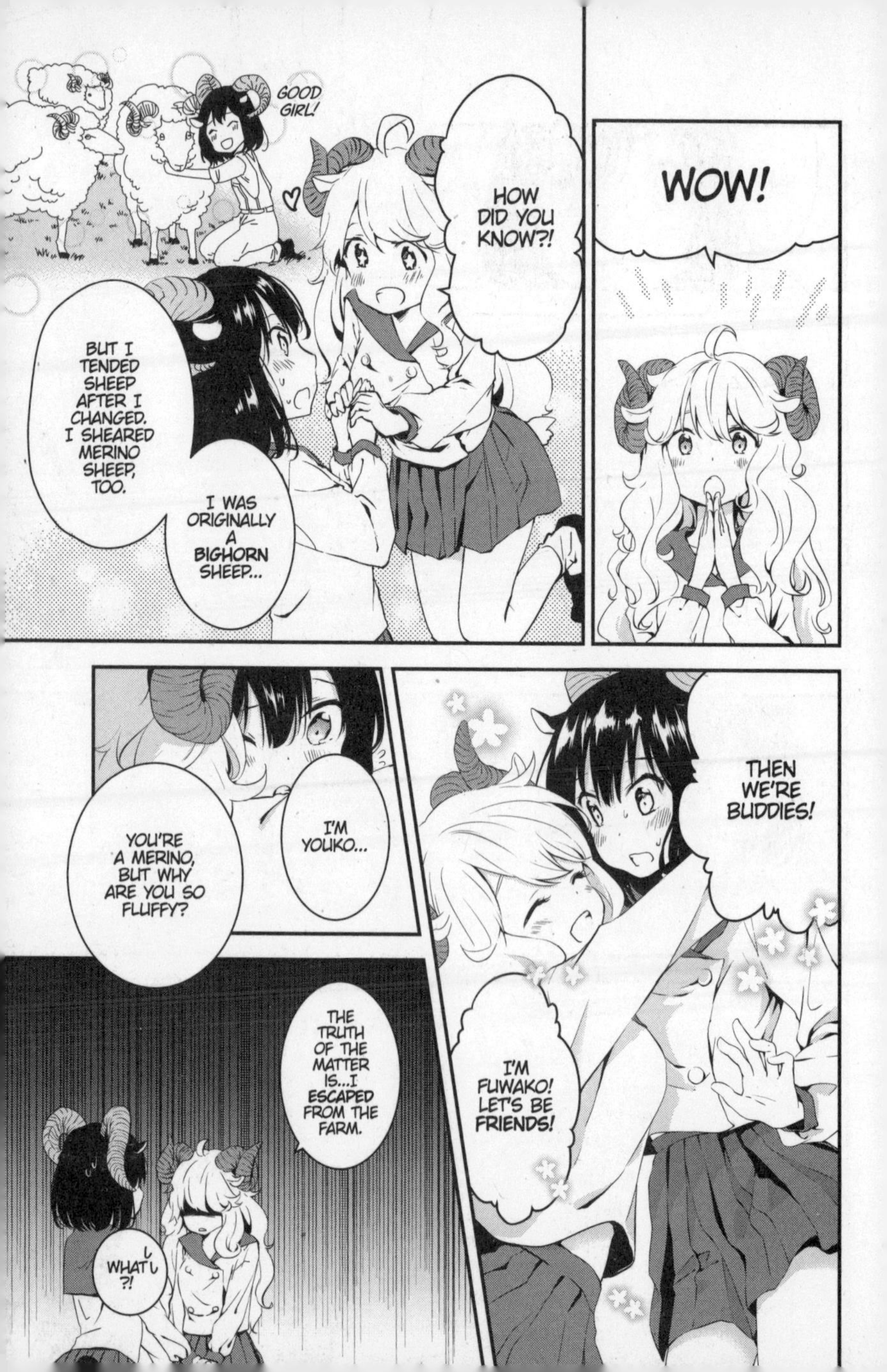
WOW!
HOW DID YOU KNOW?!
GOOD GIRL!
BUT I TENDED SHEEP AFTER I CHANGED. I SHEARED MERINO SHEEP, TOO.
I WAS ORIGINALLY A BIGHORN SHEEP...
THEN WE'RE BUDDIES!
I'M FUWAKO! LET'S BE FRIENDS!
I'M YOUKO...
YOU'RE A MERINO, BUT WHY ARE YOU SO FLUFFY?
THE TRUTH OF THE MATTER IS...I ESCAPED FROM THE FARM.
WHAT?!

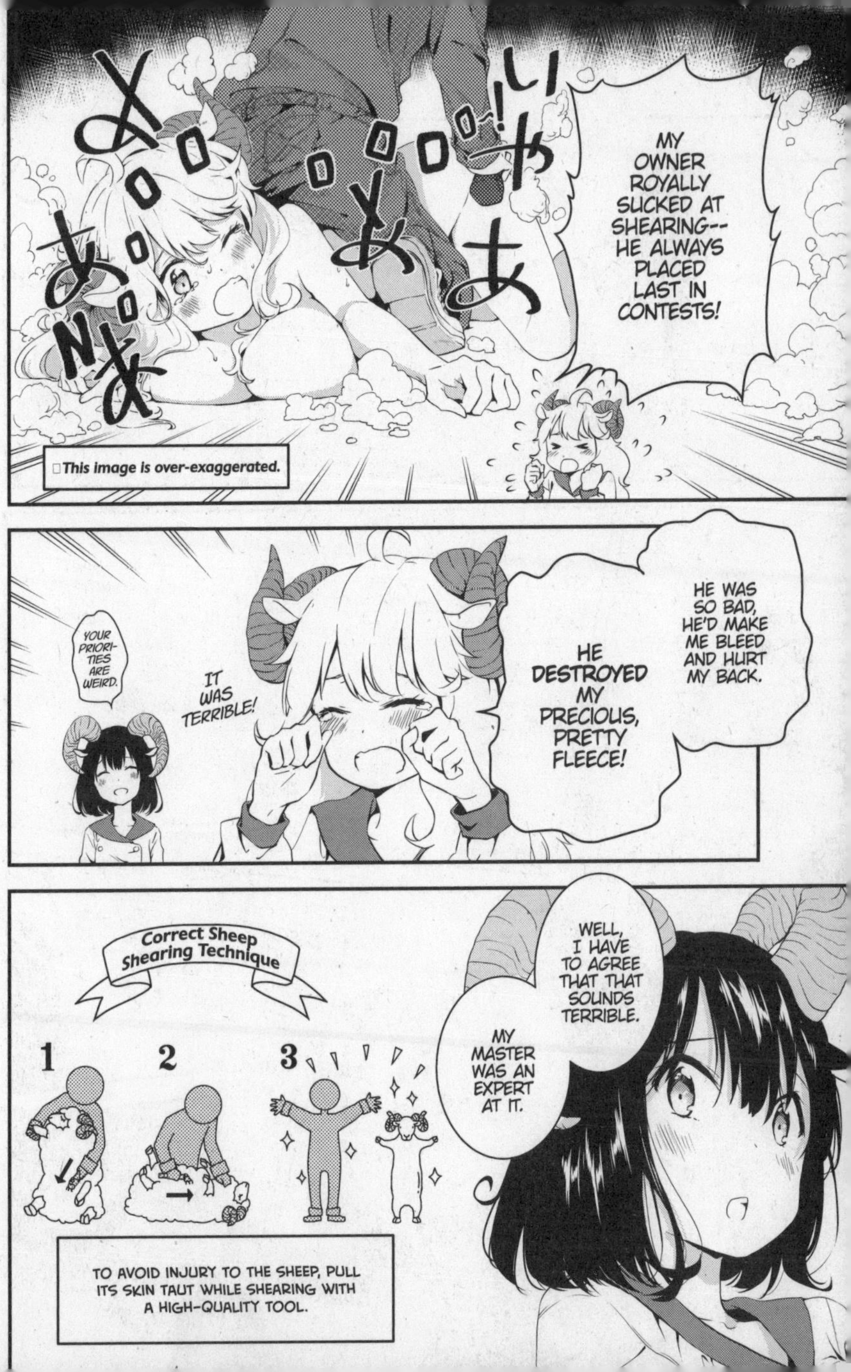
MY OWNER ROYALLY SUCKED AT SHEARING-- HE ALWAYS PLACED LAST IN CONTESTS!
※This image is over-exaggerated.
HE WAS SO BAD, HE'D MAKE ME BLEED AND HURT MY BACK.
HE DESTROYED MY PRECIOUS, PRETTY FLEECE!
IT WAS TERRIBLE!
YOUR PRIORI-TIES ARE WEIRD.
WELL, I HAVE TO AGREE THAT THAT SOUNDS TERRIBLE.
MY MASTER WAS AN EXPERT AT IT.
Correct Sheep Shearing Technique
1
2
3
TO AVOID INJURY TO THE SHEEP, PULL ITS SKIN TAUT WHILE SHEARING WITH A HIGH-QUALITY TOOL.

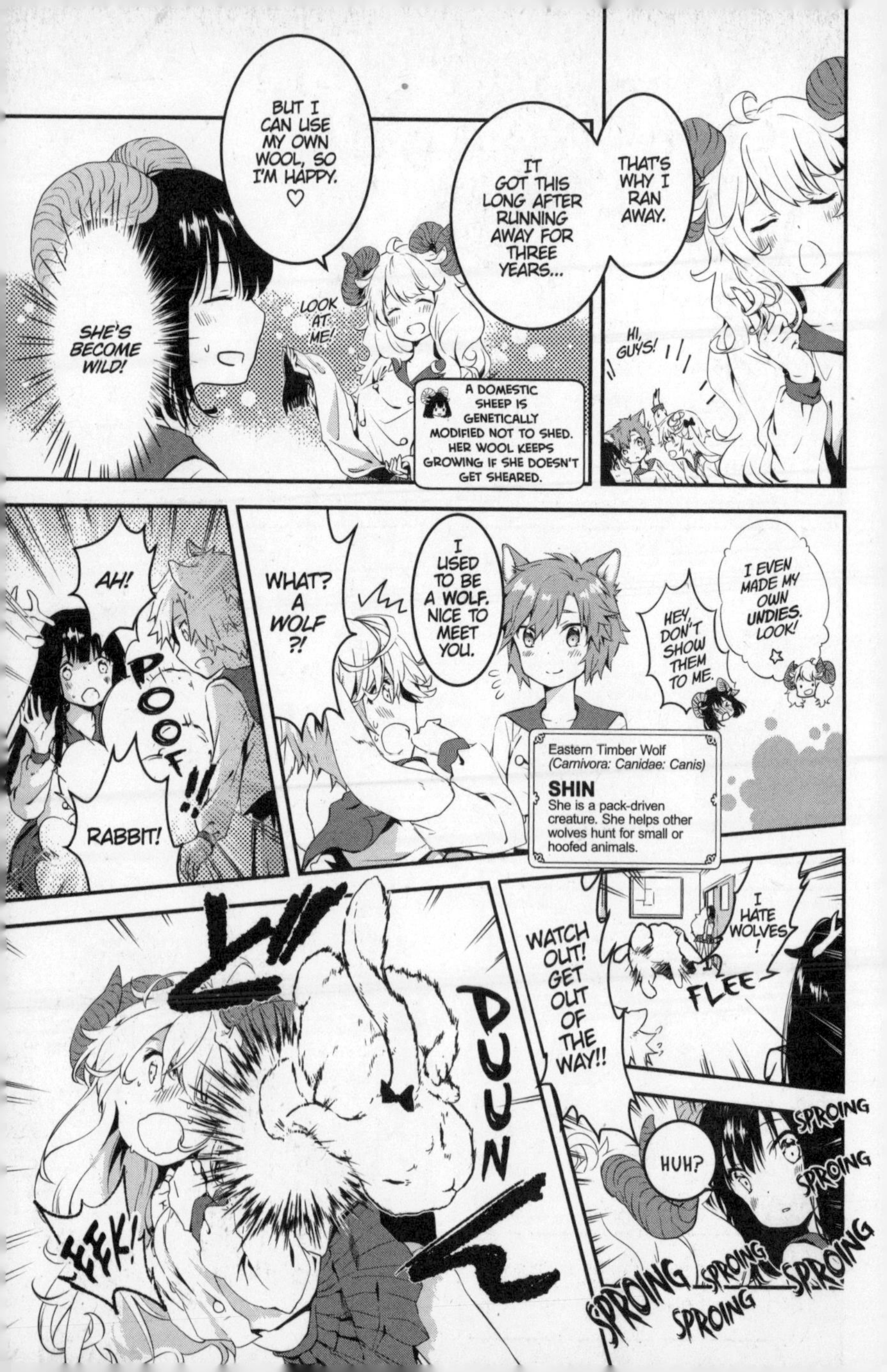
THAT'S WHY I RAN AWAY.
IT GOT THIS LONG AFTER RUNNING AWAY FOR THREE YEARS...
HI, GUYS!
BUT I CAN USE MY OWN WOOL, SO I'M HAPPY. ♡
LOOK AT ME!
A DOMESTIC SHEEP IS GENETICALLY MODIFIED NOT TO SHED. HER WOOL KEEPS GROWING IF SHE DOESN'T GET SHEARED.
SHE'S BECOME WILD!
I EVEN MADE MY OWN UNDIES. LOOK!
HEY, DON'T SHOW THEM TO ME.
I USED TO BE A WOLF. NICE TO MEET YOU.
WHAT? A WOLF?!
Eastern Timber Wolf
(Carnivora: Canidae: Canis)
SHIN
She is a pack-driven creature. She helps other wolves hunt for small or hoofed animals.
AH!
POOF!!
RABBIT!
I HATE WOLVES!
FLEE
WATCH OUT! GET OUT OF THE WAY!!
HUH?
SPROING
SPROING
SPROING
SPROING
SPROING
SPROING
DUUN
EEK!

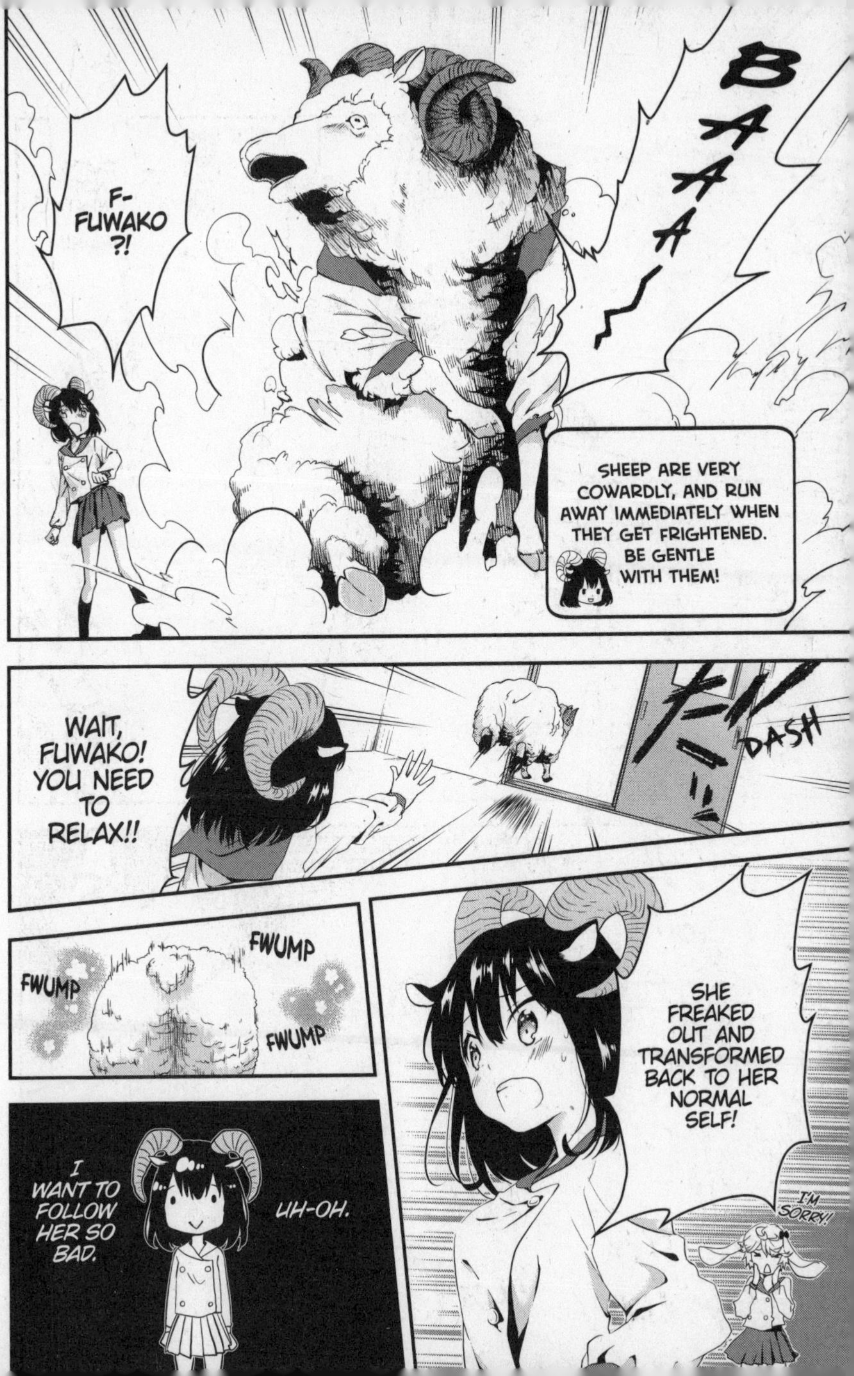
BAAAA~~
F-FUWAKO?!
SHEEP ARE VERY COWARDLY, AND RUN AWAY IMMEDIATELY WHEN THEY GET FRIGHTENED. BE GENTLE WITH THEM!
DASH
WAIT, FUWAKO! YOU NEED TO RELAX!!
SHE FREAKED OUT AND TRANSFORMED BACK TO HER NORMAL SELF!
I'M SORRY!
FWUMP
FWUMP
FWUMP
UH-OH.
I WANT TO FOLLOW HER SO BAD.

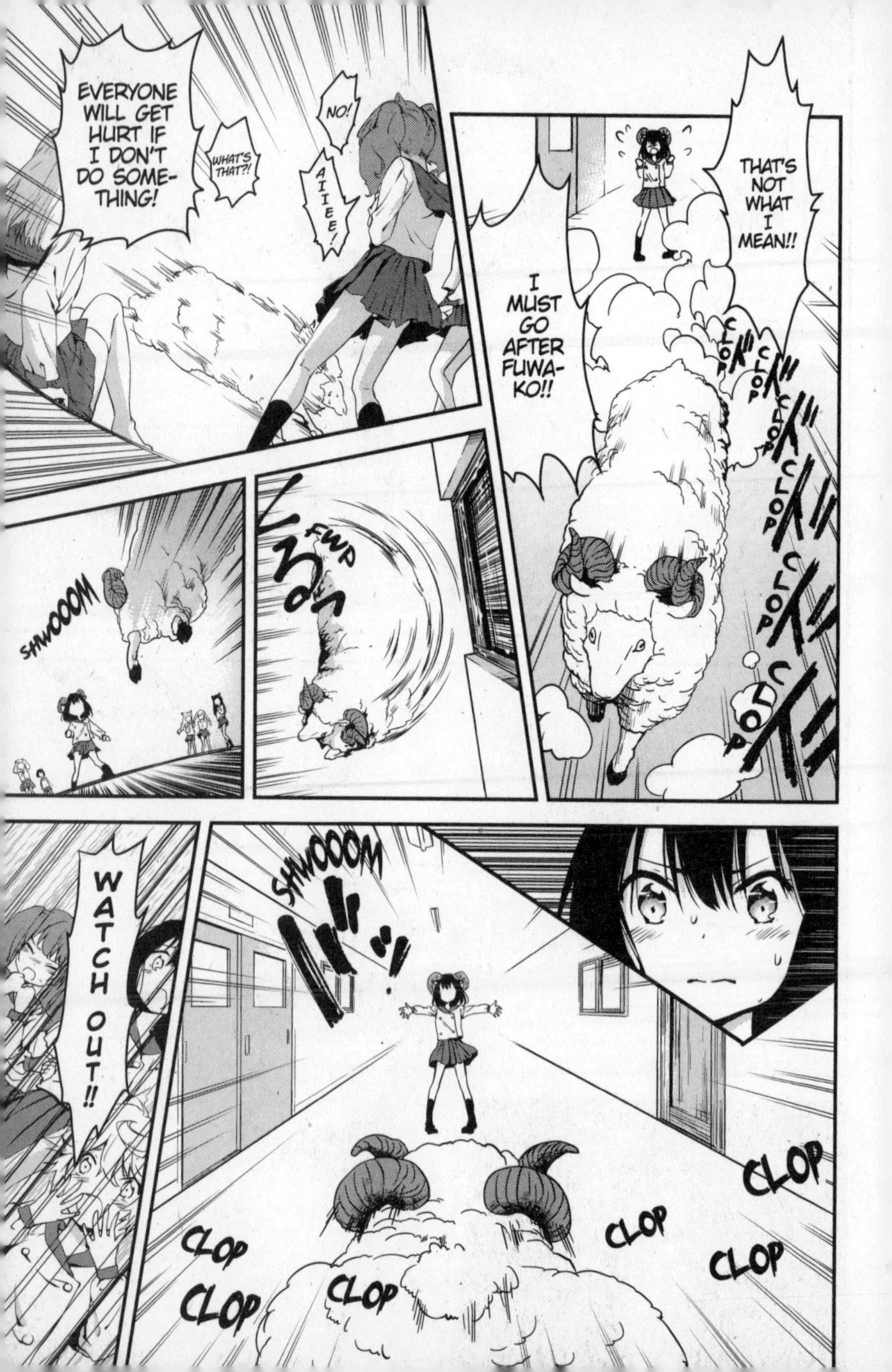
THAT'S NOT WHAT I MEAN!!
I MUST GO AFTER FUWAKO!!
CLOP CLOP CLOP CLOP CLOP CLOP CLOP
NO!
AIIEEE!
WHAT'S THAT?!
EVERYONE WILL GET HURT IF I DON'T DO SOMETHING!
FWP
SHWOOOM
SHWOOOM
CLOP
CLOP
CLOP
CLOP
CLOP
CLOP
WATCH OUT!!

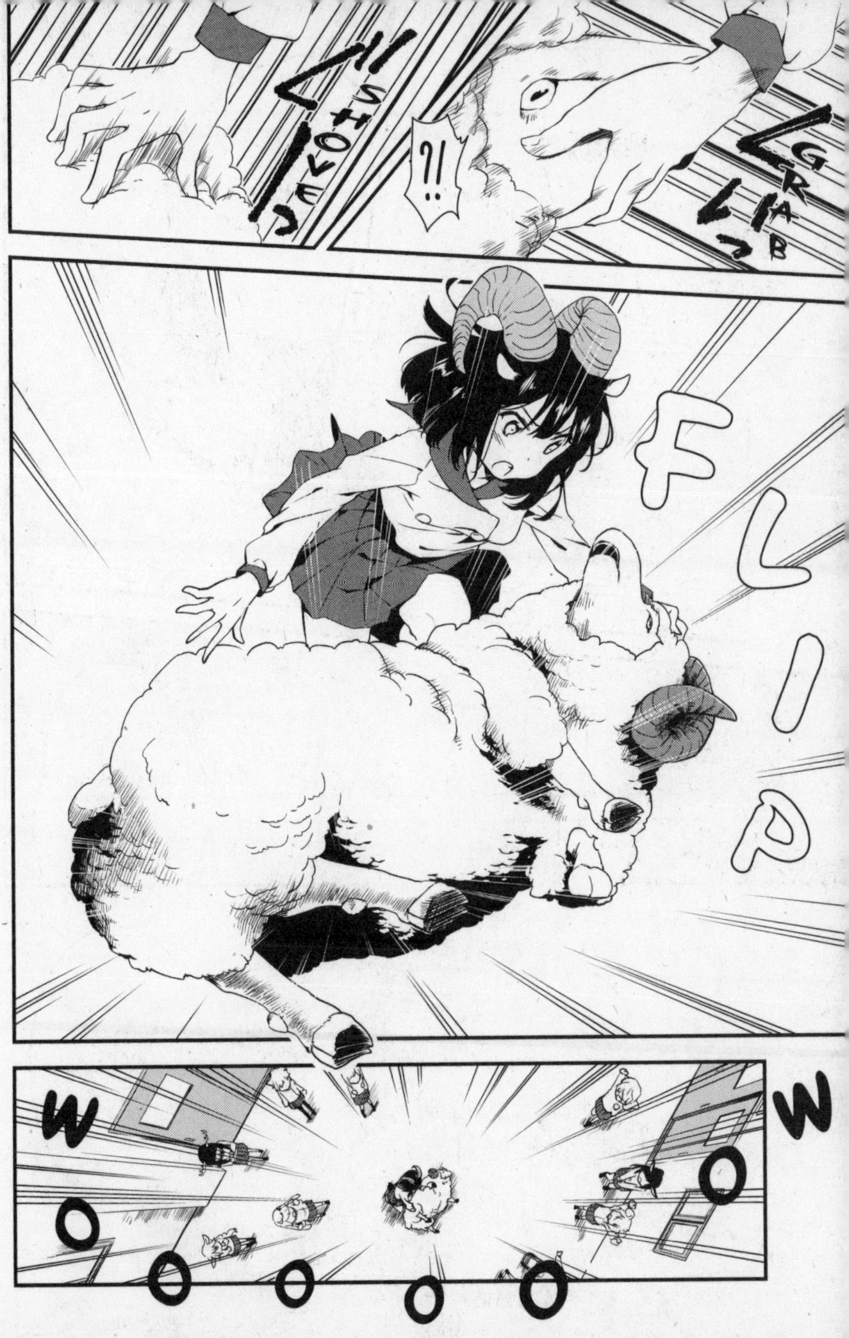
GRAB
?!!
SHOVE
FLIP
WOOOOOOW

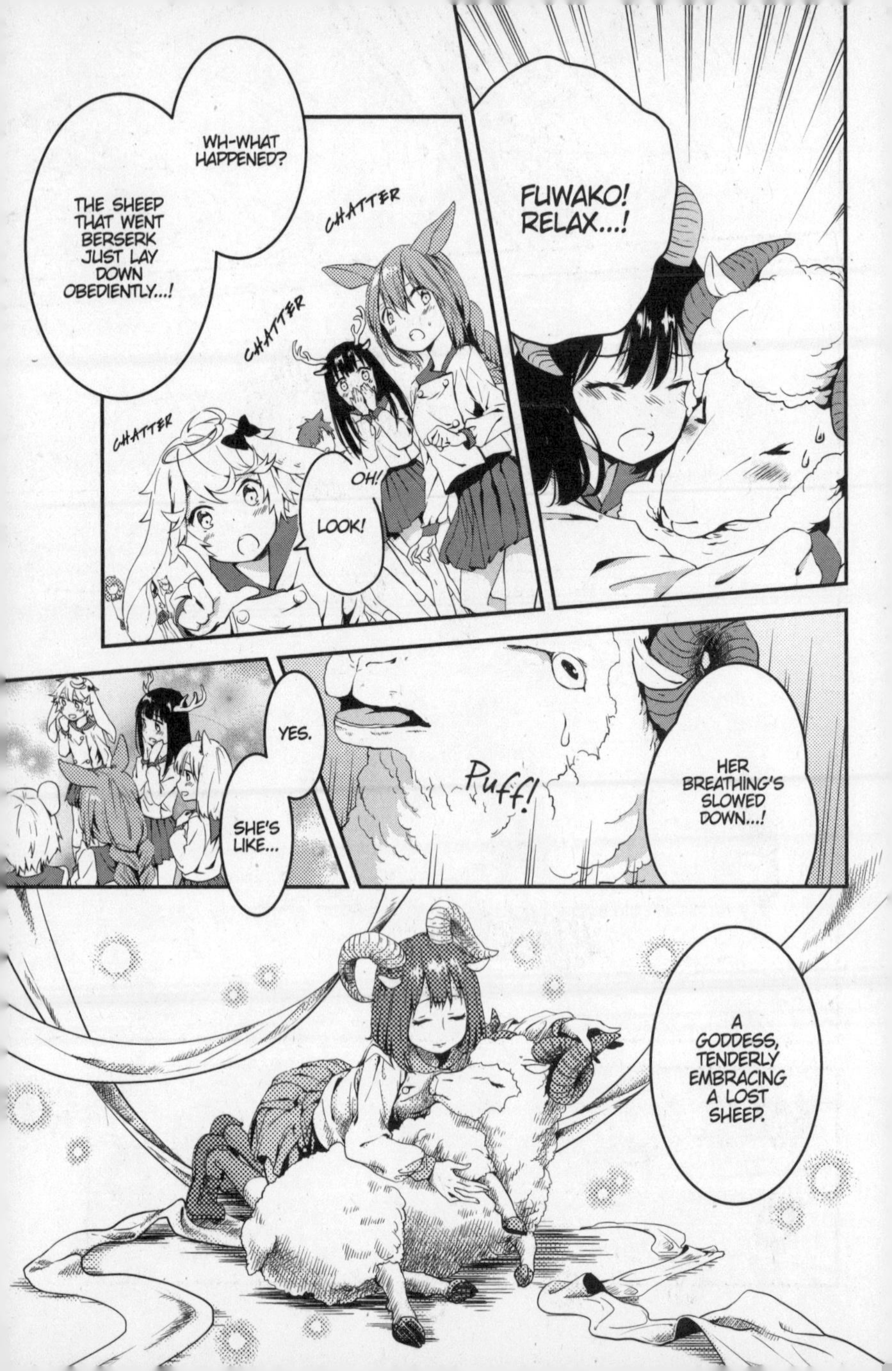
FUWAKO! RELAX...!
WH-WHAT HAPPENED?
THE SHEEP THAT WENT BERSERK JUST LAY DOWN OBEDIENTLY...!
CHATTER
CHATTER
CHATTER
OH!
LOOK!
HER BREATHING'S SLOWED DOWN...!
Puff!
YES.
SHE'S LIKE...
A GODDESS, TENDERLY EMBRACING A LOST SHEEP.

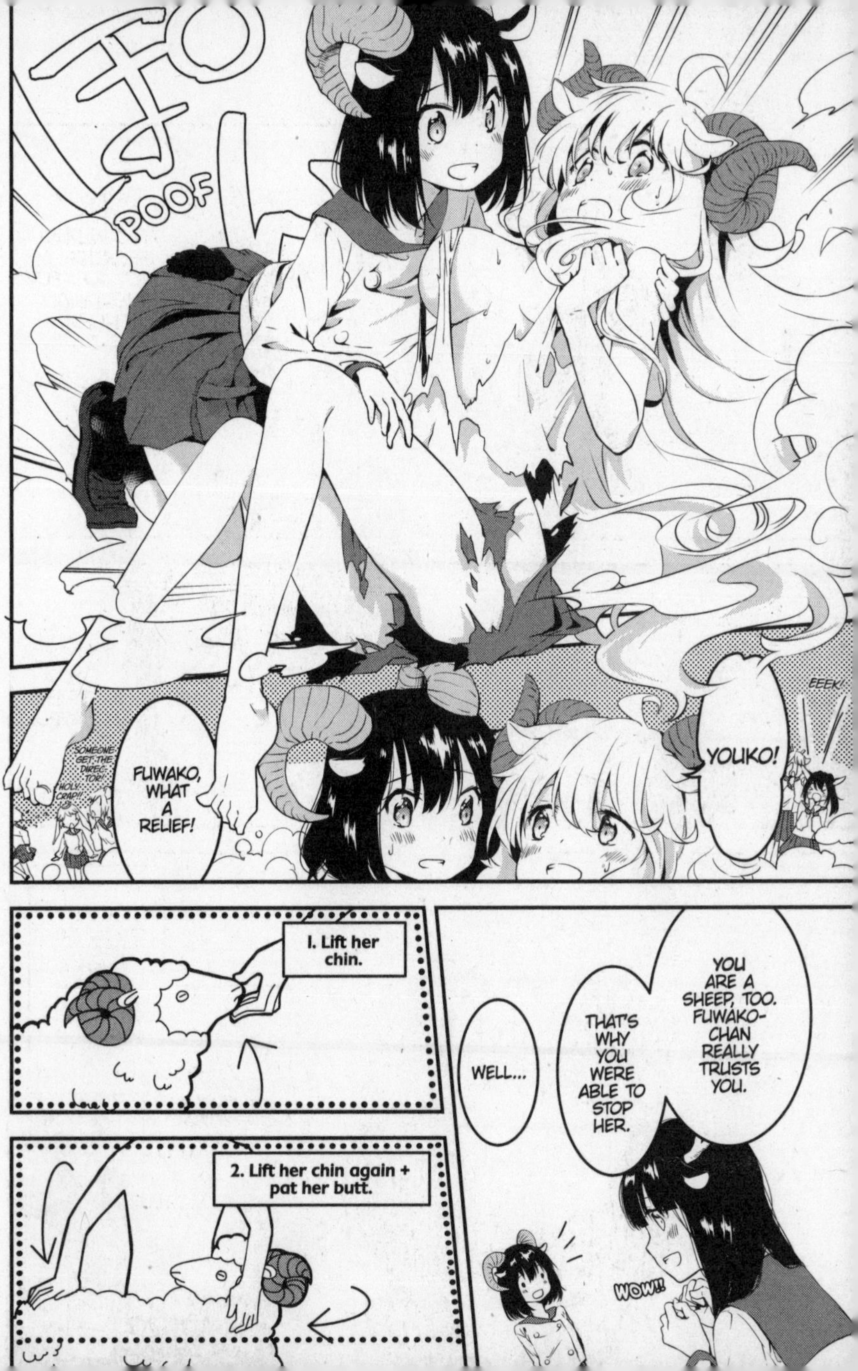
POOF
EEEK!
YOUKO!
FUWAKO, WHAT A RELIEF!
SOMEONE GET THE DIRECTOR!
HOLY CRAP!!
YOU ARE A SHEEP, TOO. FUWAKO-CHAN REALLY TRUSTS YOU.
THAT'S WHY YOU WERE ABLE TO STOP HER.
WELL...
WOW!!
1. Lift her chin.
2. Lift her chin again + pat her butt.

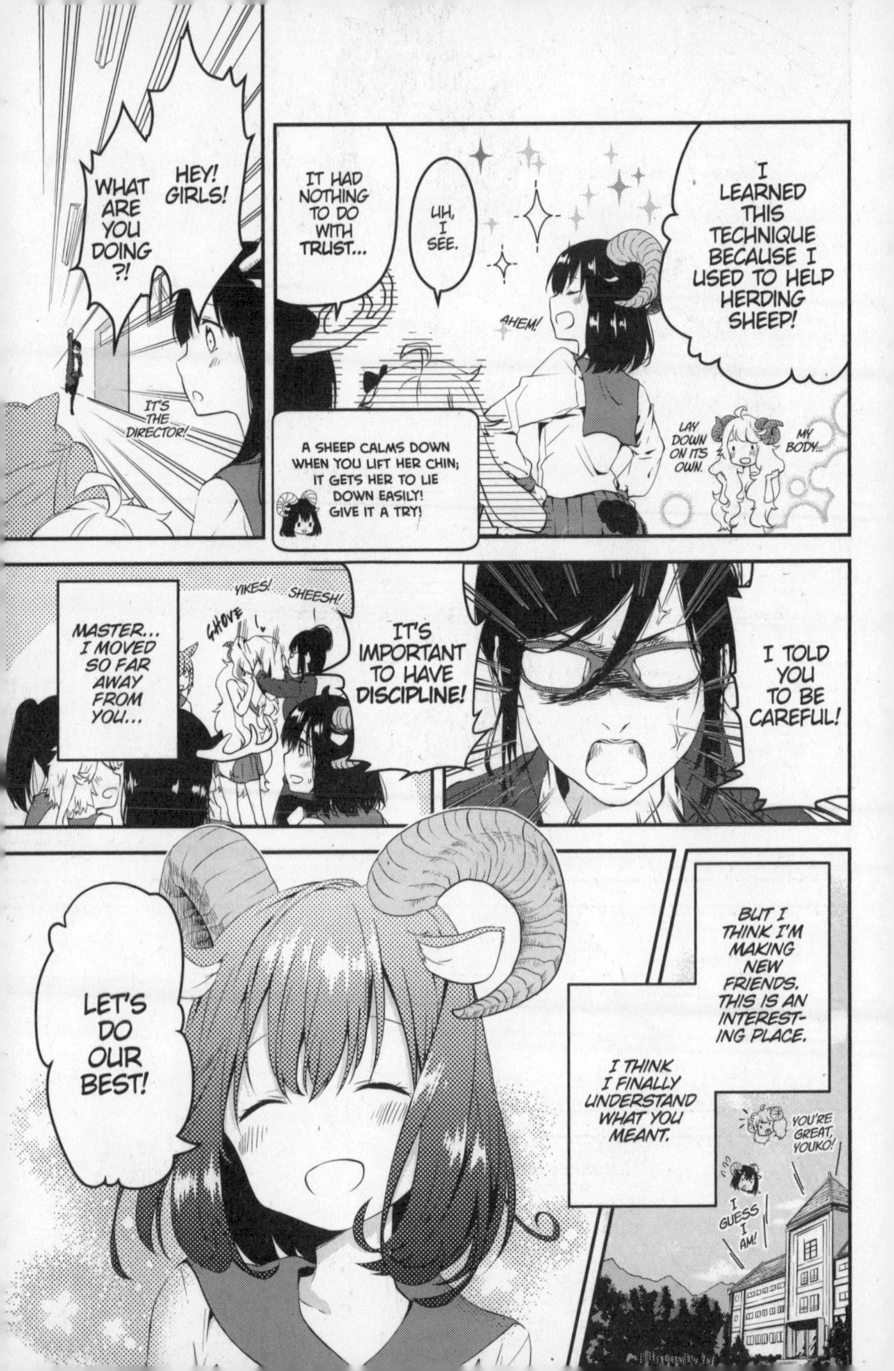

I LEARNED THIS TECHNIQUE BECAUSE I USED TO HELP HERDING SHEEP!
AHEM!
UH, I SEE.
IT HAD NOTHING TO DO WITH TRUST...
MY BODY...
LAY DOWN ON ITS OWN.
A SHEEP CALMS DOWN WHEN YOU LIFT HER CHIN; IT GETS HER TO LIE DOWN EASILY! GIVE IT A TRY!
HEY! GIRLS!
WHAT ARE YOU DOING?!
IT'S THE DIRECTOR!
I TOLD YOU TO BE CAREFUL!
IT'S IMPORTANT TO HAVE DISCIPLINE!
SHEESH!
YIKES!
SHOVE
MASTER... I MOVED SO FAR AWAY FROM YOU...
BUT I THINK I'M MAKING NEW FRIENDS. THIS IS AN INTERESTING PLACE.
I THINK I FINALLY UNDERSTAND WHAT YOU MEANT.
YOU'RE GREAT, YOUKO!
I GUESS I AM!
LET'S DO OUR BEST!

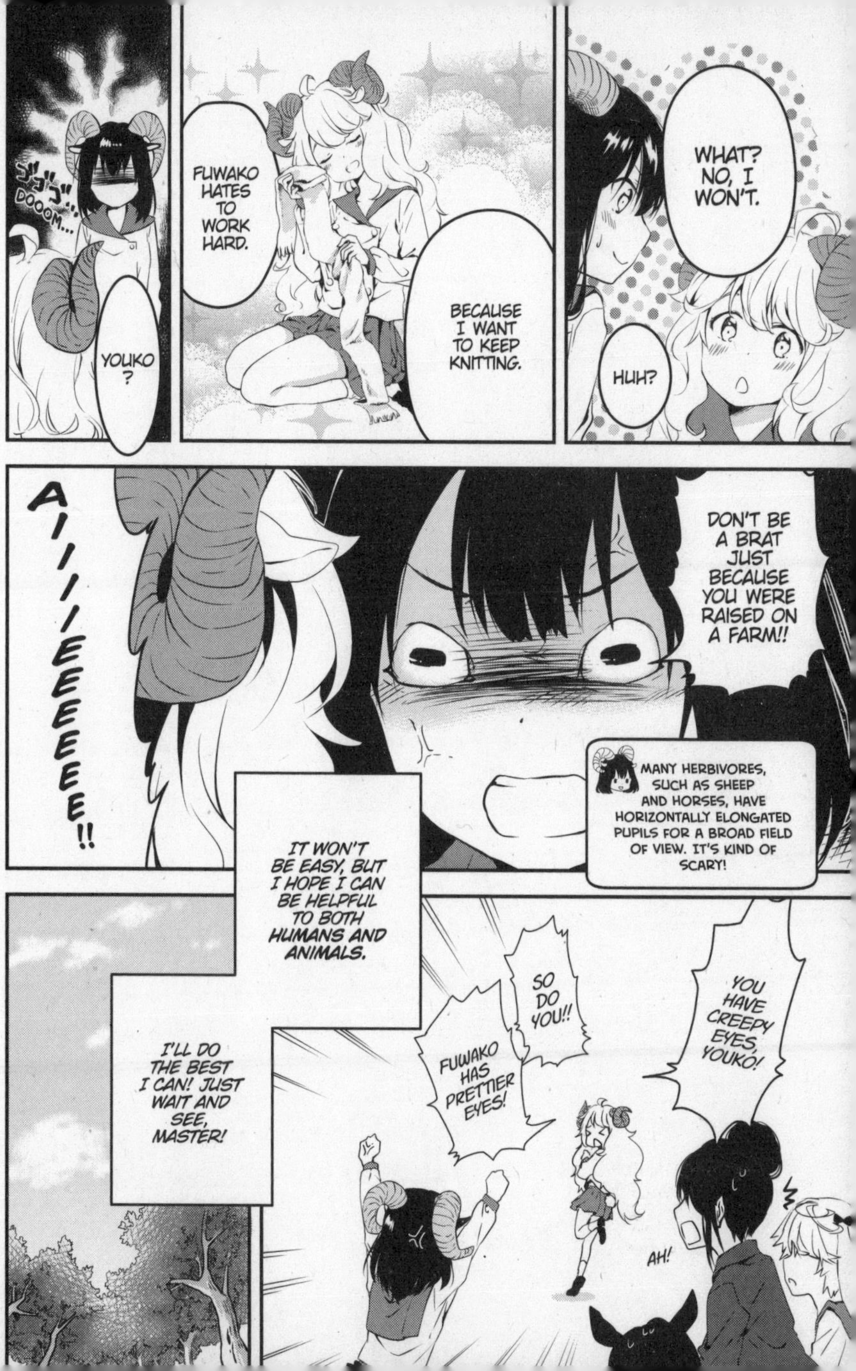
WHAT? NO, I WON'T.
HUH?
BECAUSE I WANT TO KEEP KNITTING.
FUWAKO HATES TO WORK HARD.
ゴゴゴ
DOOOM...
YOUKO?
DON'T BE A BRAT JUST BECAUSE YOU WERE RAISED ON A FARM!!
MANY HERBIVORES, SUCH AS SHEEP AND HORSES, HAVE HORIZONTALLY ELONGATED PUPILS FOR A BROAD FIELD OF VIEW. IT'S KIND OF SCARY!
AIIIIEEEEEEE!!
YOU HAVE CREEPY EYES, YOUKO!
SO DO YOU!!
FUWAKO HAS PRETTIER EYES!
AH!
IT WON'T BE EASY, BUT I HOPE I CAN BE HELPFUL TO BOTH HUMANS AND ANIMALS.
I'LL DO THE BEST I CAN! JUST WAIT AND SEE, MASTER!

Australian Merino

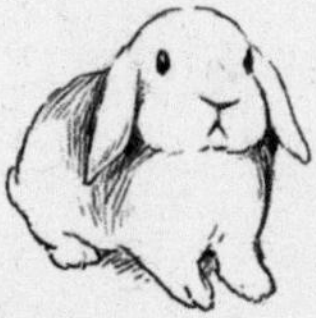
Holland Lop

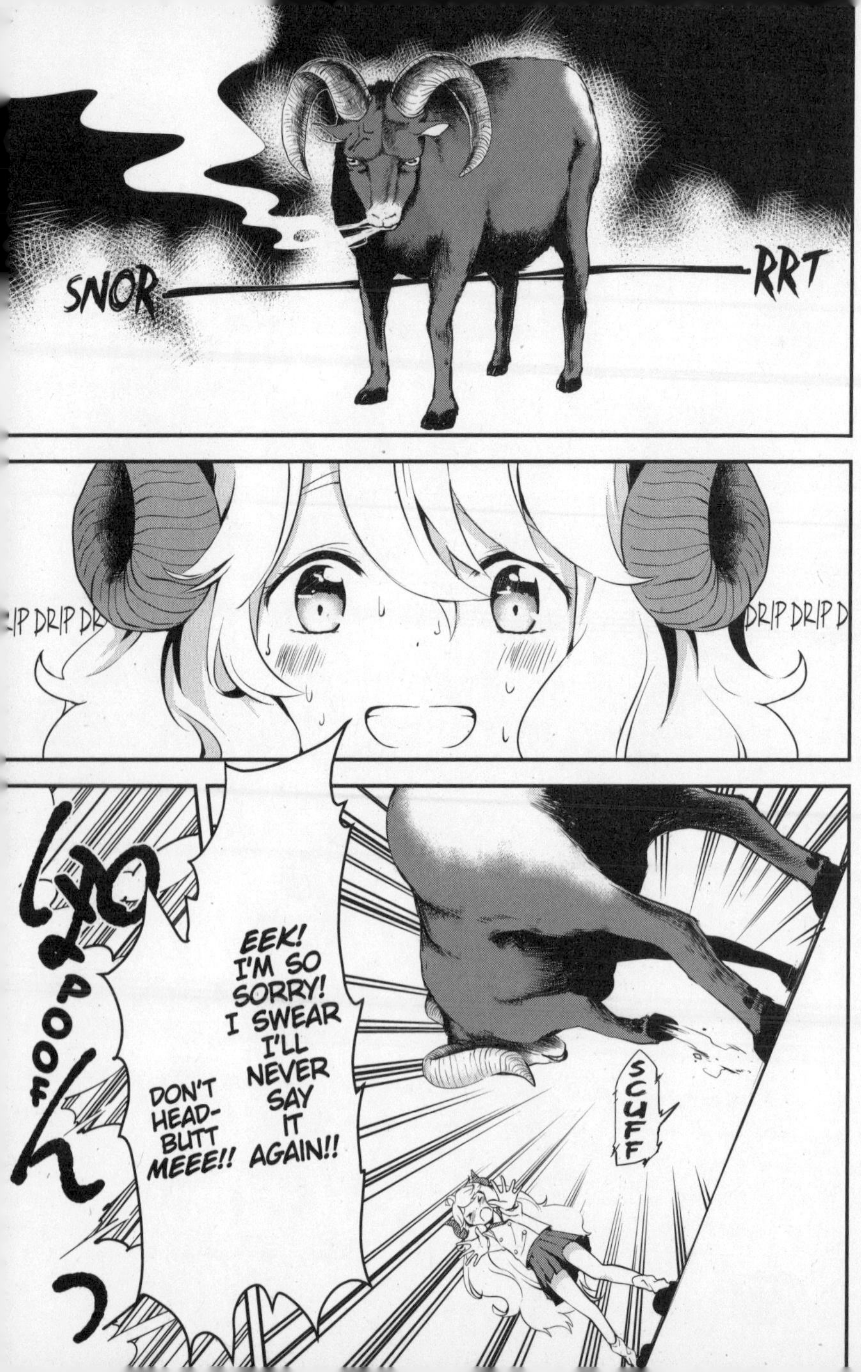
SNOR—RRT
IP DRIP DR
DRIP DRIP D
EEK! I'M SO SORRY! I SWEAR I'LL NEVER SAY IT AGAIN!!
DON'T HEAD-BUTT MEEE!!
SCUFF
POOF

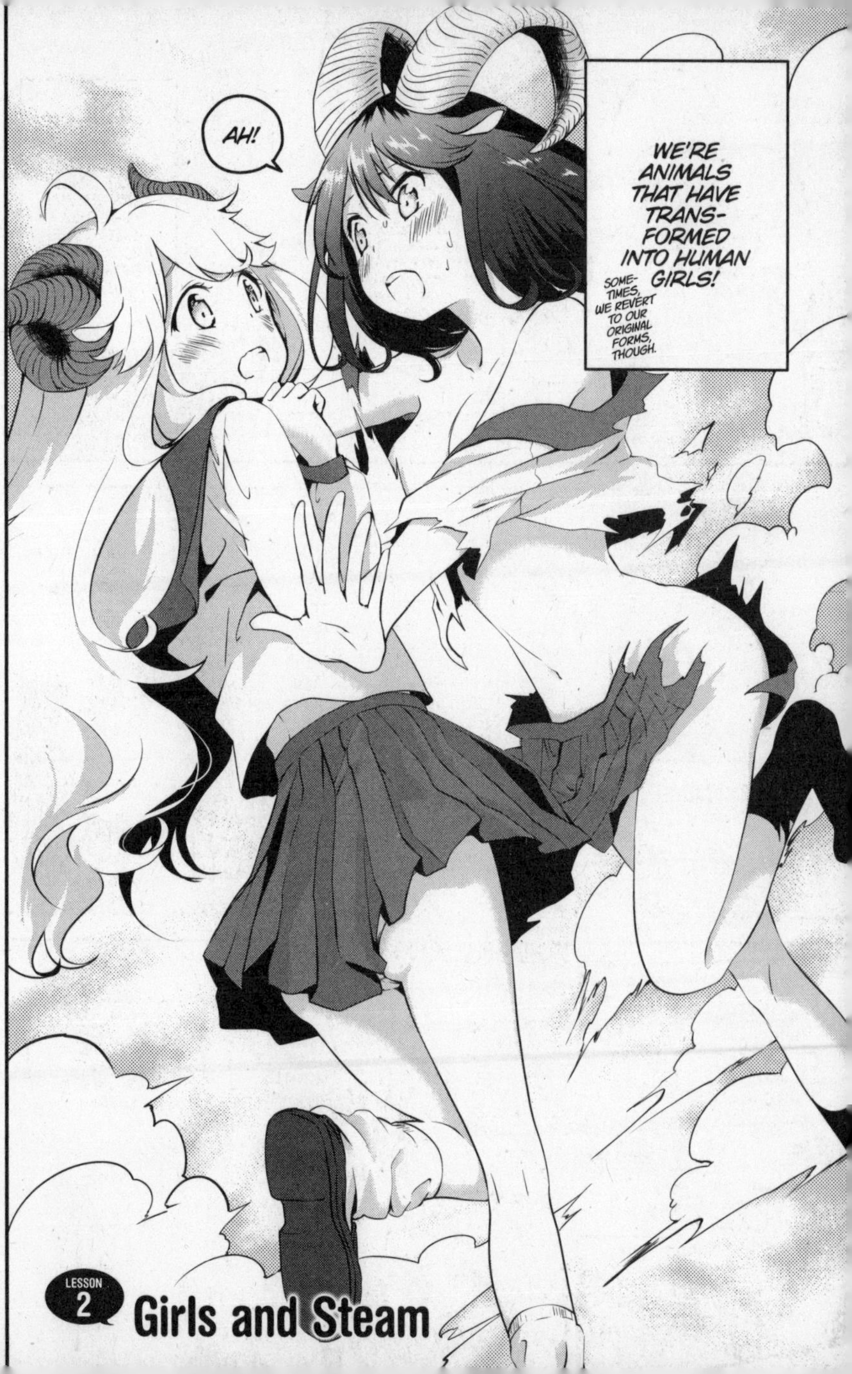
WE'RE ANIMALS THAT HAVE TRANS-FORMED INTO HUMAN GIRLS!
SOME-TIMES, WE REVERT TO OUR ORIGINAL FORMS, THOUGH.
AH!

LESSON 2 Girls and Steam

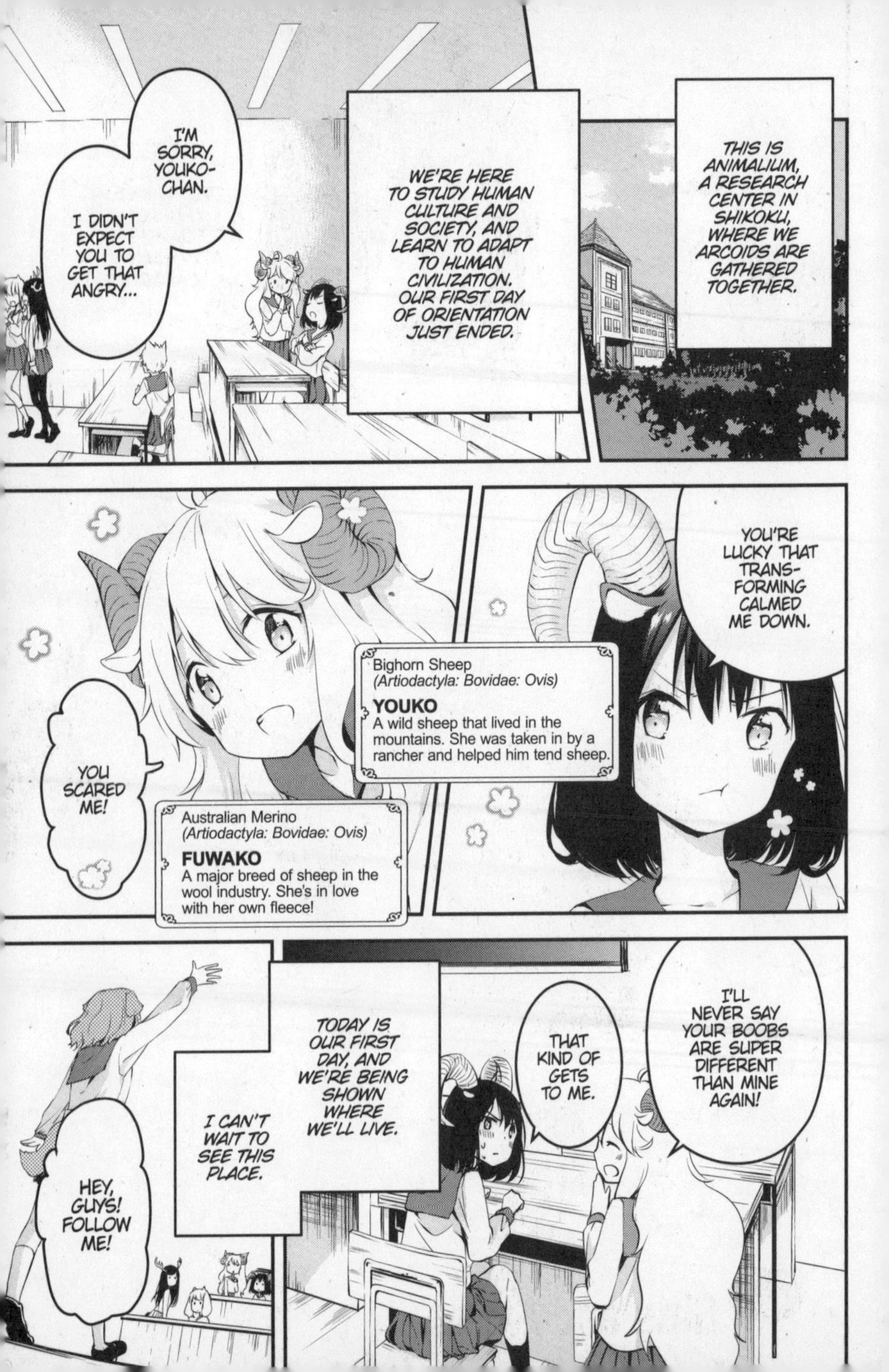
THIS IS ANIMALIUM, A RESEARCH CENTER IN SHIKOKU, WHERE WE ARCOIDS ARE GATHERED TOGETHER.
WE'RE HERE TO STUDY HUMAN CULTURE AND SOCIETY, AND LEARN TO ADAPT TO HUMAN CIVILIZATION. OUR FIRST DAY OF ORIENTATION JUST ENDED.
I'M SORRY, YOUKO-CHAN.
I DIDN'T EXPECT YOU TO GET THAT ANGRY...
YOU'RE LUCKY THAT TRANS-FORMING CALMED ME DOWN.
Bighorn Sheep (Artiodactyla: Bovidae: Ovis) YOUKO A wild sheep that lived in the mountains. She was taken in by a rancher and helped him tend sheep.
YOU SCARED ME!
Australian Merino (Artiodactyla: Bovidae: Ovis) FUWAKO A major breed of sheep in the wool industry. She's in love with her own fleece!
I'LL NEVER SAY YOUR BOOBS ARE SUPER DIFFERENT THAN MINE AGAIN!
THAT KIND OF GETS TO ME.
TODAY IS OUR FIRST DAY, AND WE'RE BEING SHOWN WHERE WE'LL LIVE.
I CAN'T WAIT TO SEE THIS PLACE.
HEY, GUYS! FOLLOW ME!

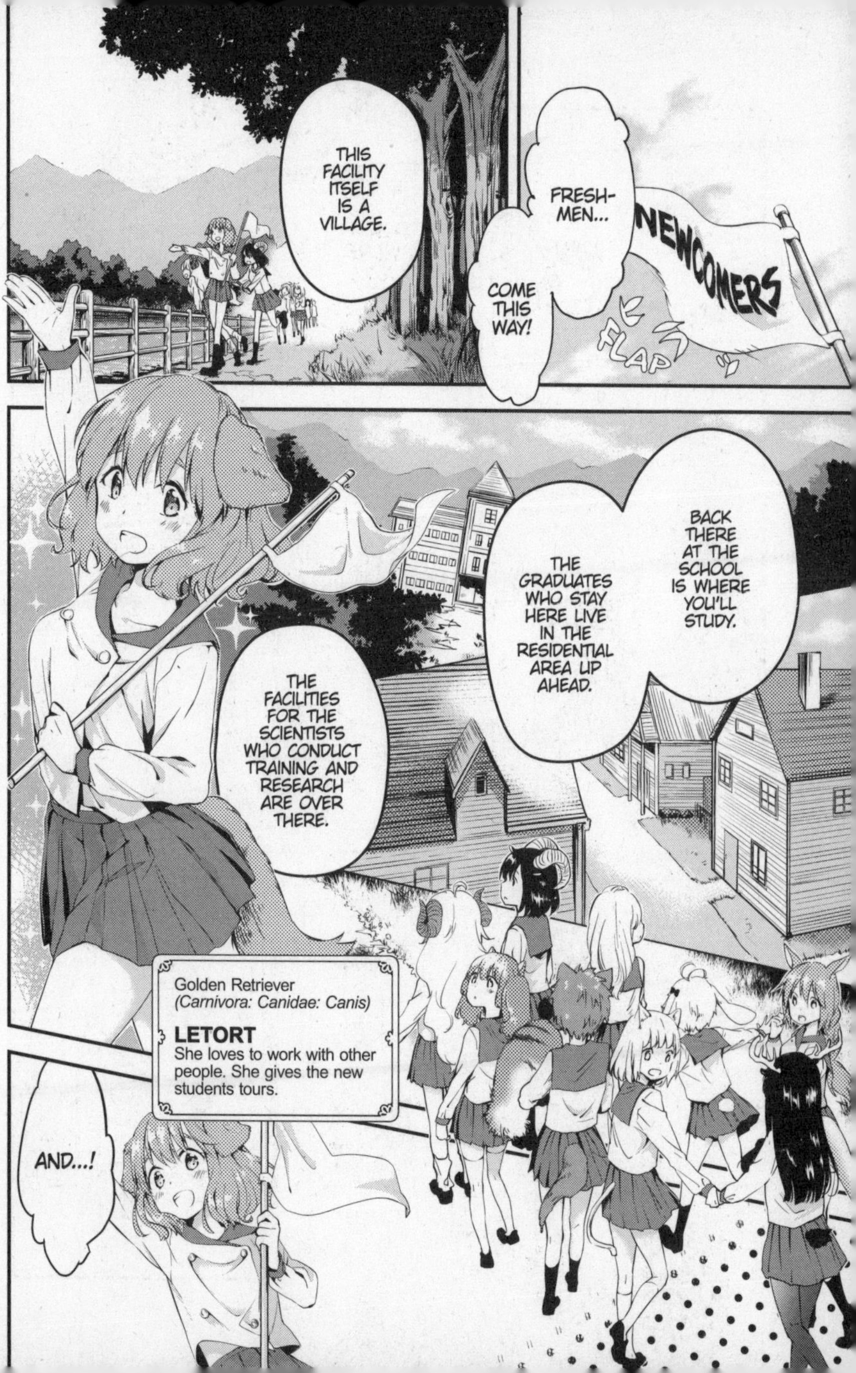
FRESHMEN...
COME THIS WAY!
NEWCOMERS
FLAP
THIS FACILITY ITSELF IS A VILLAGE.
BACK THERE AT THE SCHOOL IS WHERE YOU'LL STUDY.
THE GRADUATES WHO STAY HERE LIVE IN THE RESIDENTIAL AREA UP AHEAD.
THE FACILITIES FOR THE SCIENTISTS WHO CONDUCT TRAINING AND RESEARCH ARE OVER THERE.
Golden Retriever
(Carnivora: Canidae: Canis)
LETORT
She loves to work with other people. She gives the new students tours.
AND...!

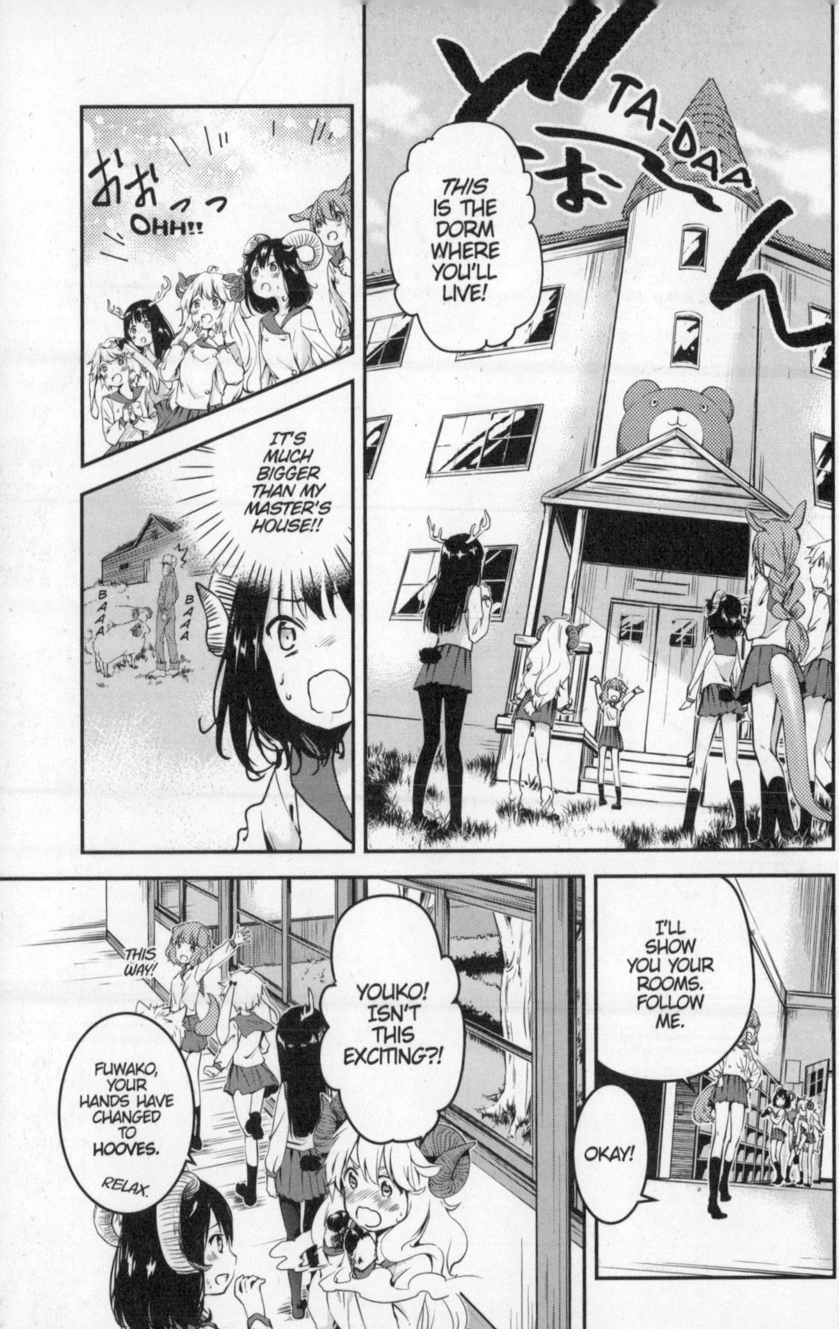
TA-DAA
THIS IS THE DORM WHERE YOU'LL LIVE!
おおっっ
OHH!!
IT'S MUCH BIGGER THAN MY MASTER'S HOUSE!!
BAAA
BAAA
I'LL SHOW YOU YOUR ROOMS. FOLLOW ME.
OKAY!
YOUKO! ISN'T THIS EXCITING?!
THIS WAY!
FUWAKO, YOUR HANDS HAVE CHANGED TO HOOVES.
RELAX.

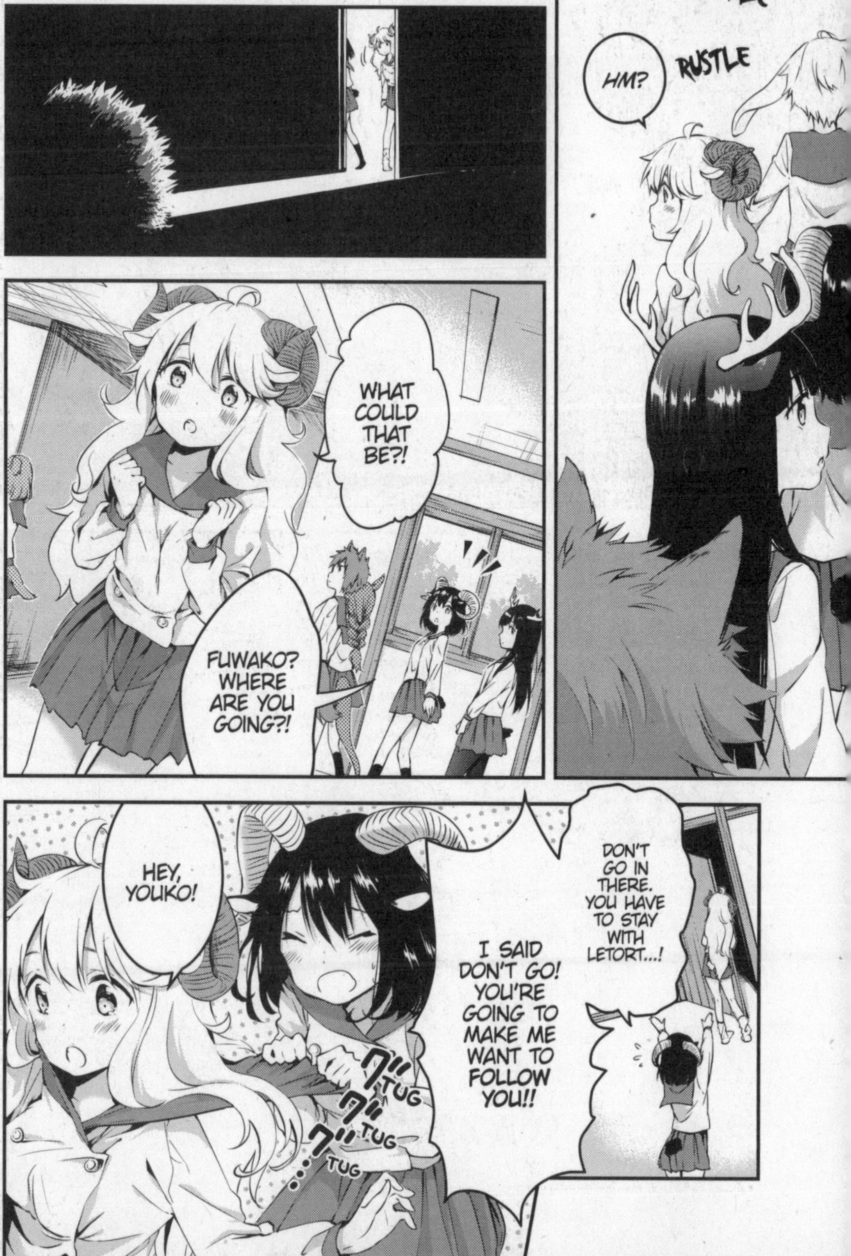
RUSTLE
HM?
RUSTLE
WHAT COULD THAT BE?!
FUWAKO? WHERE ARE YOU GOING?!
DON'T GO IN THERE. YOU HAVE TO STAY WITH LETORT...!
I SAID DON'T GO! YOU'RE GOING TO MAKE ME WANT TO FOLLOW YOU!!
HEY, YOUKO!
TUG
TUG
TUG

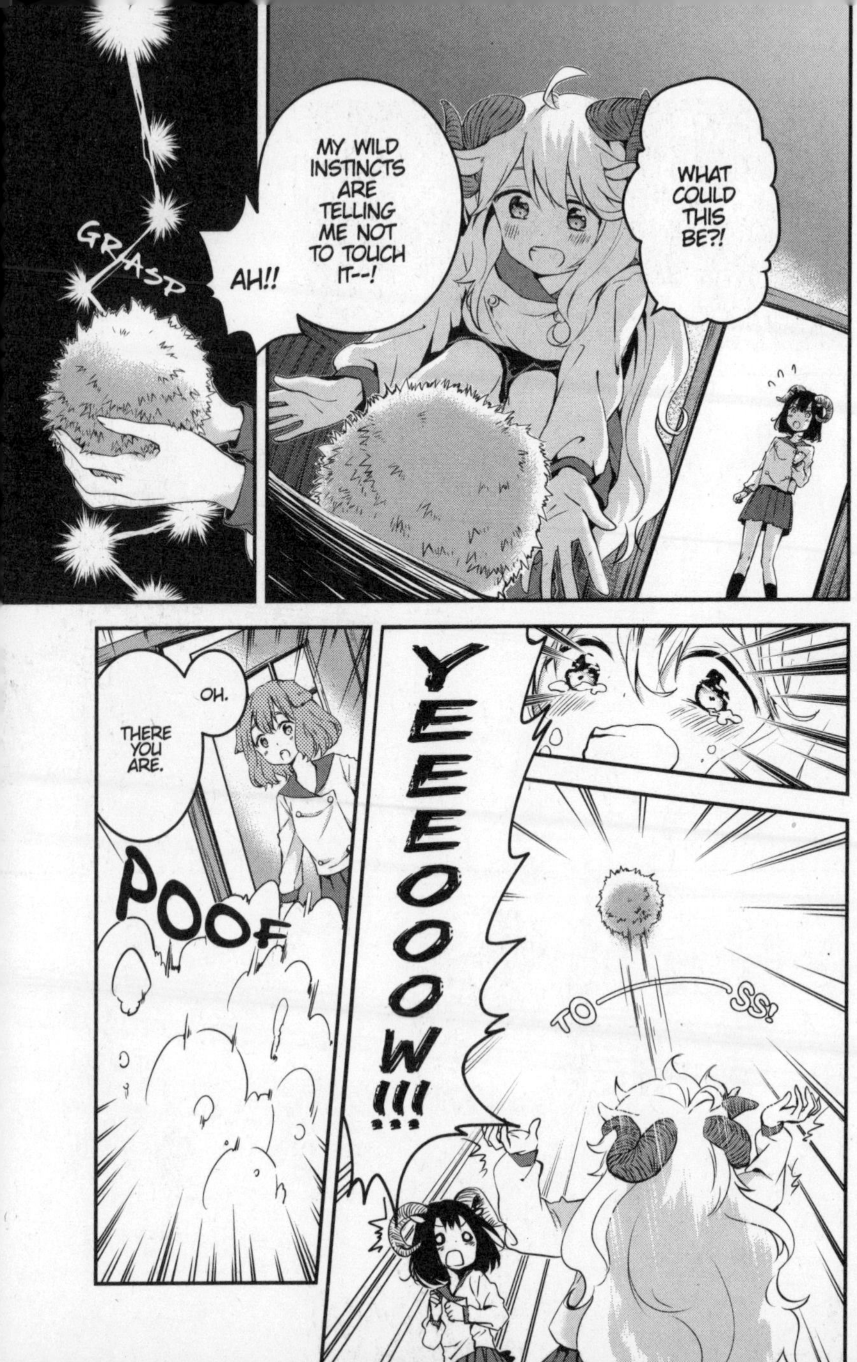

WHAT COULD THIS BE?!
MY WILD INSTINCTS ARE TELLING ME NOT TO TOUCH IT--!
AH!!
GRASP
YEEEOOOOW!!!
TO——SS!
OH.
THERE YOU ARE.
POOF

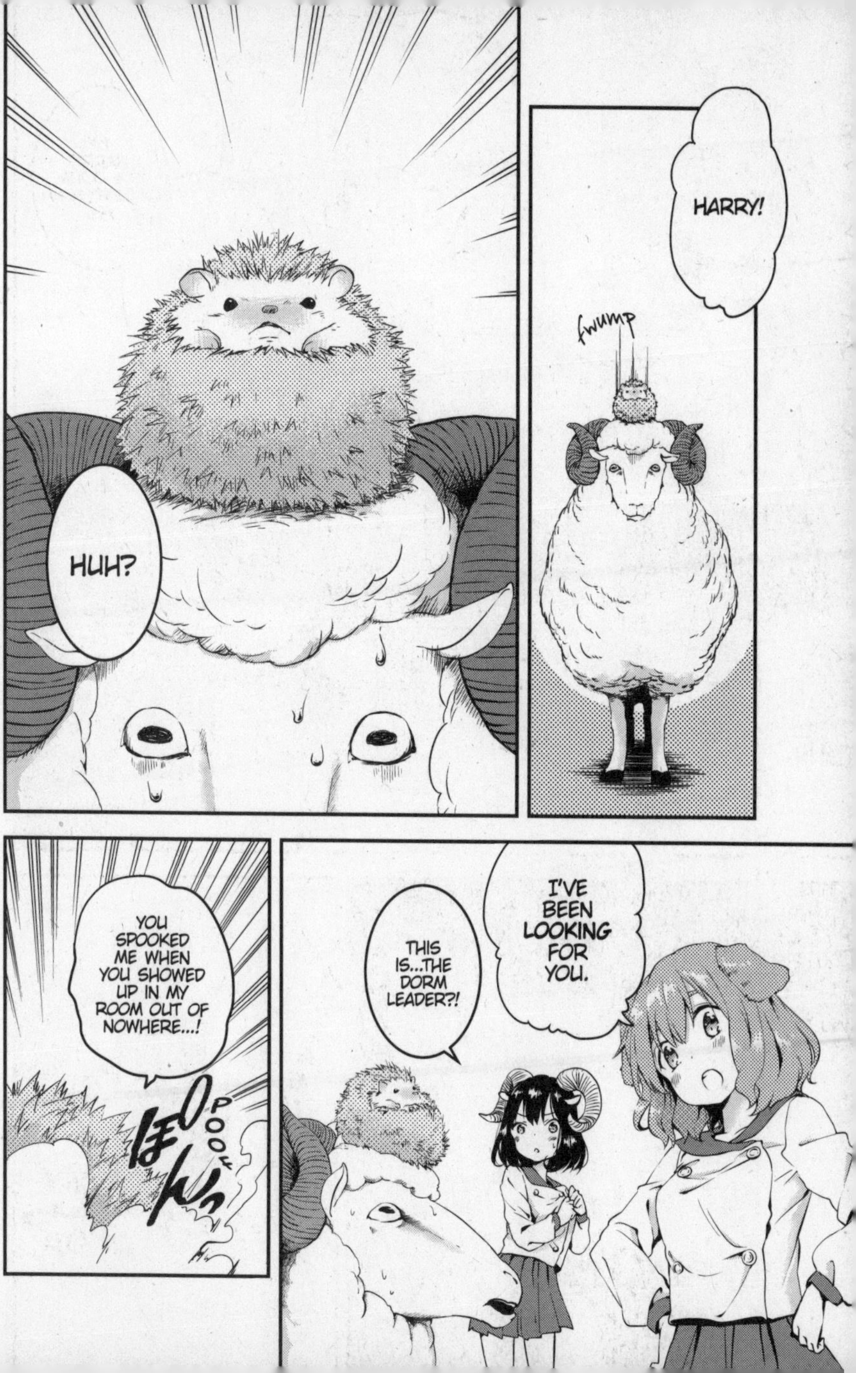
HARRY!
fwump
HUH?
I'VE BEEN LOOKING FOR YOU.
THIS IS...THE DORM LEADER?!
YOU SPOOKED ME WHEN YOU SHOWED UP IN MY ROOM OUT OF NOWHERE...!
POOF

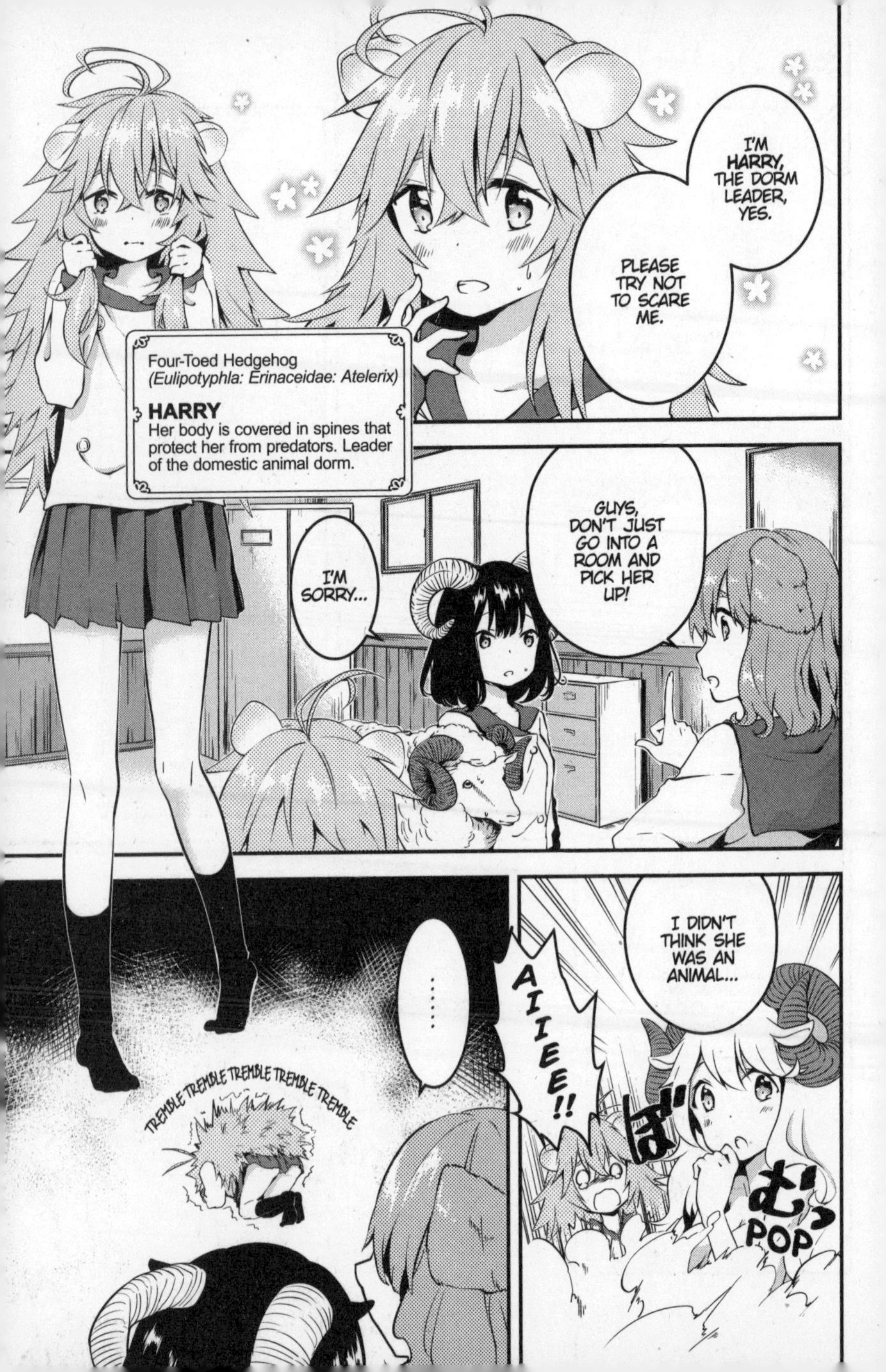
I'M HARRY, THE DORM LEADER, YES.
PLEASE TRY NOT TO SCARE ME.
GUYS, DON'T JUST GO INTO A ROOM AND PICK HER UP!
I'M SORRY...
Four-Toed Hedgehog
(Eulipotyphla: Erinaceidae: Atelerix)
HARRY
Her body is covered in spines that protect her from predators. Leader of the domestic animal dorm.
I DIDN'T THINK SHE WAS AN ANIMAL...
AIIEE!!
ぽ
むっ
POP
......
TREMBLE TREMBLE TREMBLE TREMBLE

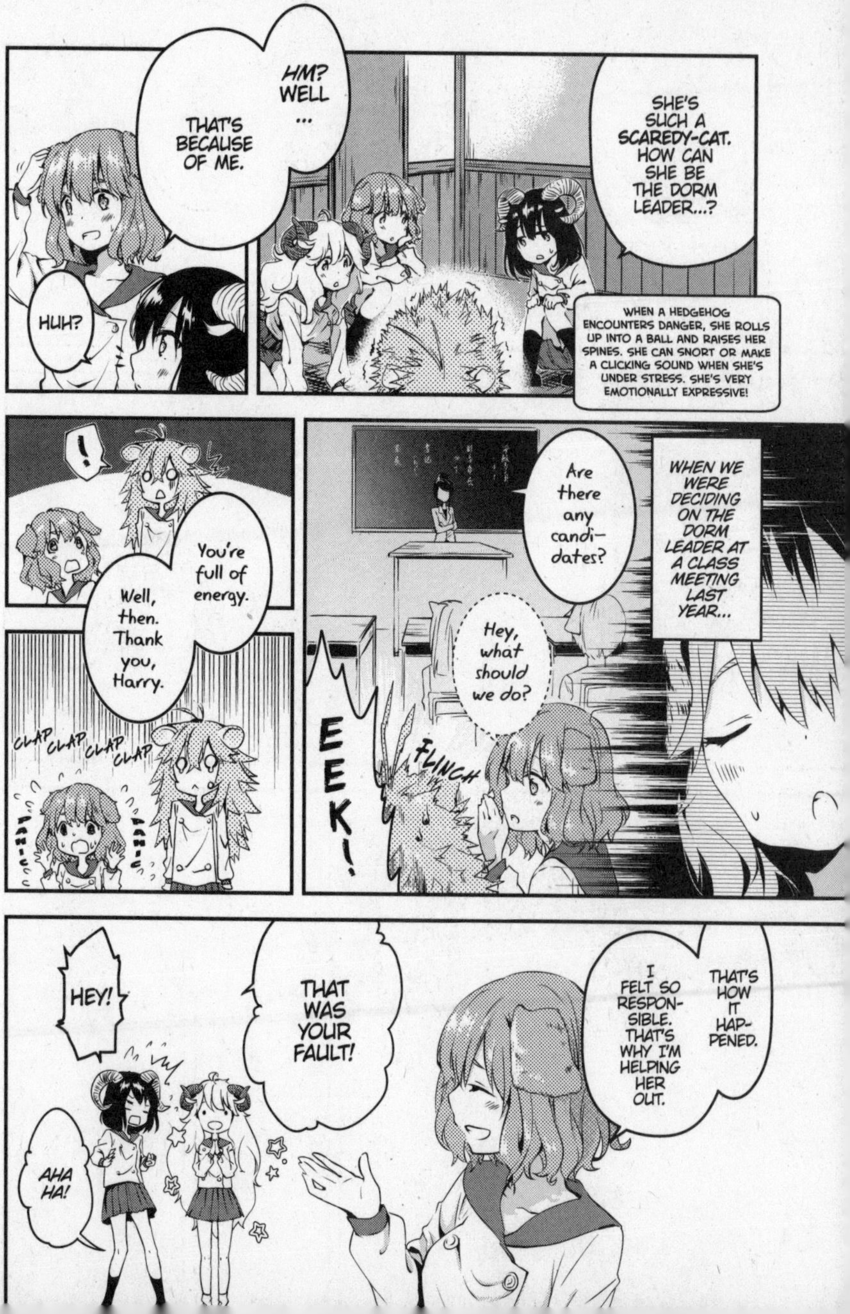
SHE'S SUCH A SCAREDY-CAT. HOW CAN SHE BE THE DORM LEADER...?
WHEN A HEDGEHOG ENCOUNTERS DANGER, SHE ROLLS UP INTO A BALL AND RAISES HER SPINES. SHE CAN SNORT OR MAKE A CLICKING SOUND WHEN SHE'S UNDER STRESS. SHE'S VERY EMOTIONALLY EXPRESSIVE!
HM? WELL ...
THAT'S BECAUSE OF ME.
HUH?
WHEN WE WERE DECIDING ON THE DORM LEADER AT A CLASS MEETING LAST YEAR...
Are there any candi-dates?
Hey, what should we do?
FLINCH
EEK!
!
You're full of energy.
Well, then. Thank you, Harry.
CLAP CLAP CLAP CLAP
PANIC PANIC
THAT'S HOW IT HAP-PENED.
I FELT SO RESPON-SIBLE. THAT'S WHY I'M HELPING HER OUT.
THAT WAS YOUR FAULT!
HEY!
AHA HA!

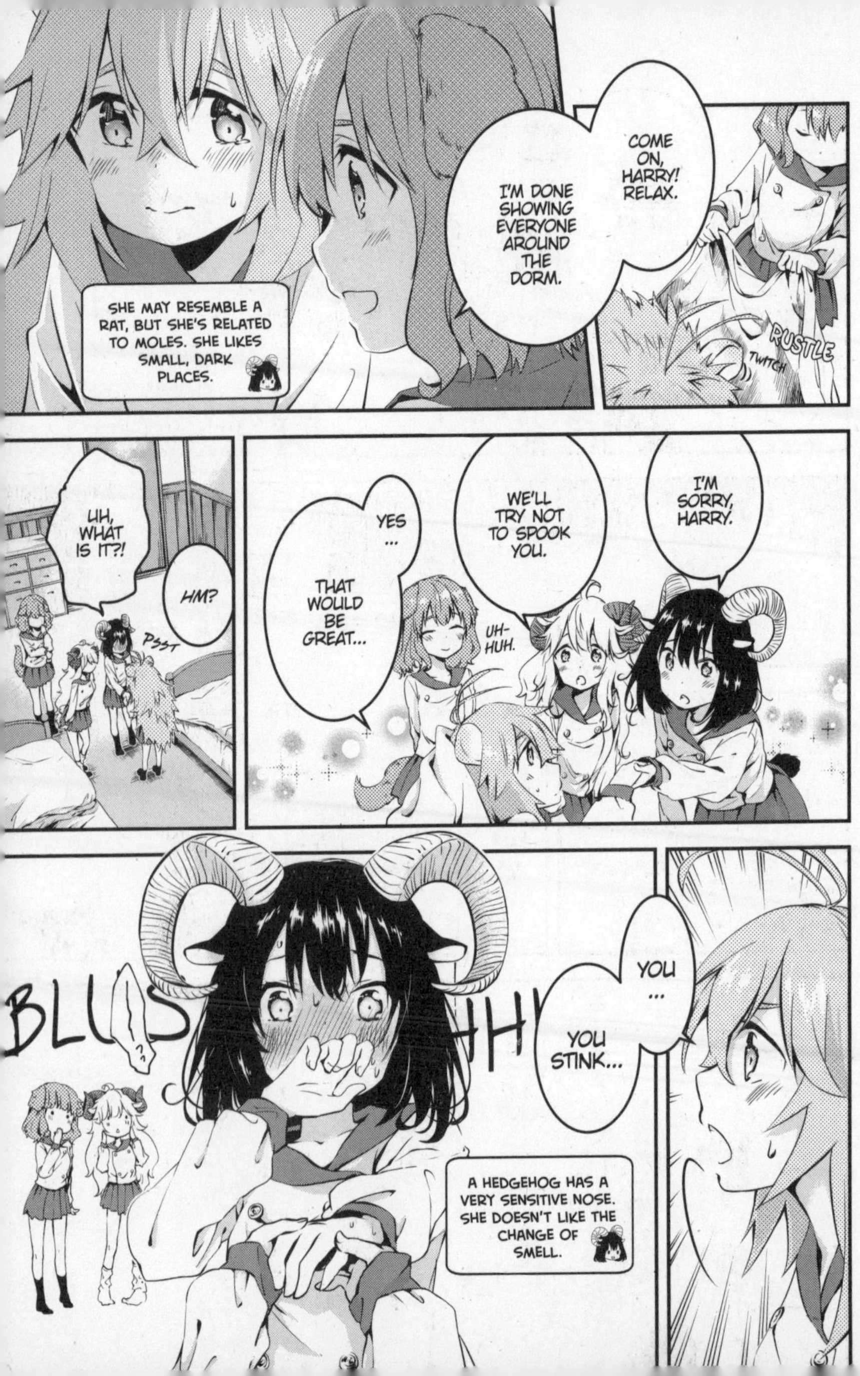
RUSTLE
TWITCH
COME ON, HARRY! RELAX.
I'M DONE SHOWING EVERYONE AROUND THE DORM.
SHE MAY RESEMBLE A RAT, BUT SHE'S RELATED TO MOLES. SHE LIKES SMALL, DARK PLACES.
I'M SORRY, HARRY.
WE'LL TRY NOT TO SPOOK YOU.
UH-HUH.
YES ...
THAT WOULD BE GREAT...
UH, WHAT IS IT?!
HM?
PSST
YOU ...
YOU STINK...
A HEDGEHOG HAS A VERY SENSITIVE NOSE. SHE DOESN'T LIKE THE CHANGE OF SMELL.
BLUSHH
?!

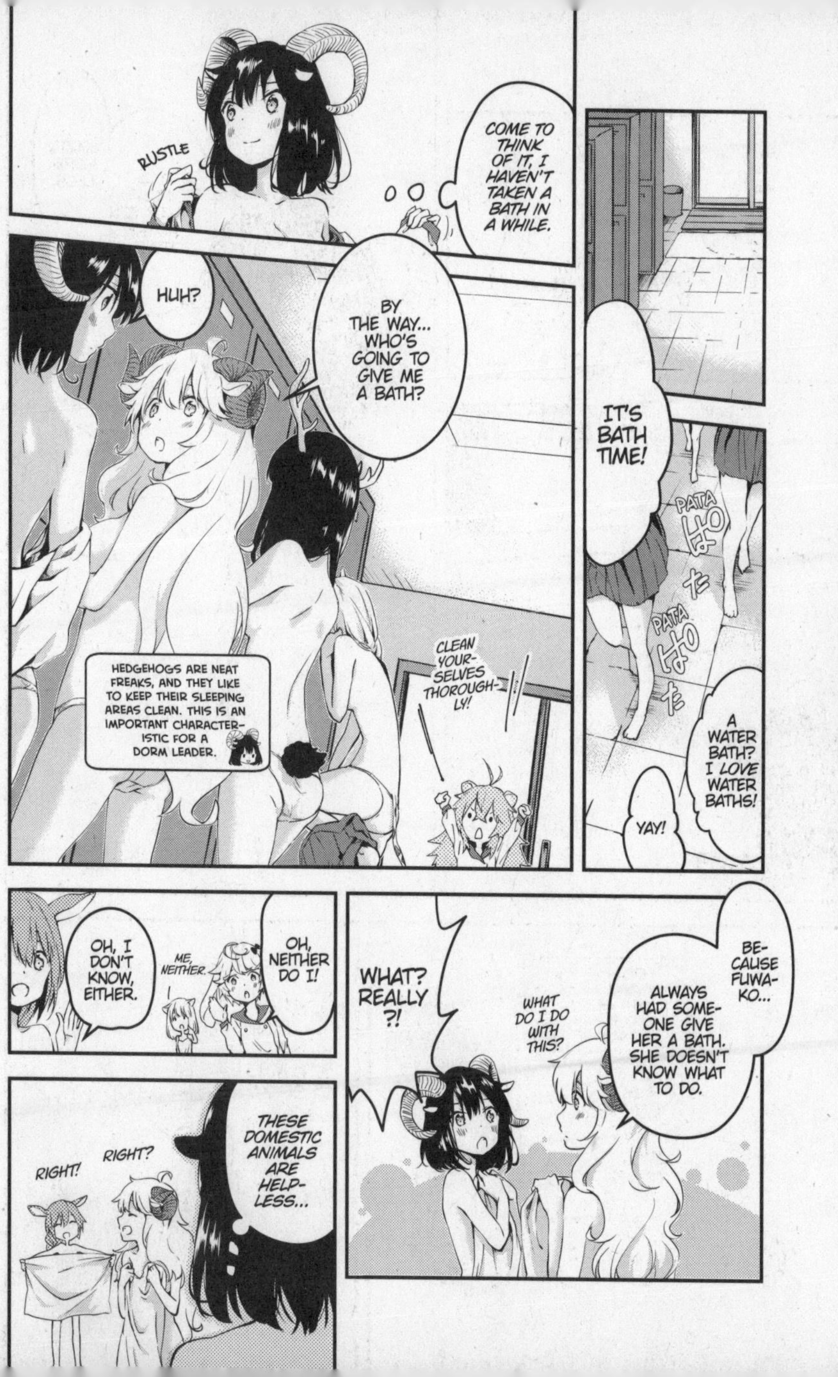
IT'S BATH TIME!
PATA
PATA
A WATER BATH? I LOVE WATER BATHS!
YAY!
RUSTLE
COME TO THINK OF IT, I HAVEN'T TAKEN A BATH IN A WHILE.
BY THE WAY... WHO'S GOING TO GIVE ME A BATH?
HUH?
CLEAN YOURSELVES THOROUGHLY!
HEDGEHOGS ARE NEAT FREAKS, AND THEY LIKE TO KEEP THEIR SLEEPING AREAS CLEAN. THIS IS AN IMPORTANT CHARACTERISTIC FOR A DORM LEADER.
BECAUSE FUWAKO...
ALWAYS HAD SOMEONE GIVE HER A BATH. SHE DOESN'T KNOW WHAT TO DO.
WHAT DO I DO WITH THIS?
WHAT? REALLY?!
OH, NEITHER DO I!
ME, NEITHER.
OH, I DON'T KNOW, EITHER.
THESE DOMESTIC ANIMALS ARE HELPLESS...
RIGHT?
RIGHT!

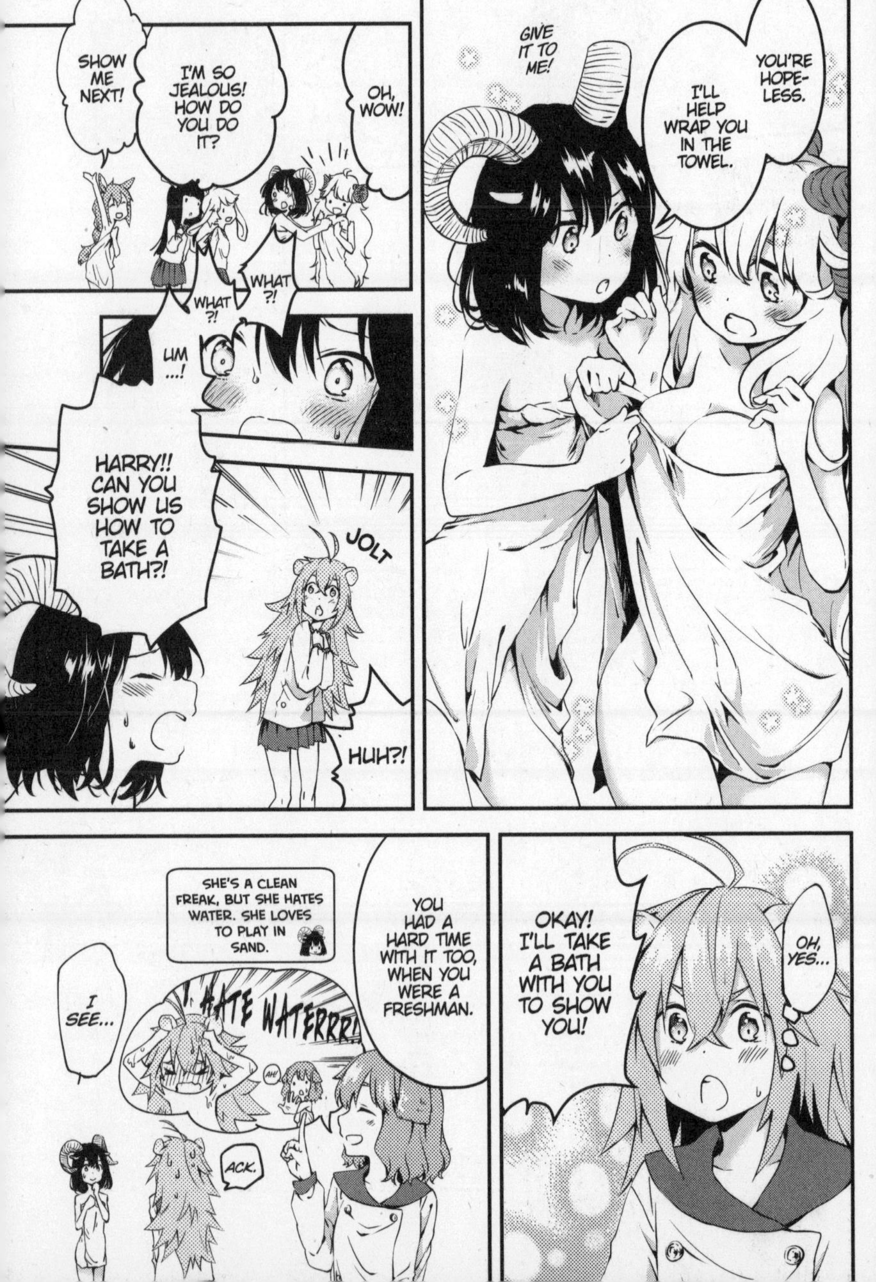
YOU'RE HOPE-LESS.
I'LL HELP WRAP YOU IN THE TOWEL.
GIVE IT TO ME!
OH, WOW!
I'M SO JEALOUS! HOW DO YOU DO IT?
SHOW ME NEXT!
WHAT?!
WHAT?!
UM ...!
HARRY!! CAN YOU SHOW US HOW TO TAKE A BATH?!
JOLT
HUH?!
OH, YES...
OKAY! I'LL TAKE A BATH WITH YOU TO SHOW YOU!
YOU HAD A HARD TIME WITH IT TOO, WHEN YOU WERE A FRESHMAN.
SHE'S A CLEAN FREAK, BUT SHE HATES WATER. SHE LOVES TO PLAY IN SAND.
I HATE WATERRR!
AH!
I SEE...
ACK.

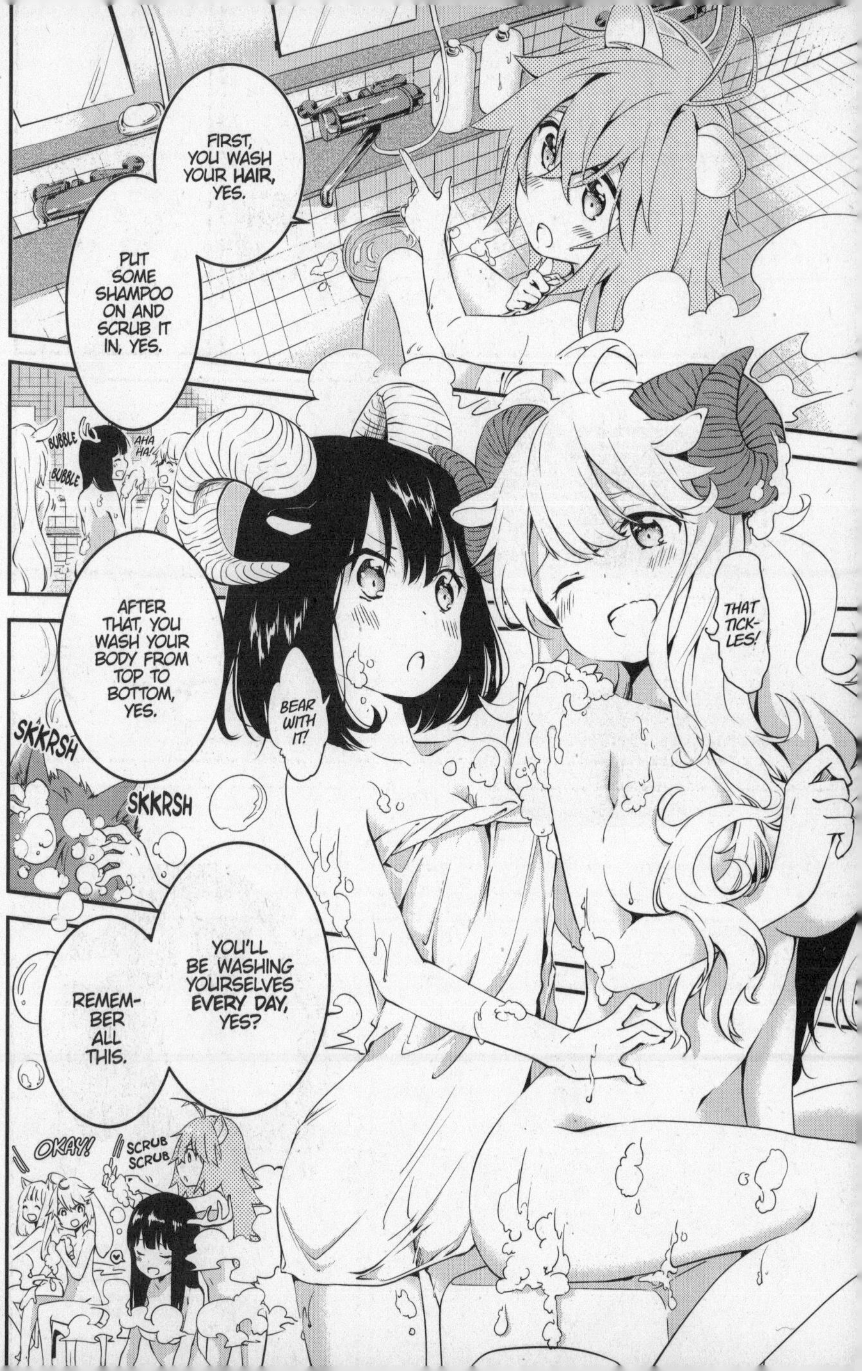
FIRST, YOU WASH YOUR HAIR, YES.
PUT SOME SHAMPOO ON AND SCRUB IT IN, YES.
THAT TICKLES!
BEAR WITH IT!
AHA HA!
BUBBLE BUBBLE
AFTER THAT, YOU WASH YOUR BODY FROM TOP TO BOTTOM, YES.
SKKRSH
SKKRSH
YOU'LL BE WASHING YOURSELVES EVERY DAY, YES?
REMEMBER ALL THIS.
SCRUB SCRUB
OKAY!

PLISH
AHHHHHHH...!♥
MY TAIL FEELS SO WARM!
DO YOU KNOW WHAT THESE ARE FOR?
EEK!
BEATS ME...
I'LL WASH YOU, BUNNY!
WAG WAG
UWAH!
CLATTER
SWISHH
NO SWIMMING, NO!
AHHH!
IT'S BEEN SO LONG SINCE I LAST TOOK A BATH! THIS IS NICE. ♥
FU-WAKO LOVES BATH TIME! ♥
I'M GLAD YOU WERE ABLE TO TAKE A BATH, YES!
MOST ANIMALS LOVE TO TAKE BATHS! THERE ARE MANY BENEFITS, SUCH AS KEEPING THEMSELVES CLEAN AND REMOVING PARASITES FROM THE SKIN.

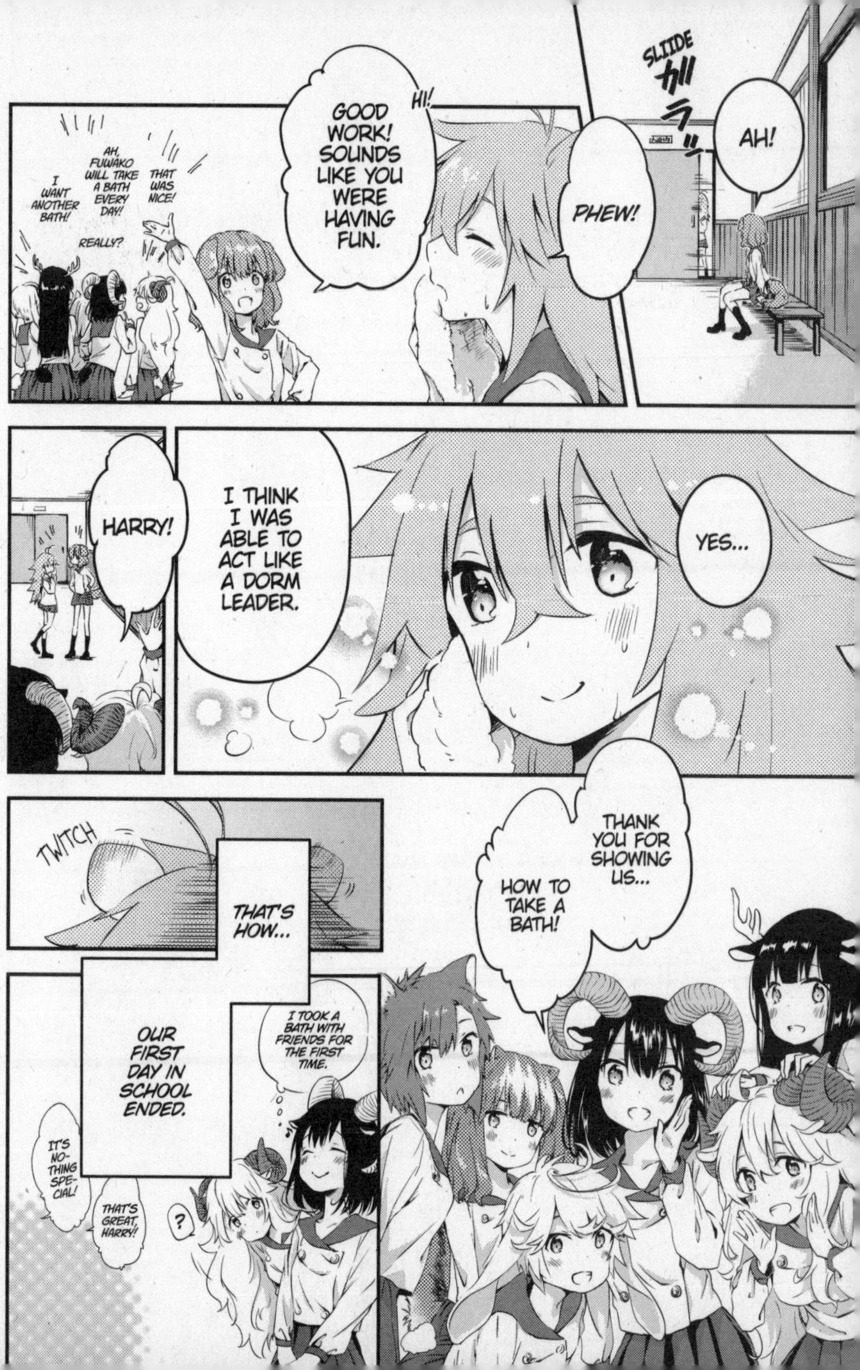
SLIIDE
ガラッ
AH!
PHEW!
HI!
GOOD WORK! SOUNDS LIKE YOU WERE HAVING FUN.
THAT WAS NICE!
AH, FUWAKO WILL TAKE A BATH EVERY DAY!
I WANT ANOTHER BATH!
REALLY?
YES...
I THINK I WAS ABLE TO ACT LIKE A DORM LEADER.
HARRY!
THANK YOU FOR SHOWING US...
HOW TO TAKE A BATH!
TWITCH
THAT'S HOW...
OUR FIRST DAY IN SCHOOL ENDED.
I TOOK A BATH WITH FRIENDS FOR THE FIRST TIME.
?
THAT'S GREAT, HARRY!
IT'S NO-THING SPE-CIAL!

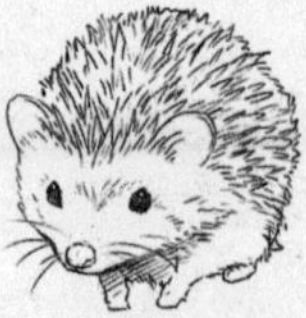

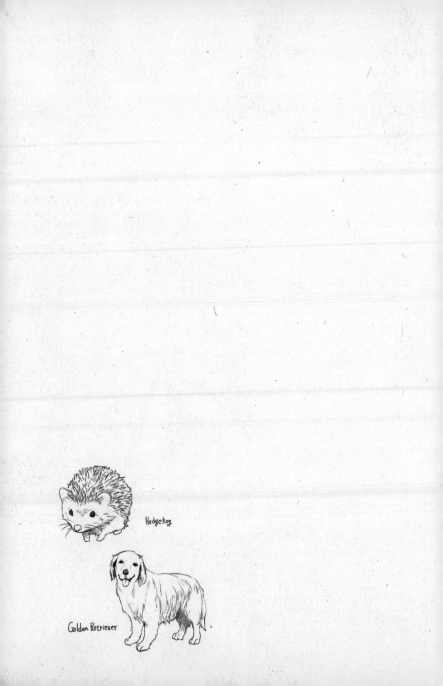

Hedgehog

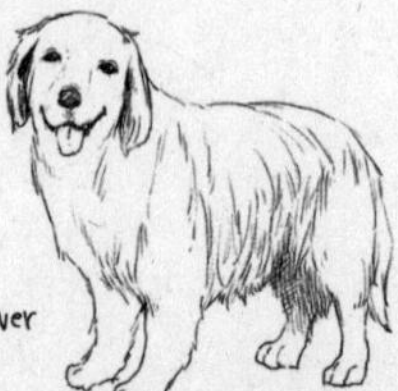

Golden Retriever

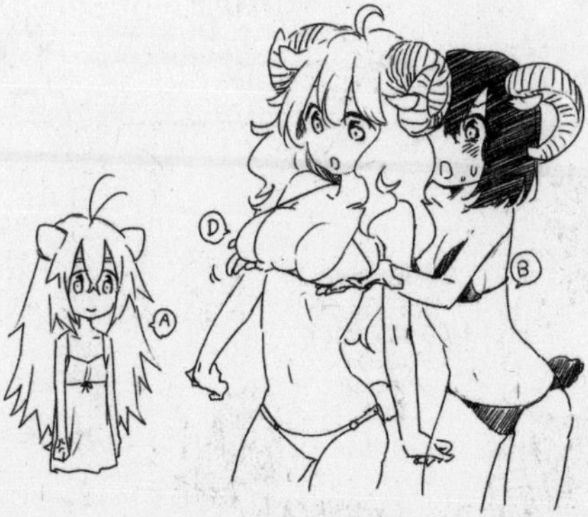
B
D
A

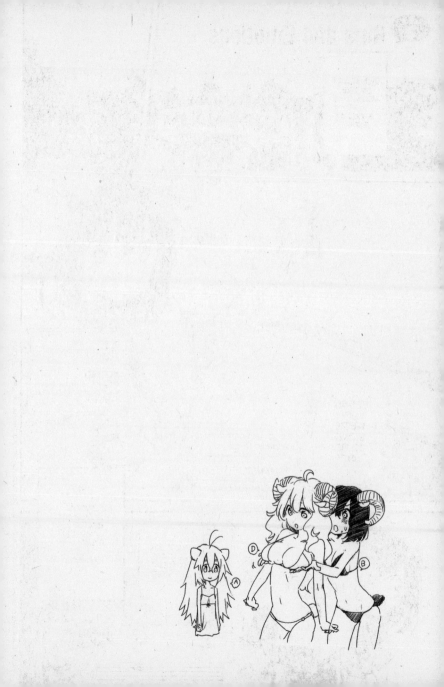

LESSON 3 Girls and Emotions

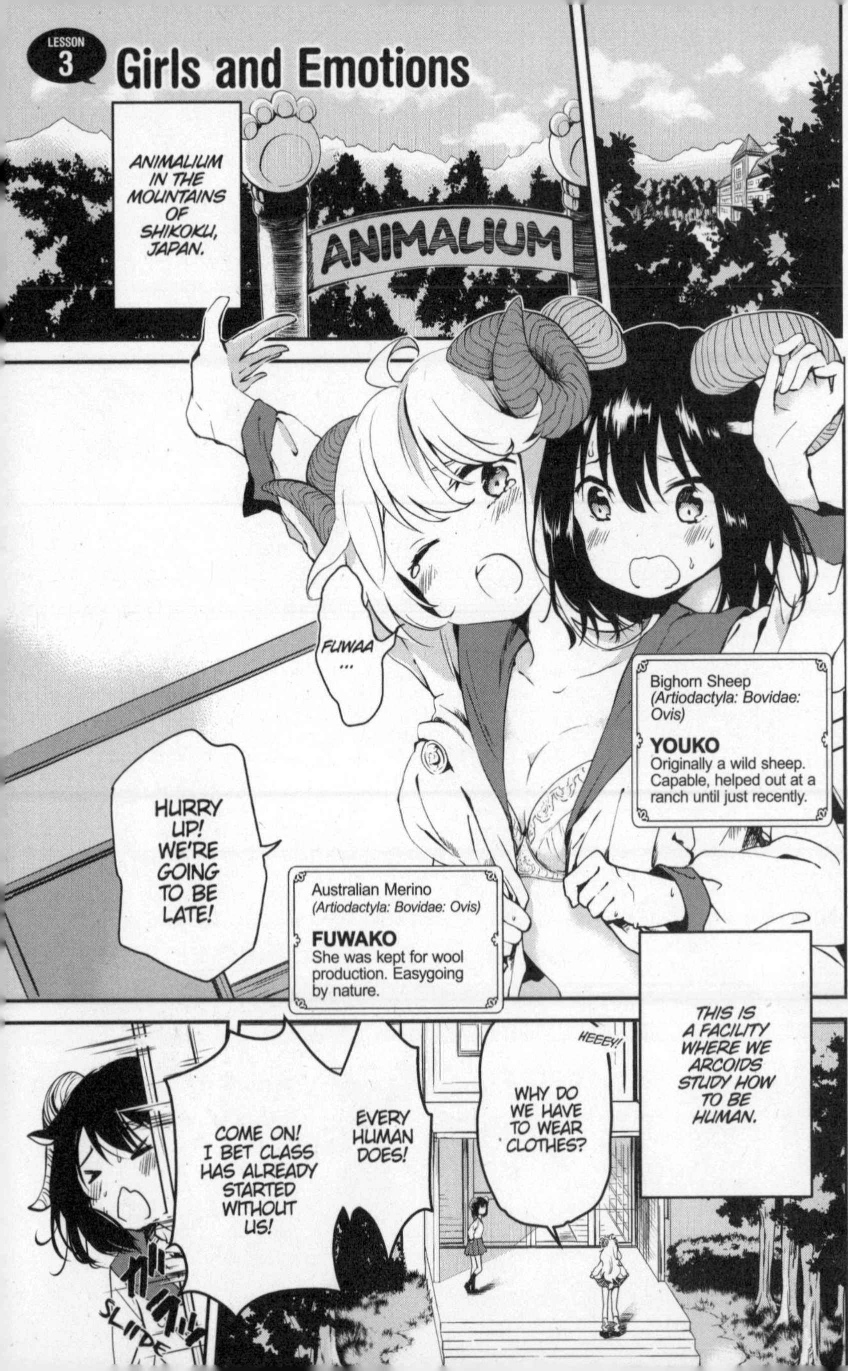
ANIMALIUM IN THE MOUNTAINS OF SHIKOKU, JAPAN.
ANIMALIUM
Bighorn Sheep (Artiodactyla: Bovidae: Ovis) YOUKO Originally a wild sheep. Capable, helped out at a ranch until just recently.
FUWAA ...
Australian Merino (Artiodactyla: Bovidae: Ovis) FUWAKO She was kept for wool production. Easygoing by nature.
HURRY UP! WE'RE GOING TO BE LATE!
THIS IS A FACILITY WHERE WE ARCOIDS STUDY HOW TO BE HUMAN.
HEEEY!
WHY DO WE HAVE TO WEAR CLOTHES?
EVERY HUMAN DOES!
COME ON! I BET CLASS HAS ALREADY STARTED WITHOUT US!
SLIIDE

※NOTE: Arcoids are animals that have morphed into human girls. Arcoids can return to their animal forms.

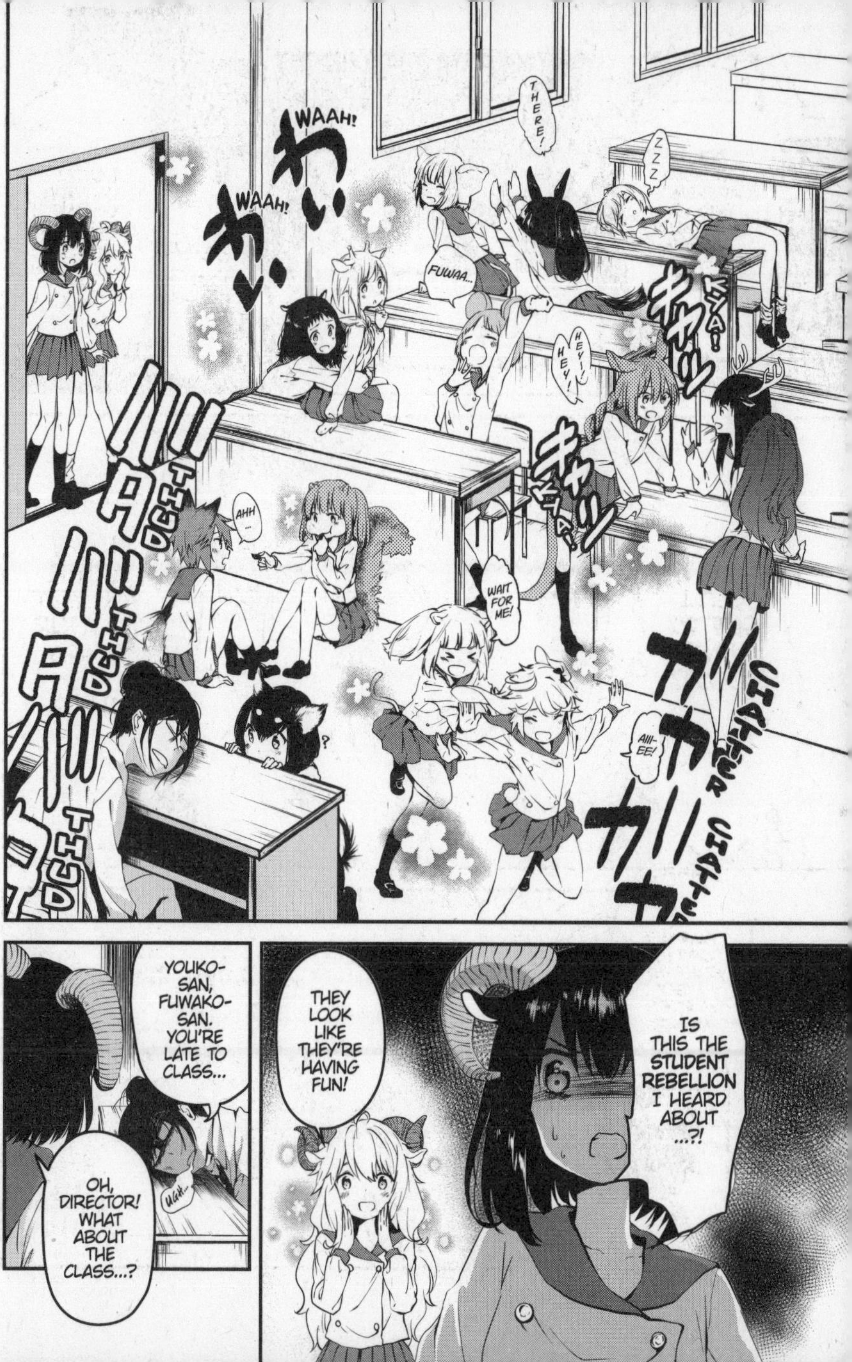
ZZZ
THERE!
KYA!
WAAH!
WAAH!
FUWAA...
HEY! HEY!
KYA!
CHATTER CHATTER
AIII-EE!
WAIT FOR ME!
AHH...
THUD THUD THUD
IS THIS THE STUDENT REBELLION I HEARD ABOUT ...?!
THEY LOOK LIKE THEY'RE HAVING FUN!
YOUKO-SAN, FUWAKO-SAN. YOU'RE LATE TO CLASS...
UGH...
OH, DIRECTOR! WHAT ABOUT THE CLASS...?

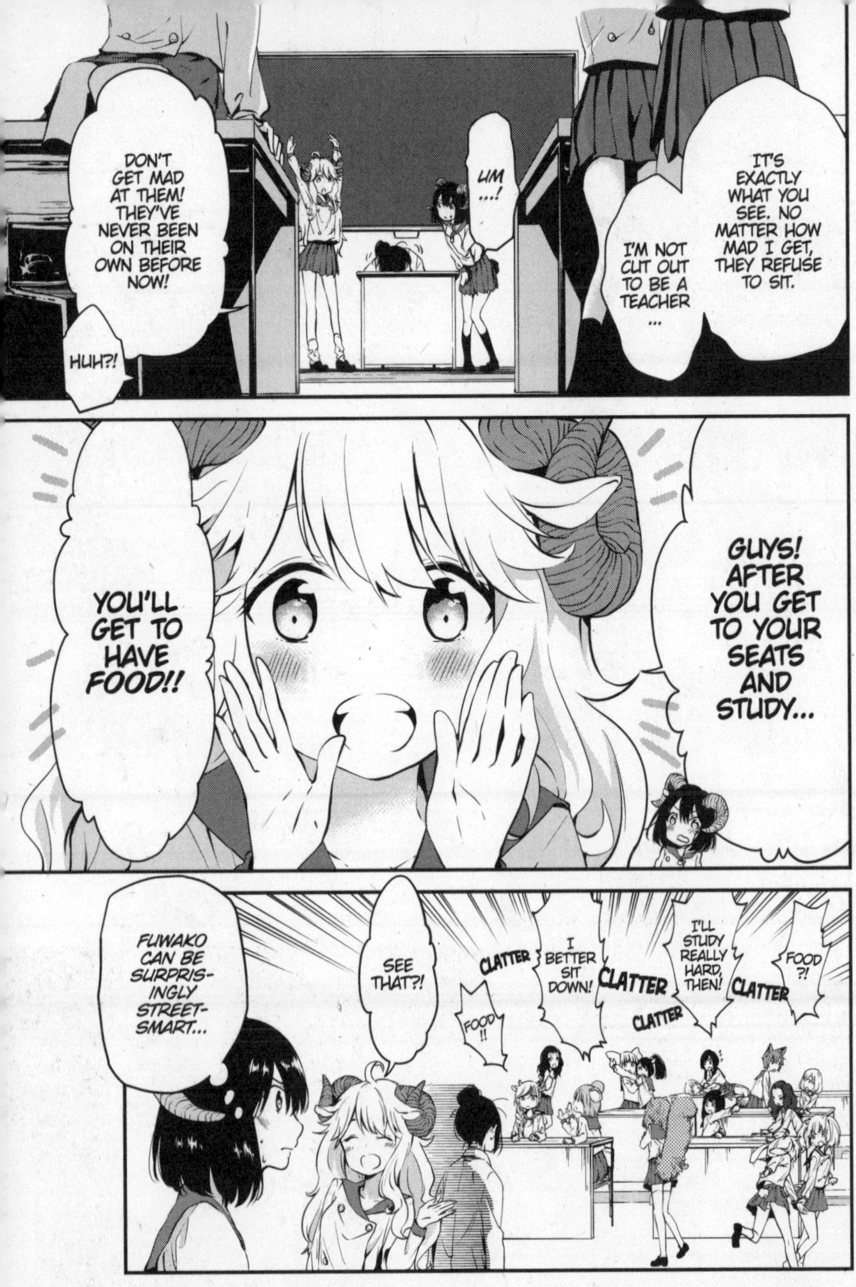
IT'S EXACTLY WHAT YOU SEE. NO MATTER HOW MAD I GET, THEY REFUSE TO SIT.
I'M NOT CUT OUT TO BE A TEACHER...
UM...!
DON'T GET MAD AT THEM! THEY'VE NEVER BEEN ON THEIR OWN BEFORE NOW!
HUH?!
GUYS! AFTER YOU GET TO YOUR SEATS AND STUDY...
YOU'LL GET TO HAVE FOOD!!
FOOD?!
CLATTER
I'LL STUDY REALLY HARD, THEN!
CLATTER
CLATTER
I BETTER SIT DOWN!
CLATTER
FOOD!!
SEE THAT?!
FUWAKO CAN BE SURPRISINGLY STREET-SMART...

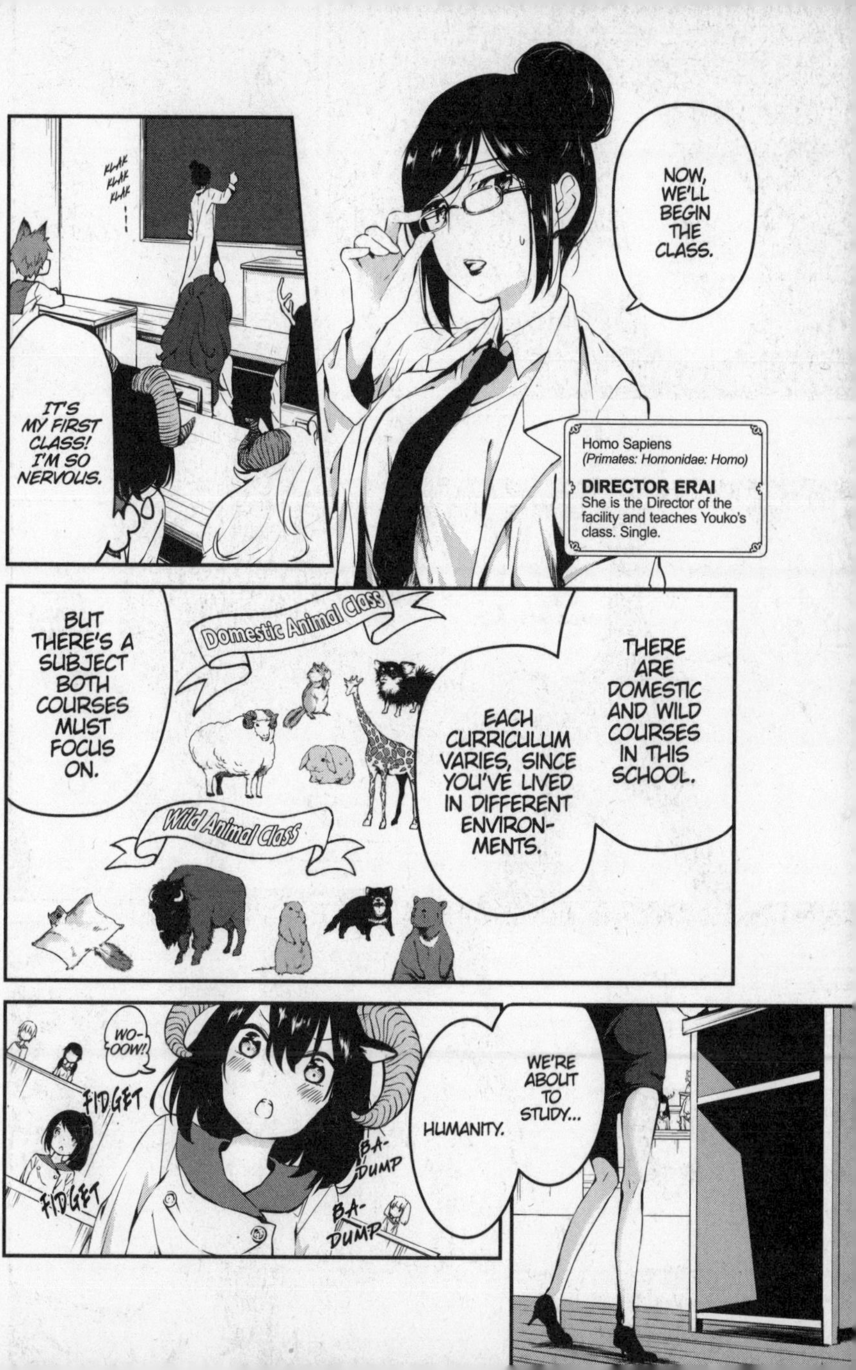
NOW, WE'LL BEGIN THE CLASS.
Homo Sapiens
(Primates: Homonidae: Homo)
DIRECTOR ERAI
She is the Director of the facility and teaches Youko's class. Single.
KLAK KLAK KLAK
IT'S MY FIRST CLASS! I'M SO NERVOUS.
THERE ARE DOMESTIC AND WILD COURSES IN THIS SCHOOL.
EACH CURRICULUM VARIES, SINCE YOU'VE LIVED IN DIFFERENT ENVIRON-MENTS.
Domestic Animal Class
Wild Animal Class
BUT THERE'S A SUBJECT BOTH COURSES MUST FOCUS ON.
WE'RE ABOUT TO STUDY...
HUMANITY.
WO-OOW!!
FIDGET
FIDGET
BA-DUMP
BA-DUMP

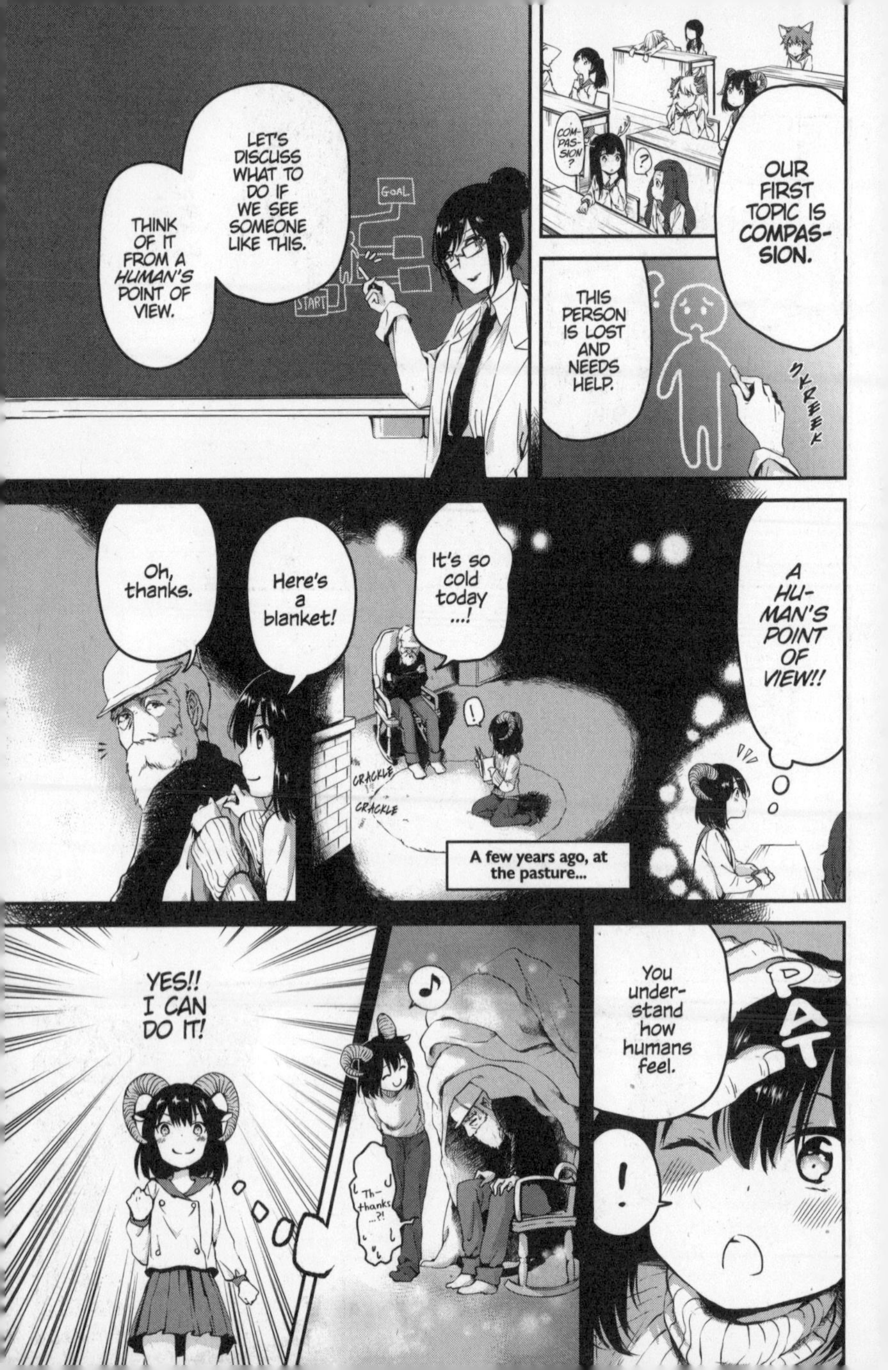
OUR FIRST TOPIC IS COMPASSION.
COMPASSION?
?
THIS PERSON IS LOST AND NEEDS HELP.
SKREEK
GOAL
START
LET'S DISCUSS WHAT TO DO IF WE SEE SOMEONE LIKE THIS.
THINK OF IT FROM A *HUMAN'S* POINT OF VIEW.
A HUMAN'S POINT OF VIEW!!
It's so cold today...!
!
Here's a blanket!
Oh, thanks.
CRACKLE
CRACKLE
A few years ago, at the pasture...
PAT
You understand how humans feel.
!
♪
Th-thanks...?!
YES!! I CAN DO IT!

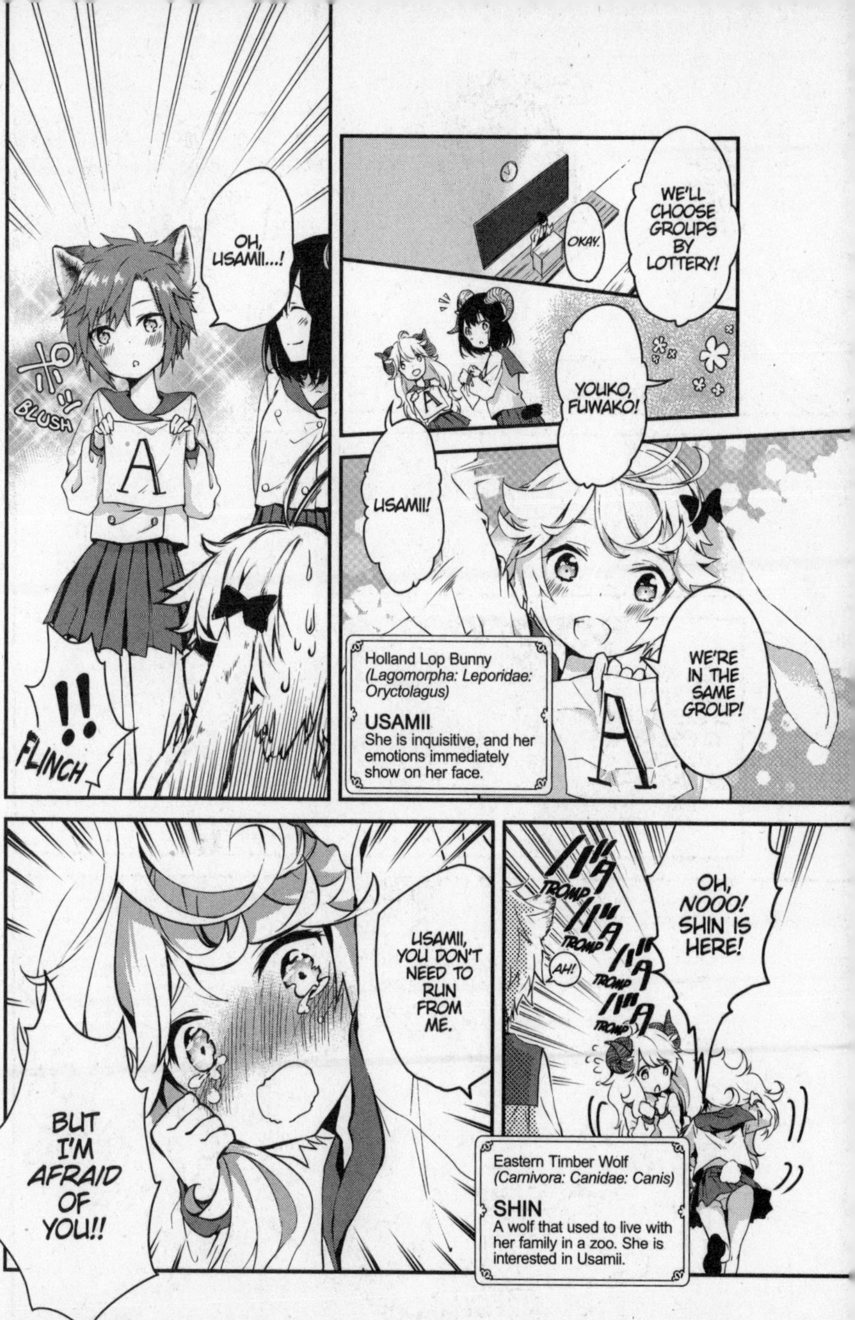
WE'LL CHOOSE GROUPS BY LOTTERY!
OKAY.
YOUKO, FUWAKO!
USAMII!
WE'RE IN THE SAME GROUP!
Holland Lop Bunny
(Lagomorpha: Leporidae: Oryctolagus)
USAMII
She is inquisitive, and her emotions immediately show on her face.
OH, USAMII...!
BLUSH
!!
FLINCH
OH, NOOO! SHIN IS HERE!
TROMP TROMP TROMP TROMP
AH!
Eastern Timber Wolf
(Carnivora: Canidae: Canis)
SHIN
A wolf that used to live with her family in a zoo. She is interested in Usamii.
USAMII, YOU DON'T NEED TO RUN FROM ME.
BUT I'M AFRAID OF YOU!!

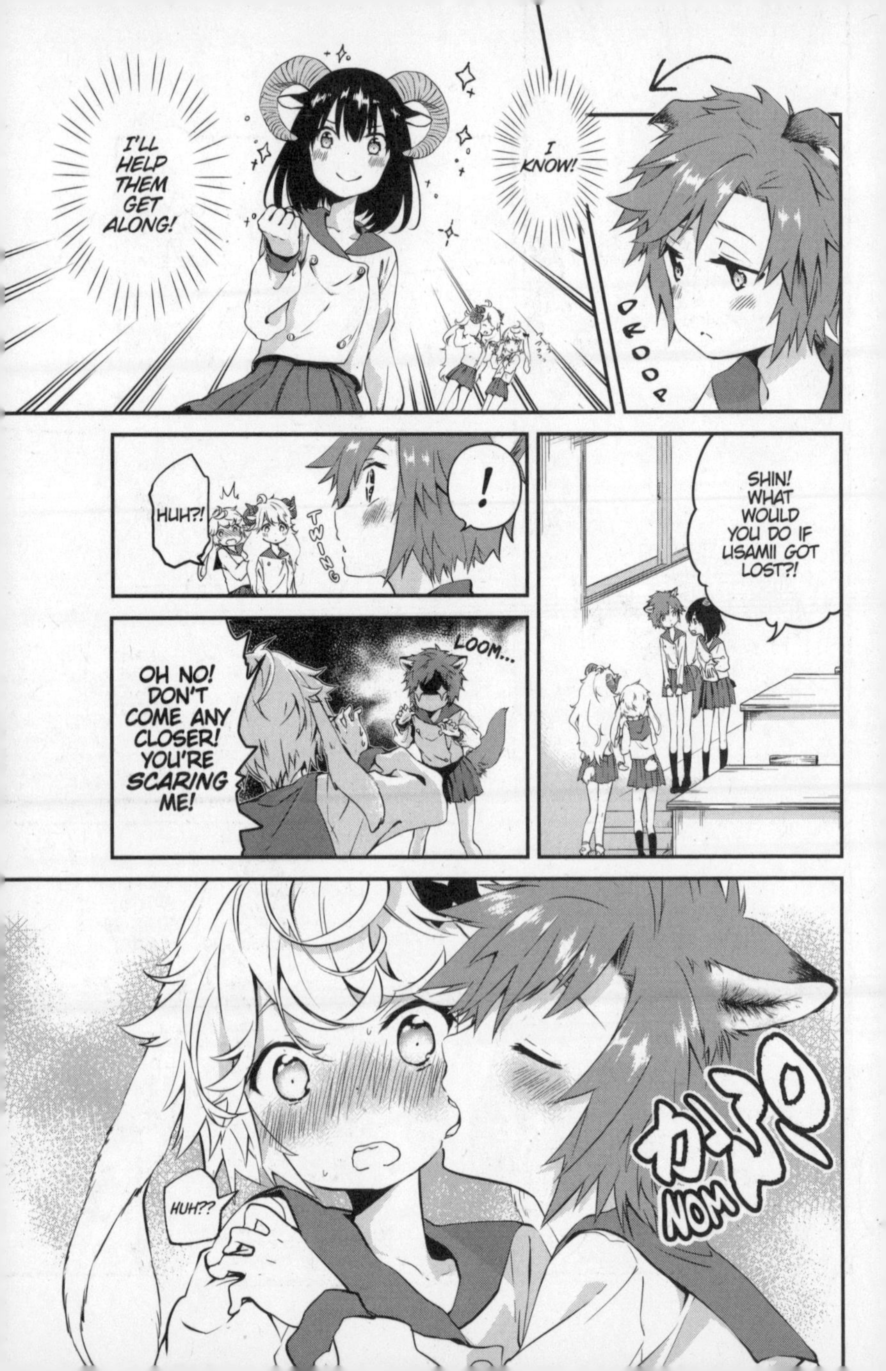
DROOP
I KNOW!
I'LL HELP THEM GET ALONG!
SHIN! WHAT WOULD YOU DO IF USAMII GOT LOST?!
!
TWING
HUH?!
LOOM...
OH NO! DON'T COME ANY CLOSER! YOU'RE SCARING ME!
かぷっ
NOM
HUH??

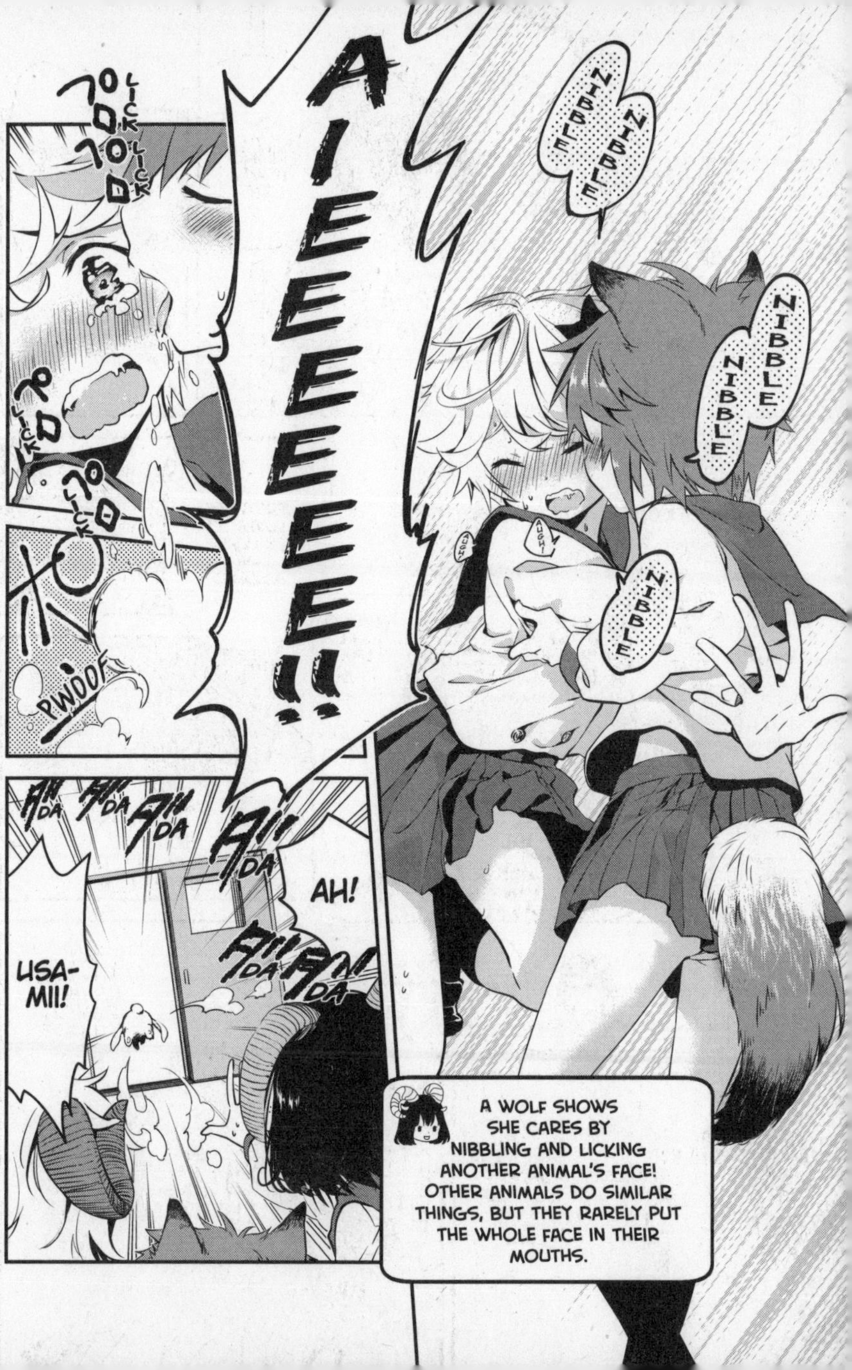
NIBBLE NIBBLE
AIEEEEEEEEEE!!
NIBBLE NIBBLE
AUGH!
AUGH!
NIBBLE
A WOLF SHOWS SHE CARES BY NIBBLING AND LICKING ANOTHER ANIMAL'S FACE! OTHER ANIMALS DO SIMILAR THINGS, BUT THEY RARELY PUT THE WHOLE FACE IN THEIR MOUTHS.
LICK LICK LICK
LICK
LICK
PWOOF
DA DA DA
DA
AH!
DA DA
USA-MII!

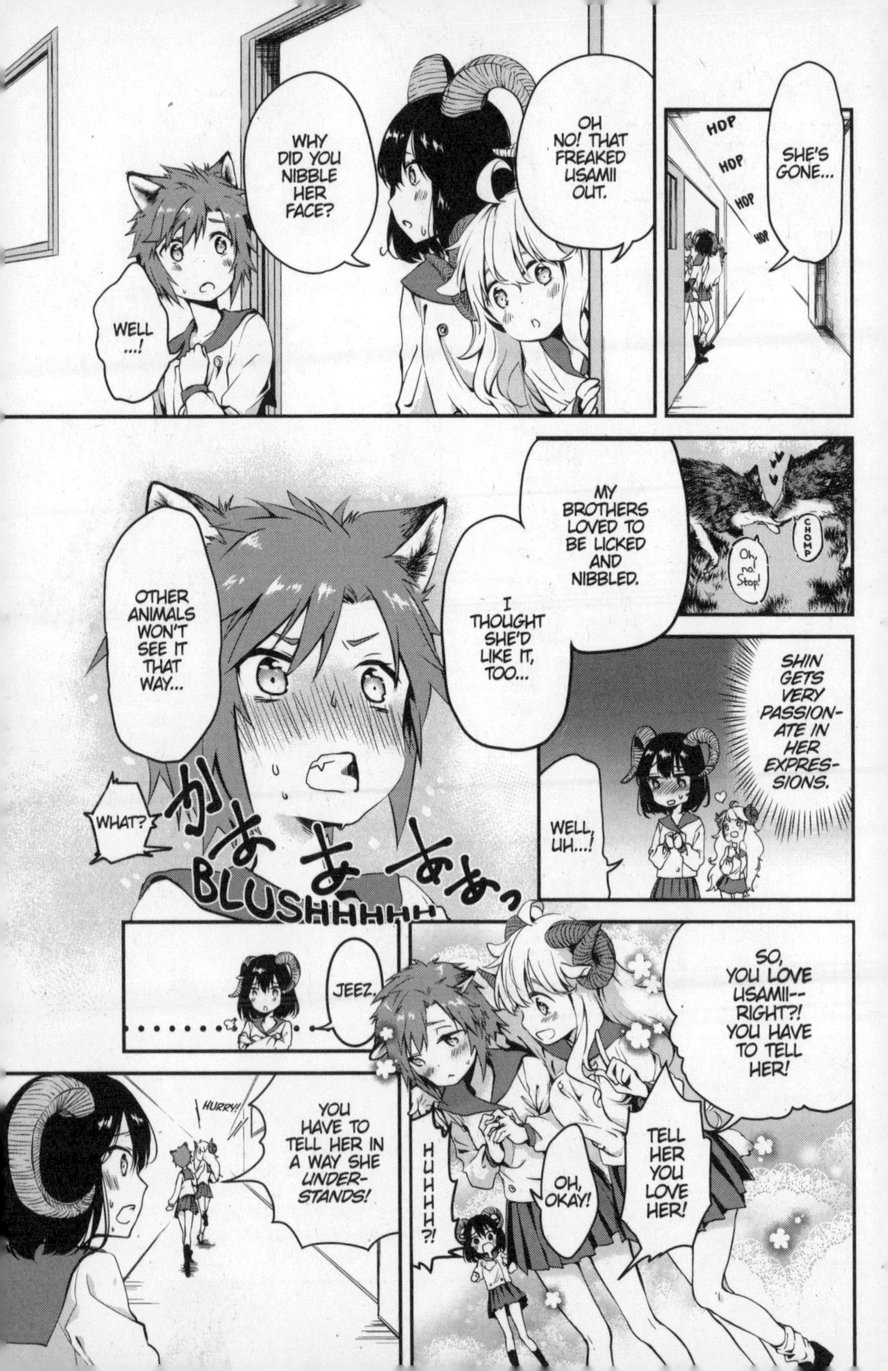
HOP
HOP
HOP
HOP
SHE'S GONE...
OH NO! THAT FREAKED USAMII OUT.
WHY DID YOU NIBBLE HER FACE?
WELL ...!
CHOMP
Oh, no! Stop!
MY BROTHERS LOVED TO BE LICKED AND NIBBLED.
I THOUGHT SHE'D LIKE IT, TOO...
OTHER ANIMALS WON'T SEE IT THAT WAY...
WHAT?
BLUSHHHHHH
SHIN GETS VERY PASSIONATE IN HER EXPRESSIONS.
WELL, UH...!
SO, YOU LOVE USAMII--RIGHT?! YOU HAVE TO TELL HER!
JEEZ.
....
TELL HER YOU LOVE HER!
OH, OKAY!
HUHHHH?!
HURRY!!
YOU HAVE TO TELL HER IN A WAY SHE UNDERSTANDS!

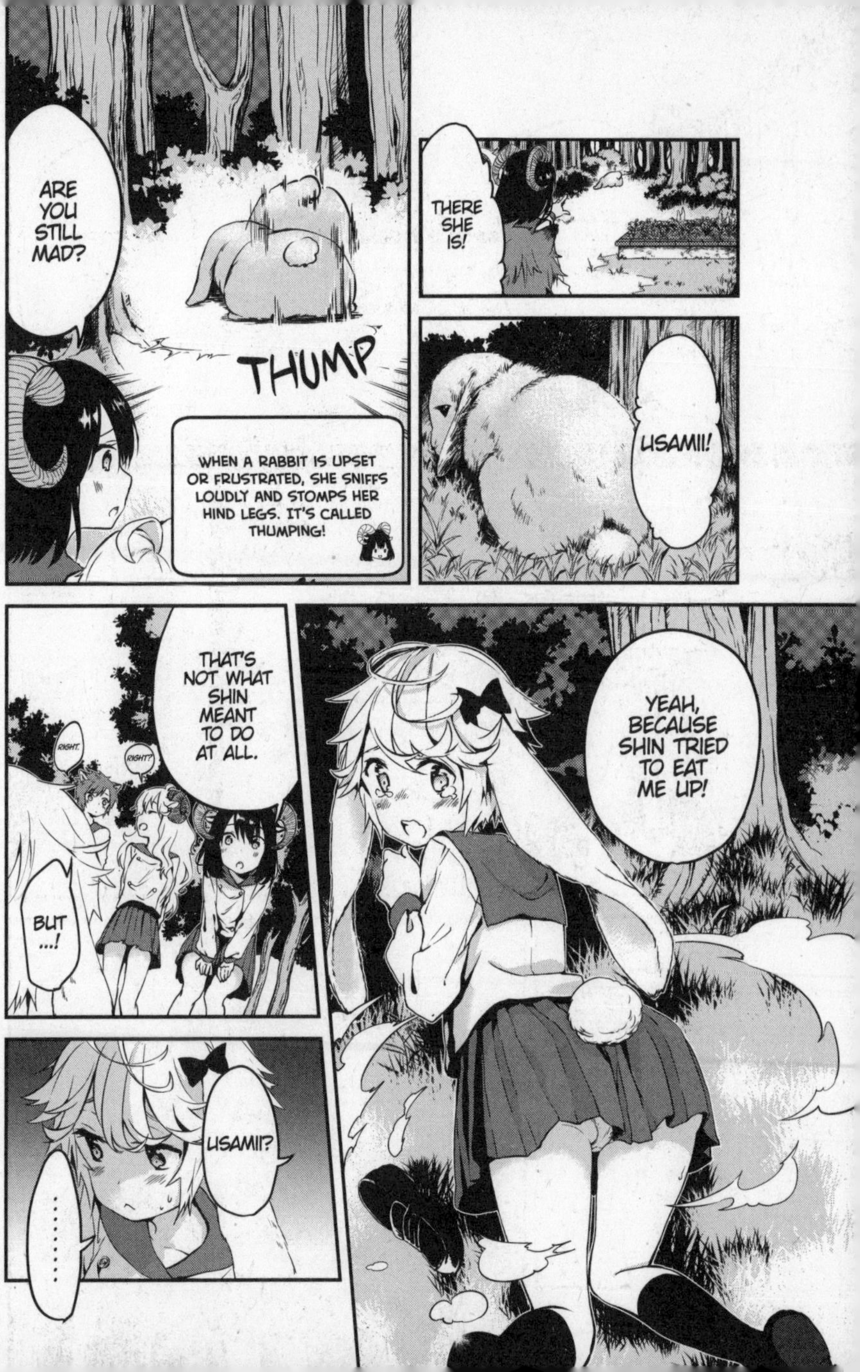
THERE SHE IS!
USAMII!
ARE YOU STILL MAD?
THUMP
WHEN A RABBIT IS UPSET OR FRUSTRATED, SHE SNIFFS LOUDLY AND STOMPS HER HIND LEGS. IT'S CALLED THUMPING!
YEAH, BECAUSE SHIN TRIED TO EAT ME UP!
THAT'S NOT WHAT SHIN MEANT TO DO AT ALL.
RIGHT?
RIGHT.
BUT ...!
USAMII?
......

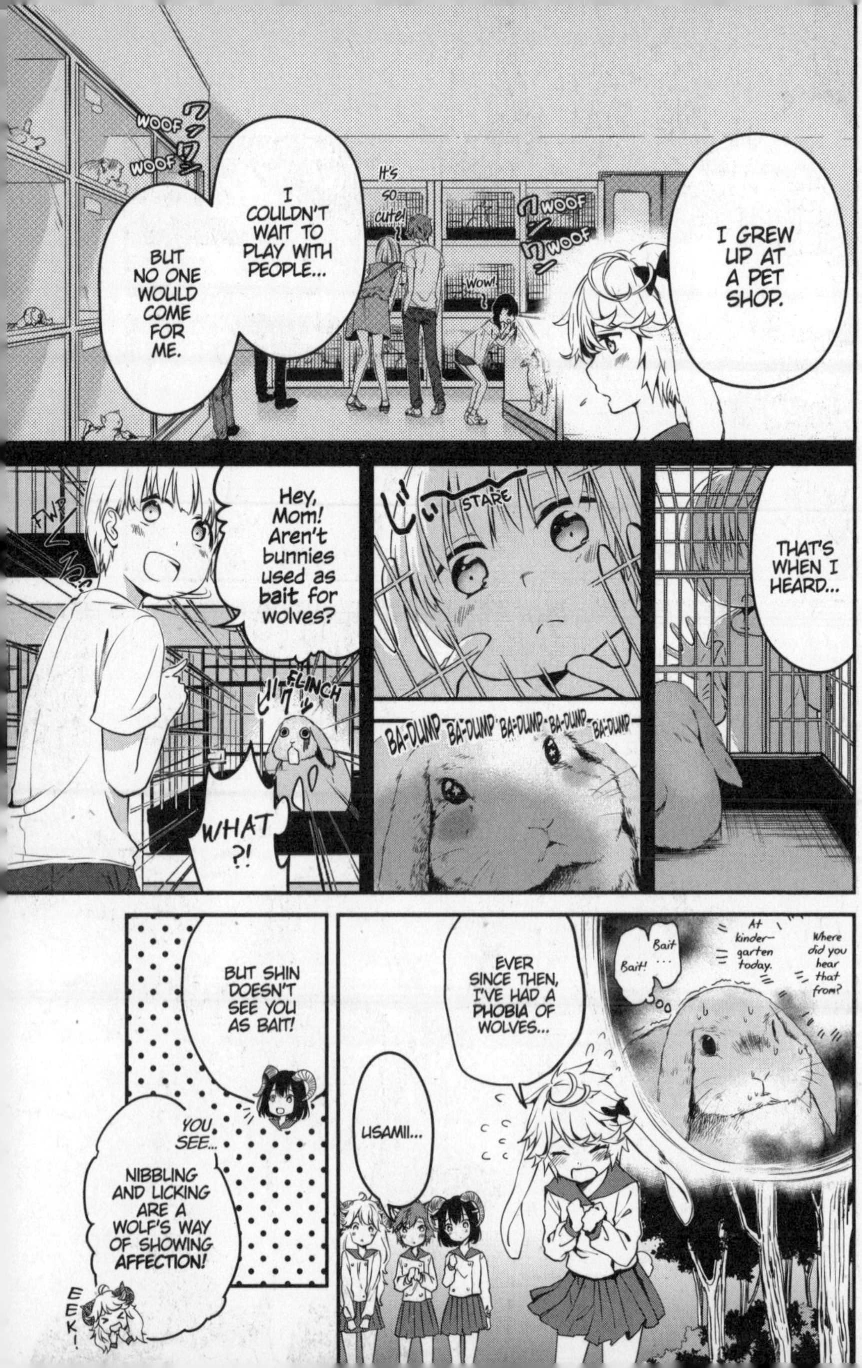
I GREW UP AT A PET SHOP.
WOOF WOOF
WOW!
It's so cute!
I COULDN'T WAIT TO PLAY WITH PEOPLE...
BUT NO ONE WOULD COME FOR ME.
WOOF WOOF
THAT'S WHEN I HEARD...
STARE
BA-DUMP BA-DUMP BA-DUMP BA-DUMP BA-DUMP
Hey, Mom! Aren't bunnies used as bait for wolves?
FWP
FLINCH
WHAT ?!
EVER SINCE THEN, I'VE HAD A PHOBIA OF WOLVES...
Where did you hear that from?
At kinder-garten today.
Bait...
Bait!
USAMI...
BUT SHIN DOESN'T SEE YOU AS BAIT!
YOU SEE...
NIBBLING AND LICKING ARE A WOLF'S WAY OF SHOWING AFFECTION!
EEK!

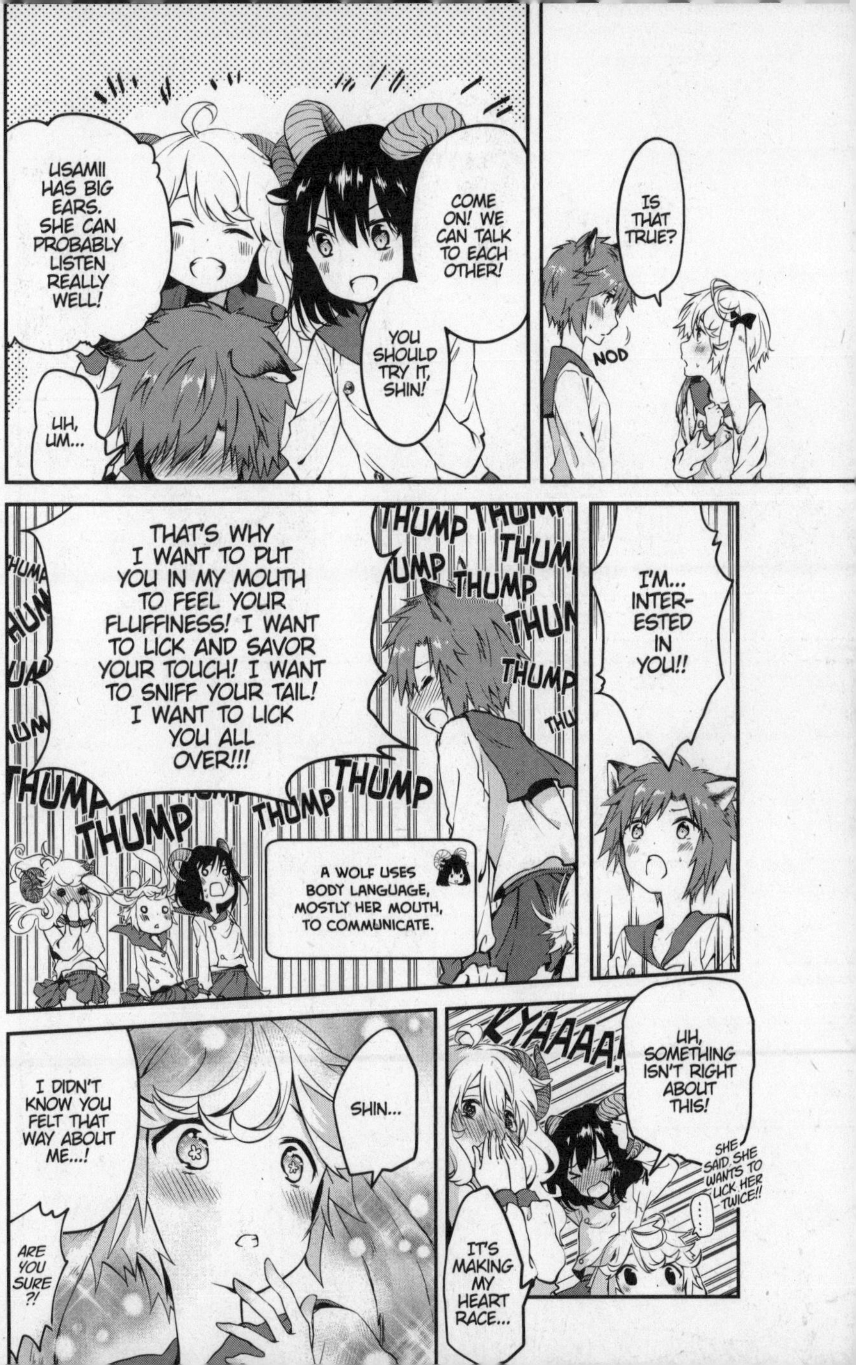
IS THAT TRUE?
NOD
COME ON! WE CAN TALK TO EACH OTHER!
YOU SHOULD TRY IT, SHIN!
USAMII HAS BIG EARS. SHE CAN PROBABLY LISTEN REALLY WELL!
UH, UM...
I'M... INTER-ESTED IN YOU!!
THUMP THUMP THUMP THUMP THUMP THUMP THUMP
THAT'S WHY I WANT TO PUT YOU IN MY MOUTH TO FEEL YOUR FLUFFINESS! I WANT TO LICK AND SAVOR YOUR TOUCH! I WANT TO SNIFF YOUR TAIL! I WANT TO LICK YOU ALL OVER!!!
THUMP THUMP THUMP THUMP
A WOLF USES BODY LANGUAGE, MOSTLY HER MOUTH, TO COMMUNICATE.
KYAAAAA!
UH, SOMETHING ISN'T RIGHT ABOUT THIS!
SHE SAID, SHE WANTS TO LICK HER TWICE!!
......
IT'S MAKING MY HEART RACE...
SHIN...
I DIDN'T KNOW YOU FELT THAT WAY ABOUT ME...!
ARE YOU SURE?!

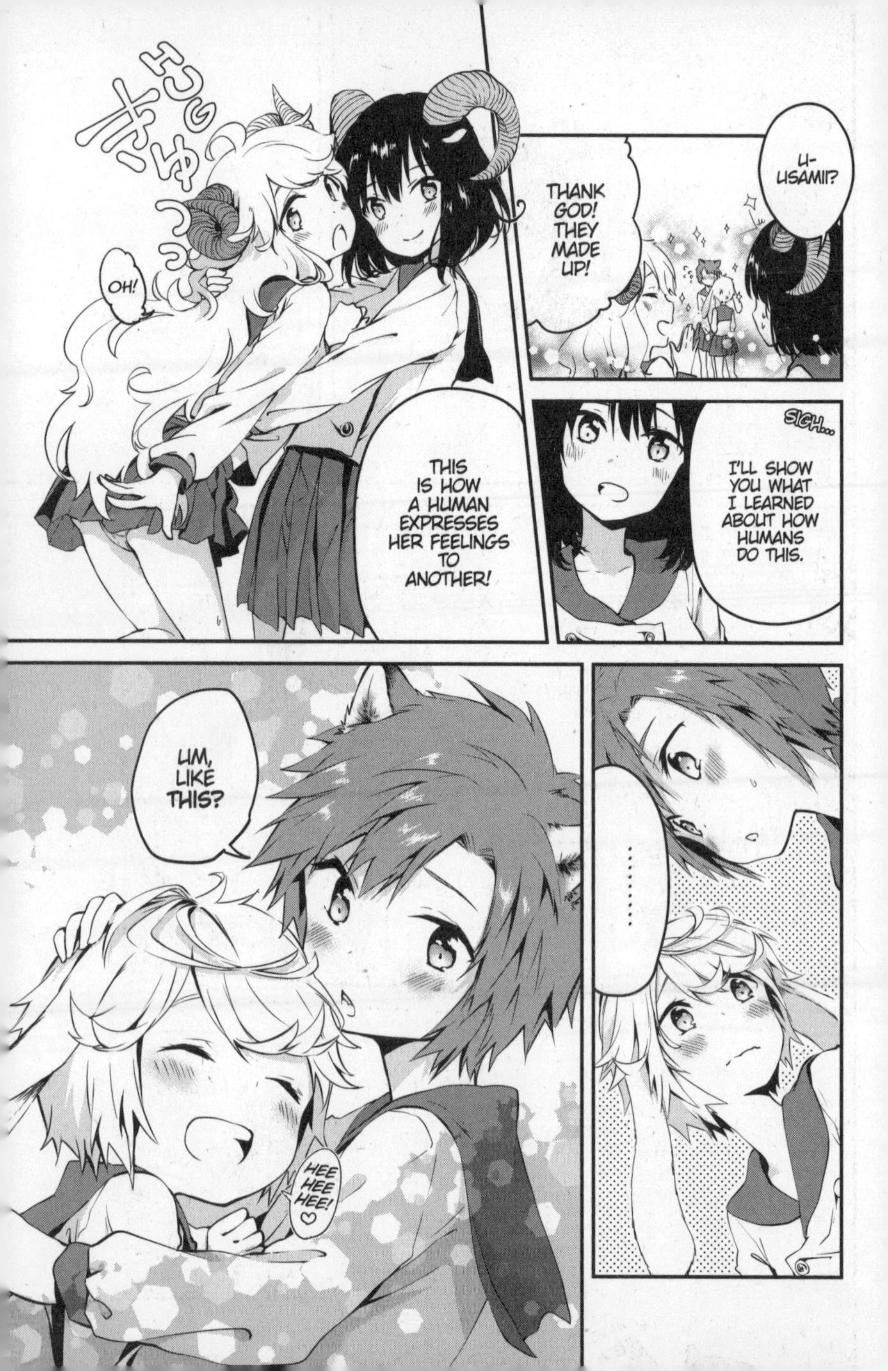
U-USAMI!?
THANK GOD! THEY MADE UP!
SIGH...
I'LL SHOW YOU WHAT I LEARNED ABOUT HOW HUMANS DO THIS.
THIS IS HOW A HUMAN EXPRESSES HER FEELINGS TO ANOTHER!
きゅっ
OH!
......
UM, LIKE THIS?
HEE HEE HEE! ♡

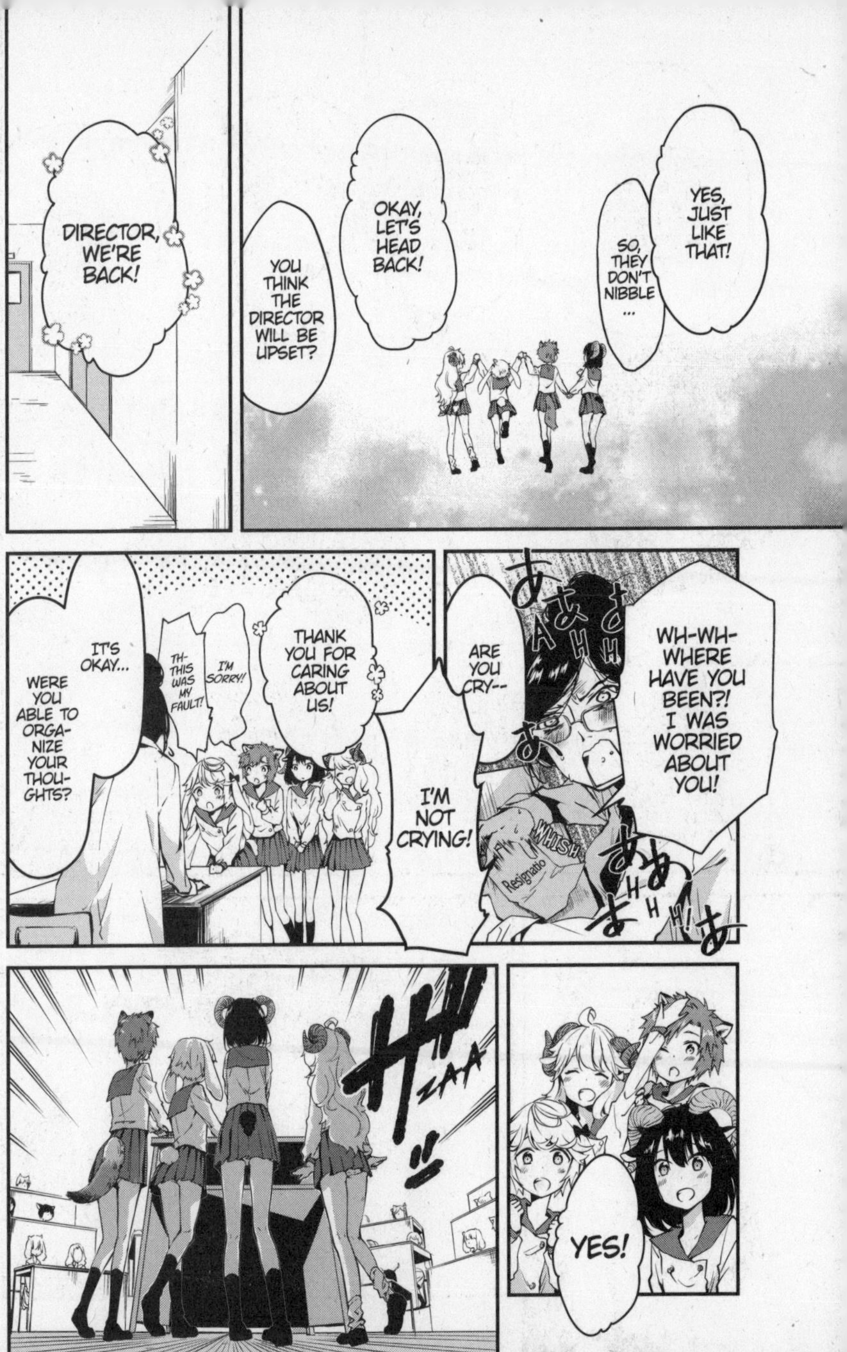
YES, JUST LIKE THAT!
SO, THEY DON'T NIBBLE ...
OKAY, LET'S HEAD BACK!
YOU THINK THE DIRECTOR WILL BE UPSET?
DIRECTOR, WE'RE BACK!
WH-WH-WHERE HAVE YOU BEEN?! I WAS WORRIED ABOUT YOU!
あああ AHH
ARE YOU CRY--
I'M NOT CRYING!
WHISH
Resignatio
あああ AHH!
THANK YOU FOR CARING ABOUT US!
I'M SORRY!
TH-THIS WAS MY FAULT!
IT'S OKAY...
WERE YOU ABLE TO ORGANIZE YOUR THOUGHTS?
YES!
ZAA

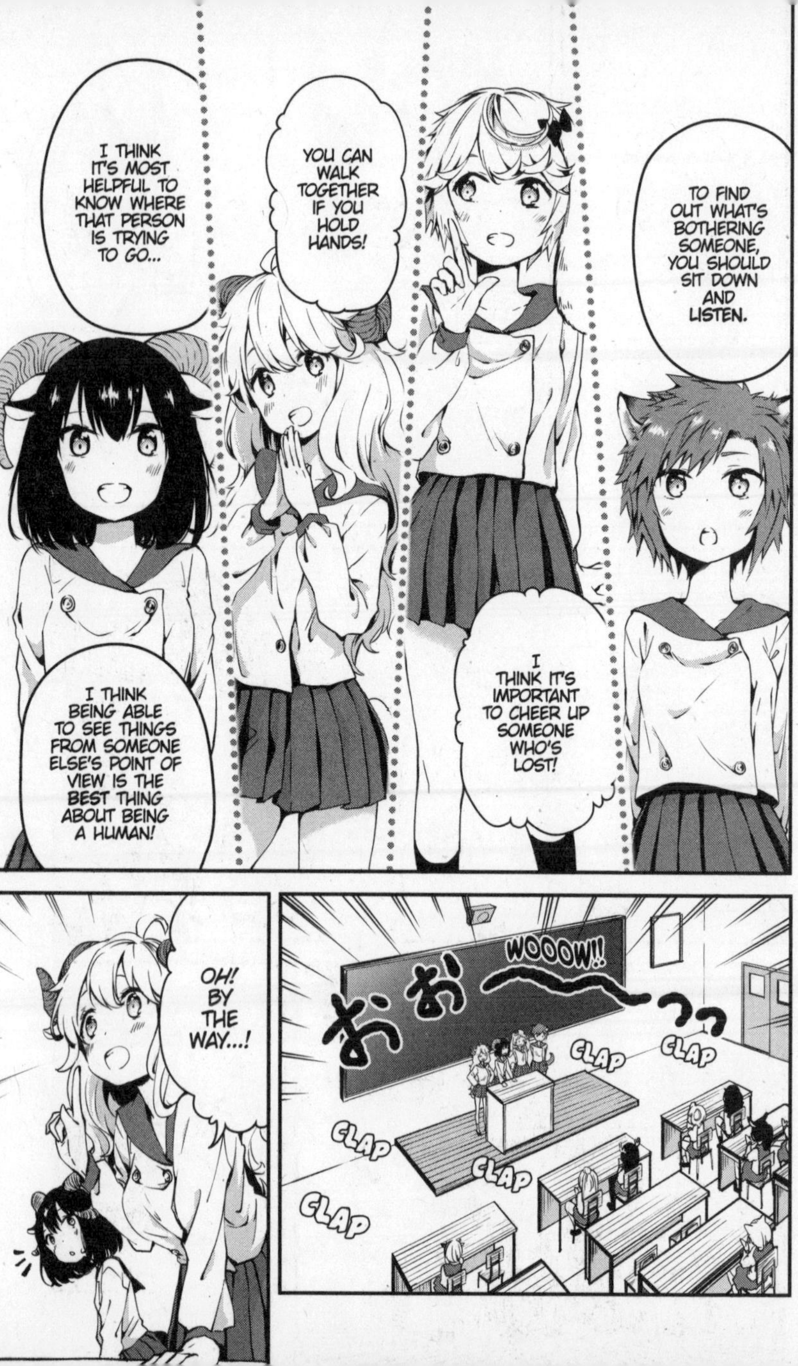
TO FIND OUT WHAT'S BOTHERING SOMEONE, YOU SHOULD SIT DOWN AND LISTEN.
I THINK IT'S IMPORTANT TO CHEER UP SOMEONE WHO'S LOST!
YOU CAN WALK TOGETHER IF YOU HOLD HANDS!
I THINK IT'S MOST HELPFUL TO KNOW WHERE THAT PERSON IS TRYING TO GO...
I THINK BEING ABLE TO SEE THINGS FROM SOMEONE ELSE'S POINT OF VIEW IS THE BEST THING ABOUT BEING A HUMAN!
WOOOW!!
おお〜〜っっ
CLAP
CLAP
CLAP
CLAP
CLAP
OH! BY THE WAY...!

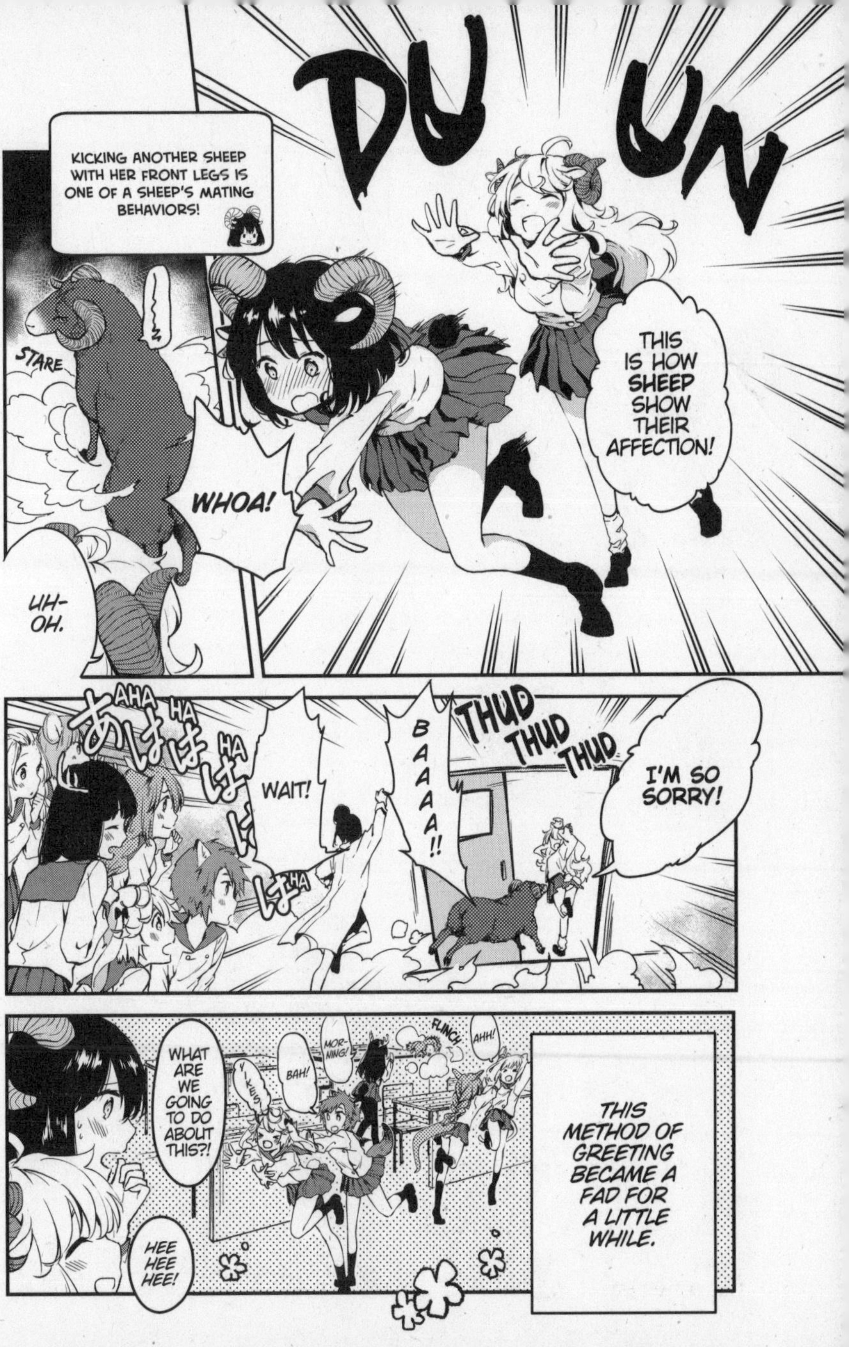
DU UN
THIS IS HOW SHEEP SHOW THEIR AFFECTION!
WHOA!
KICKING ANOTHER SHEEP WITH HER FRONT LEGS IS ONE OF A SHEEP'S MATING BEHAVIORS!
STARE
UH-OH.
I'M SO SORRY!
THUD THUD THUD
BAAAAA!!
WAIT!
あはははは
AHA HA HA HA
THIS METHOD OF GREETING BECAME A FAD FOR A LITTLE WHILE.
AHH!
FLINCH
MORNING!
BAH!
YIKES!
WHAT ARE WE GOING TO DO ABOUT THIS?!
HEE HEE HEE!

Eastern Timber Wolf

DNA
DOESN'T
TELL US.

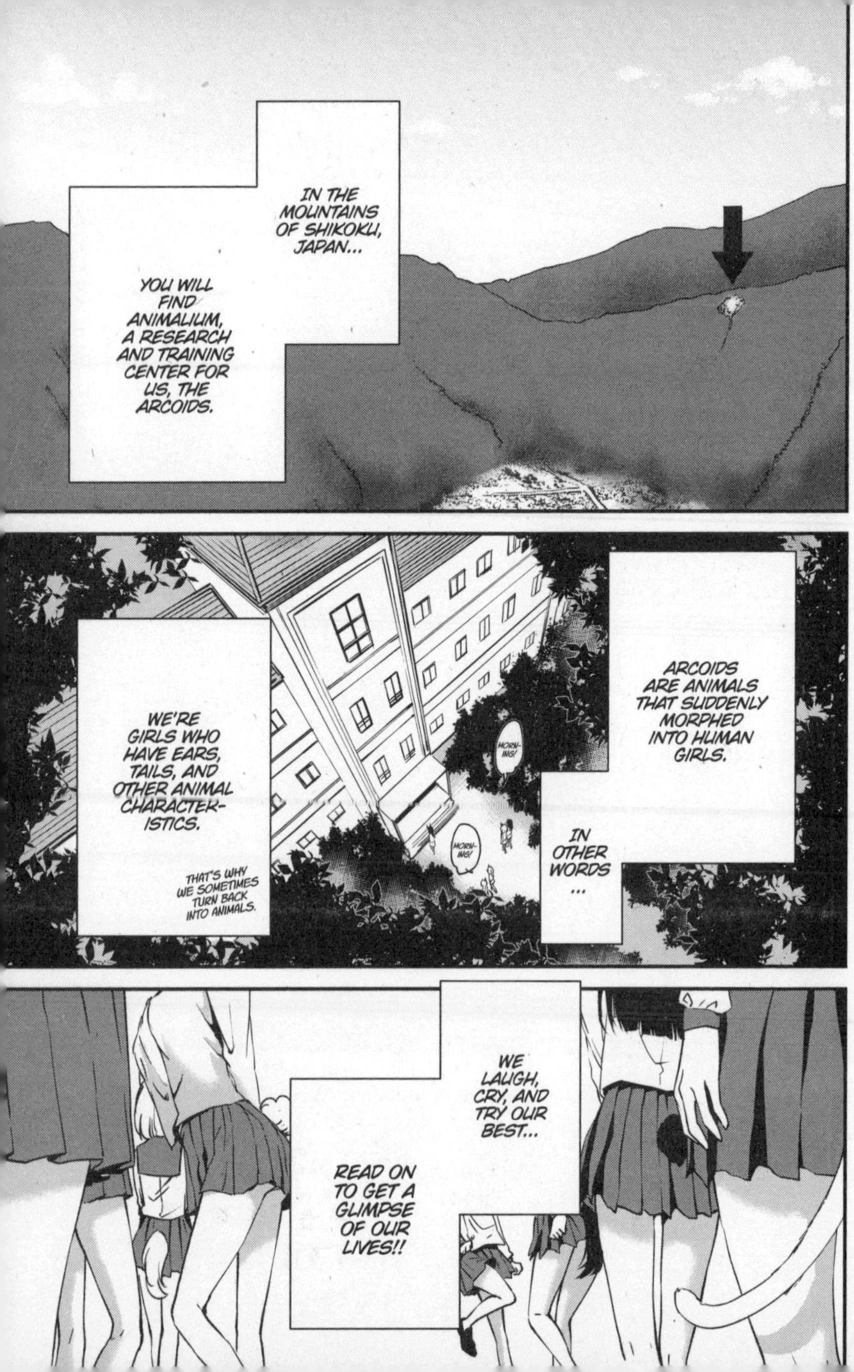

IN THE MOUNTAINS OF SHIKOKU, JAPAN...
YOU WILL FIND ANIMALIUM, A RESEARCH AND TRAINING CENTER FOR US, THE ARCOIDS.
ARCOIDS ARE ANIMALS THAT SUDDENLY MORPHED INTO HUMAN GIRLS.
IN OTHER WORDS...
MORN-ING!
MORN-ING!
WE'RE GIRLS WHO HAVE EARS, TAILS, AND OTHER ANIMAL CHARACTER-ISTICS.
THAT'S WHY WE SOMETIMES TURN BACK INTO ANIMALS.
WE LAUGH, CRY, AND TRY OUR BEST...
READ ON TO GET A GLIMPSE OF OUR LIVES!!

LESSON 4 Girls and Physical Activity

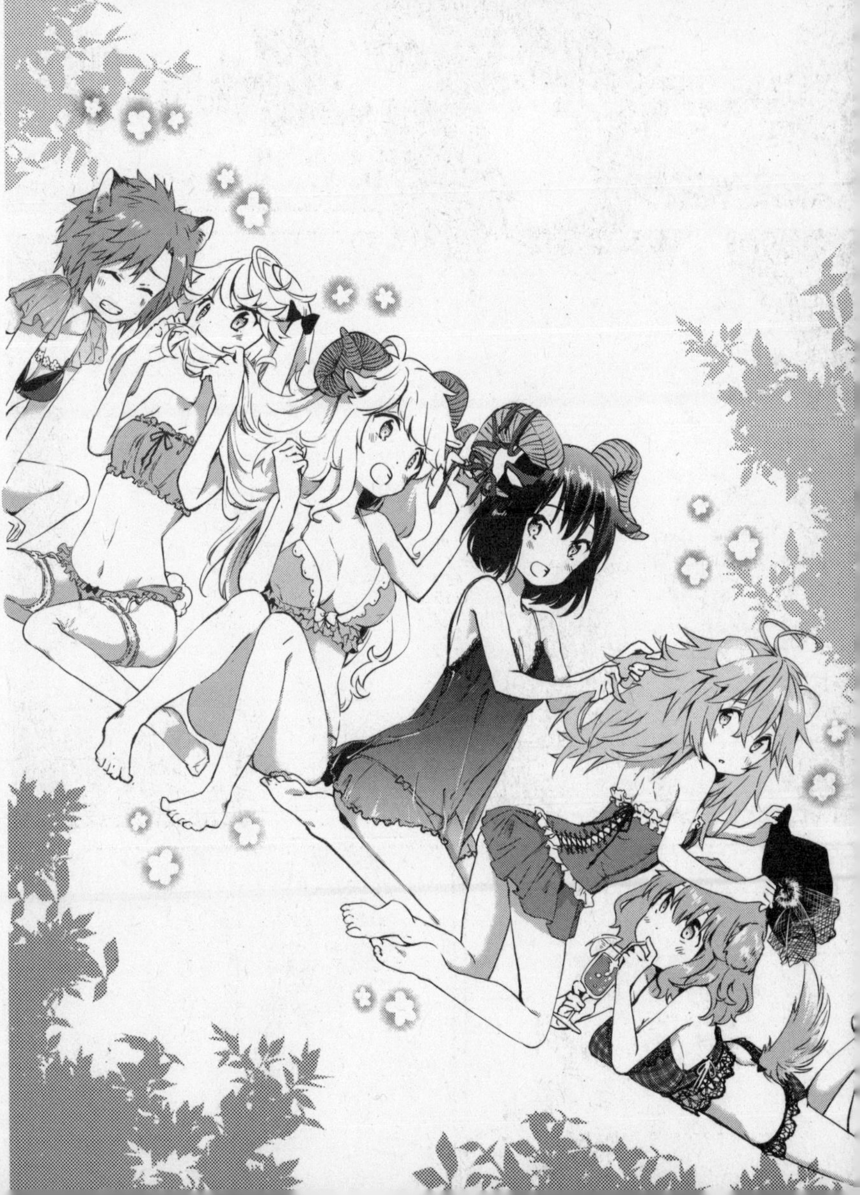

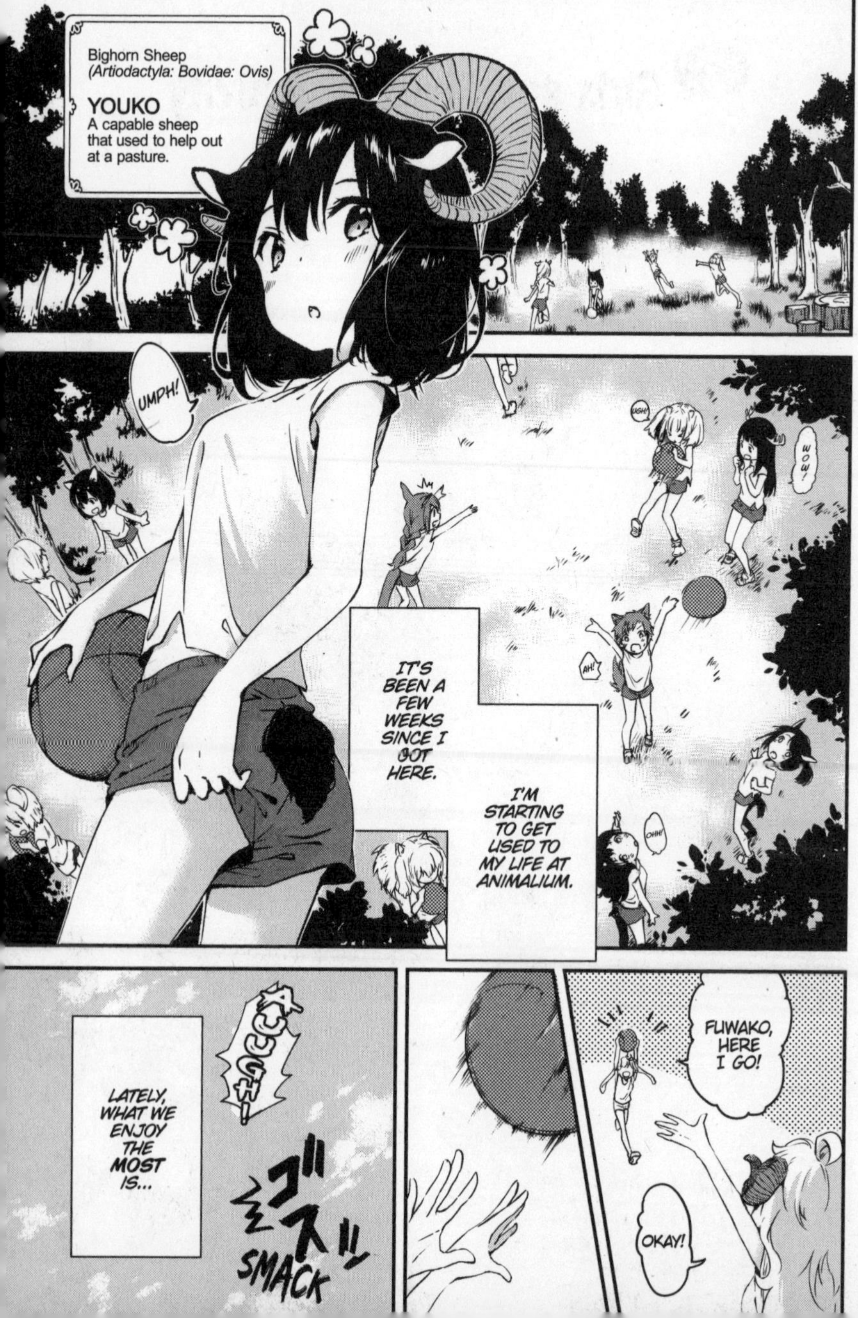

Bighorn Sheep
(Artiodactyla: Bovidae: Ovis)
YOUKO
A capable sheep that used to help out at a pasture.
WOW!
UGH!
UMPH!
IT'S BEEN A FEW WEEKS SINCE I GOT HERE.
AH!
I'M STARTING TO GET USED TO MY LIFE AT ANIMALIUM.
OHH!
FUWAKO, HERE I GO!
OKAY!
AUGH!
SMACK
LATELY, WHAT WE ENJOY THE MOST IS...

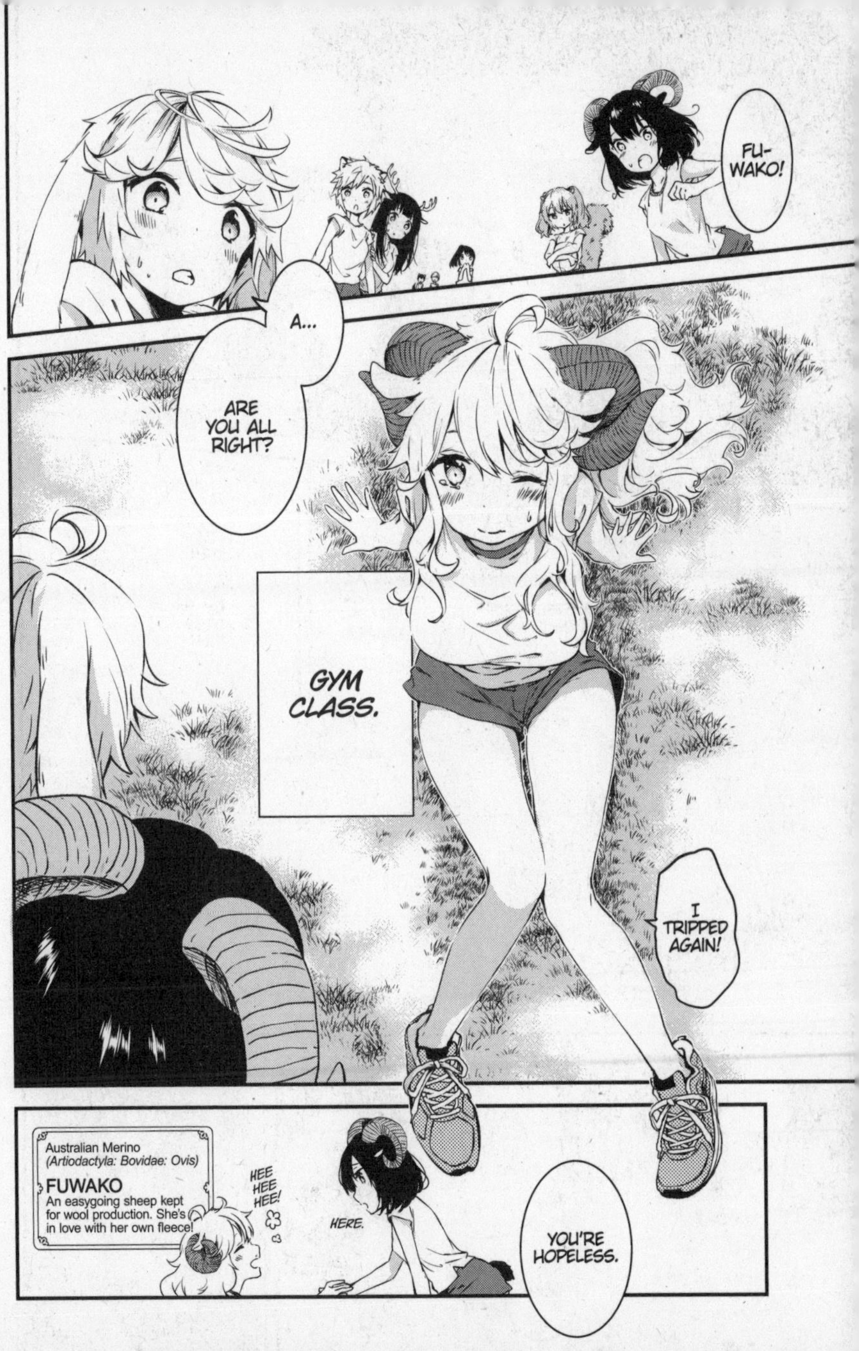
FU-WAKO!
A...
ARE YOU ALL RIGHT?
GYM CLASS.
I TRIPPED AGAIN!
YOU'RE HOPELESS.
HERE.
HEE HEE HEE!
Australian Merino
(Artiodactyla: Bovidae: Ovis)
FUWAKO
An easygoing sheep kept for wool production. She's in love with her own fleece!

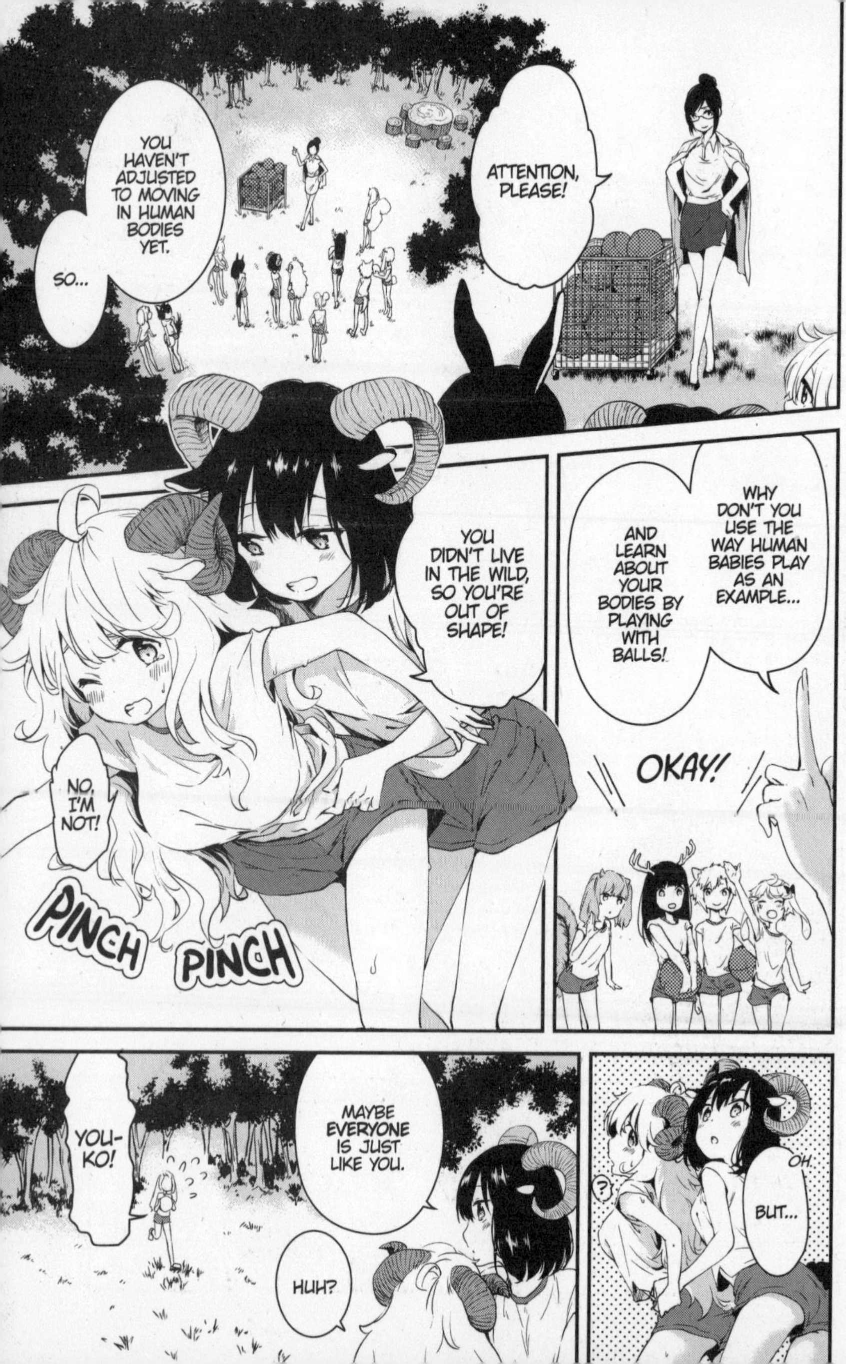
ATTENTION, PLEASE!
YOU HAVEN'T ADJUSTED TO MOVING IN HUMAN BODIES YET.
SO...
WHY DON'T YOU USE THE WAY HUMAN BABIES PLAY AS AN EXAMPLE...
AND LEARN ABOUT YOUR BODIES BY PLAYING WITH BALLS!
OKAY!
YOU DIDN'T LIVE IN THE WILD, SO YOU'RE OUT OF SHAPE!
NO, I'M NOT!
PINCH PINCH
OH.
BUT...
?
MAYBE EVERYONE IS JUST LIKE YOU.
HUH?
YOU-KO!

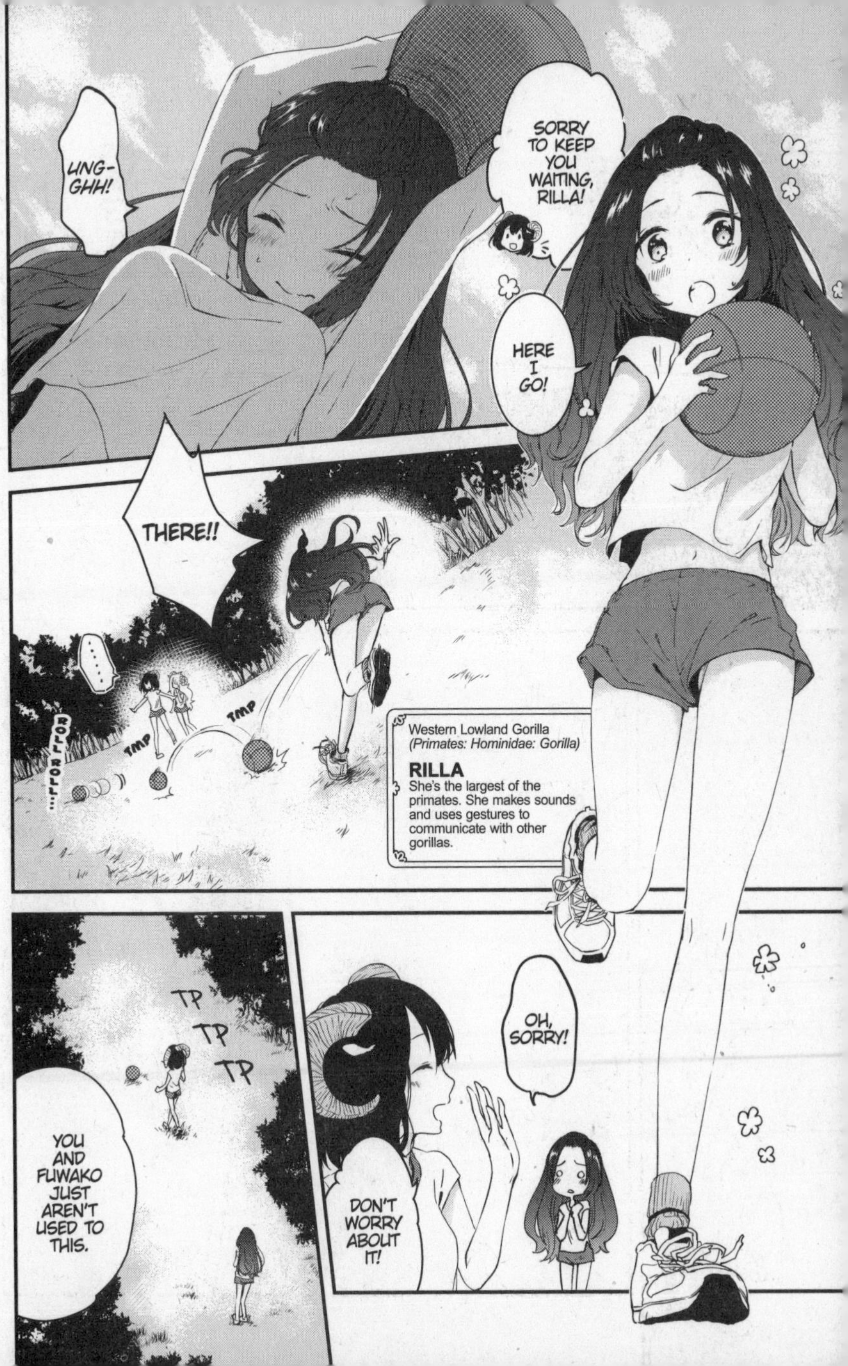
SORRY TO KEEP YOU WAITING, RILLA!
UNG-GHH!
HERE I GO!
THERE!!
. . . . .
TMP
TMP
ROLL ROLL...
Western Lowland Gorilla
(Primates: Hominidae: Gorilla)
RILLA
She's the largest of the primates. She makes sounds and uses gestures to communicate with other gorillas.
OH, SORRY!
DON'T WORRY ABOUT IT!
TP
TP
TP
YOU AND FUWAKO JUST AREN'T USED TO THIS.

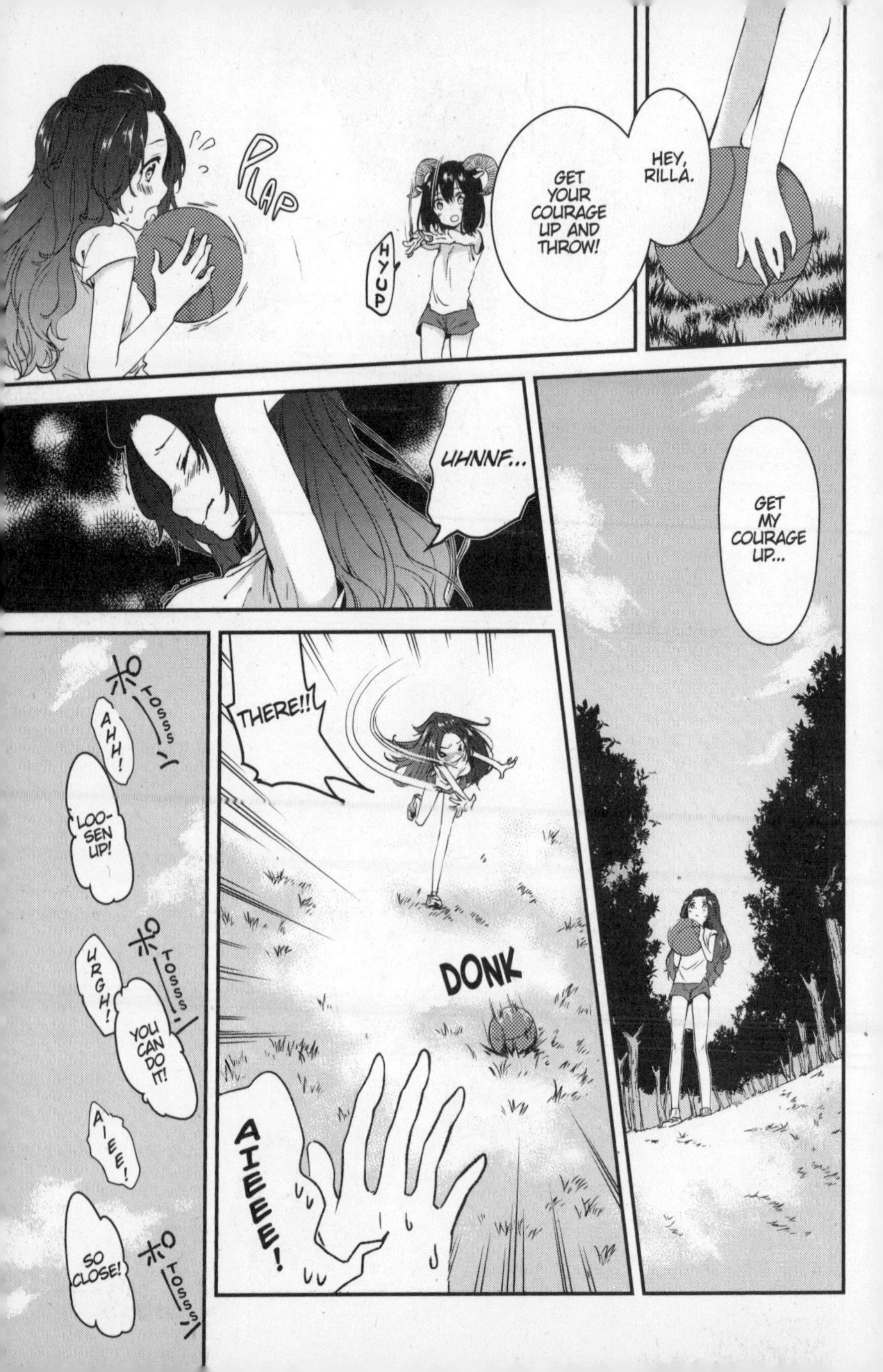
HEY, RILLA.
GET YOUR COURAGE UP AND THROW!
HYUP
PLAP
GET MY COURAGE UP...
UHNNF...
THERE!!
DONK
AIEEEE!
ホ TOSSS
AHH!
LOO-SEN UP!
ホ TOSSS
URGH!
YOU CAN DO IT!
AIEE!
ホ TOSSS
SO CLOSE!

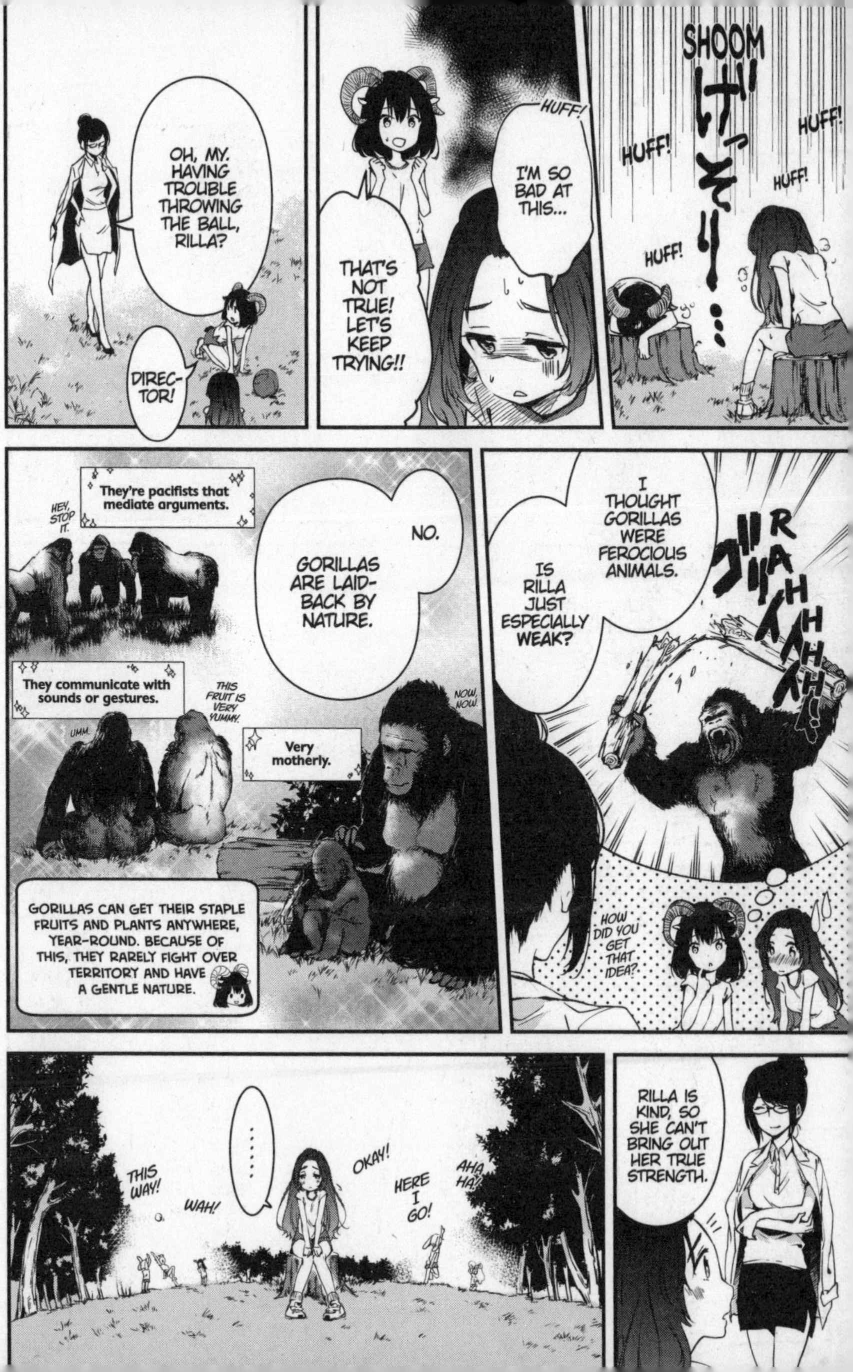
SHOOM
げっそり…
HUFF!
HUFF!
HUFF!
HUFF!
HUFF!
I'M SO BAD AT THIS...
THAT'S NOT TRUE! LET'S KEEP TRYING!!
OH, MY. HAVING TROUBLE THROWING THE BALL, RILLA?
DIRECTOR!
I THOUGHT GORILLAS WERE FEROCIOUS ANIMALS.
IS RILLA JUST ESPECIALLY WEAK?
RAHHHHH!
HOW DID YOU GET THAT IDEA?
NO.
GORILLAS ARE LAID-BACK BY NATURE.
They're pacifists that mediate arguments.
HEY, STOP IT.
They communicate with sounds or gestures.
THIS FRUIT IS VERY YUMMY.
UMM.
Very motherly.
NOW, NOW.
GORILLAS CAN GET THEIR STAPLE FRUITS AND PLANTS ANYWHERE, YEAR-ROUND. BECAUSE OF THIS, THEY RARELY FIGHT OVER TERRITORY AND HAVE A GENTLE NATURE.
RILLA IS KIND, SO SHE CAN'T BRING OUT HER TRUE STRENGTH.
......
AHA HA!
HERE I GO!
OKAY!
WAH!
THIS WAY!

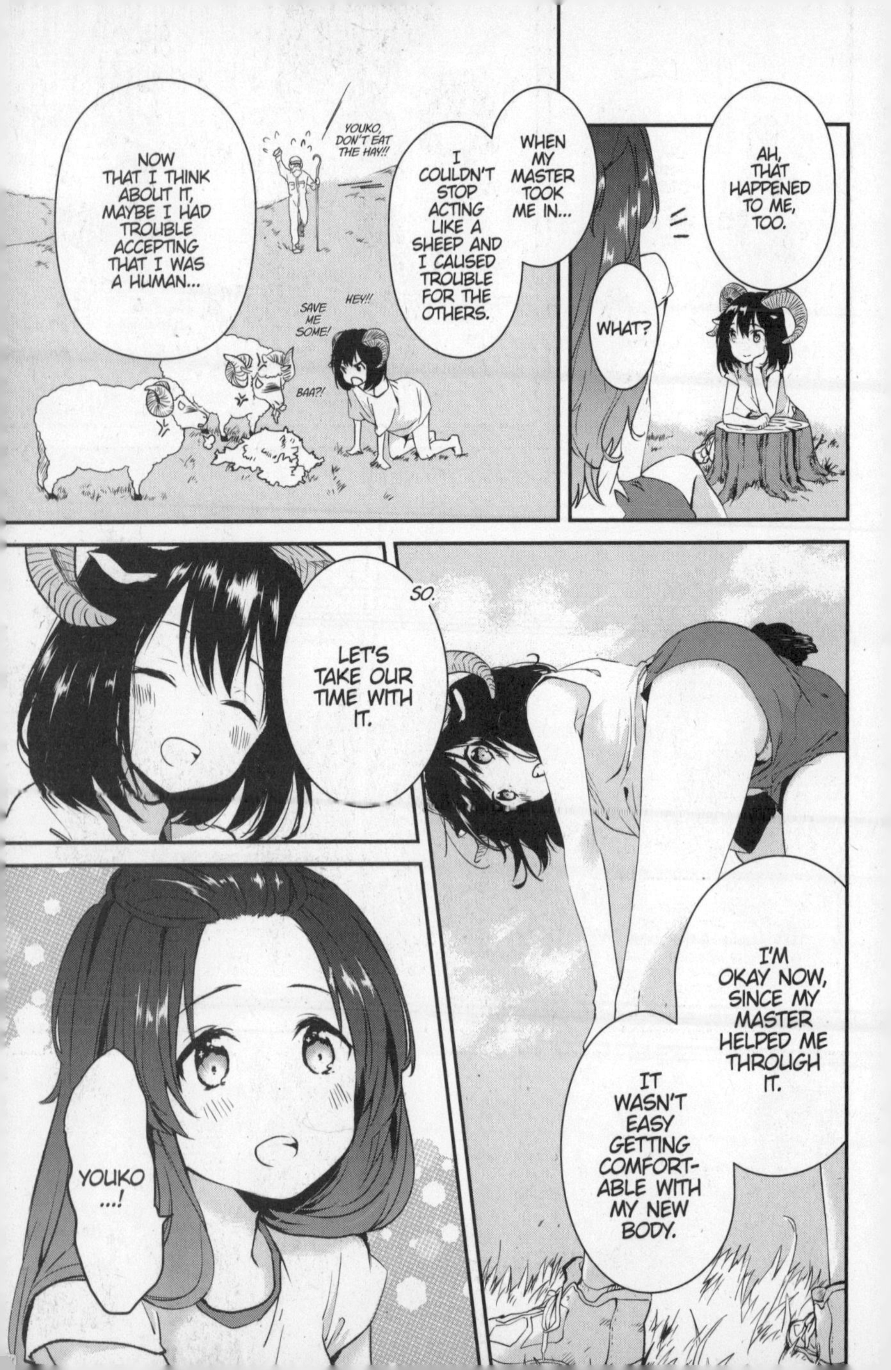
AH, THAT HAPPENED TO ME, TOO.
WHAT?
WHEN MY MASTER TOOK ME IN...
I COULDN'T STOP ACTING LIKE A SHEEP AND I CAUSED TROUBLE FOR THE OTHERS.
YOUKO, DON'T EAT THE HAY!!
NOW THAT I THINK ABOUT IT, MAYBE I HAD TROUBLE ACCEPTING THAT I WAS A HUMAN...
HEY!!
SAVE ME SOME!
BAA?!
I'M OKAY NOW, SINCE MY MASTER HELPED ME THROUGH IT.
IT WASN'T EASY GETTING COMFORTABLE WITH MY NEW BODY.
SO.
LET'S TAKE OUR TIME WITH IT.
YOUKO ...!

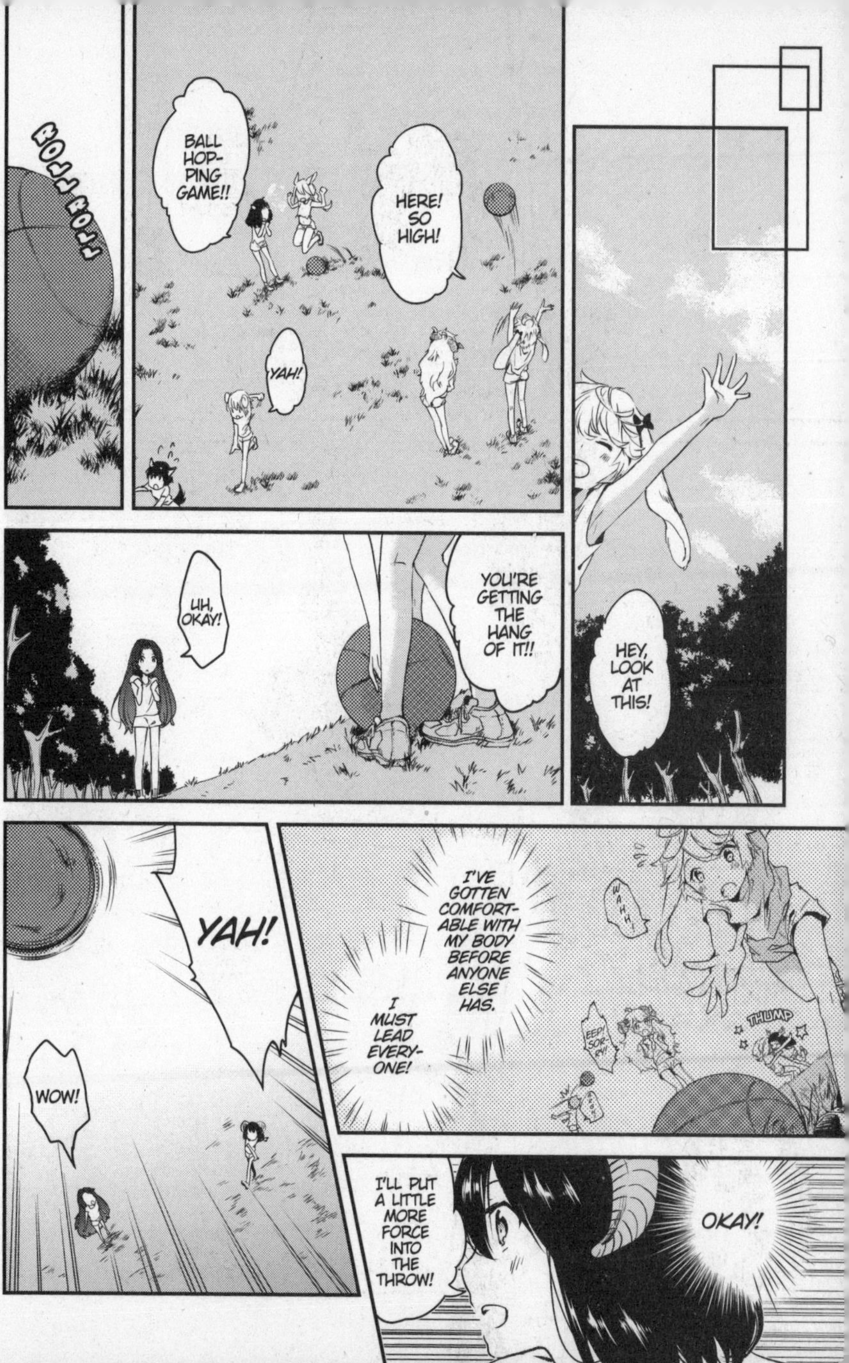
HEY, LOOK AT THIS!
BALL HOP-PING GAME!!
HERE! SO HIGH!
YAH!
ROLL ROLL
YOU'RE GETTING THE HANG OF IT!!
UH, OKAY!
I'VE GOTTEN COMFORT-ABLE WITH MY BODY BEFORE ANYONE ELSE HAS.
I MUST LEAD EVERY-ONE!
WAHH!
THUMP
EEP! SOR-RY!
OKAY!
I'LL PUT A LITTLE MORE FORCE INTO THE THROW!
YAH!
WOW!

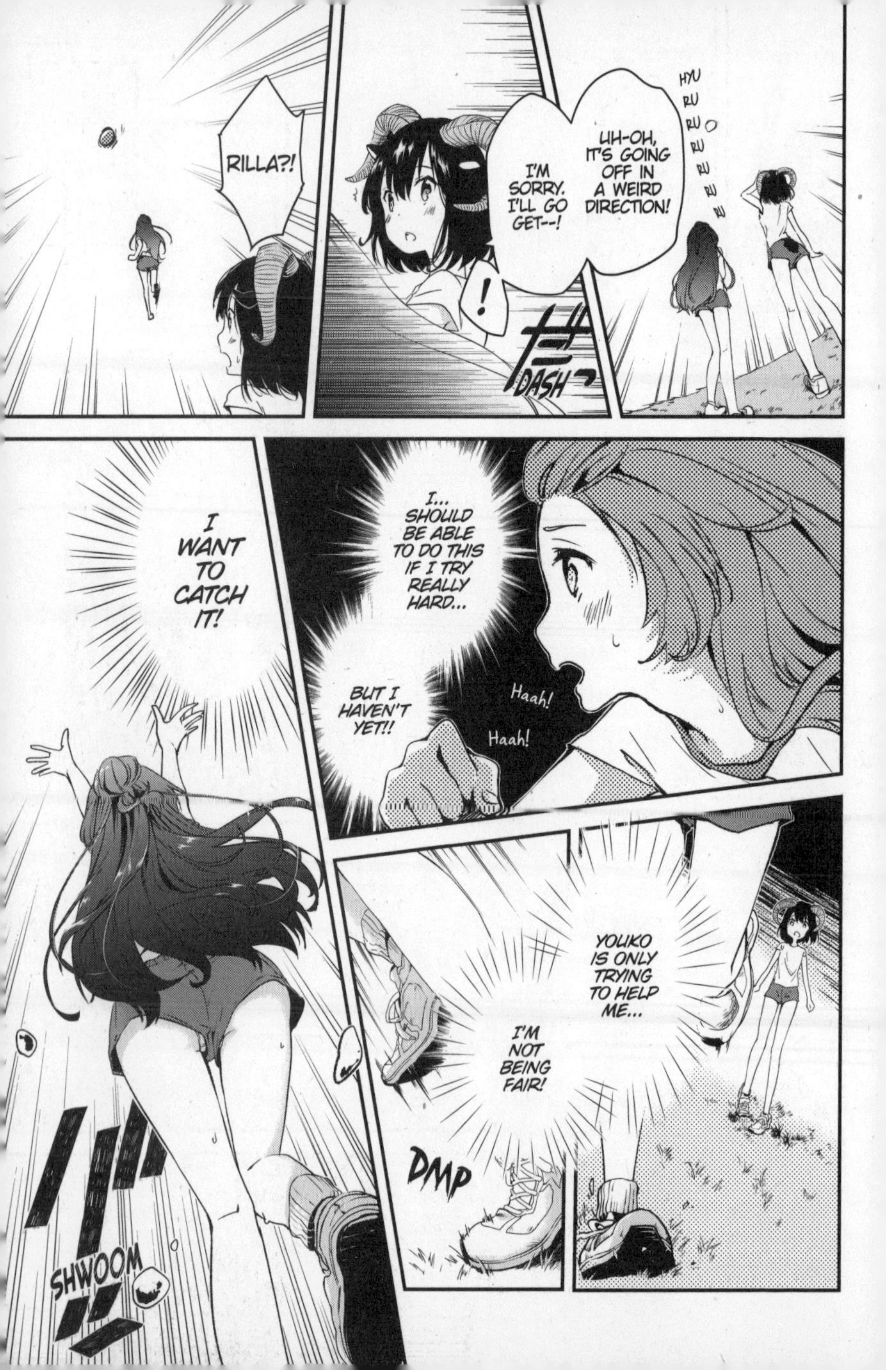
HYU RU RU RU RU RU RU
UH-OH, IT'S GOING OFF IN A WEIRD DIRECTION!
I'M SORRY. I'LL GO GET--!
!
DASH
RILLA?!
I... SHOULD BE ABLE TO DO THIS IF I TRY REALLY HARD...
BUT I HAVEN'T YET!!
Haah!
Haah!
YOUKO IS ONLY TRYING TO HELP ME...
I'M NOT BEING FAIR!
DMP
I WANT TO CATCH IT!
SHWOOM

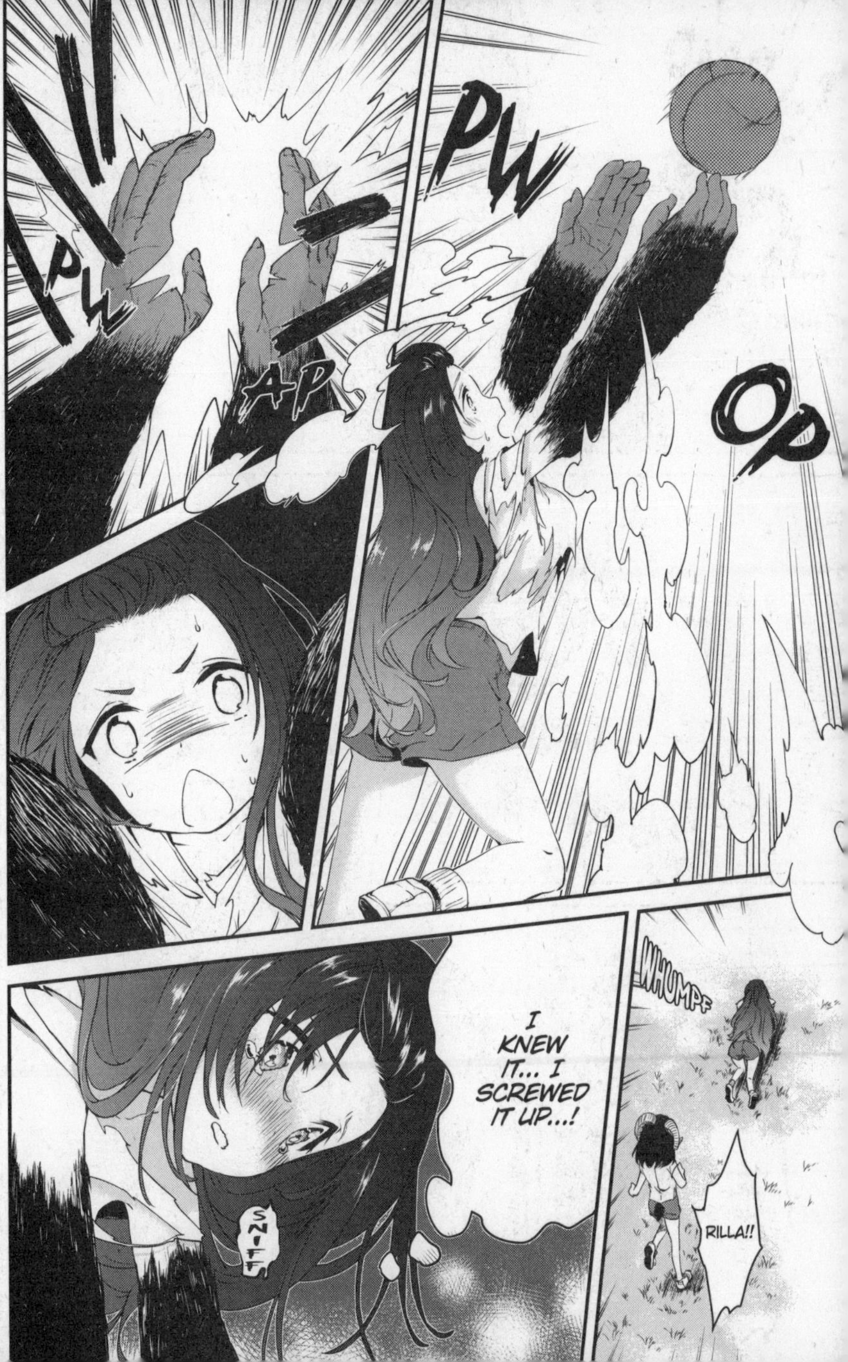
PWOP
PWAP
WHUMPF
I KNEW IT... I SCREWED IT UP...!
SNIFF
RILLA!!

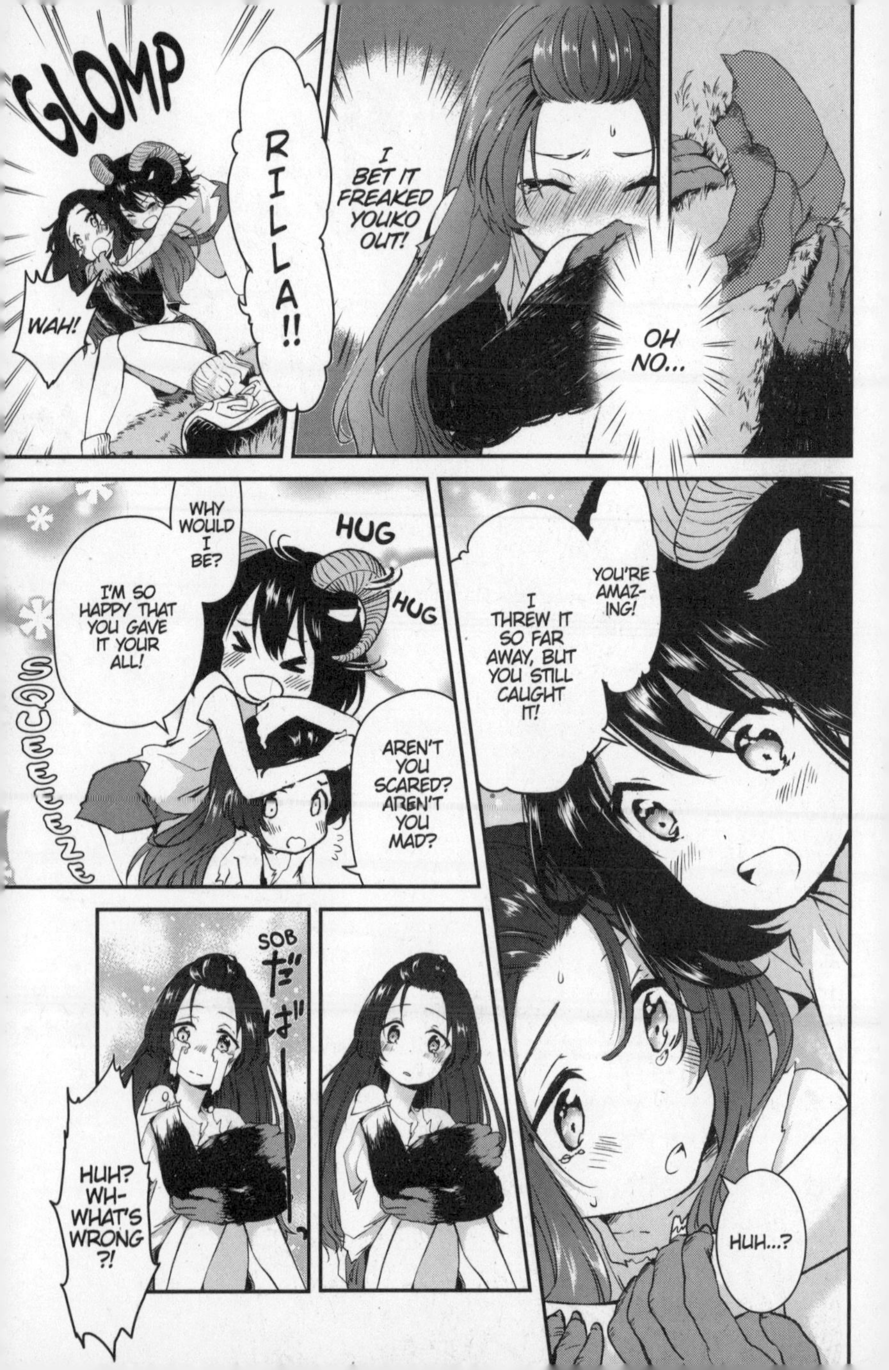
OH NO...
I BET IT FREAKED YOUKO OUT!
RILLA!!
GLOMP
WAH!
YOU'RE AMAZING!
I THREW IT SO FAR AWAY, BUT YOU STILL CAUGHT IT!
HUH...?
AREN'T YOU SCARED? AREN'T YOU MAD?
WHY WOULD I BE?
I'M SO HAPPY THAT YOU GAVE IT YOUR ALL!
HUG
HUG
SQUEEEEEZE
SOB
だばー
HUH? WH-WHAT'S WRONG?!

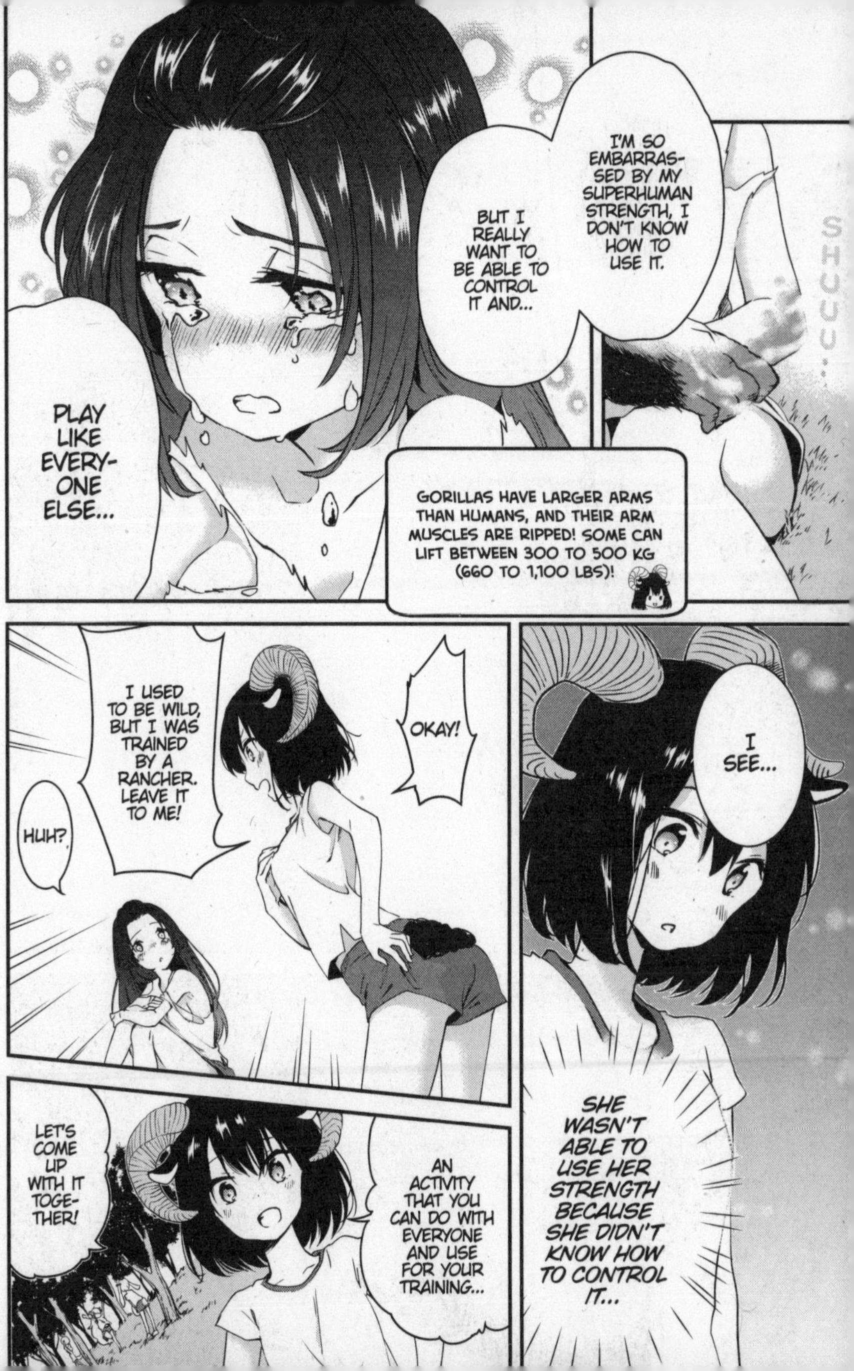
SHUUU...
I'M SO EMBARRASSED BY MY SUPERHUMAN STRENGTH, I DON'T KNOW HOW TO USE IT.
BUT I REALLY WANT TO BE ABLE TO CONTROL IT AND...
PLAY LIKE EVERYONE ELSE...
GORILLAS HAVE LARGER ARMS THAN HUMANS, AND THEIR ARM MUSCLES ARE RIPPED! SOME CAN LIFT BETWEEN 300 TO 500 KG (660 TO 1,100 LBS)!
I SEE...
OKAY!
I USED TO BE WILD, BUT I WAS TRAINED BY A RANCHER. LEAVE IT TO ME!
HUH?
SHE WASN'T ABLE TO USE HER STRENGTH BECAUSE SHE DIDN'T KNOW HOW TO CONTROL IT...
AN ACTIVITY THAT YOU CAN DO WITH EVERYONE AND USE FOR YOUR TRAINING...
LET'S COME UP WITH IT TOGETHER!

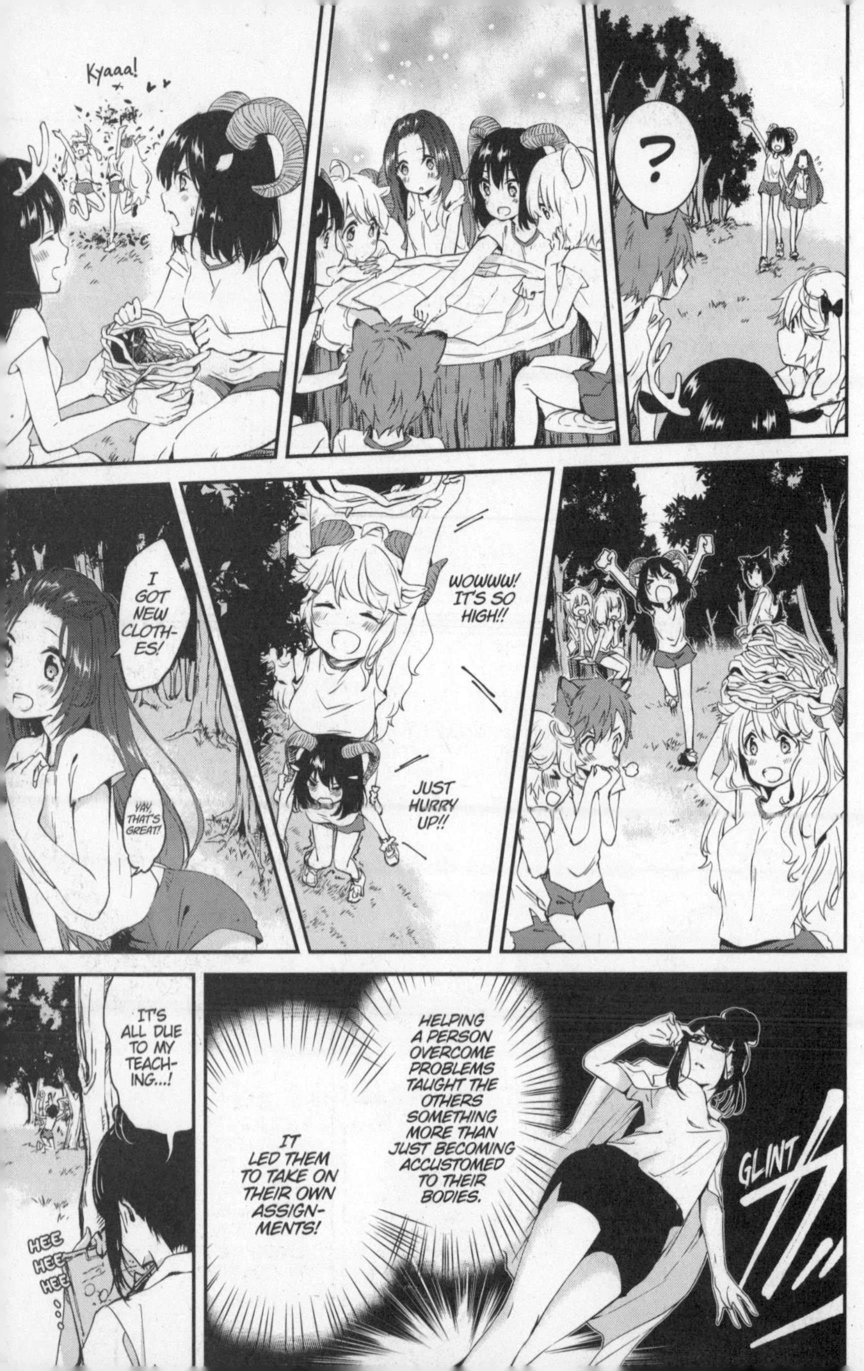
?
Kyaaa!
WOWWW! IT'S SO HIGH!!
JUST HURRY UP!!
I GOT NEW CLOTH-ES!
YAY, THAT'S GREAT!
HELPING A PERSON OVERCOME PROBLEMS TAUGHT THE OTHERS SOMETHING MORE THAN JUST BECOMING ACCUSTOMED TO THEIR BODIES.
IT LED THEM TO TAKE ON THEIR OWN ASSIGN-MENTS!
GLINT
IT'S ALL DUE TO MY TEACH-ING...!
HEE HEE HEE

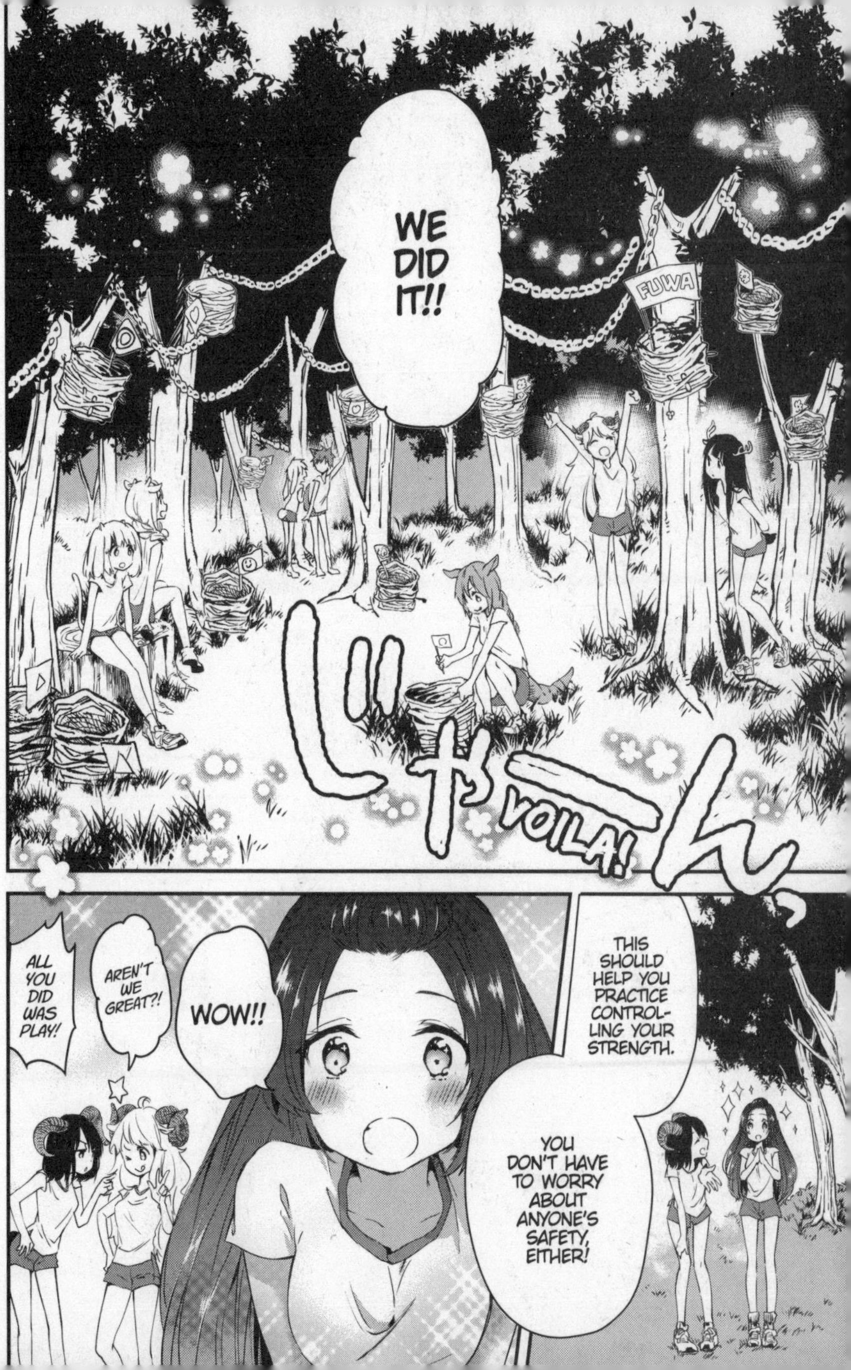
WE DID IT!!
FUWA
VOILA!
THIS SHOULD HELP YOU PRACTICE CONTROL-LING YOUR STRENGTH.
YOU DON'T HAVE TO WORRY ABOUT ANYONE'S SAFETY, EITHER!
WOW!!
AREN'T WE GREAT?!
ALL YOU DID WAS PLAY!

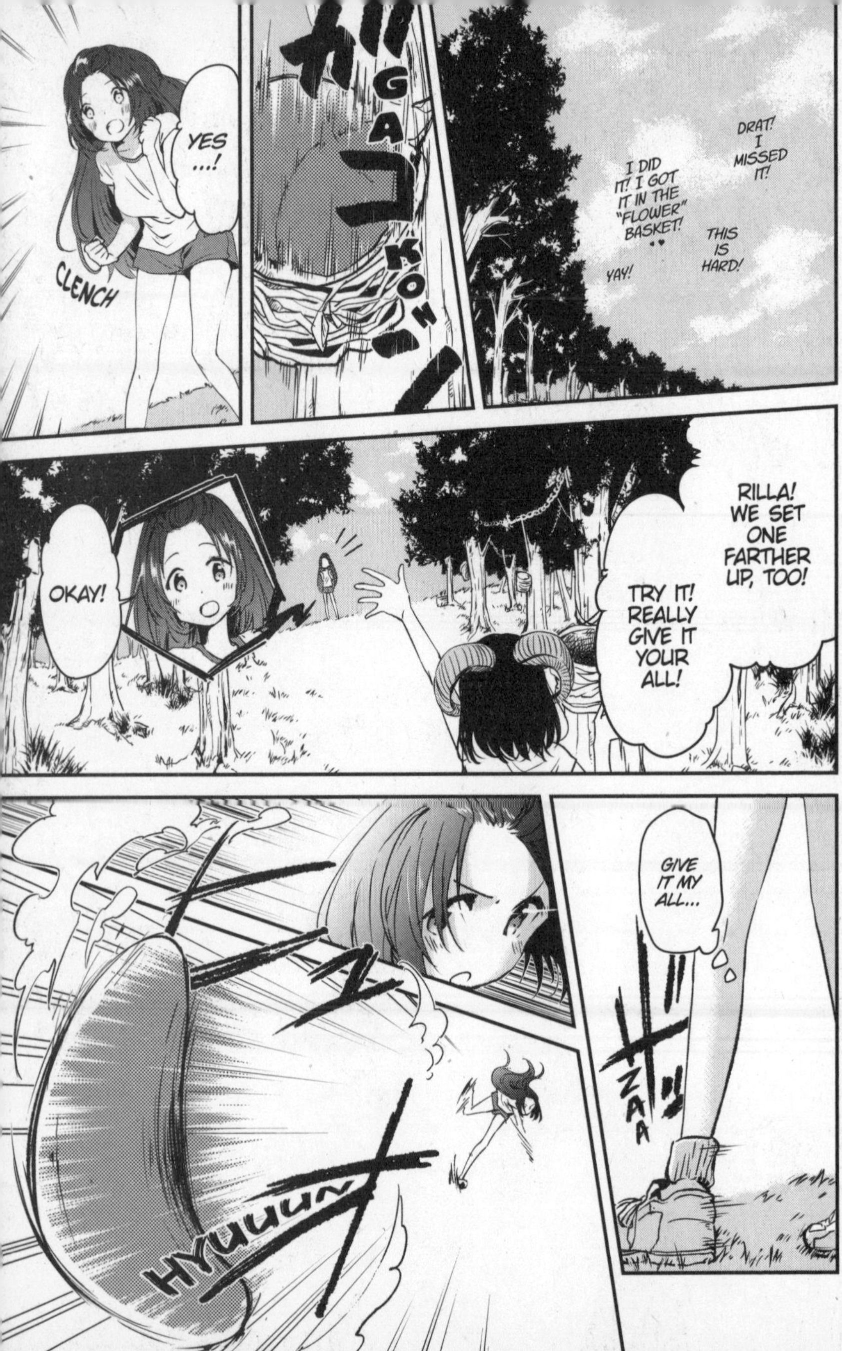
DRAT! I MISSED IT!
I DID IT! I GOT IT IN THE "FLOWER" BASKET! ♥
THIS IS HARD!
YAY!
GAKON
YES ...!
CLENCH
RILLA! WE SET ONE FARTHER UP, TOO!
TRY IT! REALLY GIVE IT YOUR ALL!
OKAY!
GIVE IT MY ALL...
ZAA
HYUUUN

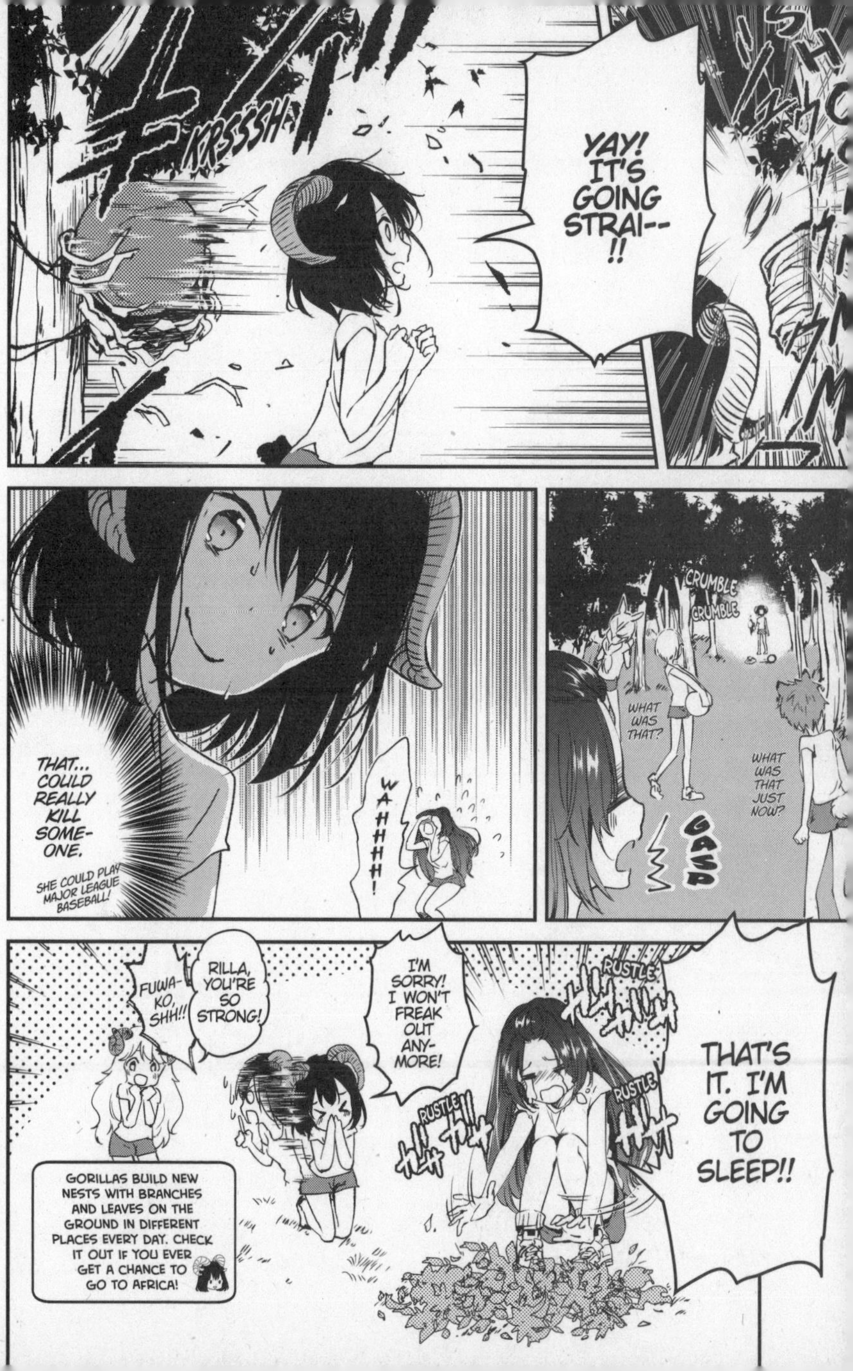
KRSSSH
YAY! IT'S GOING STRAI-- !!
CRUMBLE
CRUMBLE
WHAT WAS THAT JUST NOW?
WHAT WAS THAT?
GASP
WAHHHHH!
THAT... COULD REALLY KILL SOME-ONE.
SHE COULD PLAY MAJOR LEAGUE BASEBALL!
THAT'S IT. I'M GOING TO SLEEP!!
RUSTLE
RUSTLE
RUSTLE
I'M SORRY! I WON'T FREAK OUT ANY-MORE!
RILLA, YOU'RE SO STRONG!
FUWA-KO, SHH!!
GORILLAS BUILD NEW NESTS WITH BRANCHES AND LEAVES ON THE GROUND IN DIFFERENT PLACES EVERY DAY. CHECK IT OUT IF YOU EVER GET A CHANCE TO GO TO AFRICA!

Western Lowland Gorilla

DNAは教えてくれない

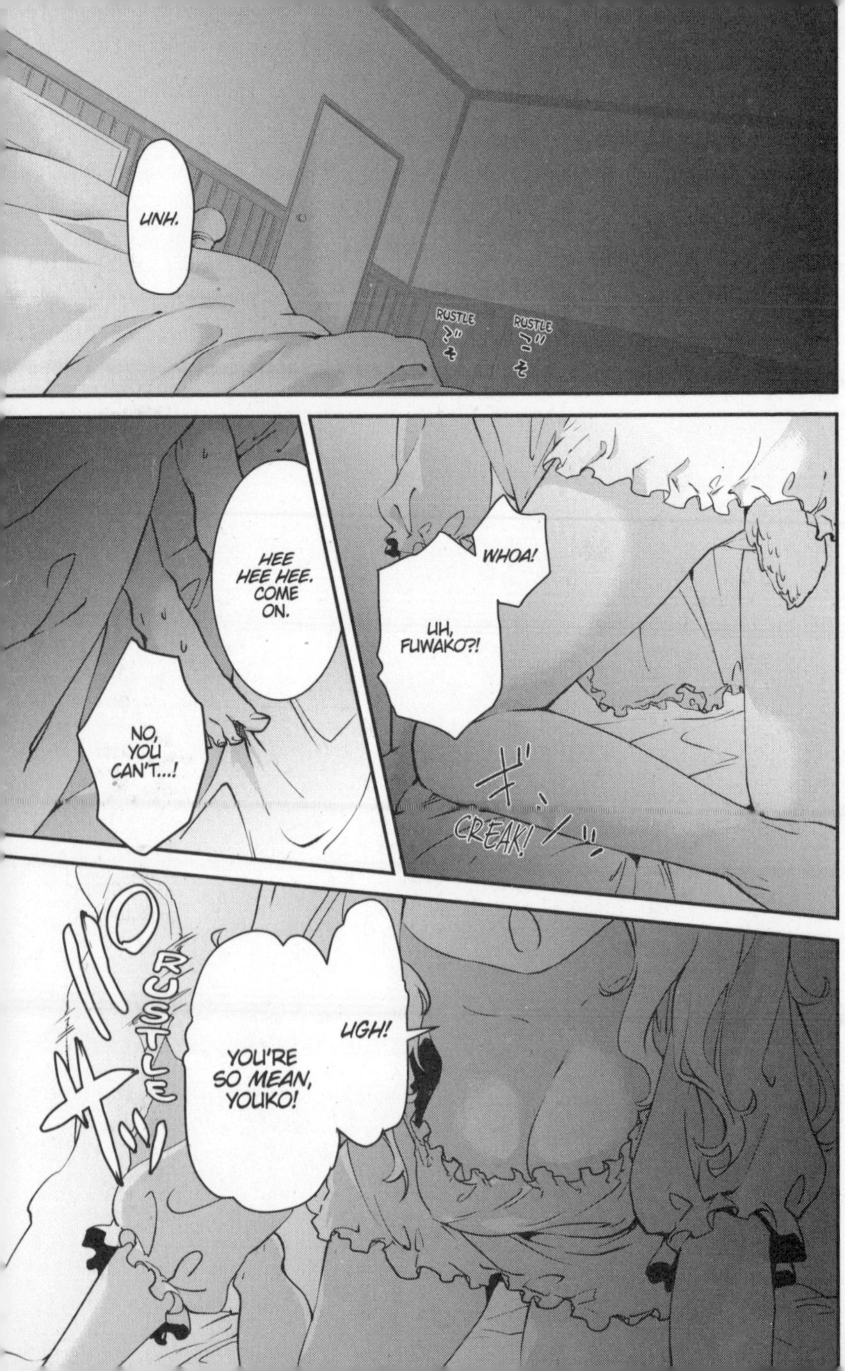
UNH.
RUSTLE ごそ
RUSTLE ごそ
WHOA!
UH, FUWAKO?!
CREAK!
HEE HEE HEE. COME ON.
NO, YOU CAN'T...!
UGH!
YOU'RE SO MEAN, YOUKO!
RUSTLE

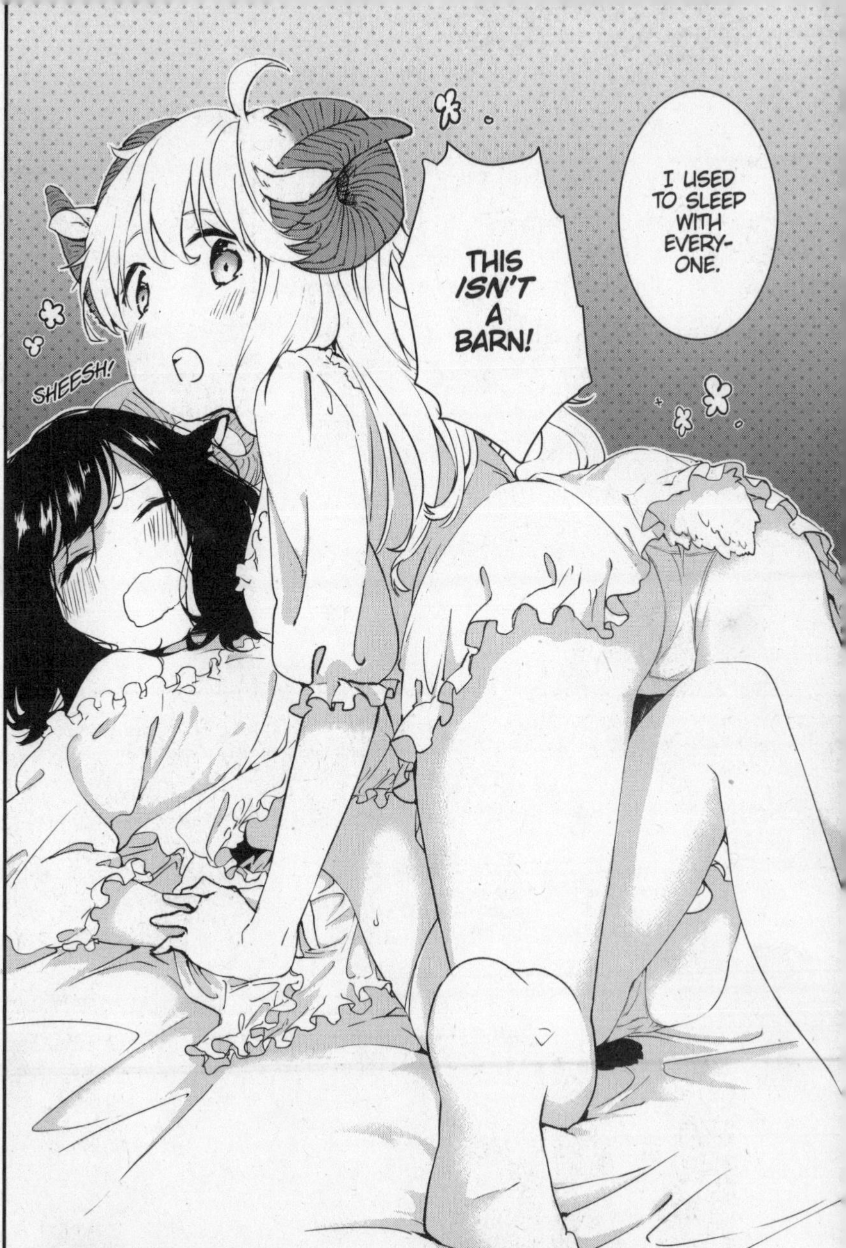
I USED TO SLEEP WITH EVERY-ONE.
THIS ISN'T A BARN!
SHEESH!

LESSON 5

Working Girls at a Café

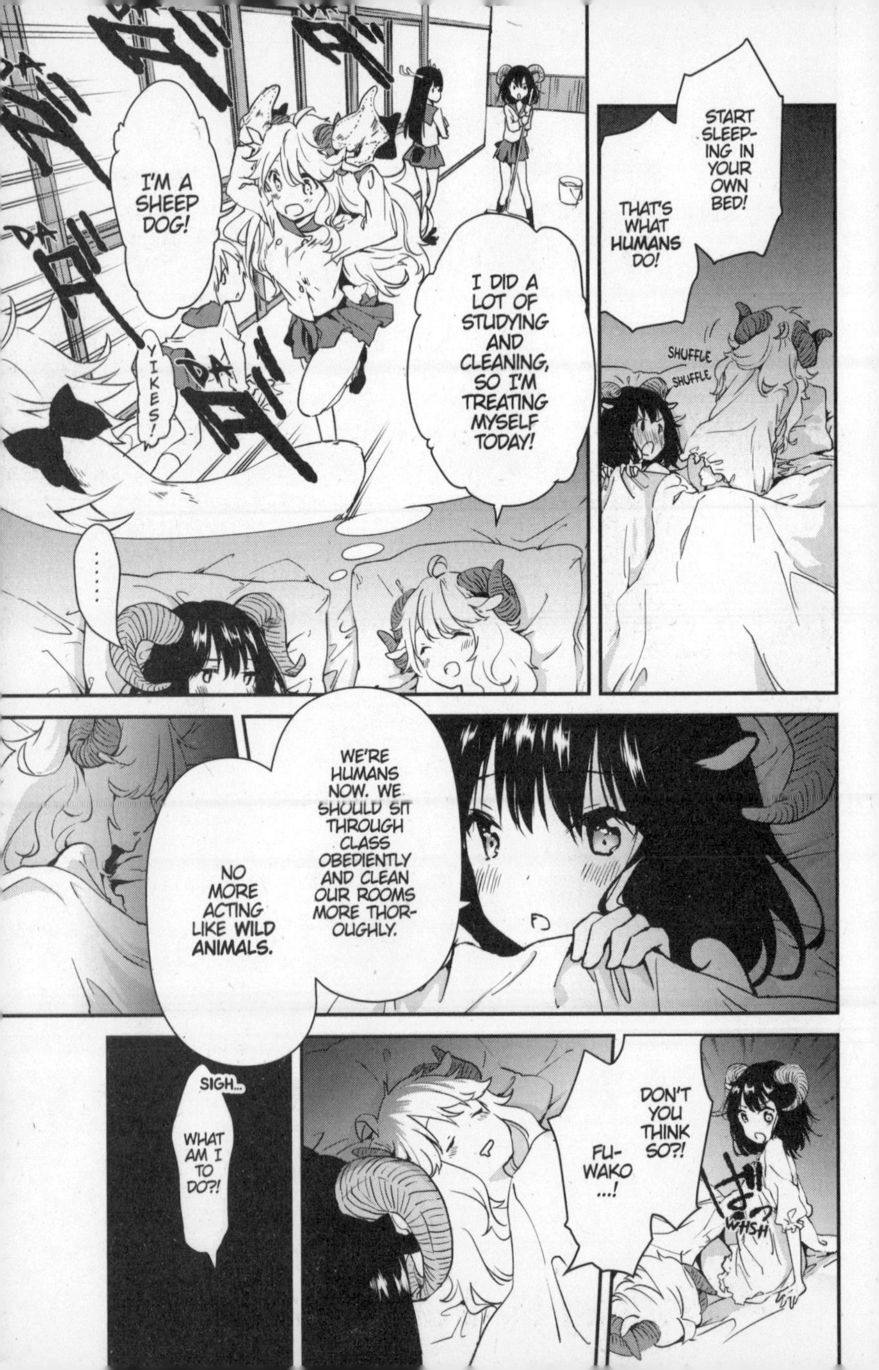
START SLEEPING IN YOUR OWN BED!
THAT'S WHAT HUMANS DO!
SHUFFLE
SHUFFLE
I DID A LOT OF STUDYING AND CLEANING, SO I'M TREATING MYSELF TODAY!
I'M A SHEEP DOG!
DA
DA
DA
YIKES!
......
WE'RE HUMANS NOW. WE SHOULD SIT THROUGH CLASS OBEDIENTLY AND CLEAN OUR ROOMS MORE THOR-OUGHLY.
NO MORE ACTING LIKE WILD ANIMALS.
DON'T YOU THINK SO?!
FU-WAKO ...!
WHSH
SIGH...
WHAT AM I TO DO?!

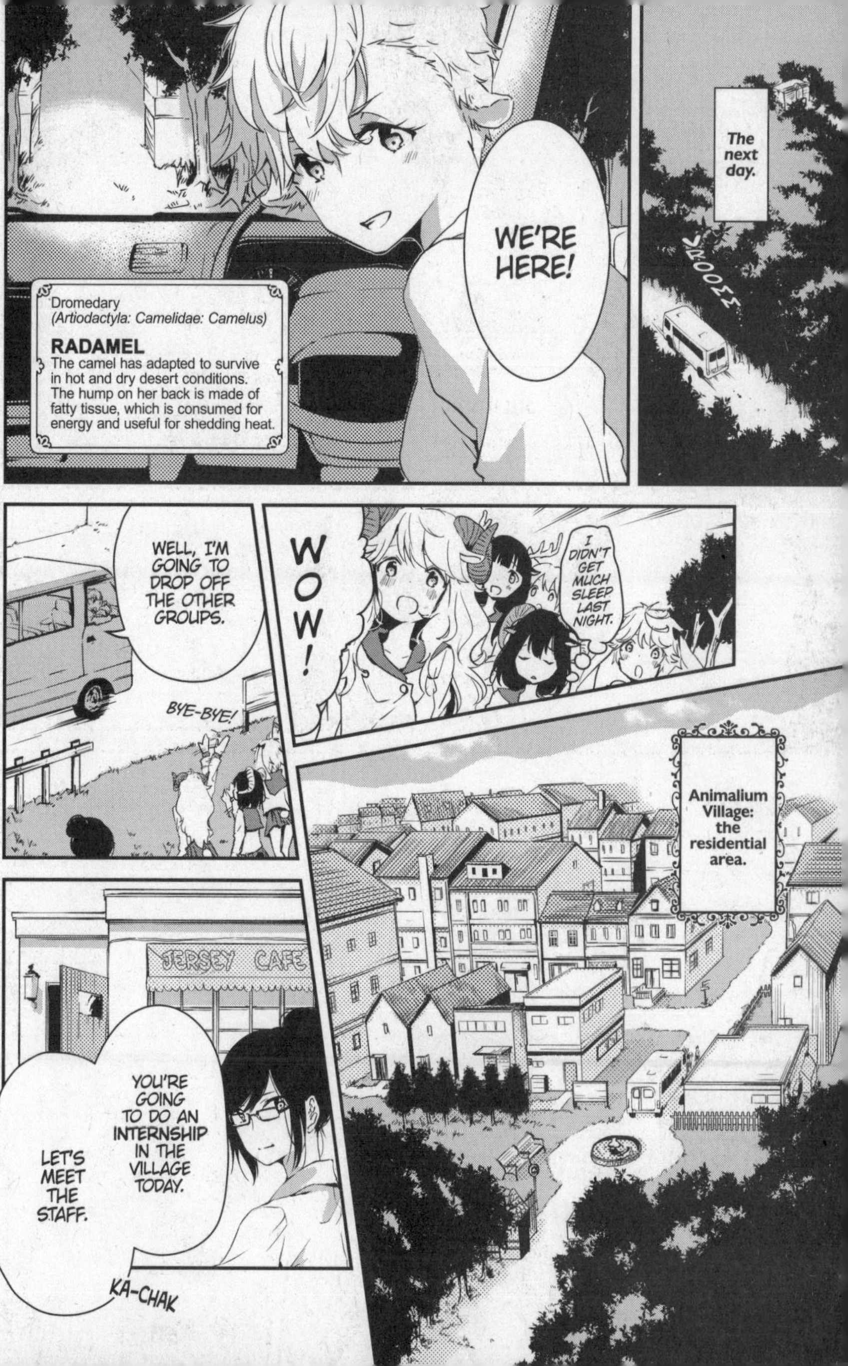
The next day.
VROOM
WE'RE HERE!
Dromedary
(Artiodactyla: Camelidae: Camelus)
RADAMEL
The camel has adapted to survive in hot and dry desert conditions. The hump on her back is made of fatty tissue, which is consumed for energy and useful for shedding heat.
WOW!
I DIDN'T GET MUCH SLEEP LAST NIGHT.
WELL, I'M GOING TO DROP OFF THE OTHER GROUPS.
BYE-BYE!
Animalium Village: the residential area.
JERSEY CAFE
YOU'RE GOING TO DO AN INTERNSHIP IN THE VILLAGE TODAY.
LET'S MEET THE STAFF.
KA-CHAK

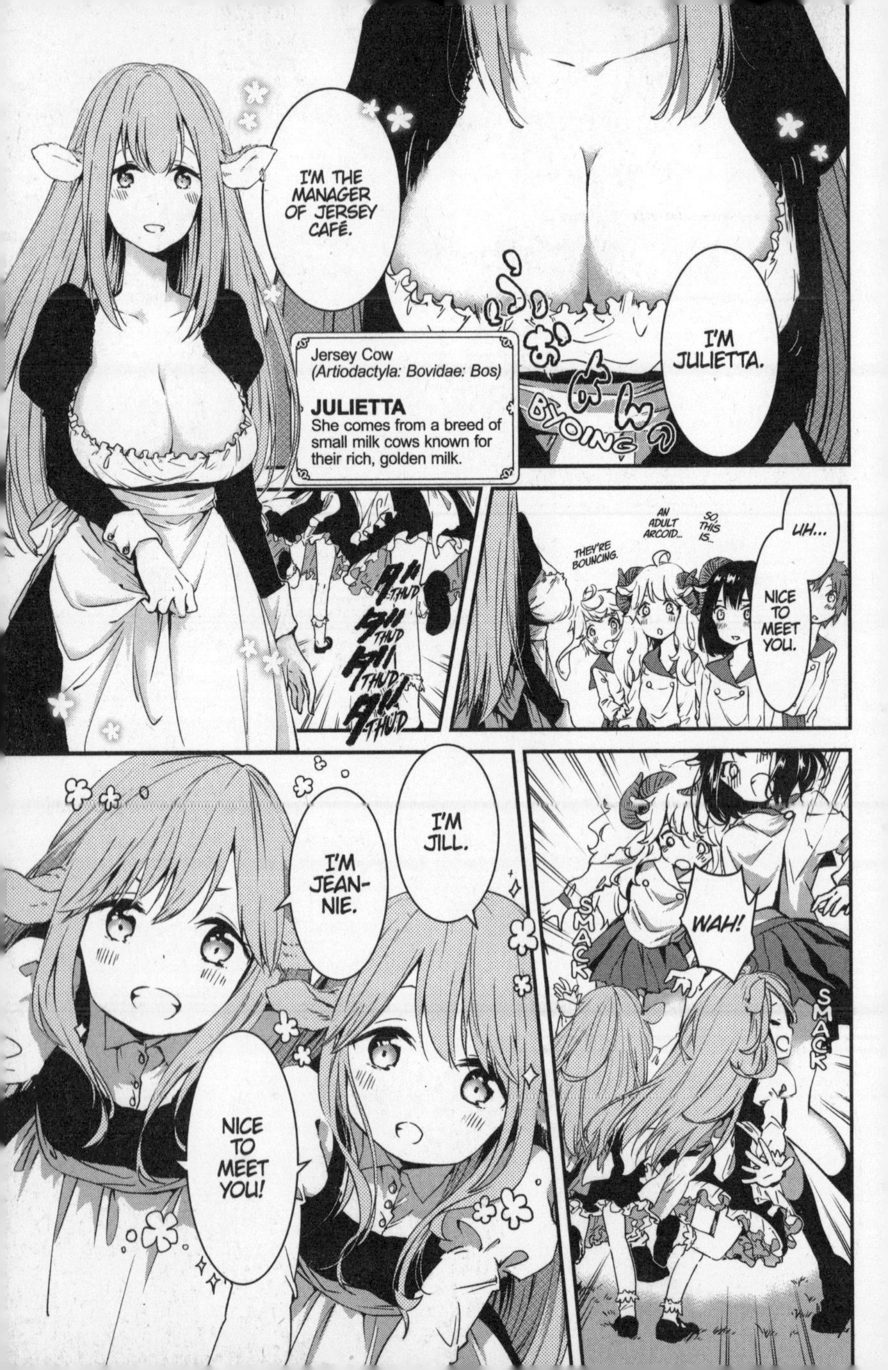
I'M JULIETTA.
BYOING
I'M THE MANAGER OF JERSEY CAFÉ.
Jersey Cow
(Artiodactyla: Bovidae: Bos)
JULIETTA
She comes from a breed of small milk cows known for their rich, golden milk.
UH...
NICE TO MEET YOU.
SO, THIS IS...
AN ADULT ARCOID...
THEY'RE BOUNCING.
THUD
THUD
THUD
THUD
SMACK
WAH!
SMACK
I'M JILL.
I'M JEAN-NIE.
NICE TO MEET YOU!

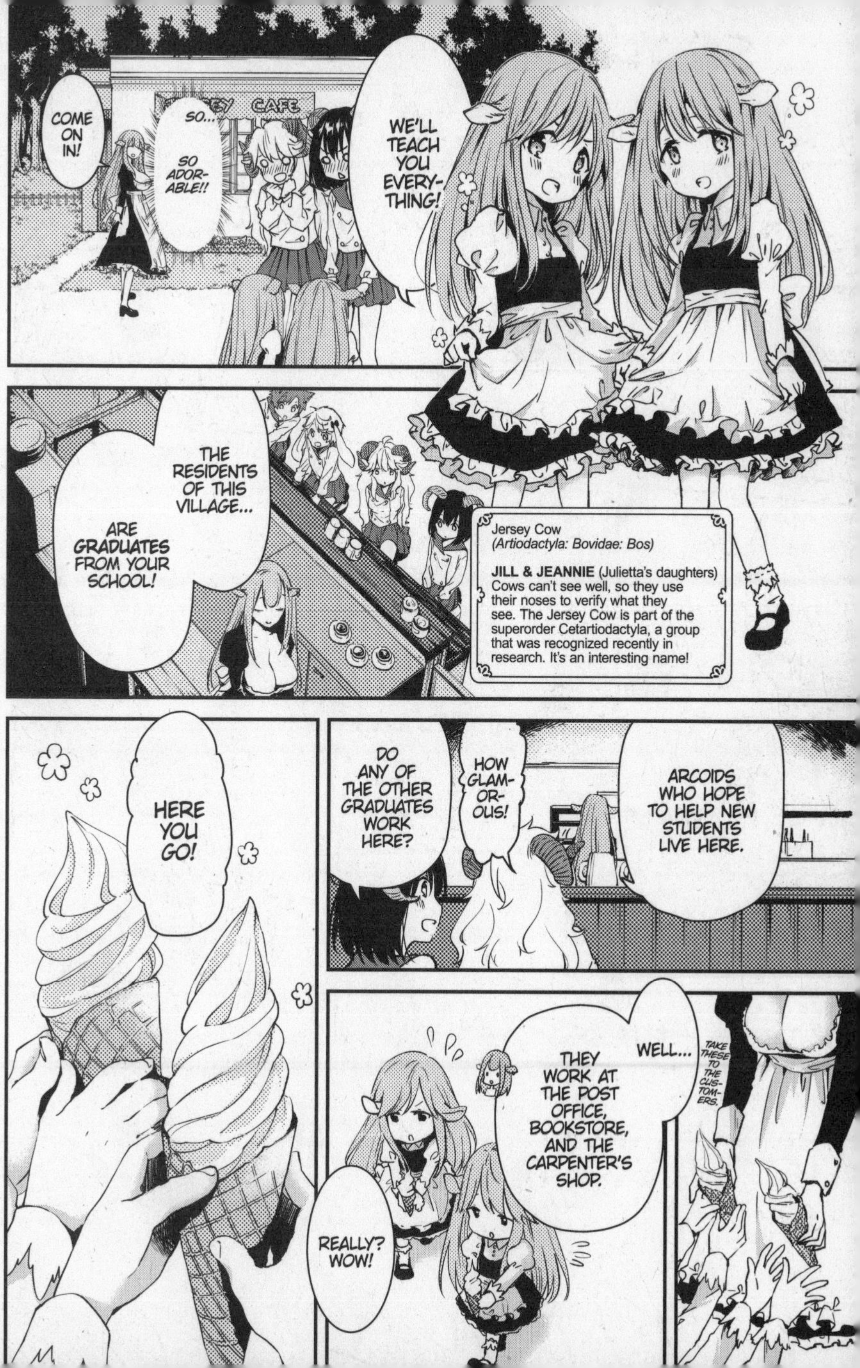
WE'LL TEACH YOU EVERYTHING!
SO... SO ADORABLE!!
COME ON IN!
THE RESIDENTS OF THIS VILLAGE...
ARE GRADUATES FROM YOUR SCHOOL!
Jersey Cow
(Artiodactyla: Bovidae: Bos)
JILL & JEANNIE (Julietta's daughters) Cows can't see well, so they use their noses to verify what they see. The Jersey Cow is part of the superorder Cetartiodactyla, a group that was recognized recently in research. It's an interesting name!
ARCOIDS WHO HOPE TO HELP NEW STUDENTS LIVE HERE.
HOW GLAMOROUS!
DO ANY OF THE OTHER GRADUATES WORK HERE?
TAKE THESE TO THE CUSTOMERS.
WELL...
THEY WORK AT THE POST OFFICE, BOOKSTORE, AND THE CARPENTER'S SHOP.
REALLY? WOW!
HERE YOU GO!

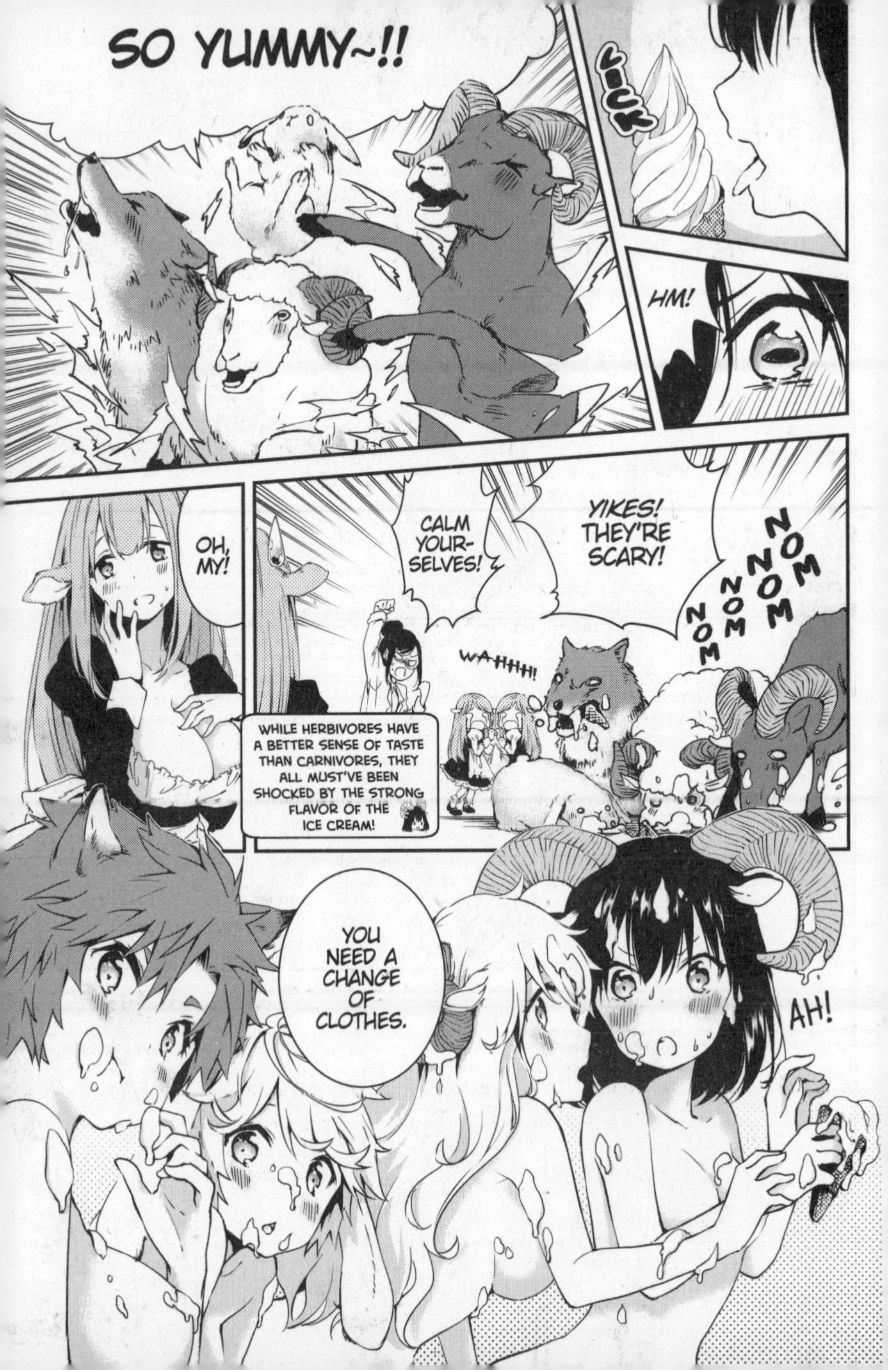
LICK
HM!
SO YUMMY~!!
NOM NOM NOM NOM
YIKES! THEY'RE SCARY!
CALM YOUR-SELVES!
WAHHHH!
WHILE HERBIVORES HAVE A BETTER SENSE OF TASTE THAN CARNIVORES, THEY ALL MUST'VE BEEN SHOCKED BY THE STRONG FLAVOR OF THE ICE CREAM!
OH, MY!
AH!
YOU NEED A CHANGE OF CLOTHES.

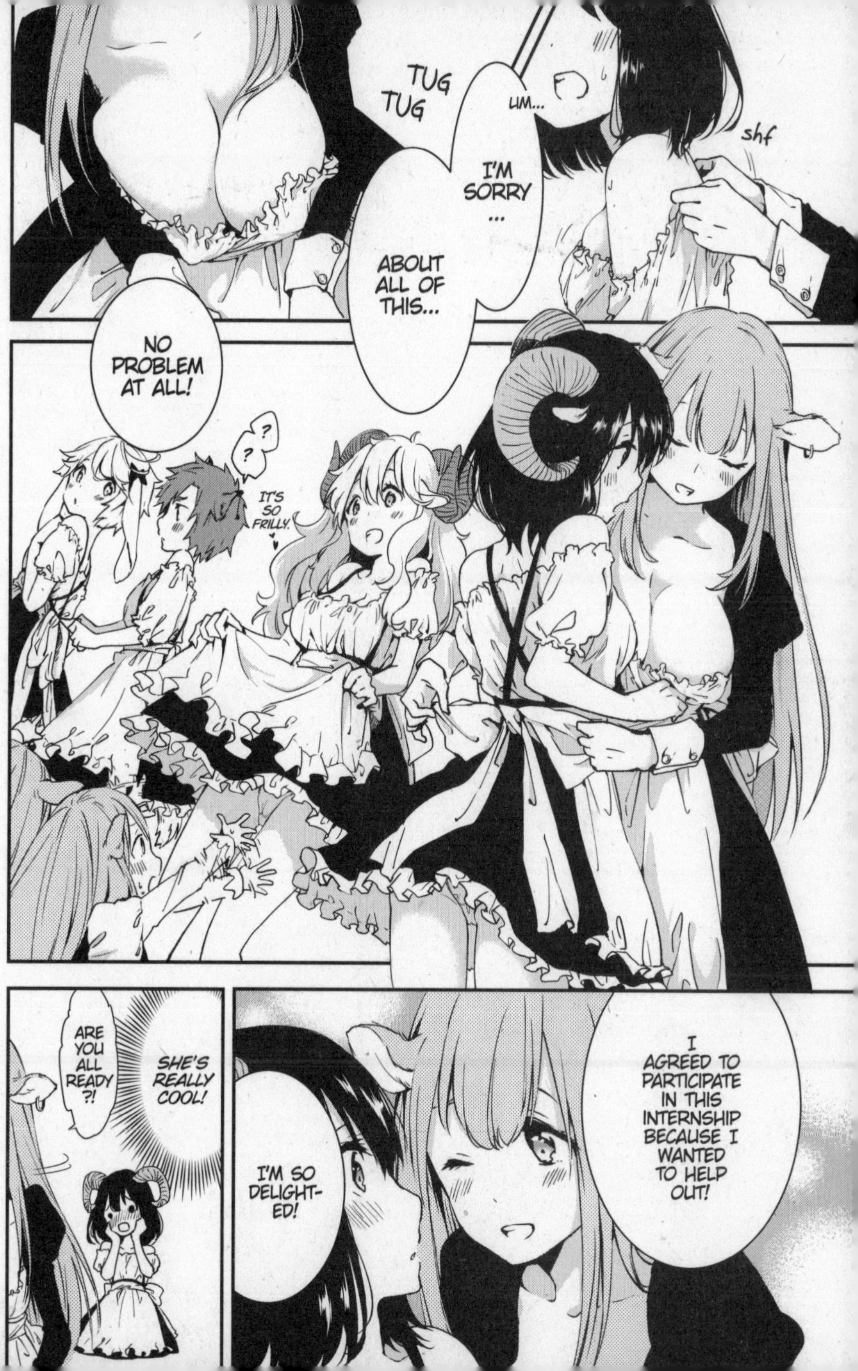
UM...
shf
TUG TUG
I'M SORRY ...
ABOUT ALL OF THIS...
NO PROBLEM AT ALL!
? ?
IT'S SO FRILLY.
I AGREED TO PARTICIPATE IN THIS INTERNSHIP BECAUSE I WANTED TO HELP OUT!
I'M SO DELIGHT-ED!
SHE'S REALLY COOL!
ARE YOU ALL READY ?!

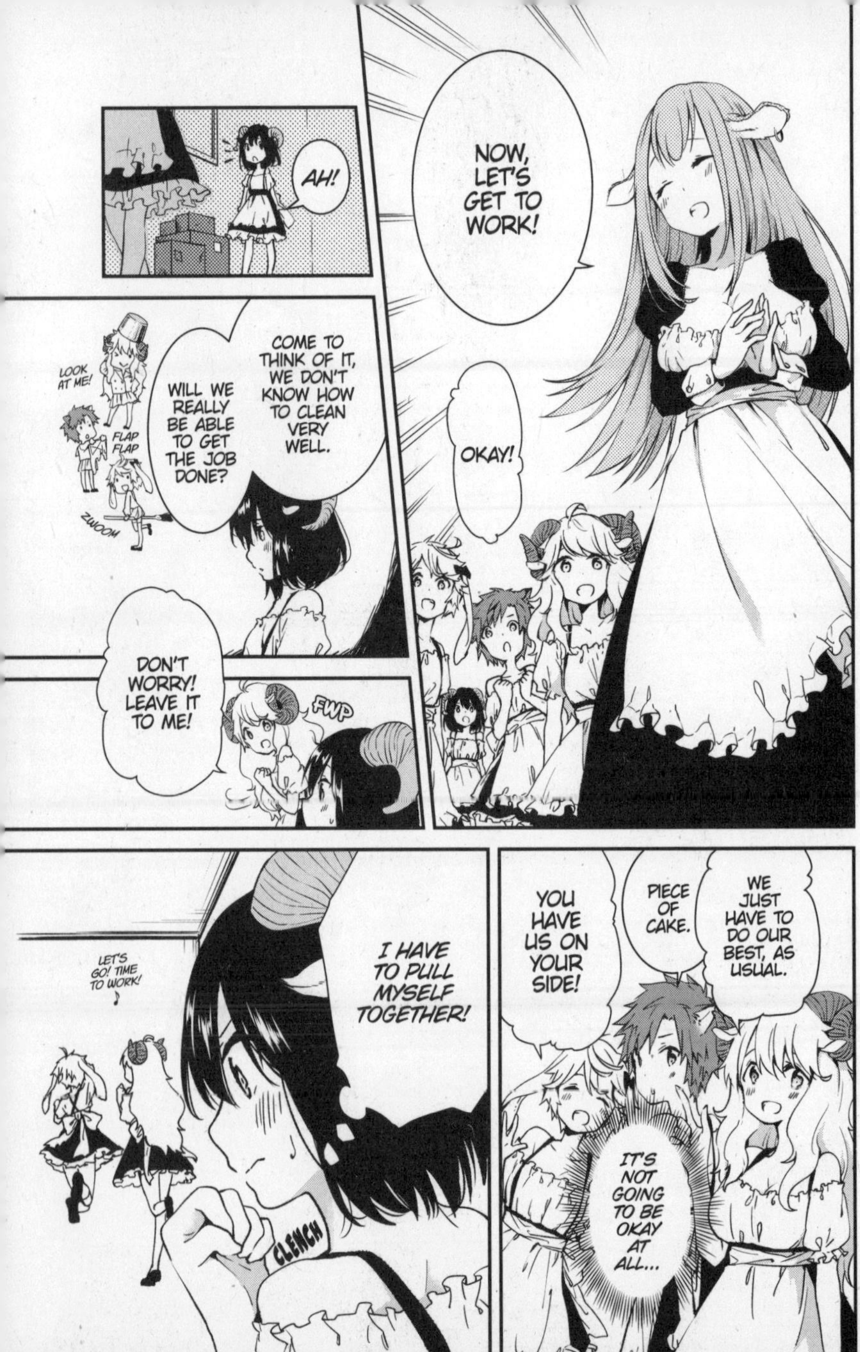
NOW, LET'S GET TO WORK!
OKAY!
AH!
COME TO THINK OF IT, WE DON'T KNOW HOW TO CLEAN VERY WELL.
WILL WE REALLY BE ABLE TO GET THE JOB DONE?
LOOK AT ME!
FLAP FLAP
ZWOOM
DON'T WORRY! LEAVE IT TO ME!
FWP
WE JUST HAVE TO DO OUR BEST, AS USUAL.
PIECE OF CAKE.
YOU HAVE US ON YOUR SIDE!
IT'S NOT GOING TO BE OKAY AT ALL...
I HAVE TO PULL MYSELF TOGETHER!
CLENCH
LET'S GO! TIME TO WORK!

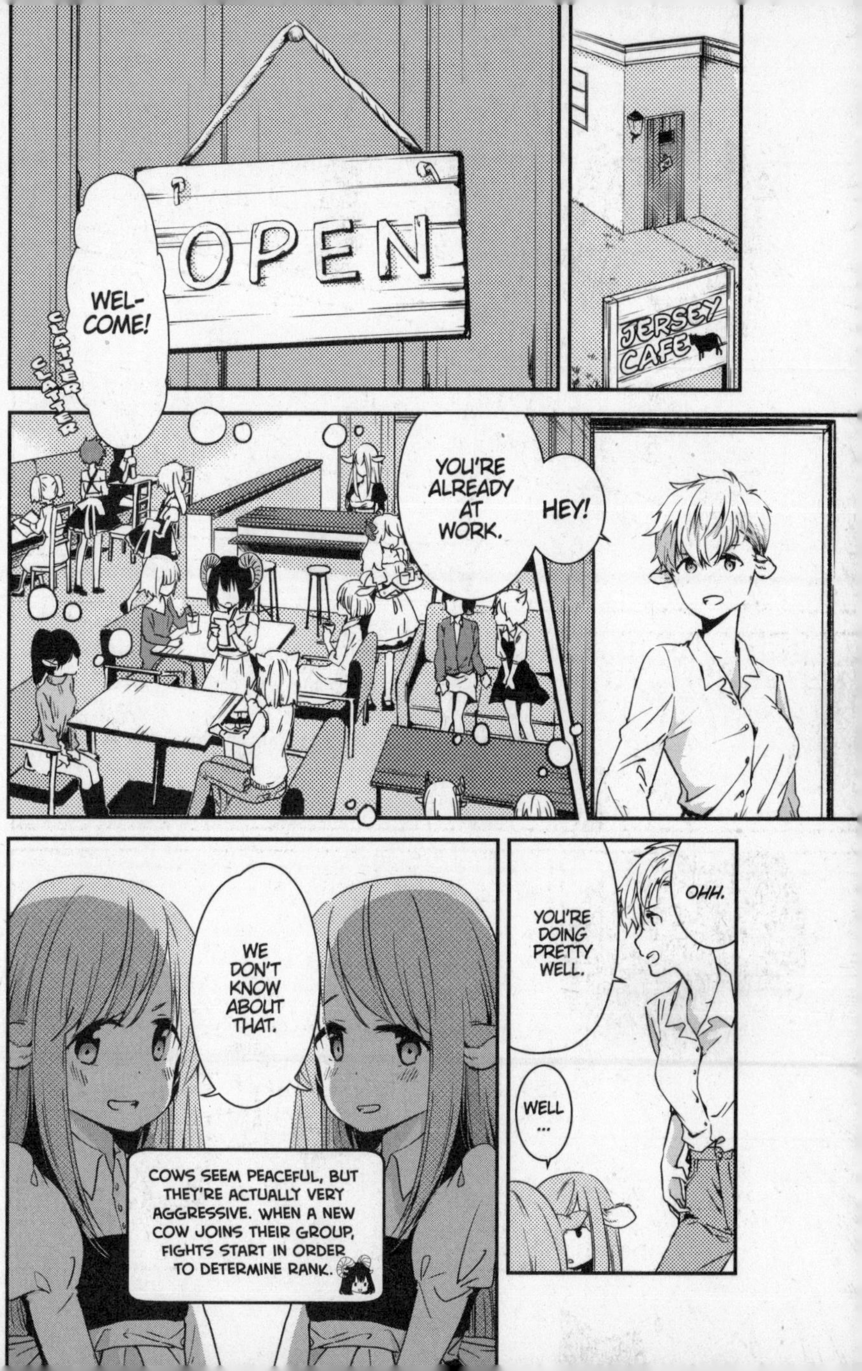
JERSEY CAFE
OPEN
WEL-COME!
CLATTER CLATTER
HEY!
YOU'RE ALREADY AT WORK.
OHH.
YOU'RE DOING PRETTY WELL.
WELL ...
WE DON'T KNOW ABOUT THAT.
COWS SEEM PEACEFUL, BUT THEY'RE ACTUALLY VERY AGGRESSIVE. WHEN A NEW COW JOINS THEIR GROUP, FIGHTS START IN ORDER TO DETERMINE RANK.

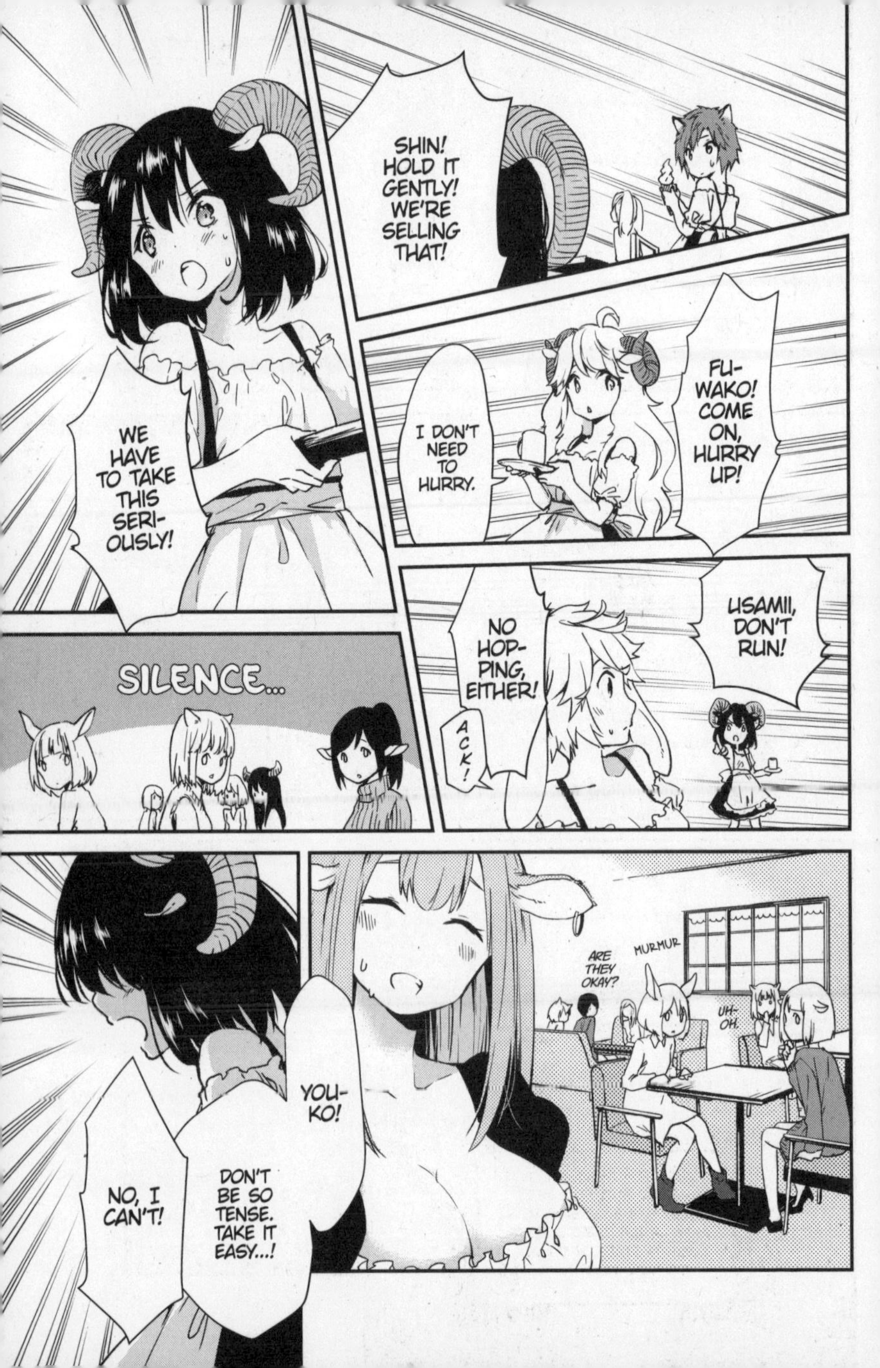
SHIN! HOLD IT GENTLY! WE'RE SELLING THAT!
FU-WAKO! COME ON, HURRY UP!
I DON'T NEED TO HURRY.
WE HAVE TO TAKE THIS SERI-OUSLY!
USAMII, DON'T RUN!
NO HOP-PING, EITHER!
ACK!
SILENCE...
MURMUR
ARE THEY OKAY?
UH-OH.
YOU-KO!
DON'T BE SO TENSE. TAKE IT EASY...!
NO, I CAN'T!

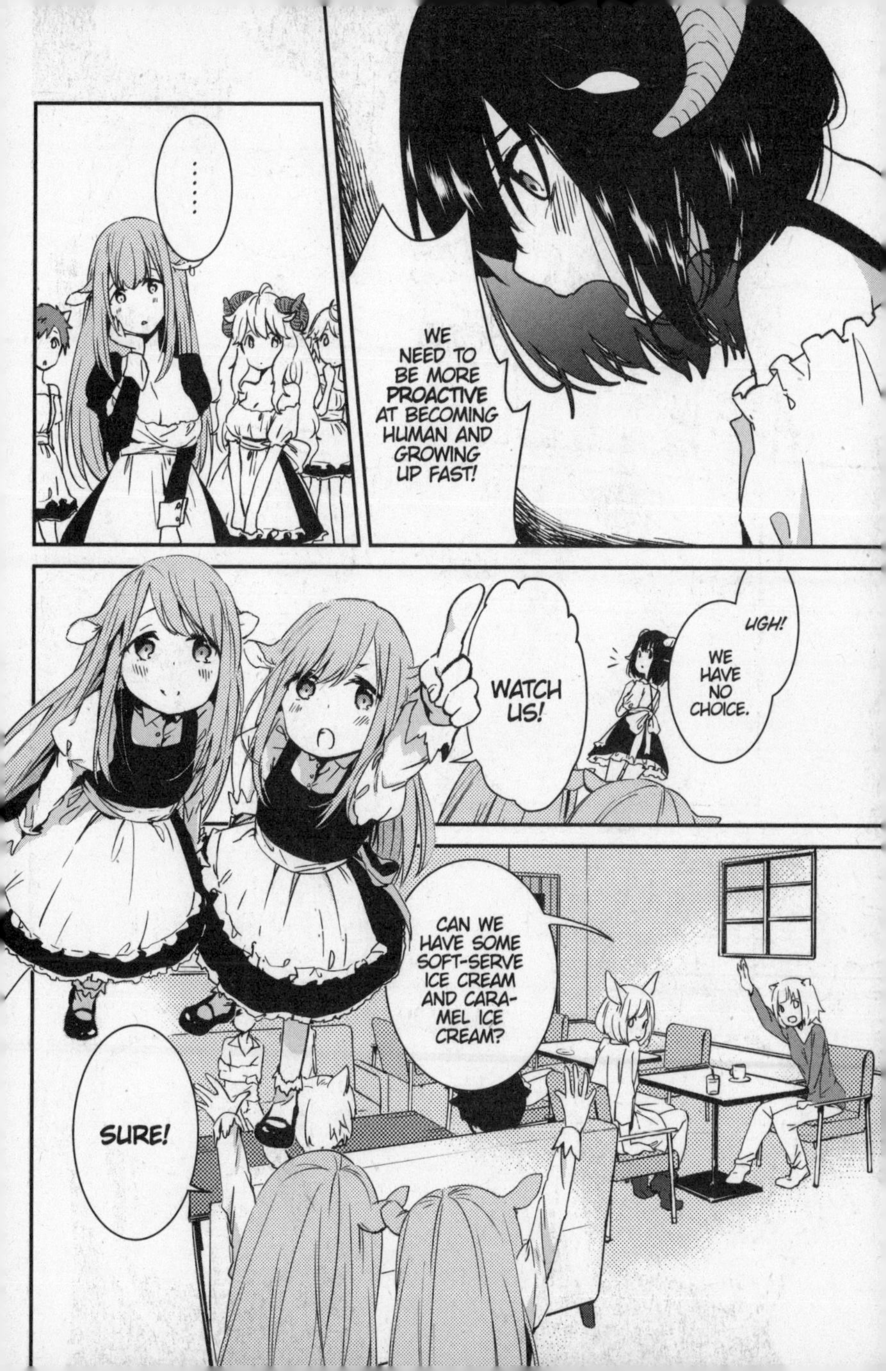
WE NEED TO BE MORE PROACTIVE AT BECOMING HUMAN AND GROWING UP FAST!
......
UGH!
WE HAVE NO CHOICE.
WATCH US!
CAN WE HAVE SOME SOFT-SERVE ICE CREAM AND CARA-MEL ICE CREAM?
SURE!

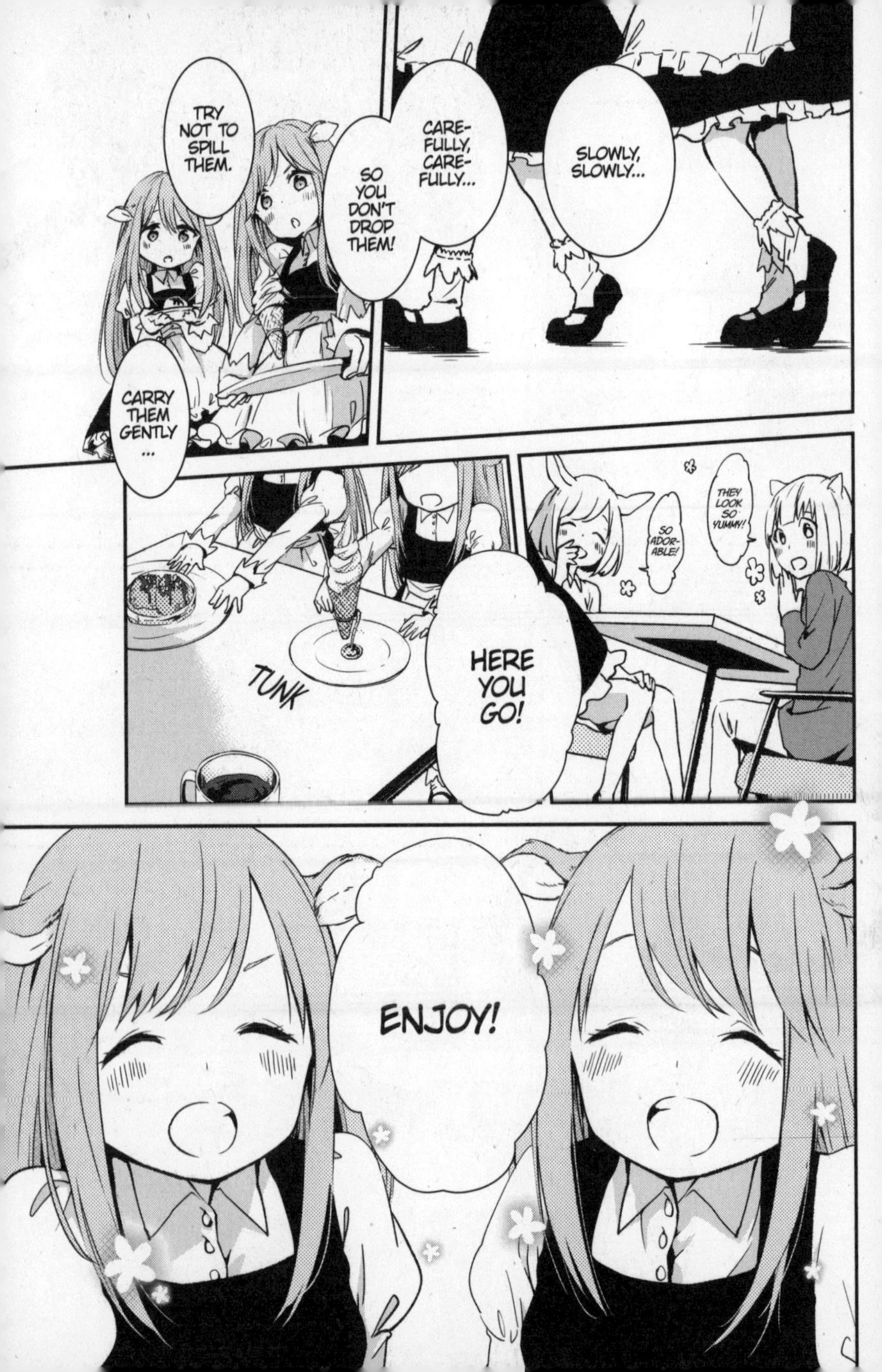
SLOWLY, SLOWLY...
CARE-FULLY, CARE-FULLY...
SO YOU DON'T DROP THEM!
TRY NOT TO SPILL THEM.
CARRY THEM GENTLY ...
THEY LOOK SO YUMMY!
SO ADORABLE!
HERE YOU GO!
TUNK
ENJOY!

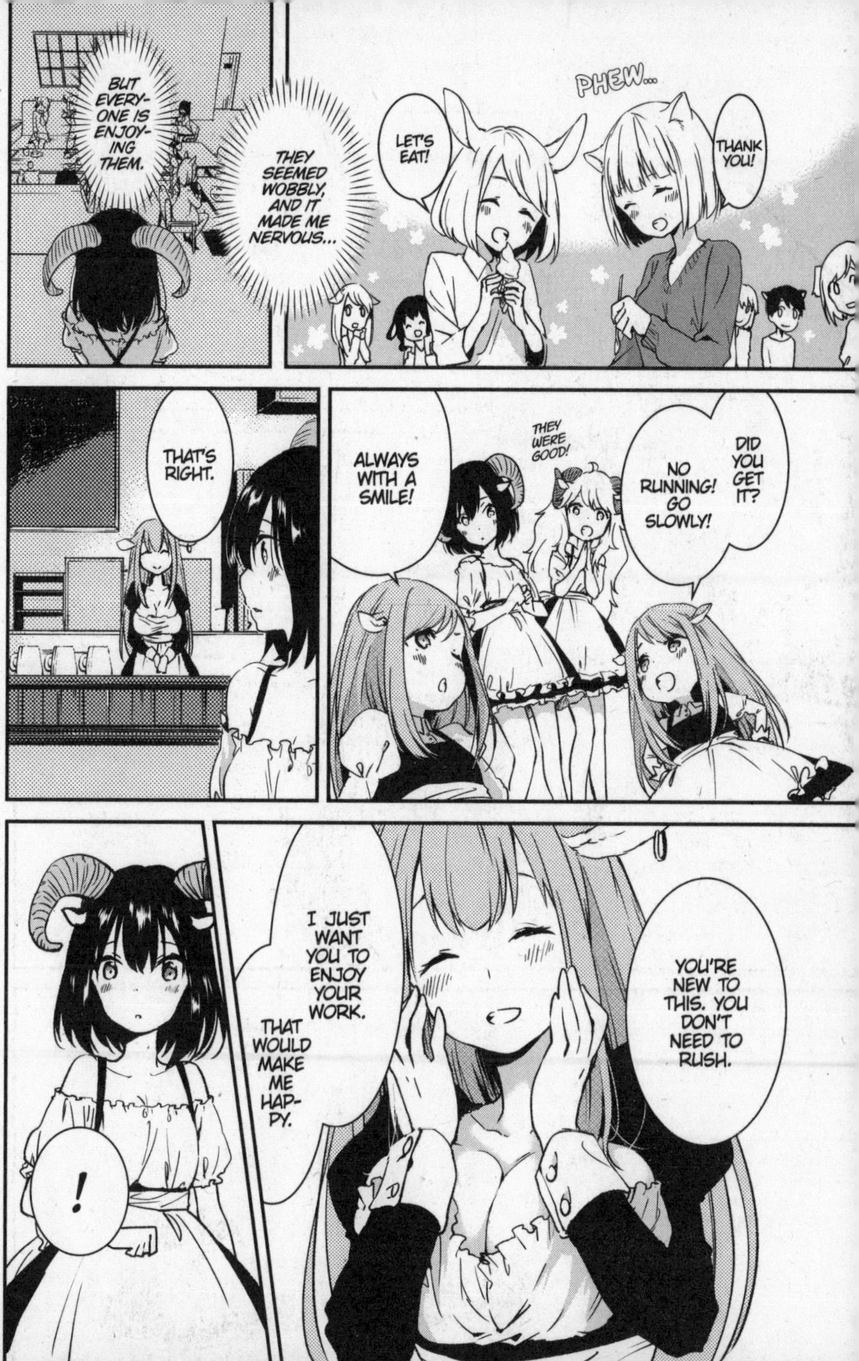
PHEW...
THANK YOU!
LET'S EAT!
THEY SEEMED WOBBLY, AND IT MADE ME NERVOUS...
BUT EVERYONE IS ENJOYING THEM.
DID YOU GET IT?
NO RUNNING! GO SLOWLY!
THEY WERE GOOD!
ALWAYS WITH A SMILE!
THAT'S RIGHT.
YOU'RE NEW TO THIS. YOU DON'T NEED TO RUSH.
I JUST WANT YOU TO ENJOY YOUR WORK.
THAT WOULD MAKE ME HAPPY.
!

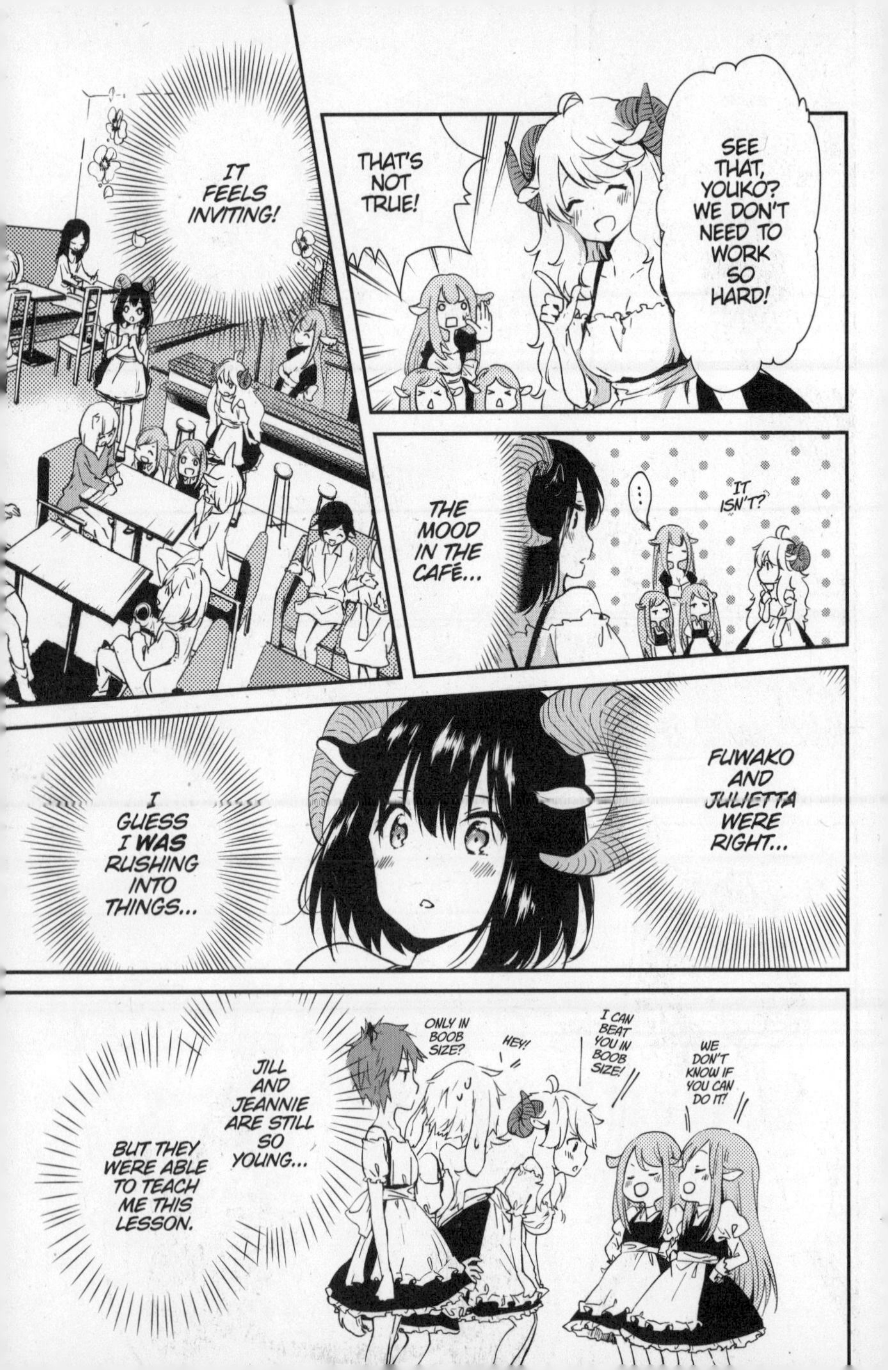
SEE THAT, YOUKO? WE DON'T NEED TO WORK SO HARD!
THAT'S NOT TRUE!
IT ISN'T?
...
THE MOOD IN THE CAFÉ...
IT FEELS INVITING!
FUWAKO AND JULIETTA WERE RIGHT...
I GUESS I WAS RUSHING INTO THINGS...
WE DON'T KNOW IF YOU CAN DO IT!
I CAN BEAT YOU IN BOOB SIZE!
ONLY IN BOOB SIZE?
HEY!
JILL AND JEANNIE ARE STILL SO YOUNG...
BUT THEY WERE ABLE TO TEACH ME THIS LESSON.

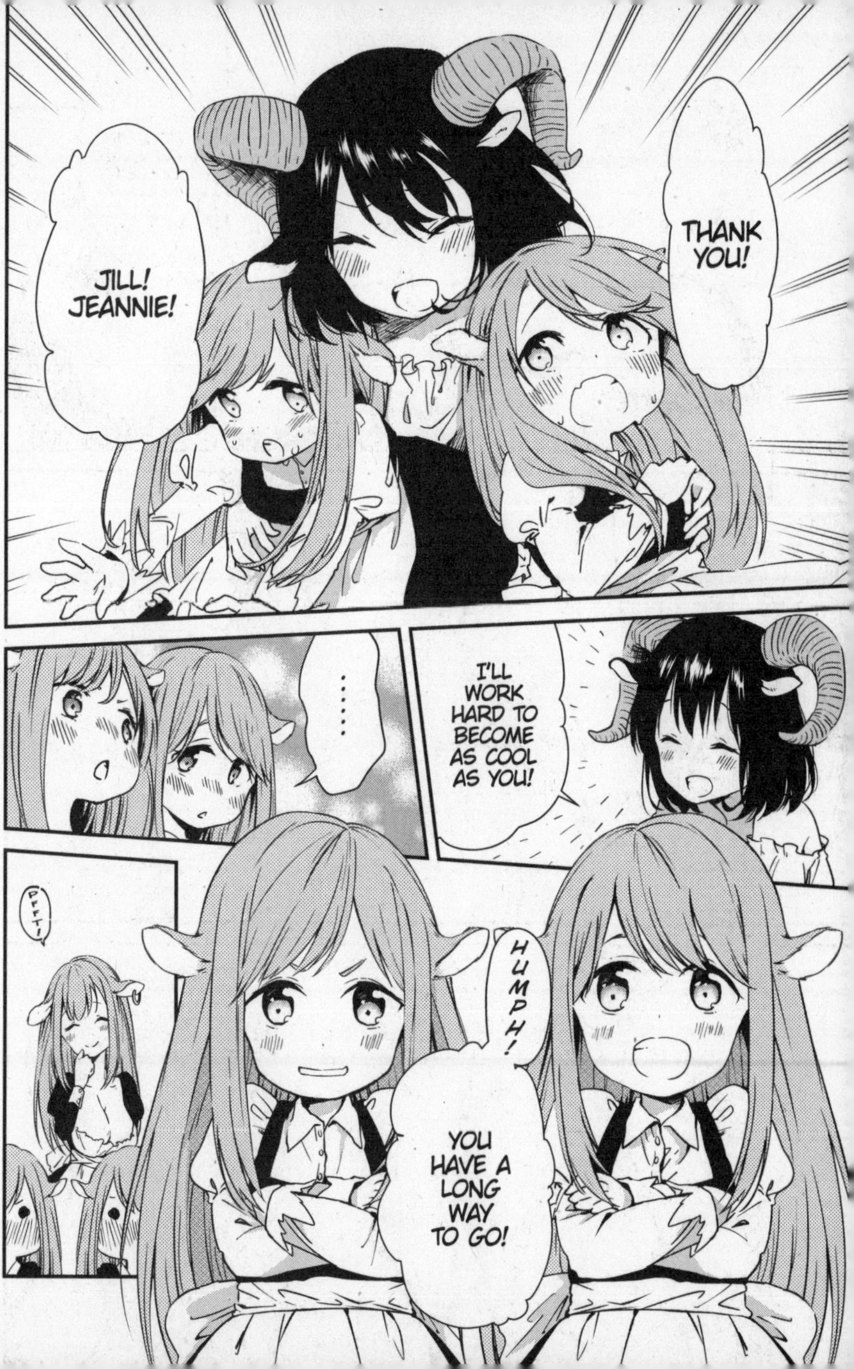
THANK YOU!
JILL! JEANNIE!
I'LL WORK HARD TO BECOME AS COOL AS YOU!
......
HUMPH!
YOU HAVE A LONG WAY TO GO!
PFFT!

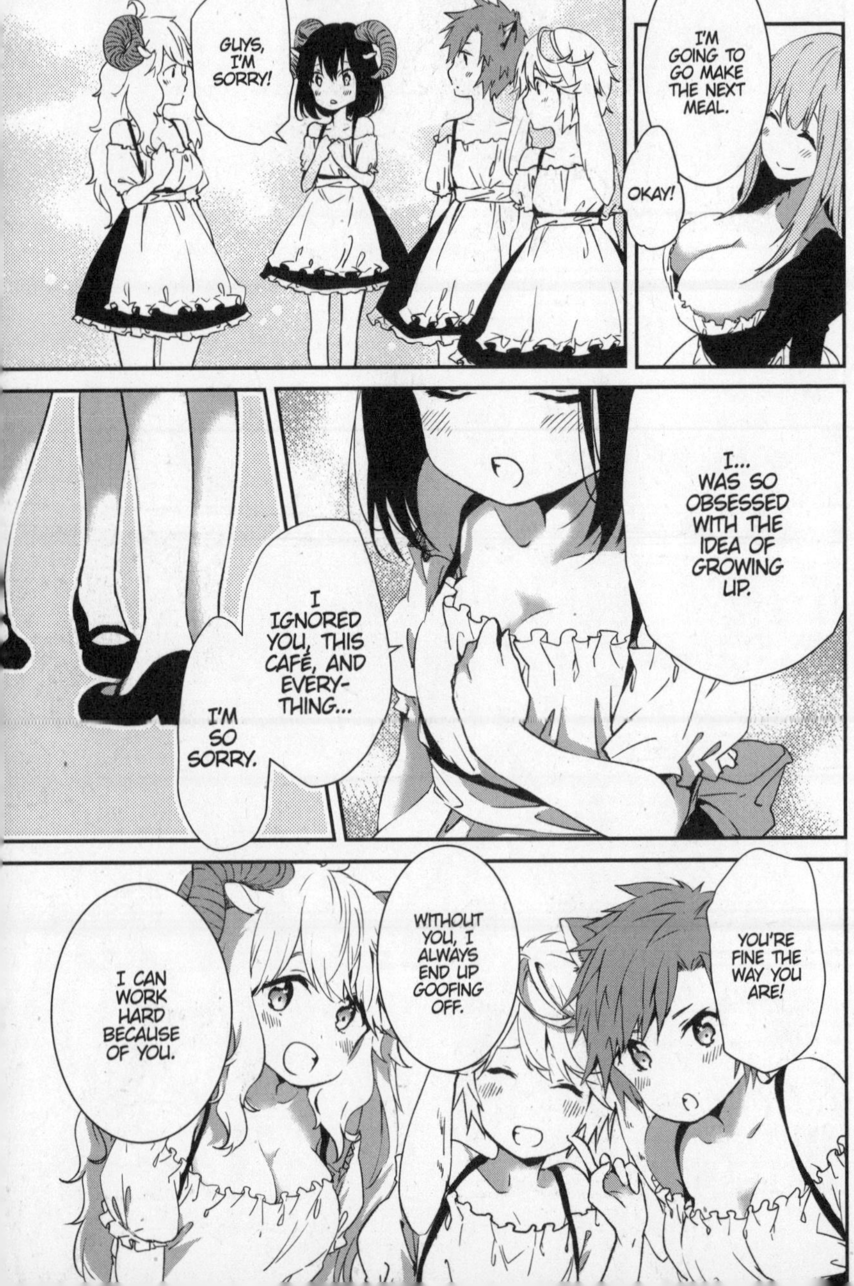
I'M GOING TO GO MAKE THE NEXT MEAL.
OKAY!
GUYS, I'M SORRY!
I... WAS SO OBSESSED WITH THE IDEA OF GROWING UP.
I IGNORED YOU, THIS CAFÉ, AND EVERY-THING...
I'M SO SORRY.
YOU'RE FINE THE WAY YOU ARE!
WITHOUT YOU, I ALWAYS END UP GOOFING OFF.
I CAN WORK HARD BECAUSE OF YOU.

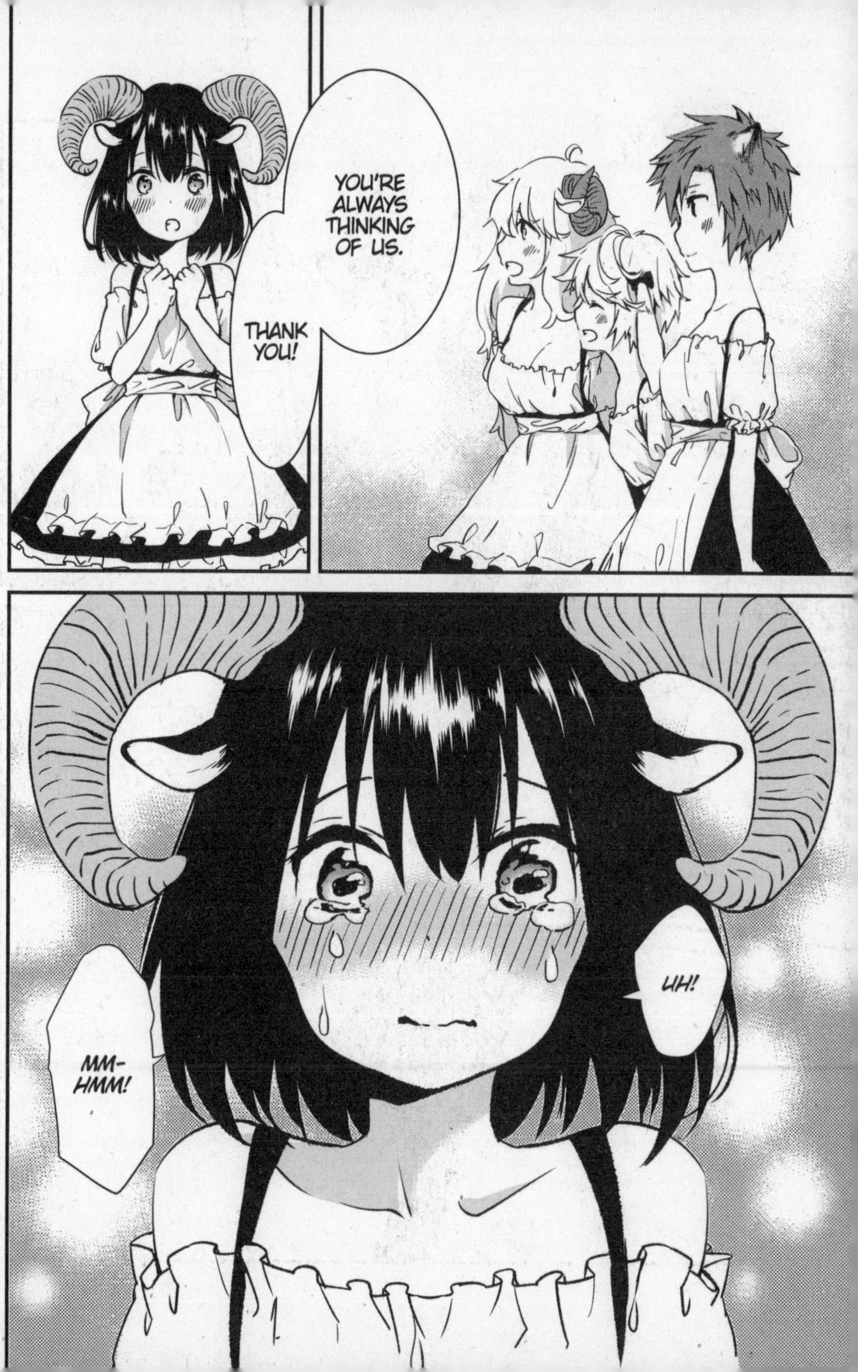
YOU'RE ALWAYS THINKING OF US.
THANK YOU!
UH!
MM-HMM!

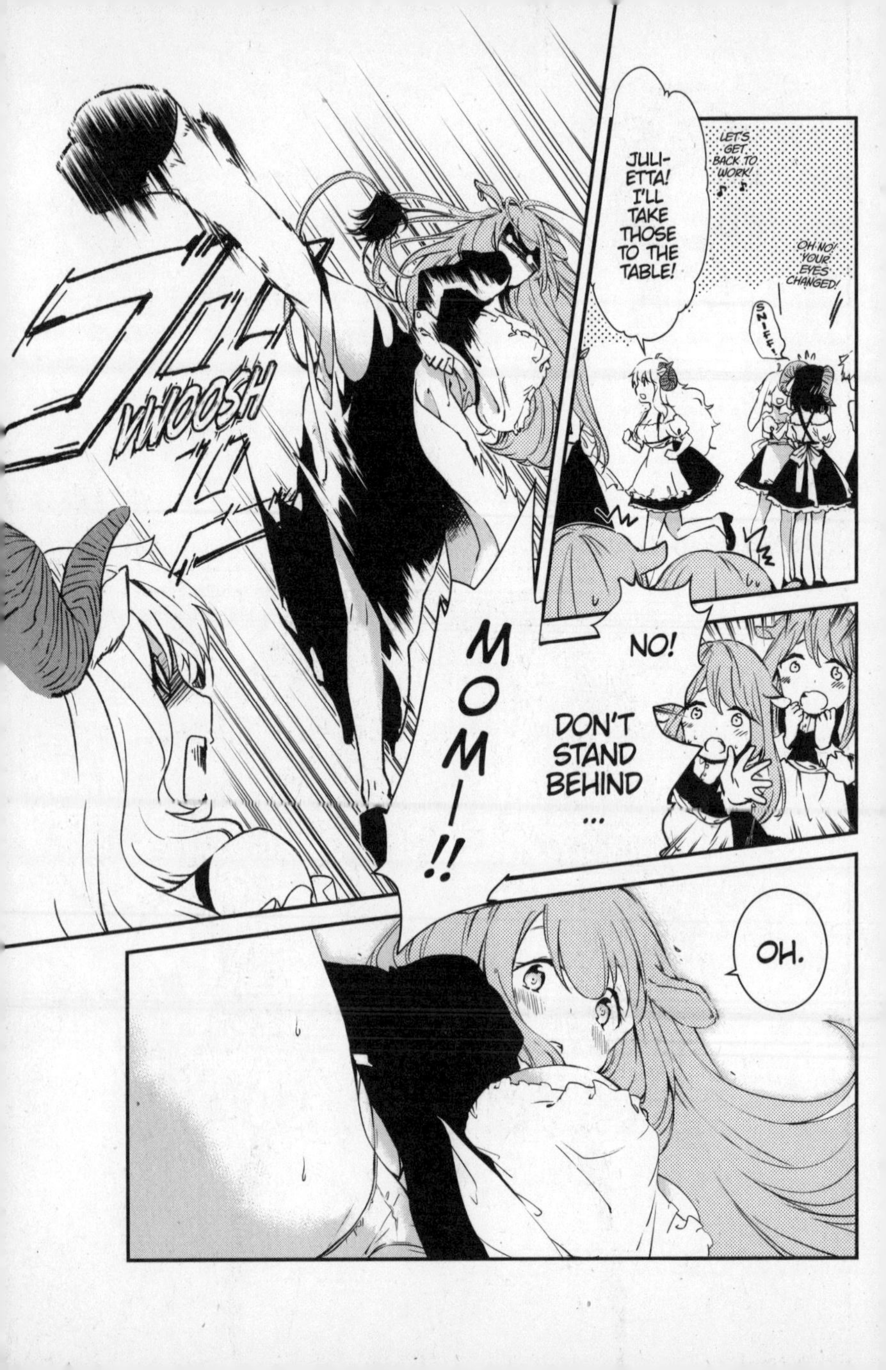
LET'S GET BACK TO WORK! ♪ ♪
JULI-ETTA! I'LL TAKE THOSE TO THE TABLE!
OH NO! YOUR EYES CHANGED!
SNIFF!
NO!
DON'T STAND BEHIND ...
VWOOSH
MOMI--!!
OH.

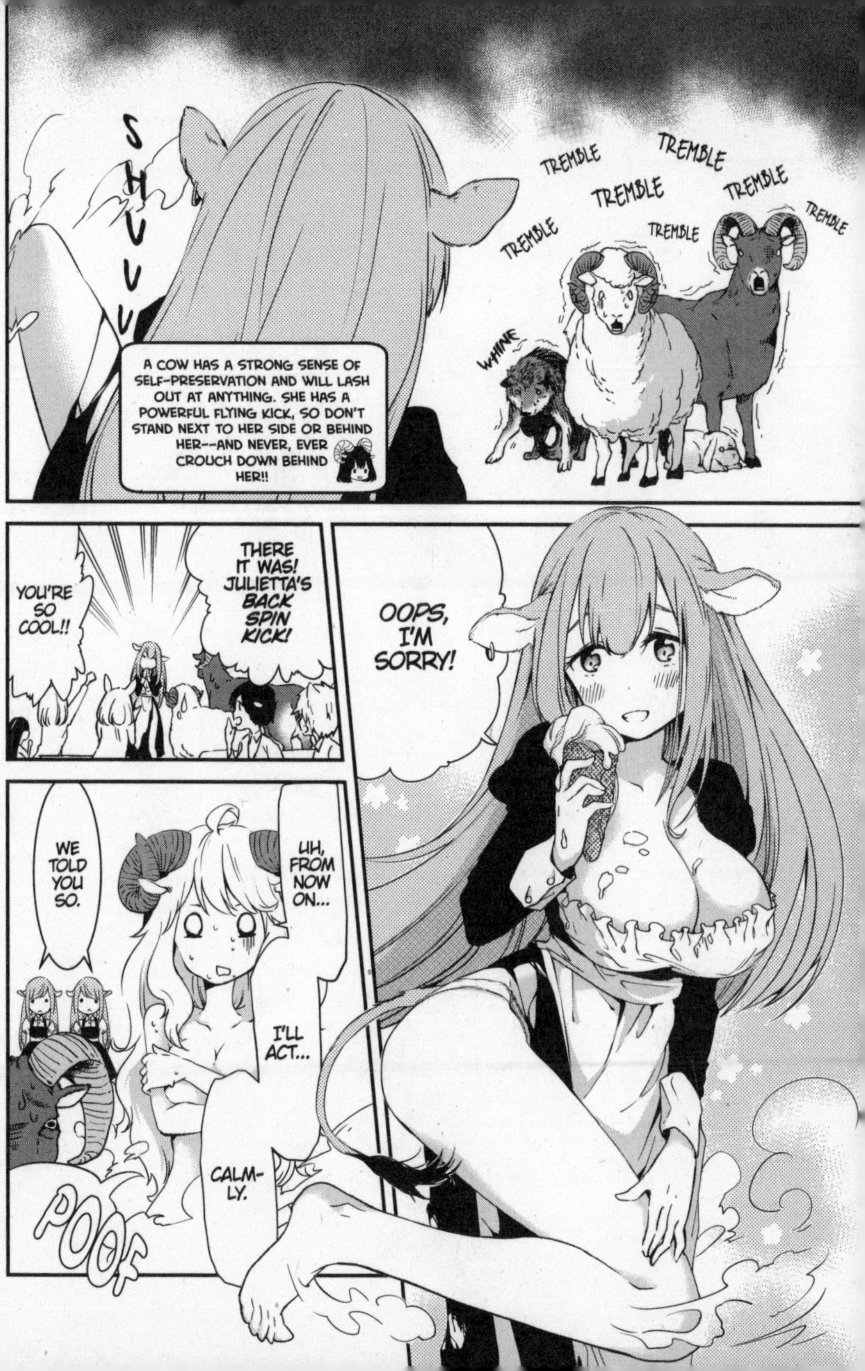
TREMBLE
TREMBLE
TREMBLE
TREMBLE
TREMBLE
TREMBLE
TREMBLE
WHINE
SHUVUU
A COW HAS A STRONG SENSE OF SELF-PRESERVATION AND WILL LASH OUT AT ANYTHING. SHE HAS A POWERFUL FLYING KICK, SO DON'T STAND NEXT TO HER SIDE OR BEHIND HER--AND NEVER, EVER CROUCH DOWN BEHIND HER!!
OOPS, I'M SORRY!
THERE IT WAS! JULIETTA'S BACK SPIN KICK!
YOU'RE SO COOL!!
UH, FROM NOW ON...
I'LL ACT...
CALM-LY.
WE TOLD YOU SO.
POOF

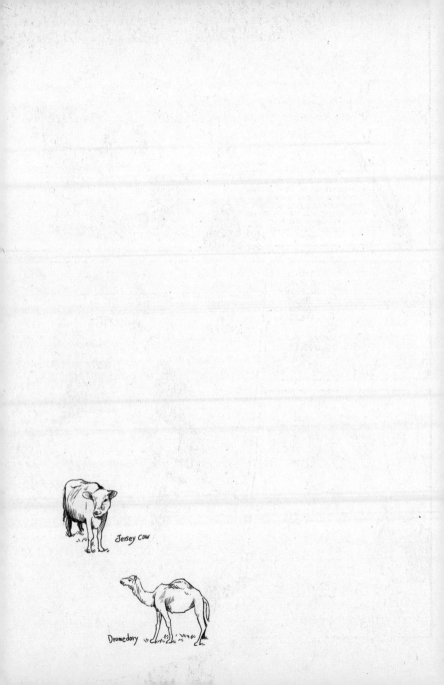

Jersey Cow

Dromedary

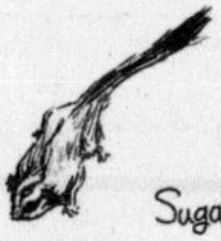

Sugar Glider

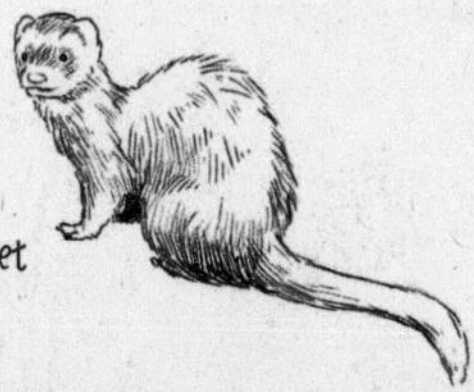

Ferret

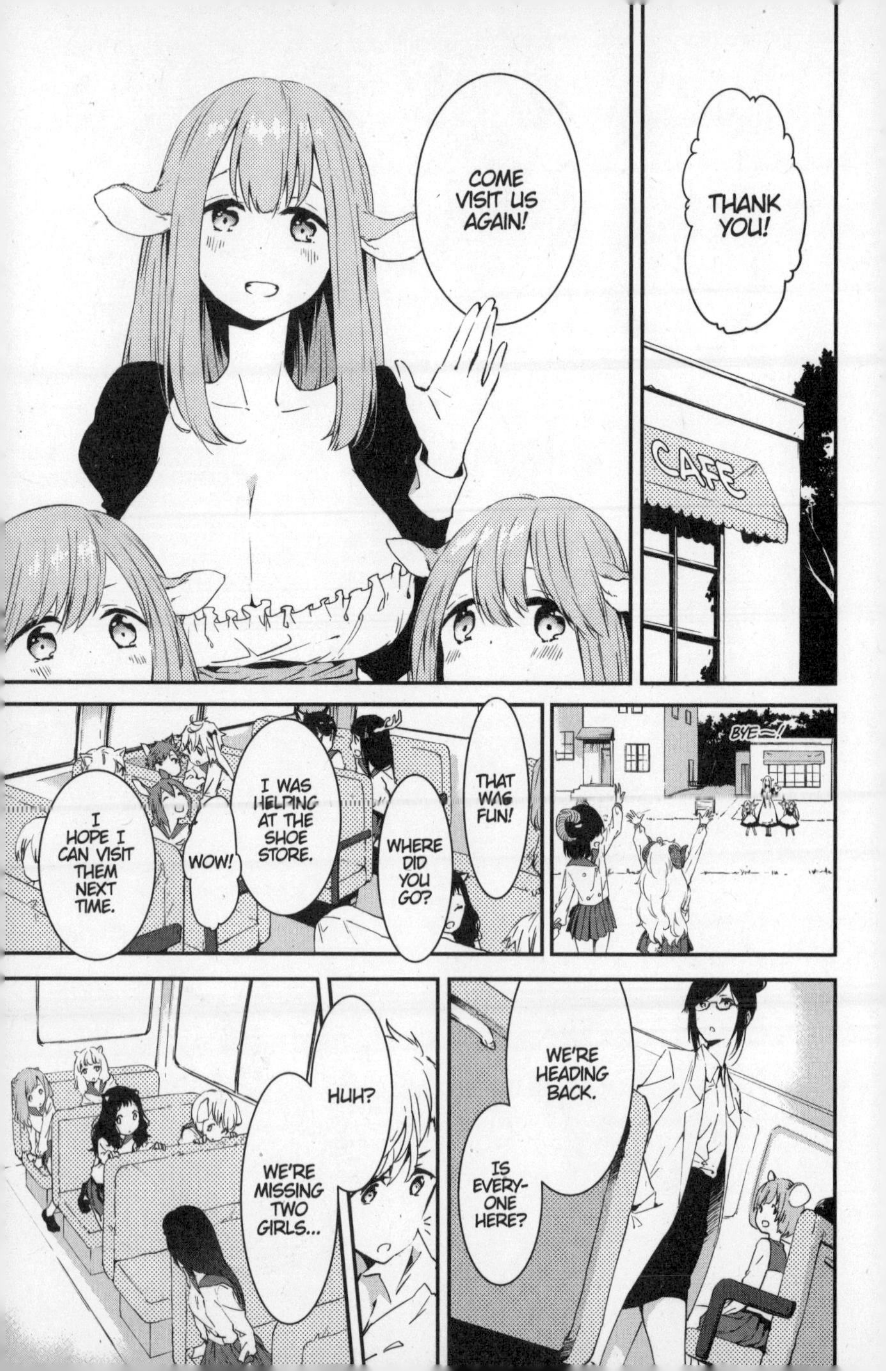
THANK YOU!
COME VISIT US AGAIN!
BYE~!
THAT WAS FUN!
WHERE DID YOU GO?
I WAS HELPING AT THE SHOE STORE.
WOW!
I HOPE I CAN VISIT THEM NEXT TIME.
WE'RE HEADING BACK.
IS EVERY-ONE HERE?
HUH?
WE'RE MISSING TWO GIRLS...

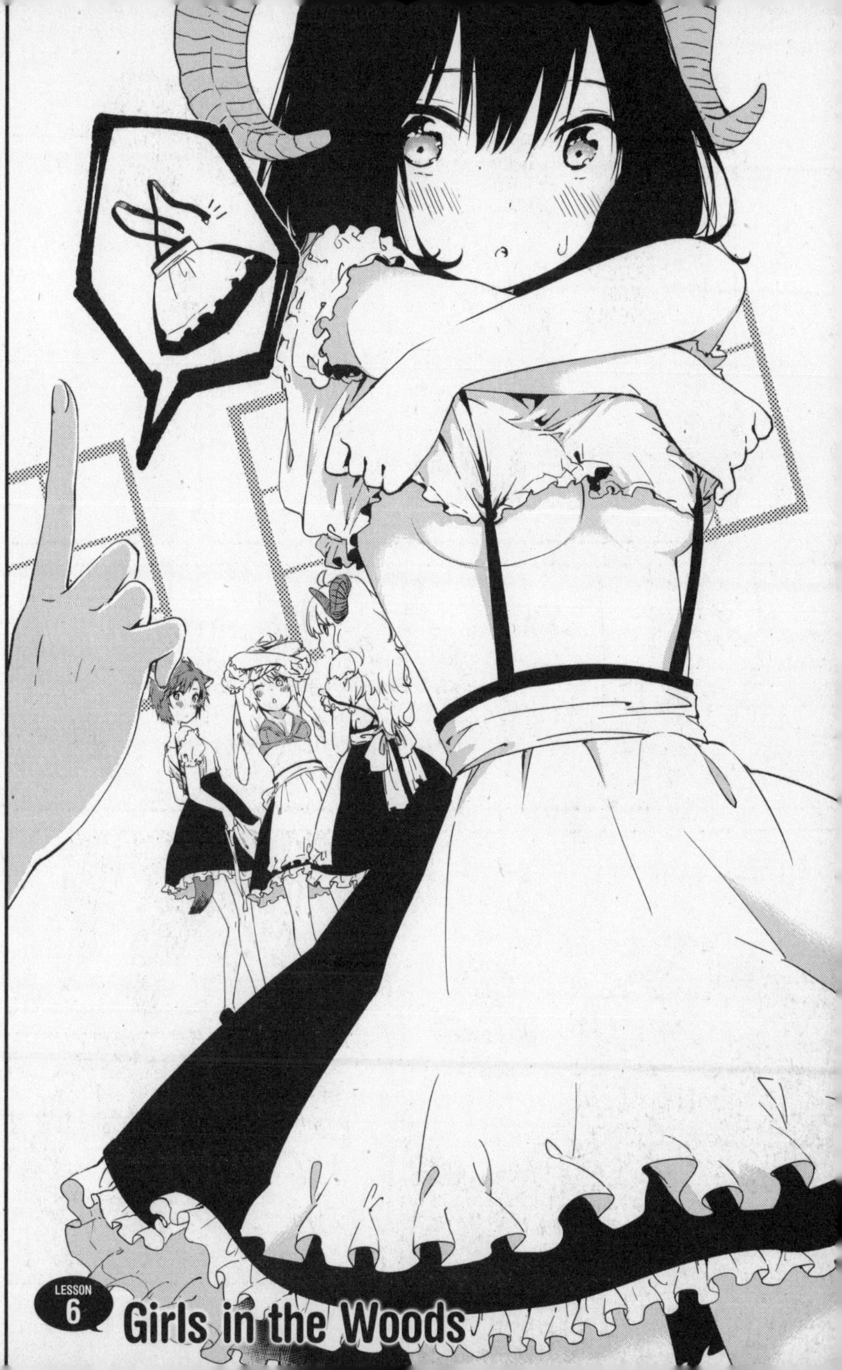

LESSON 6 Girls in the Woods

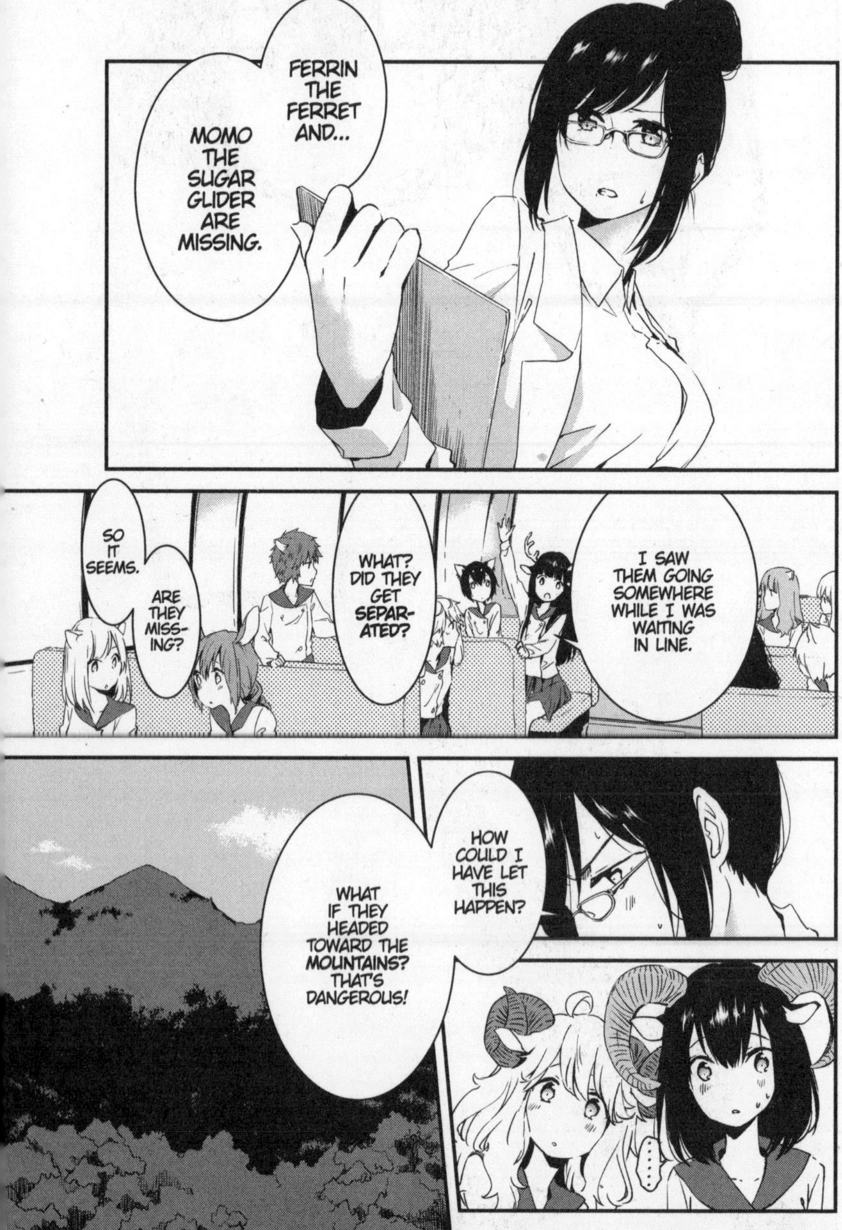
FERRIN THE FERRET AND...
MOMO THE SUGAR GLIDER ARE MISSING.
I SAW THEM GOING SOMEWHERE WHILE I WAS WAITING IN LINE.
WHAT? DID THEY GET SEPAR-ATED?
ARE THEY MISS-ING?
SO IT SEEMS.
HOW COULD I HAVE LET THIS HAPPEN?
WHAT IF THEY HEADED TOWARD THE MOUNTAINS? THAT'S DANGEROUS!

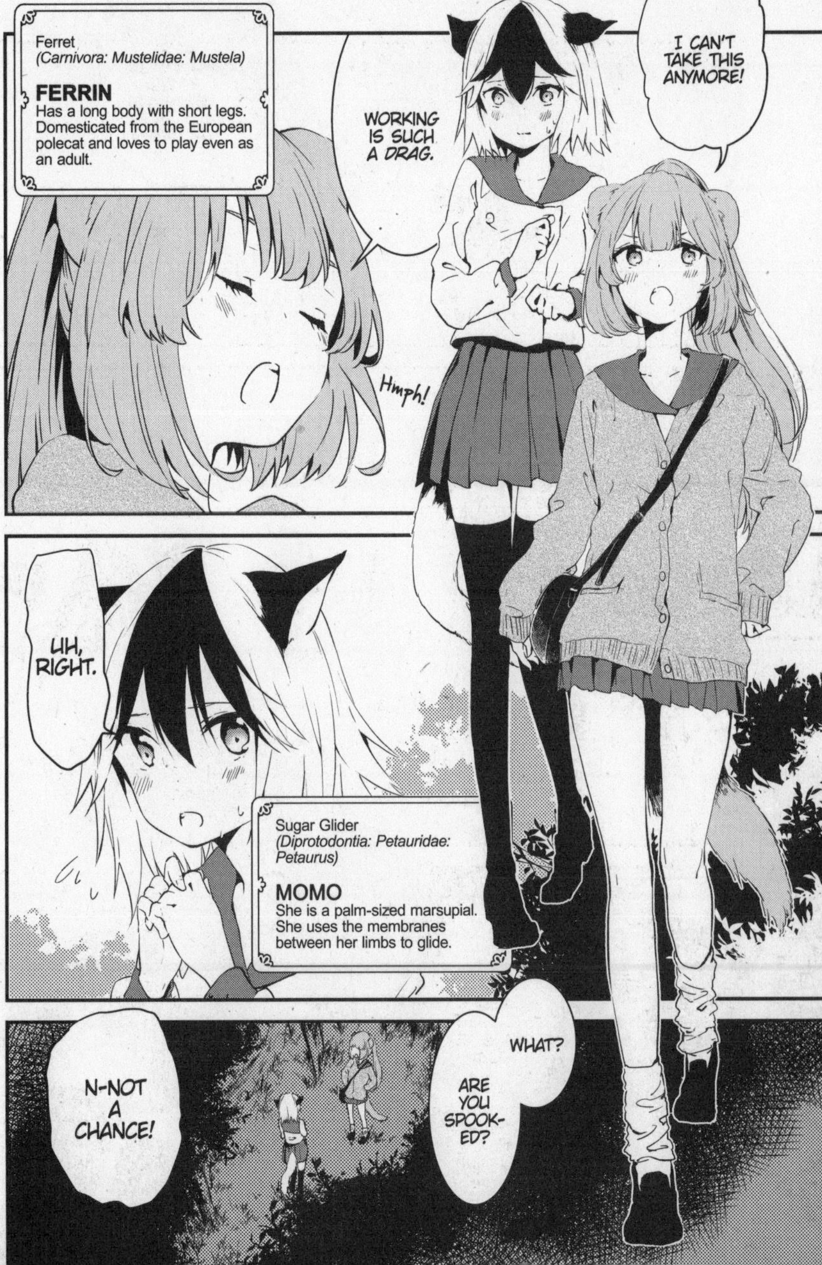
I CAN'T TAKE THIS ANYMORE!
WORKING IS SUCH A DRAG.
Hmph!
Ferret
(Carnivora: Mustelidae: Mustela)
FERRIN
Has a long body with short legs. Domesticated from the European polecat and loves to play even as an adult.
UH, RIGHT.
Sugar Glider
(Diprotodontia: Petauridae: Petaurus)
MOMO
She is a palm-sized marsupial. She uses the membranes between her limbs to glide.
WHAT?
ARE YOU SPOOK-ED?
N-NOT A CHANCE!

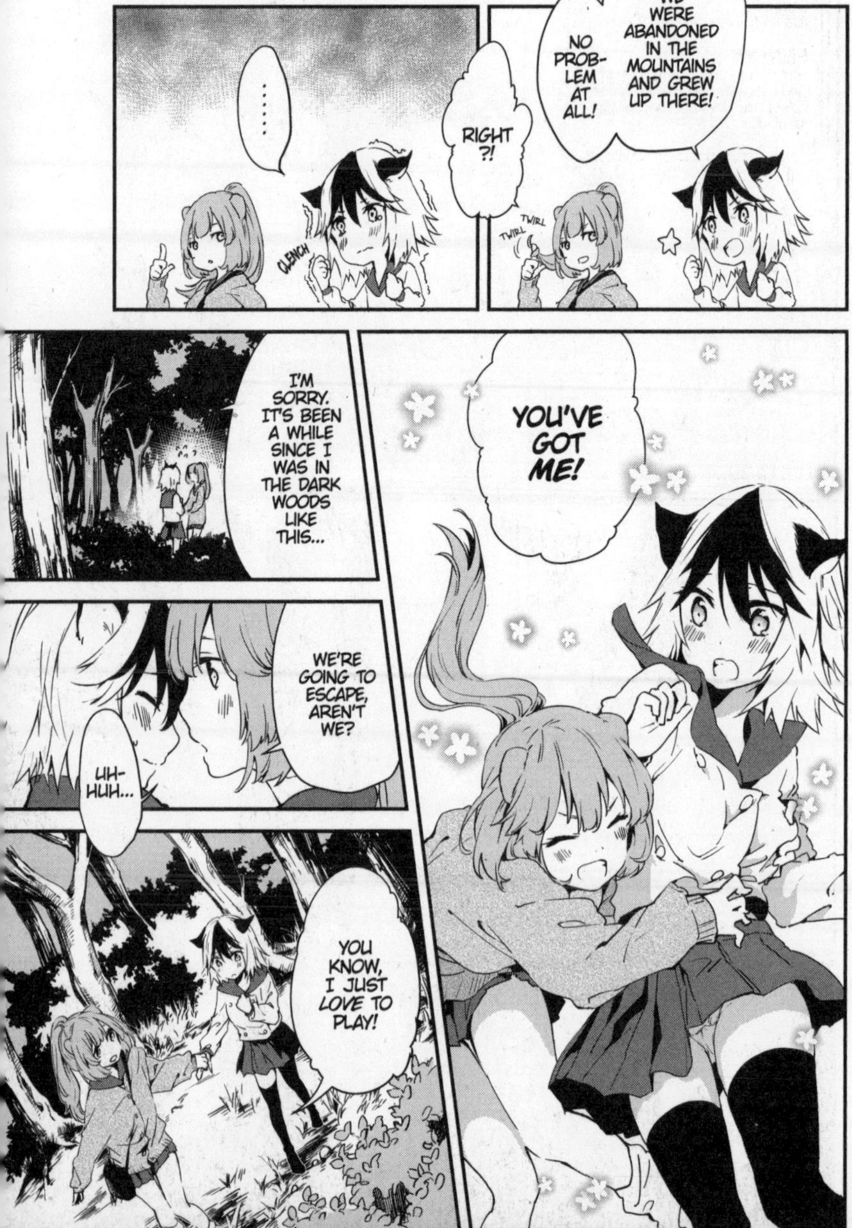
WE WERE ABANDONED IN THE MOUNTAINS AND GREW UP THERE!
NO PROBLEM AT ALL!
TWIRL TWIRL
RIGHT ?!
CLENCH
......
YOU'VE GOT ME!
I'M SORRY. IT'S BEEN A WHILE SINCE I WAS IN THE DARK WOODS LIKE THIS...
WE'RE GOING TO ESCAPE, AREN'T WE?
UH-HUH...
YOU KNOW, I JUST LOVE TO PLAY!

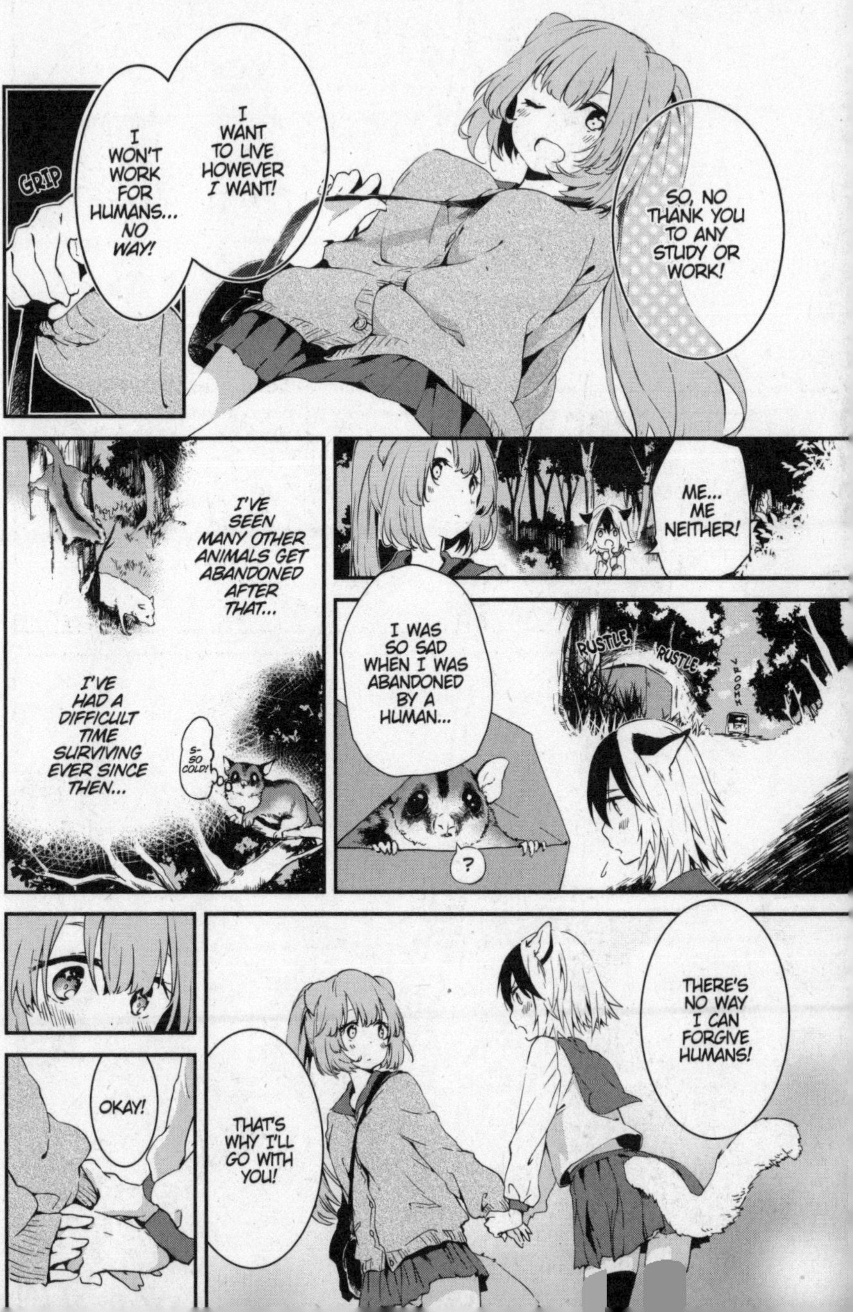
SO, NO THANK YOU TO ANY STUDY OR WORK!
I WANT TO LIVE HOWEVER I WANT!
I WON'T WORK FOR HUMANS... NO WAY!
GRIP
ME... ME NEITHER!
RUSTLE
RUSTLE
VROOMM
I WAS SO SAD WHEN I WAS ABANDONED BY A HUMAN...
?
I'VE SEEN MANY OTHER ANIMALS GET ABANDONED AFTER THAT...
I'VE HAD A DIFFICULT TIME SURVIVING EVER SINCE THEN...
S-SO COLD!
THERE'S NO WAY I CAN FORGIVE HUMANS!
THAT'S WHY I'LL GO WITH YOU!
OKAY!

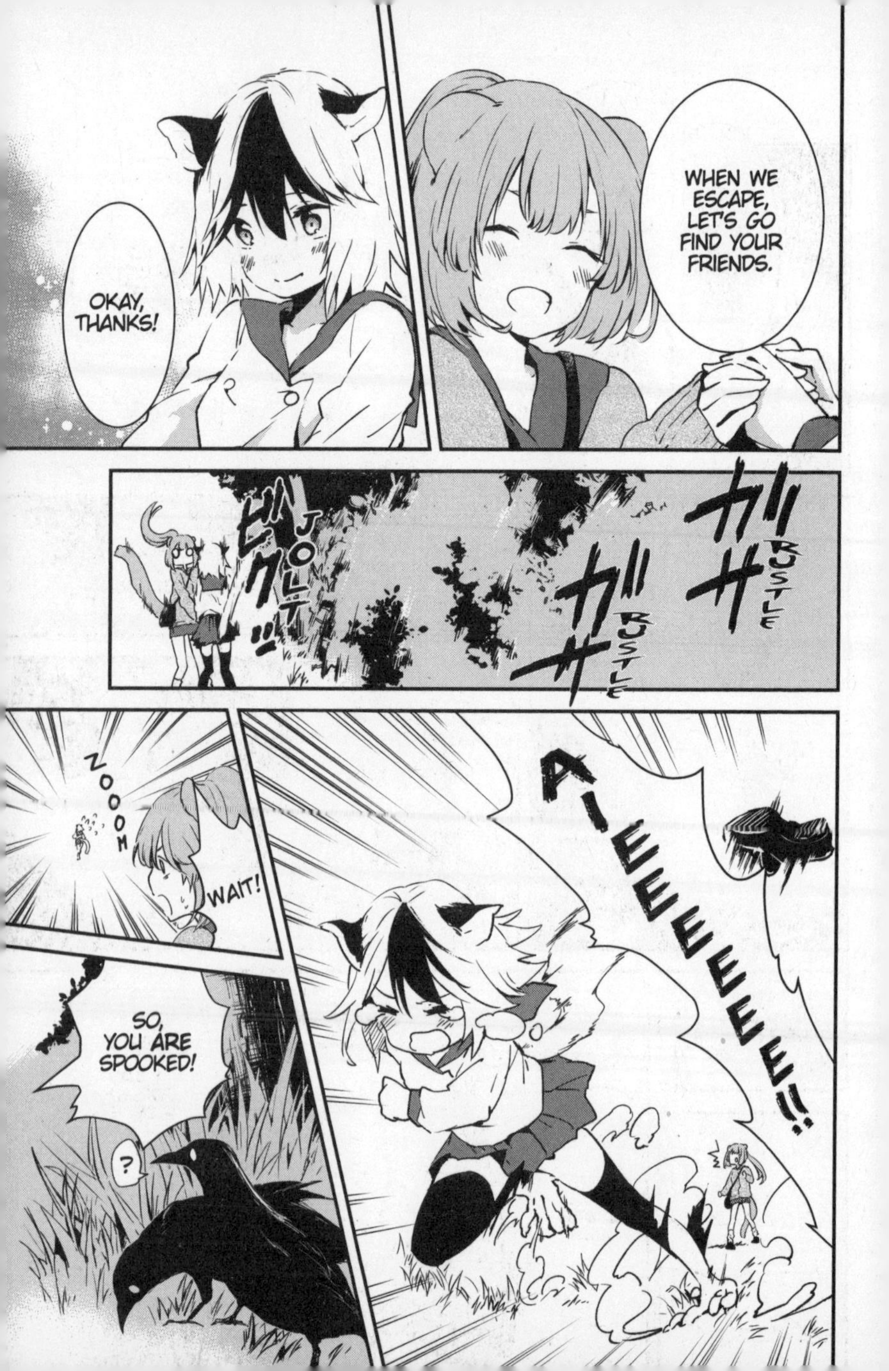
WHEN WE ESCAPE, LET'S GO FIND YOUR FRIENDS.
OKAY, THANKS!
RUSTLE
RUSTLE
JOLT!!
ZOOOM
WAIT!
AIEEEEEEEE!!
SO, YOU ARE SPOOKED!
?

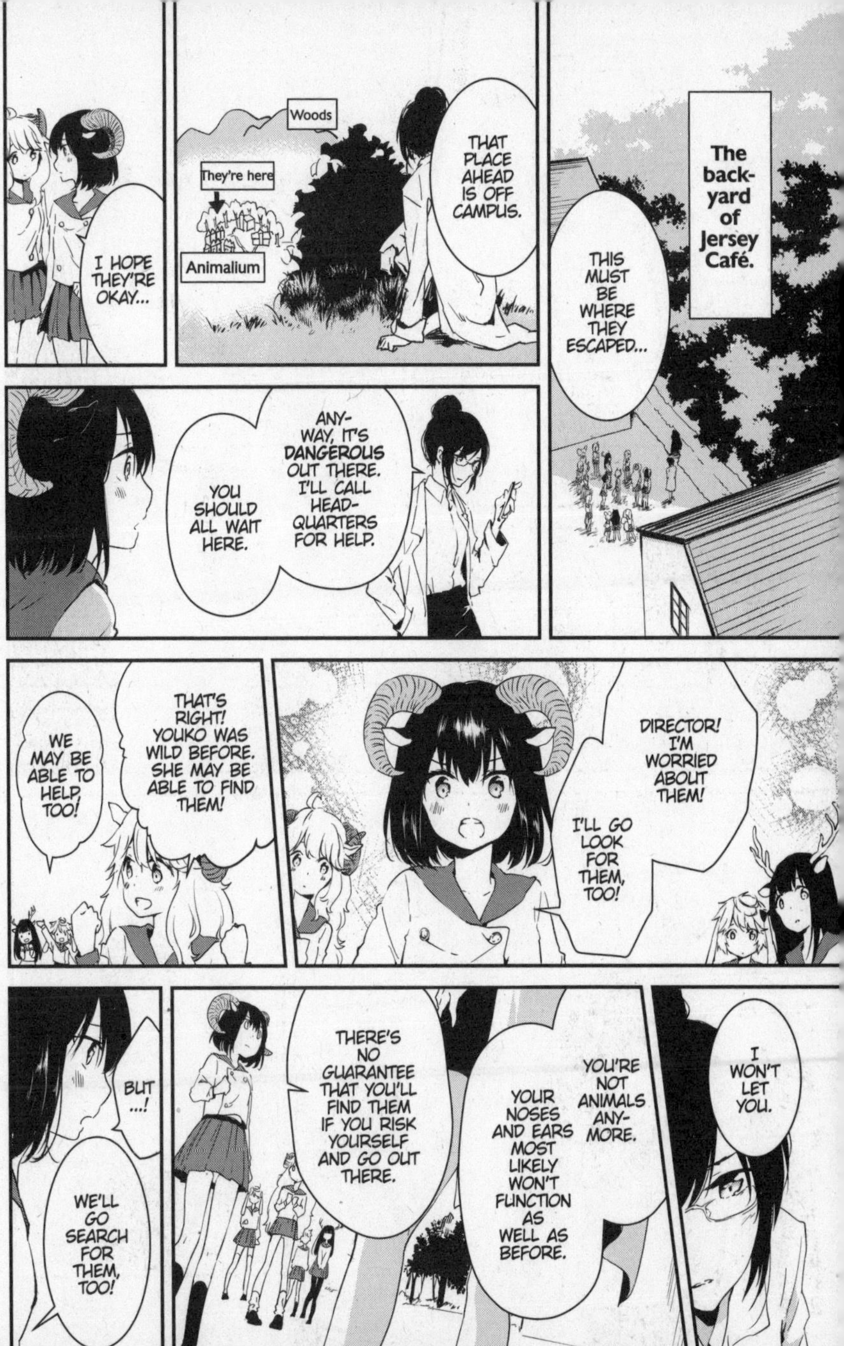
The backyard of Jersey Café.
THIS MUST BE WHERE THEY ESCAPED...
THAT PLACE AHEAD IS OFF CAMPUS.
Woods
They're here
Animalium
I HOPE THEY'RE OKAY...
ANYWAY, IT'S DANGEROUS OUT THERE. I'LL CALL HEADQUARTERS FOR HELP.
YOU SHOULD ALL WAIT HERE.
DIRECTOR! I'M WORRIED ABOUT THEM!
I'LL GO LOOK FOR THEM, TOO!
THAT'S RIGHT! YOUKO WAS WILD BEFORE. SHE MAY BE ABLE TO FIND THEM!
WE MAY BE ABLE TO HELP TOO!
I WON'T LET YOU.
YOU'RE NOT ANIMALS ANYMORE.
YOUR NOSES AND EARS MOST LIKELY WON'T FUNCTION AS WELL AS BEFORE.
THERE'S NO GUARANTEE THAT YOU'LL FIND THEM IF YOU RISK YOURSELF AND GO OUT THERE.
BUT...!
WE'LL GO SEARCH FOR THEM, TOO!

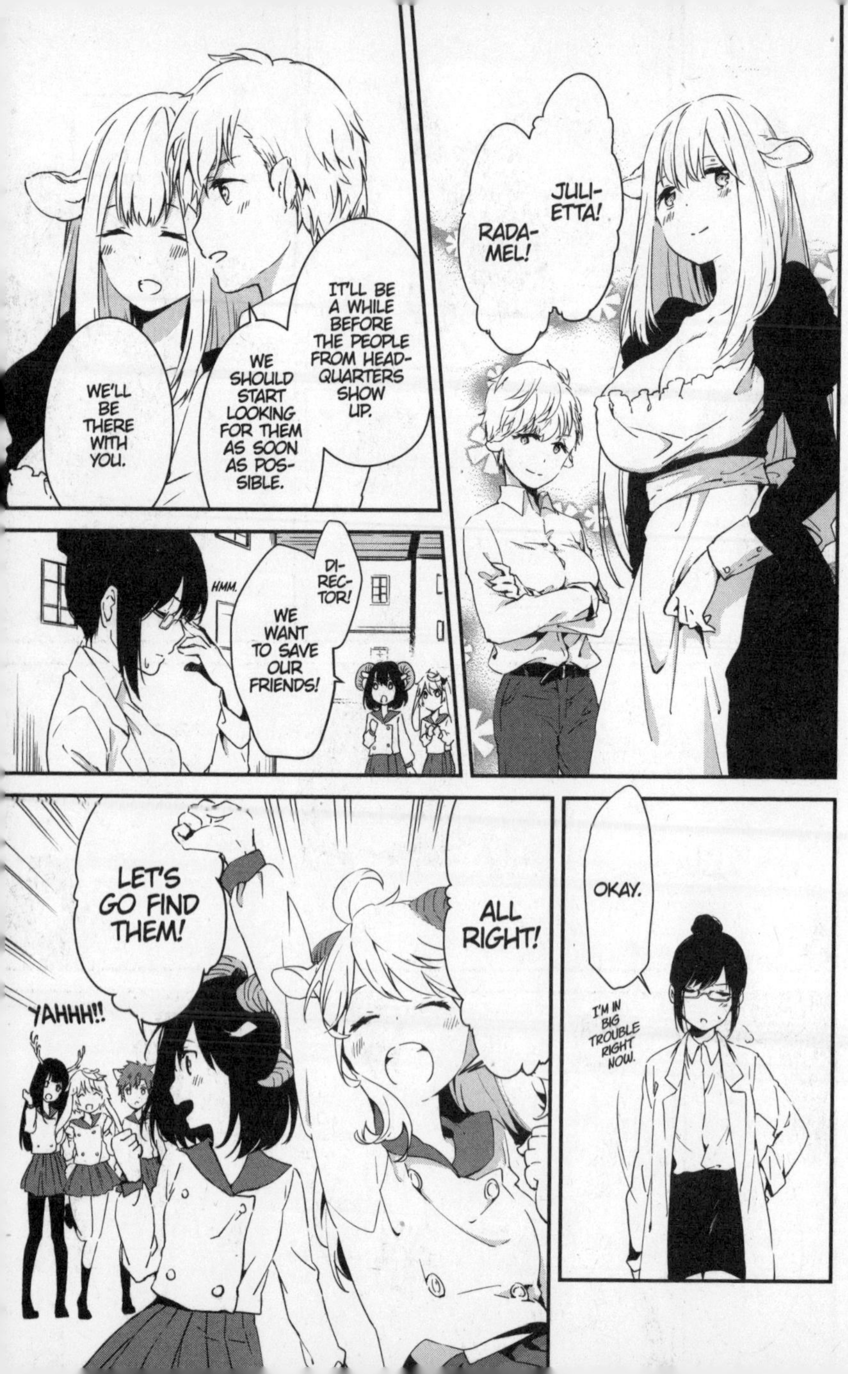
JULI-ETTA! RADA-MEL!
IT'LL BE A WHILE BEFORE THE PEOPLE FROM HEAD-QUARTERS SHOW UP.
WE SHOULD START LOOKING FOR THEM AS SOON AS POS-SIBLE.
WE'LL BE THERE WITH YOU.
DI-REC-TOR! WE WANT TO SAVE OUR FRIENDS!
HMM.
OKAY.
I'M IN BIG TROUBLE RIGHT NOW.
ALL RIGHT!
LET'S GO FIND THEM!
YAHHH!!

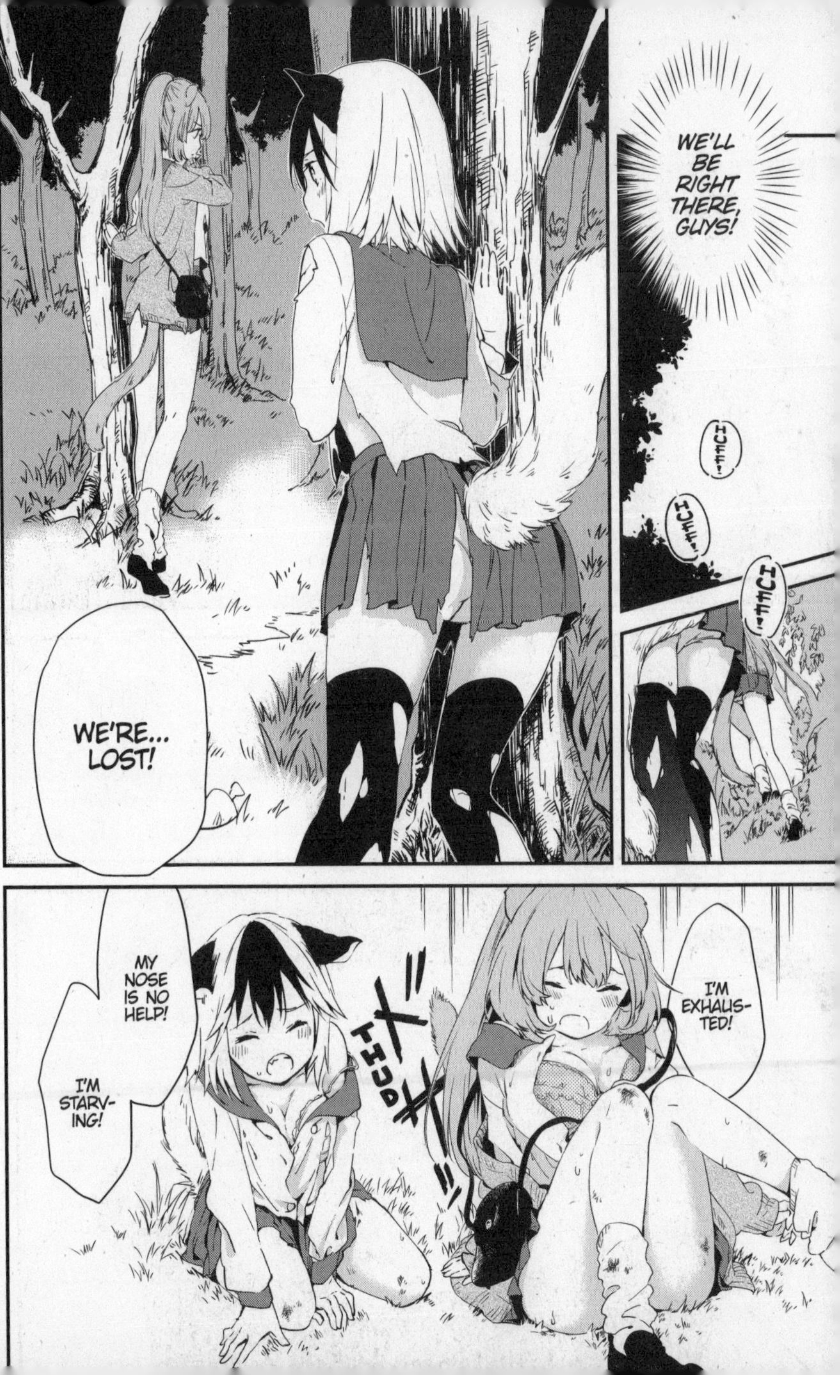
WE'LL BE RIGHT THERE, GUYS!
HUFF!
HUFF!
HUFF!
WE'RE... LOST!
I'M EXHAUS-TED!
THUD
MY NOSE IS NO HELP!
I'M STARV-ING!

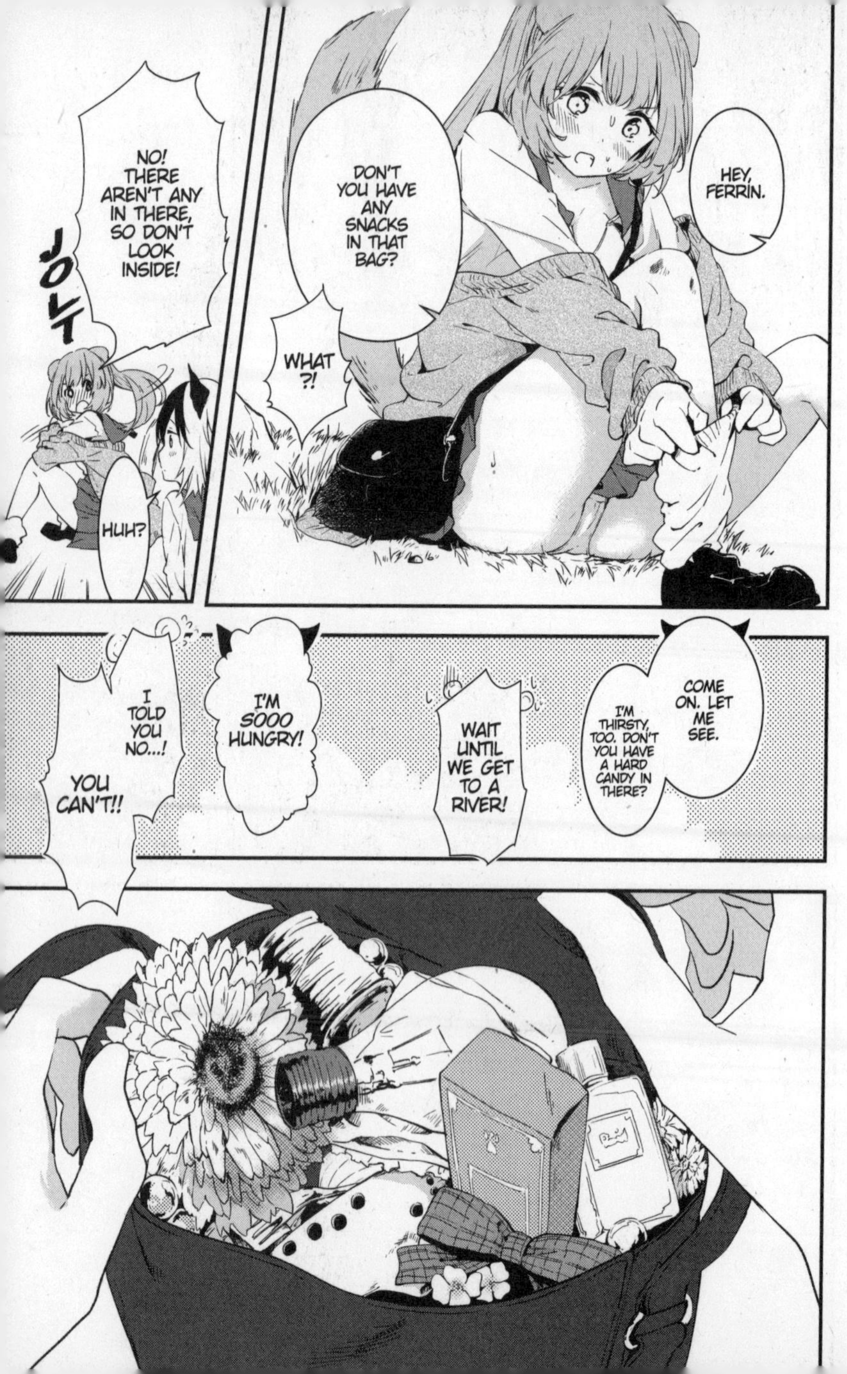
HEY, FERRIN.
DON'T YOU HAVE ANY SNACKS IN THAT BAG?
WHAT ?!
JOLT
NO! THERE AREN'T ANY IN THERE, SO DON'T LOOK INSIDE!
HUH?
COME ON. LET ME SEE.
I'M THIRSTY, TOO. DON'T YOU HAVE A HARD CANDY IN THERE?
WAIT UNTIL WE GET TO A RIVER!
I'M SOOO HUNGRY!
I TOLD YOU NO...!
YOU CAN'T!!

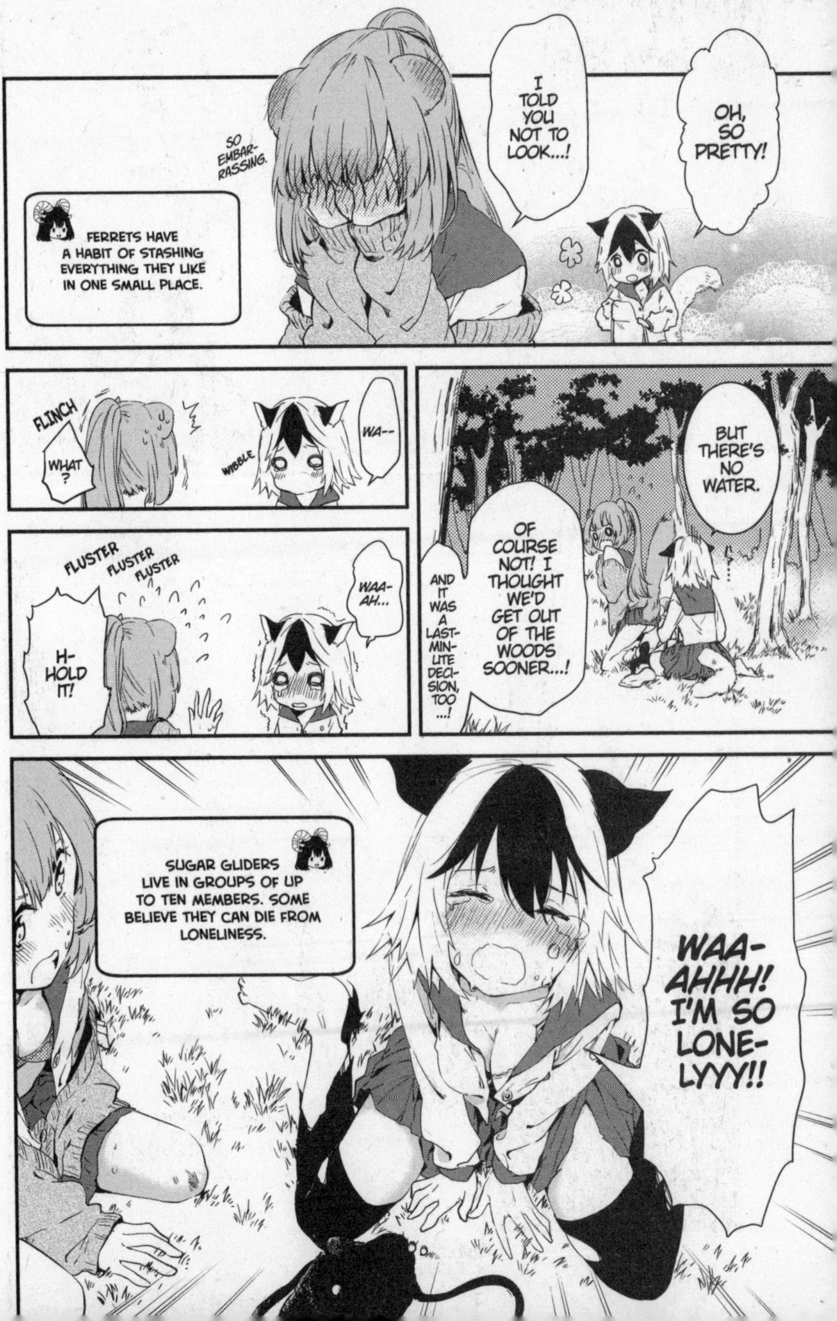
OH, SO PRETTY!
I TOLD YOU NOT TO LOOK...!
SO EMBARRASSING.
FERRETS HAVE A HABIT OF STASHING EVERYTHING THEY LIKE IN ONE SMALL PLACE.
BUT THERE'S NO WATER.
...
OF COURSE NOT! I THOUGHT WE'D GET OUT OF THE WOODS SOONER...!
AND IT WAS A LAST-MINUTE DECISION, TOO...!
WA--
WIBBLE
FLINCH
WHAT?
WAA-AH...
FLUSTER FLUSTER FLUSTER
H-HOLD IT!
WAA-AHHH! I'M SO LONE-LYYY!!
SUGAR GLIDERS LIVE IN GROUPS OF UP TO TEN MEMBERS. SOME BELIEVE THEY CAN DIE FROM LONELINESS.

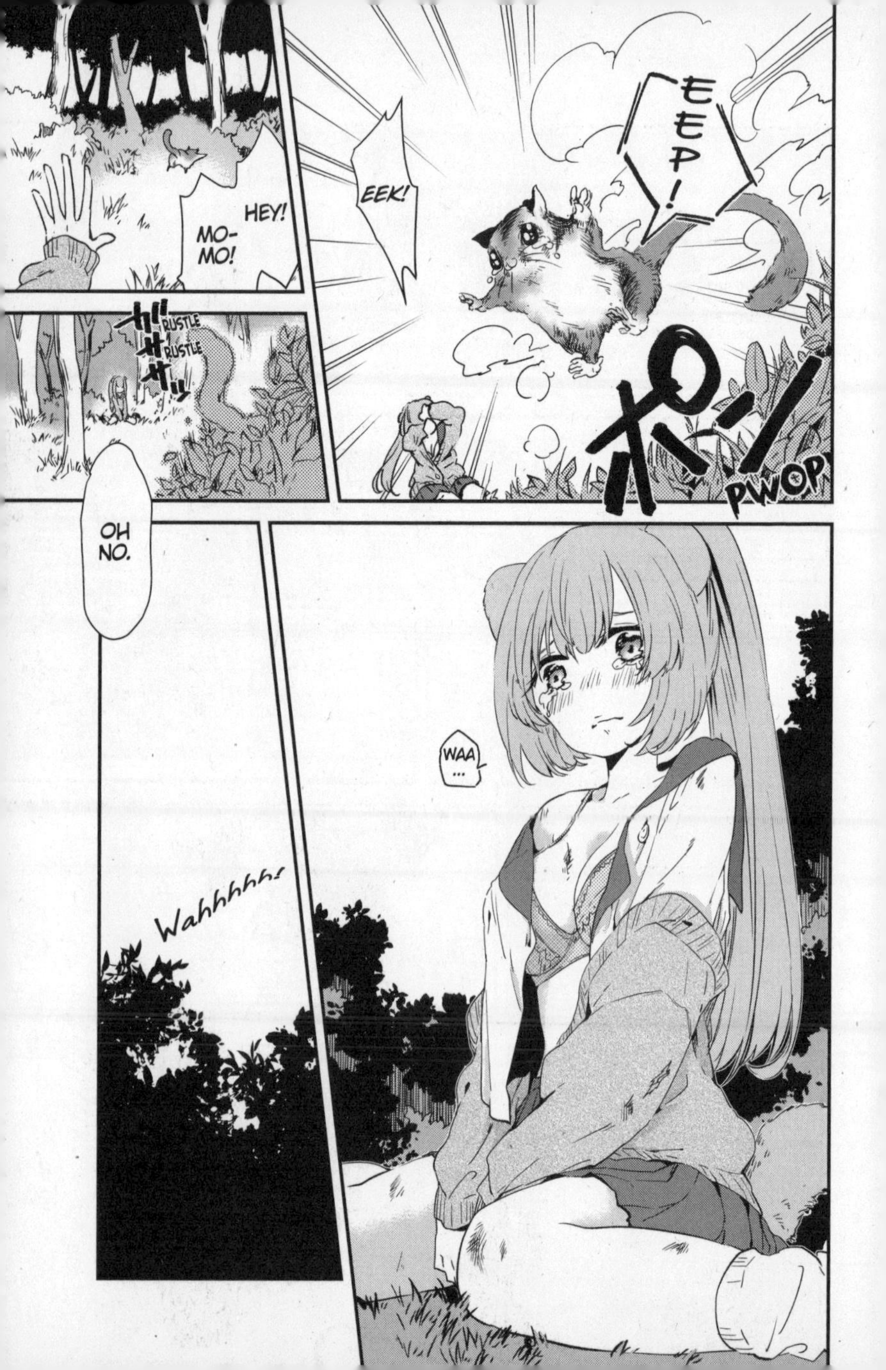
EEK!
EEP!
PWOP
HEY!
MO-MO!
RUSTLE
RUSTLE
WAA...
OH NO.
Wahhhhh!

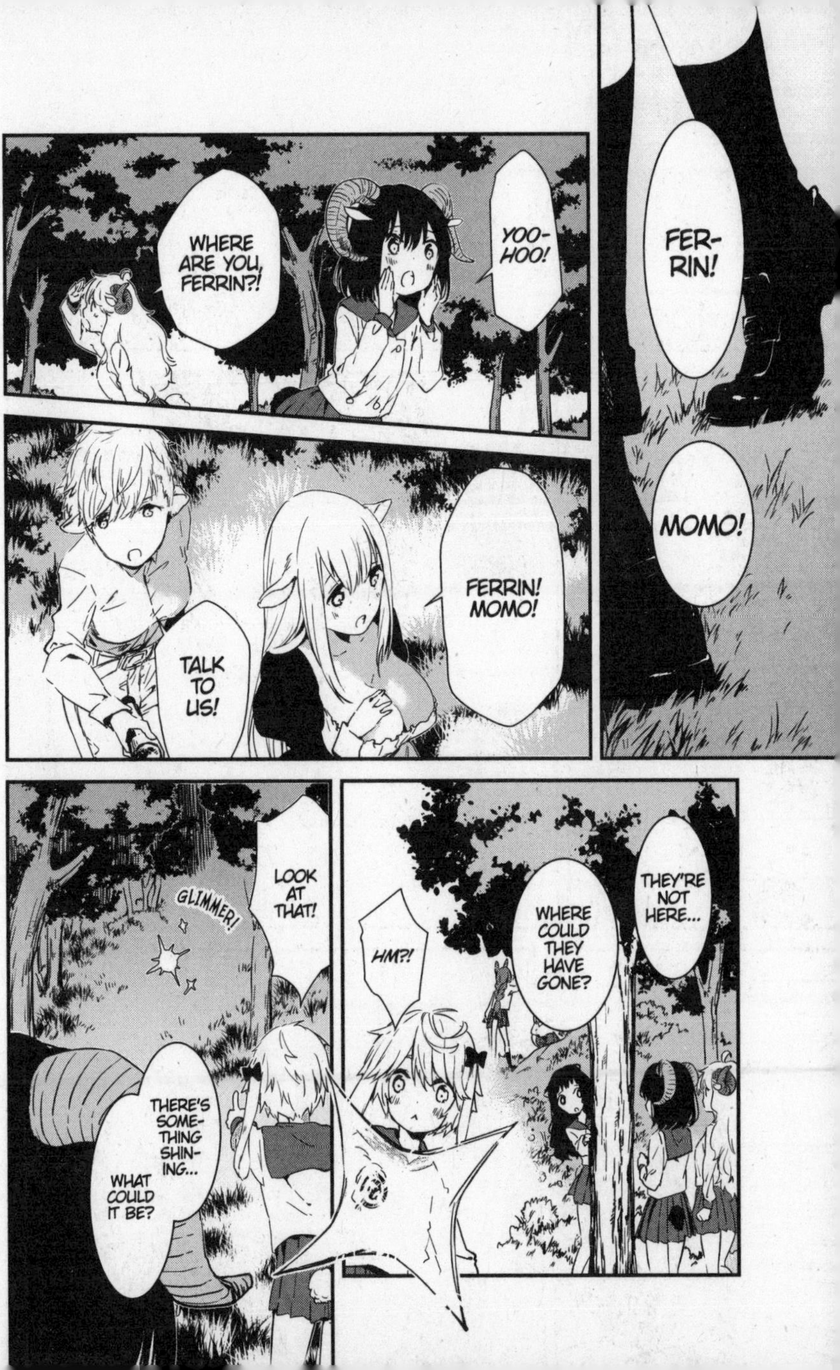
FER-RIN!
MOMO!
YOO-HOO!
WHERE ARE YOU, FERRIN?!
FERRIN! MOMO!
TALK TO US!
THEY'RE NOT HERE...
WHERE COULD THEY HAVE GONE?
HM?!
LOOK AT THAT!
GLIMMER!
THERE'S SOME-THING SHIN-ING... WHAT COULD IT BE?

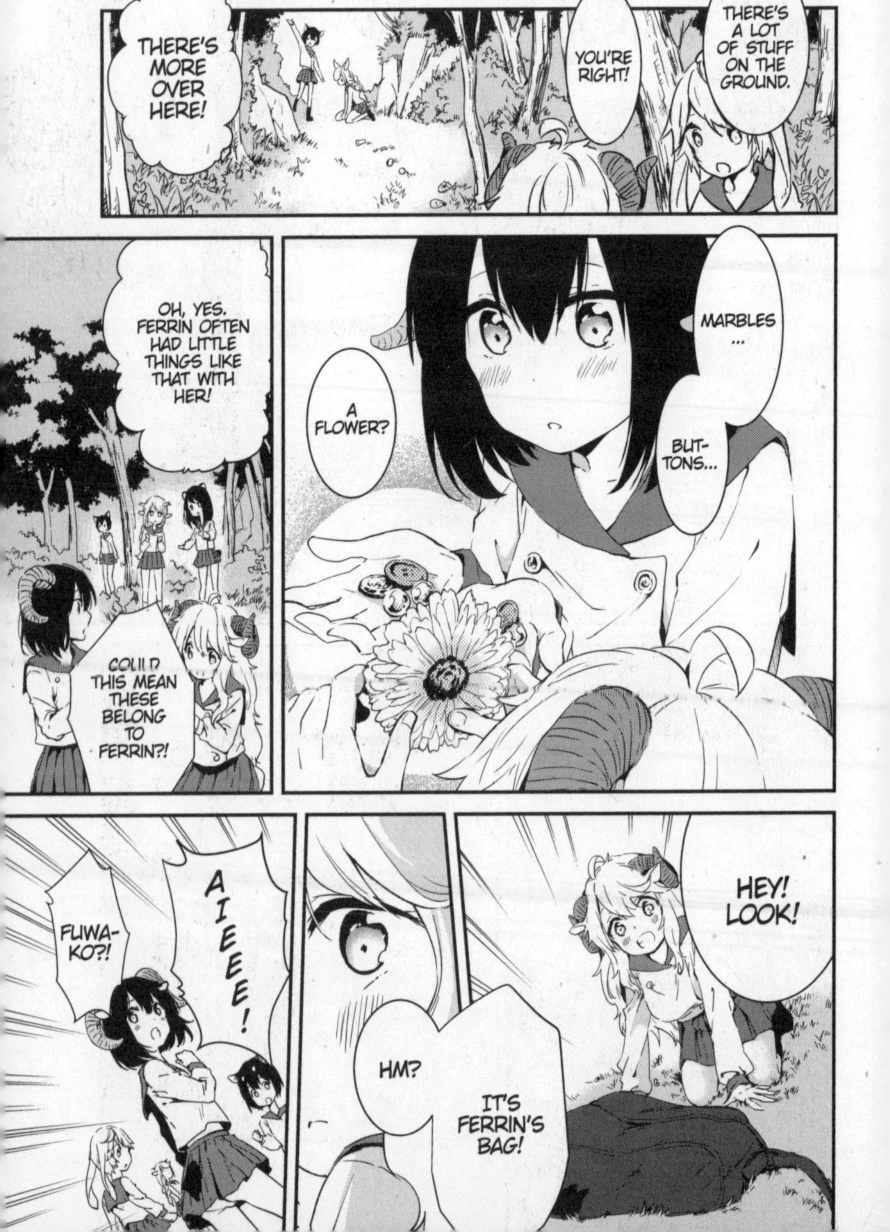
THERE'S A LOT OF STUFF ON THE GROUND.
YOU'RE RIGHT!
THERE'S MORE OVER HERE!
MARBLES ...
BUT-TONS...
A FLOWER?
OH, YES. FERRIN OFTEN HAD LITTLE THINGS LIKE THAT WITH HER!
COULD THIS MEAN THESE BELONG TO FERRIN?!
HEY! LOOK!
IT'S FERRIN'S BAG!
HM?
AIEEE!
FUWA-KO?!

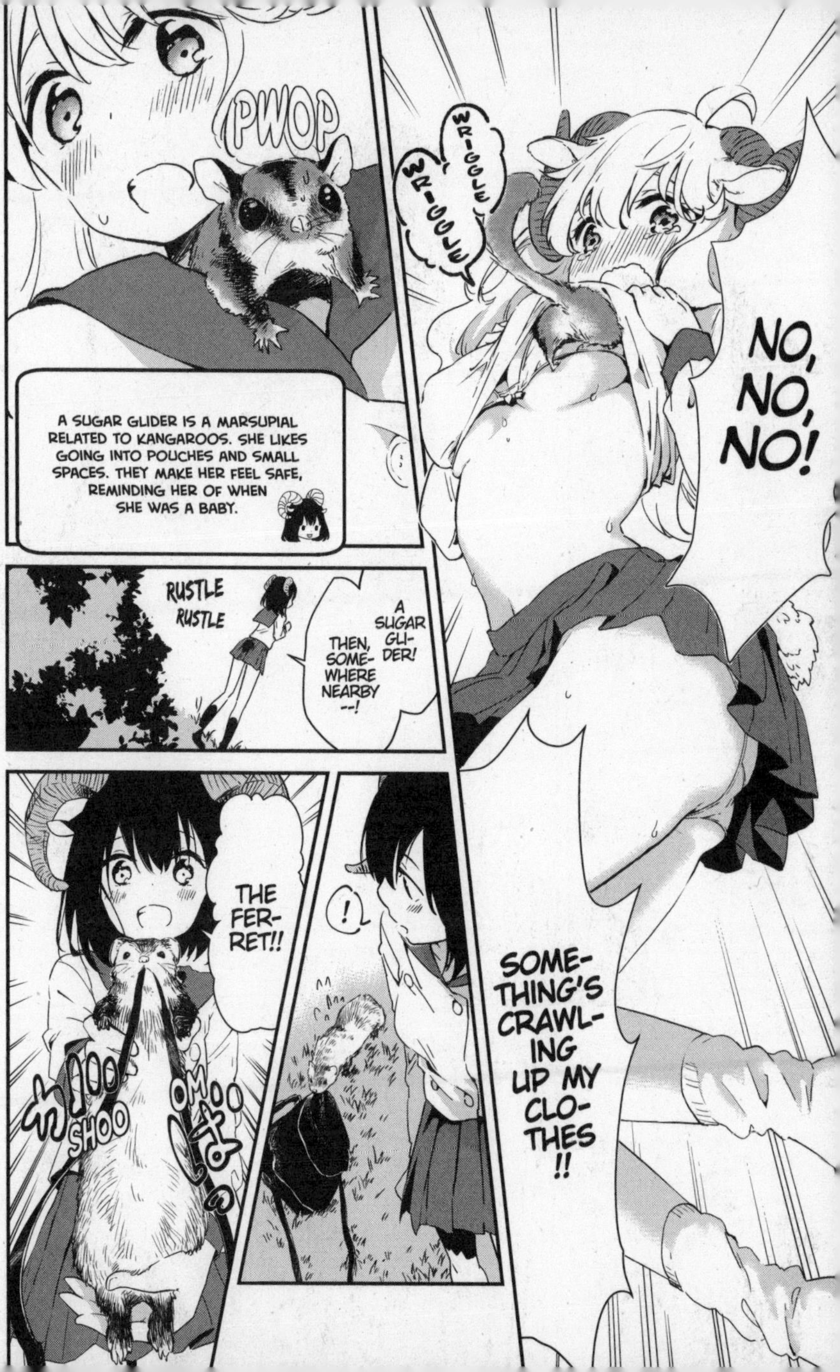
WRIGGLE
WRIGGLE
NO, NO, NO!
SOMETHING'S CRAWLING UP MY CLOTHES!!
PWOP
A SUGAR GLIDER IS A MARSUPIAL RELATED TO KANGAROOS. SHE LIKES GOING INTO POUCHES AND SMALL SPACES. THEY MAKE HER FEEL SAFE, REMINDING HER OF WHEN SHE WAS A BABY.
RUSTLE
RUSTLE
A SUGAR GLIDER!
THEN, SOMEWHERE NEARBY--!
!
THE FERRET!!
SHOO
SHOO

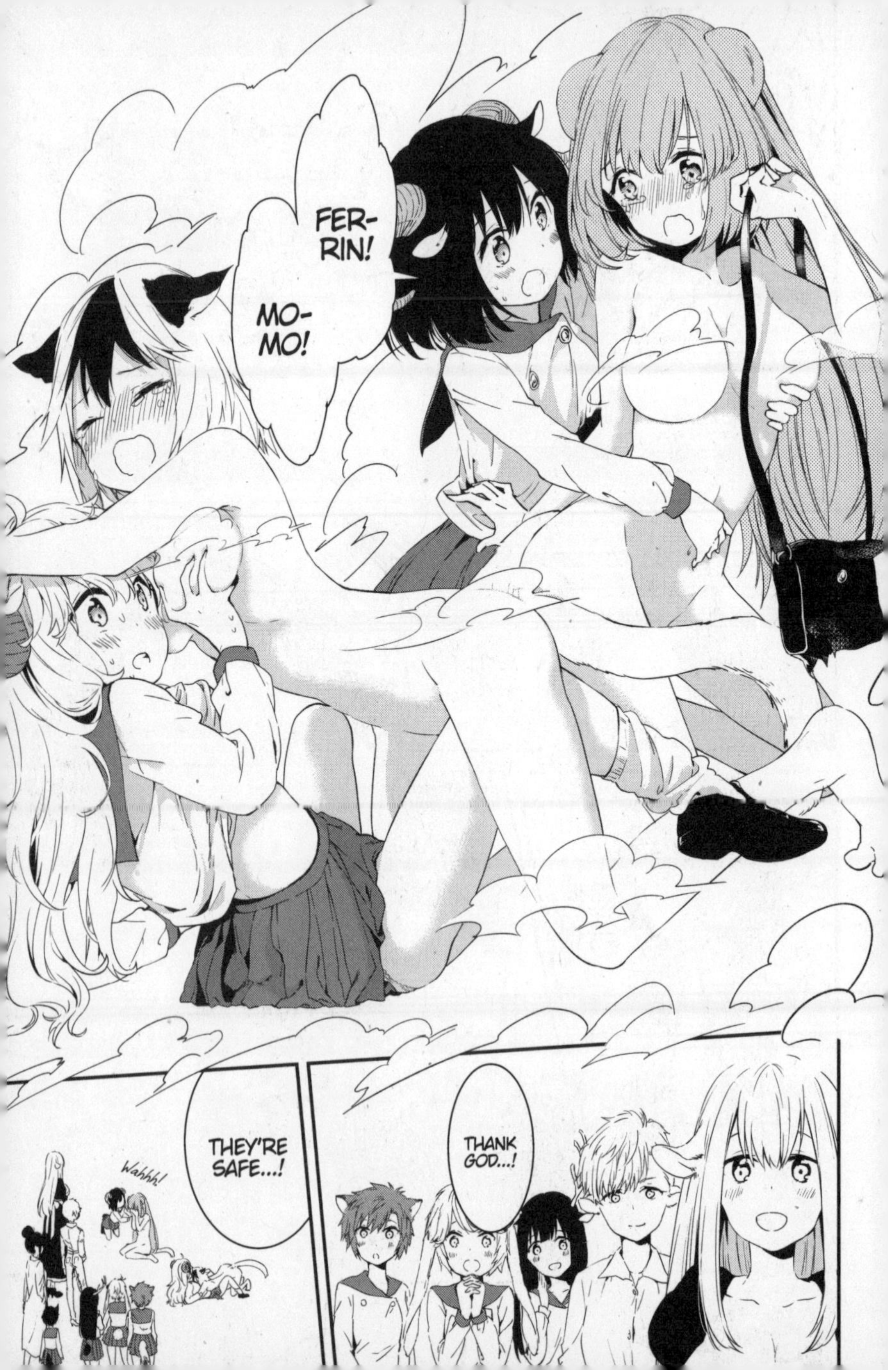
FER-RIN!
MO-MO!
THANK GOD...!
THEY'RE SAFE...!
Wahhh!

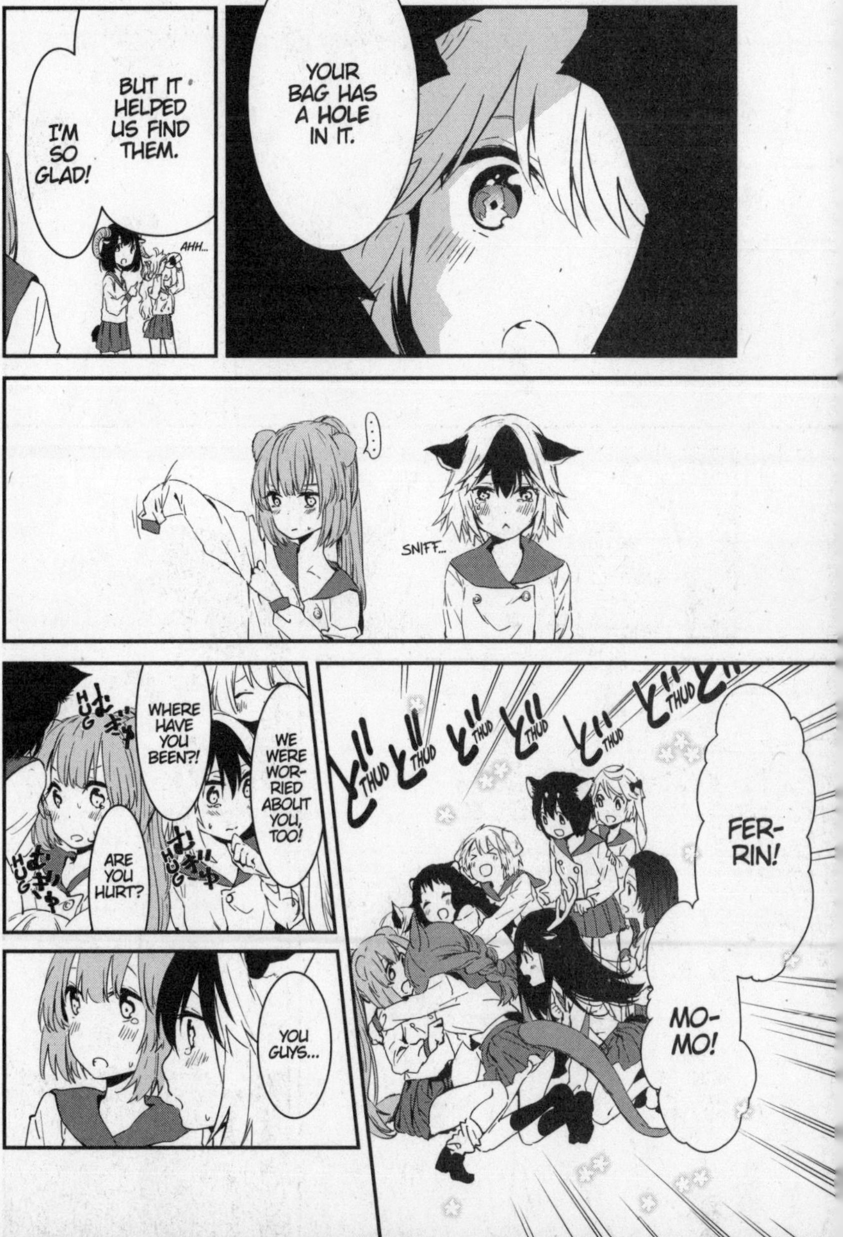
YOUR BAG HAS A HOLE IN IT.
BUT IT HELPED US FIND THEM.
I'M SO GLAD!
AHH...
...
SNIFF...
THUD THUD THUD THUD THUD THUD
FER-RIN!
MO-MO!
HUG
WHERE HAVE YOU BEEN?!
WE WERE WOR-RIED ABOUT YOU, TOO!
HUG
ARE YOU HURT?
HUG
YOU GUYS...

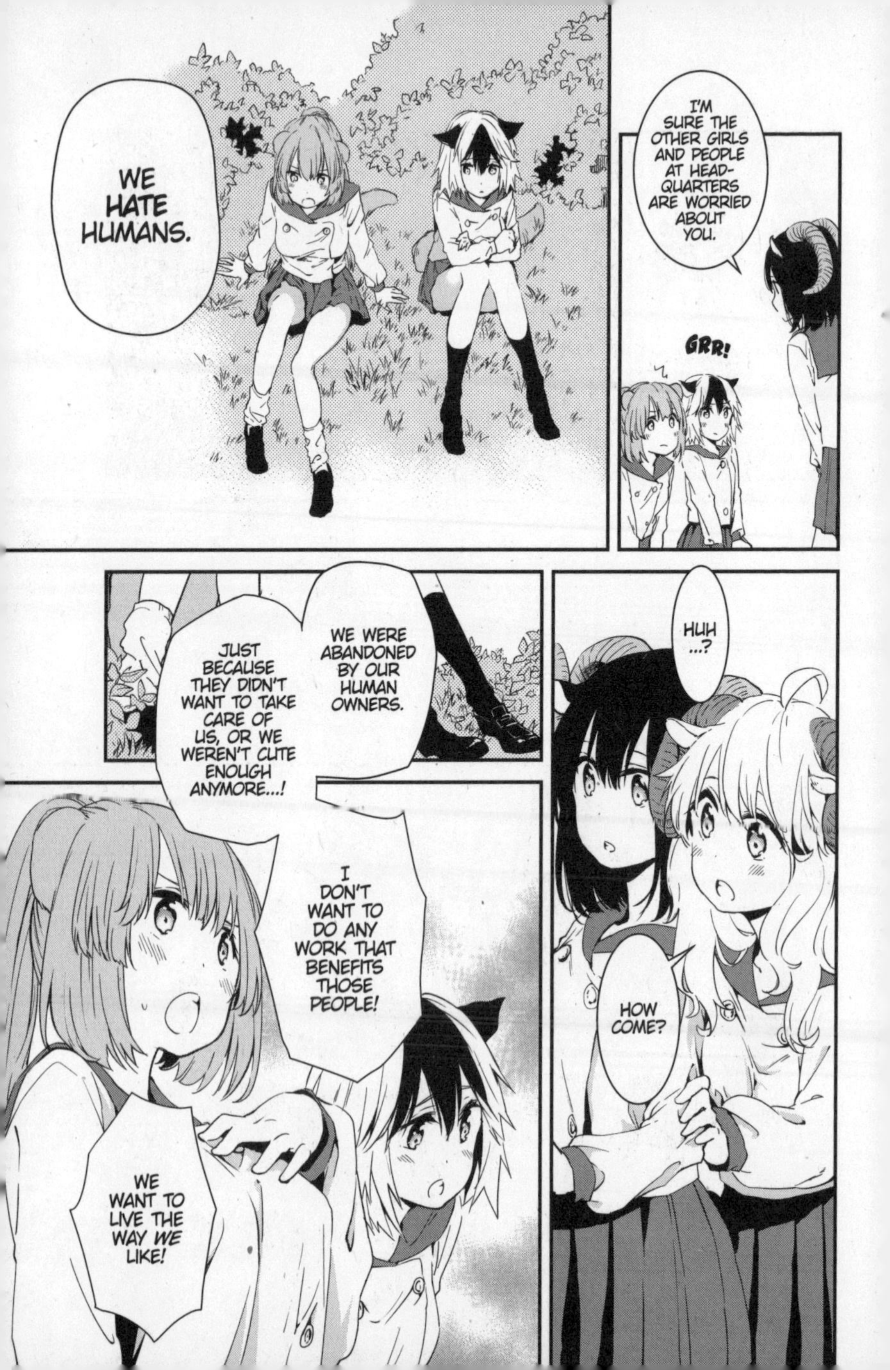
I'M SURE THE OTHER GIRLS AND PEOPLE AT HEAD-QUARTERS ARE WORRIED ABOUT YOU.
GRR!
WE HATE HUMANS.
HUH ...?
HOW COME?
WE WERE ABANDONED BY OUR HUMAN OWNERS.
JUST BECAUSE THEY DIDN'T WANT TO TAKE CARE OF US, OR WE WEREN'T CUTE ENOUGH ANYMORE...!
I DON'T WANT TO DO ANY WORK THAT BENEFITS THOSE PEOPLE!
WE WANT TO LIVE THE WAY WE LIKE!

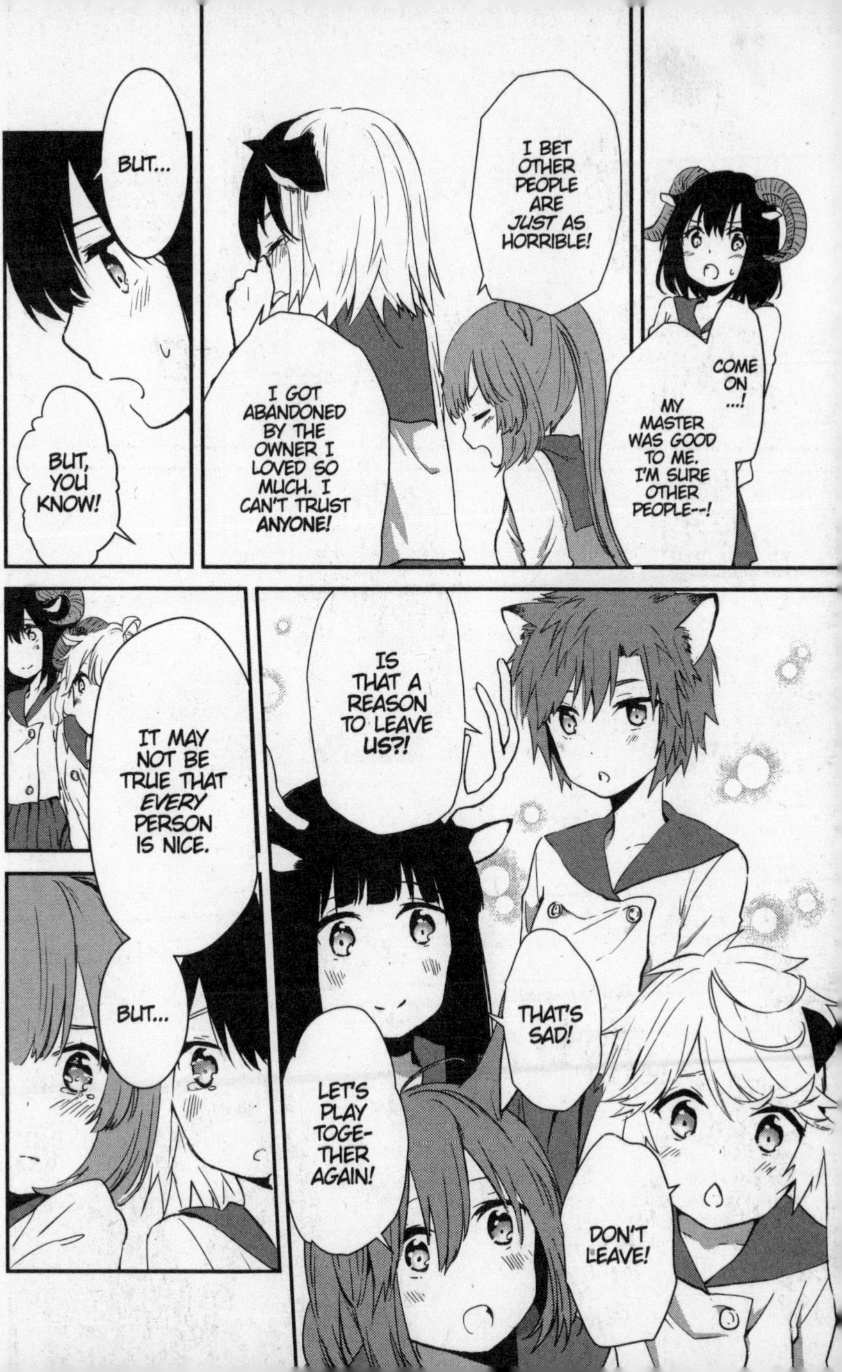
COME ON ...!
MY MASTER WAS GOOD TO ME. I'M SURE OTHER PEOPLE--!
I BET OTHER PEOPLE ARE *JUST* AS HORRIBLE!
I GOT ABANDONED BY THE OWNER I LOVED SO MUCH. I CAN'T TRUST ANYONE!
BUT...
BUT, YOU KNOW!
IS THAT A REASON TO LEAVE US?!
THAT'S SAD!
LET'S PLAY TOGE-THER AGAIN!
DON'T LEAVE!
IT MAY NOT BE TRUE THAT *EVERY* PERSON IS NICE.
BUT...

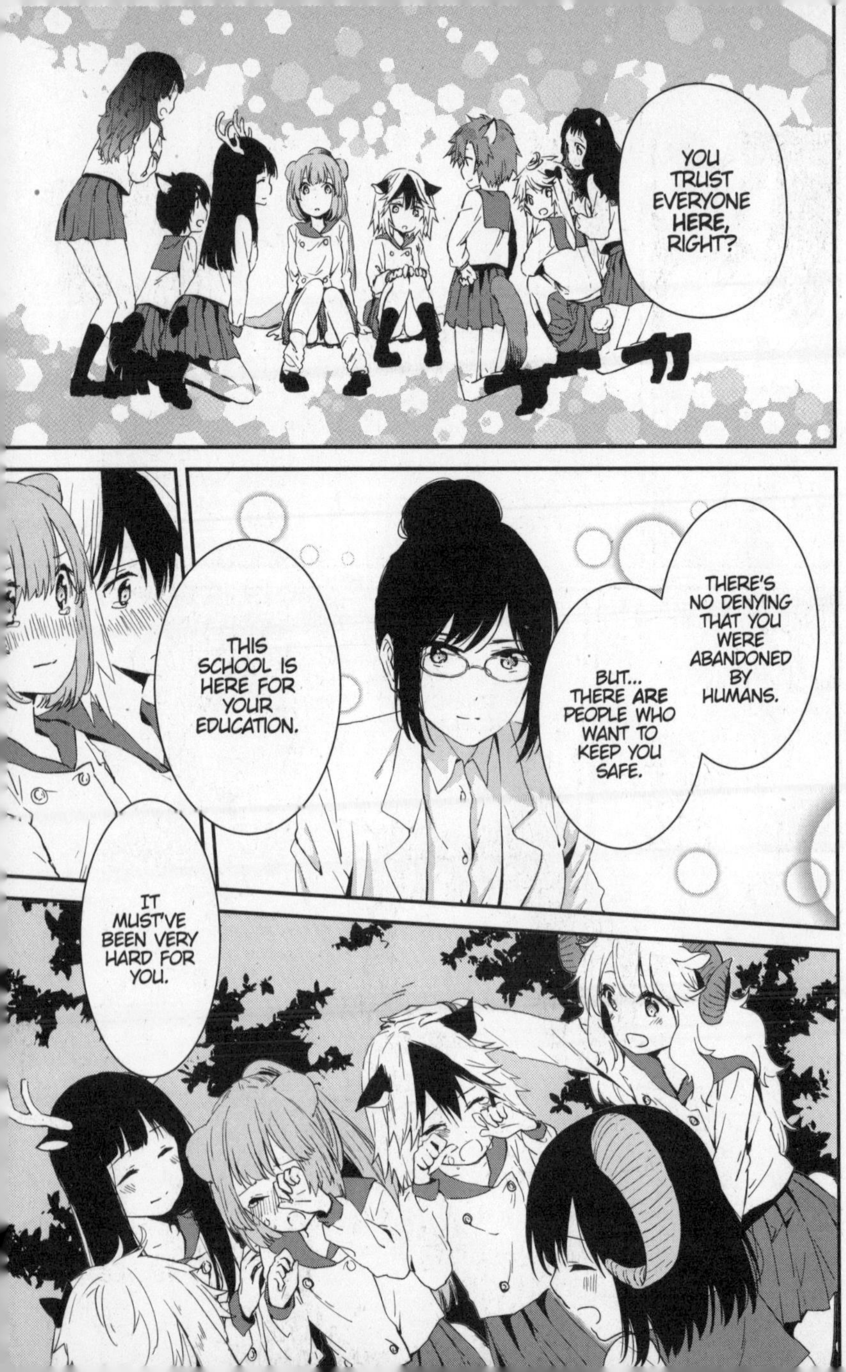
YOU TRUST EVERYONE HERE, RIGHT?
THERE'S NO DENYING THAT YOU WERE ABANDONED BY HUMANS.
BUT... THERE ARE PEOPLE WHO WANT TO KEEP YOU SAFE.
THIS SCHOOL IS HERE FOR YOUR EDUCATION.
IT MUST'VE BEEN VERY HARD FOR YOU.

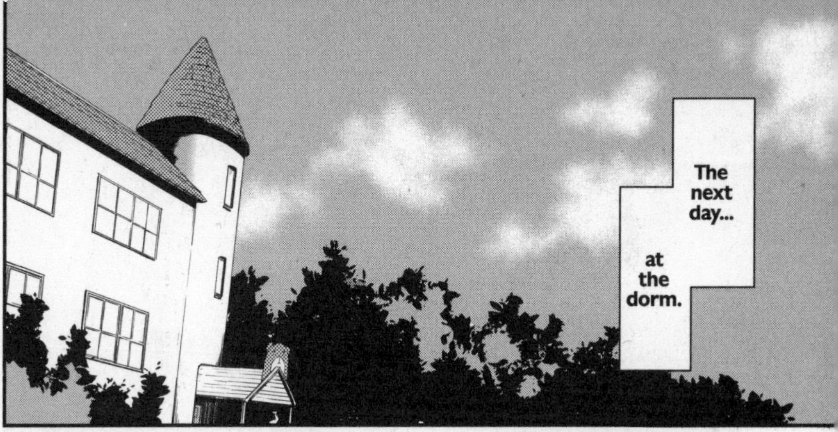
The next day...
at the dorm.

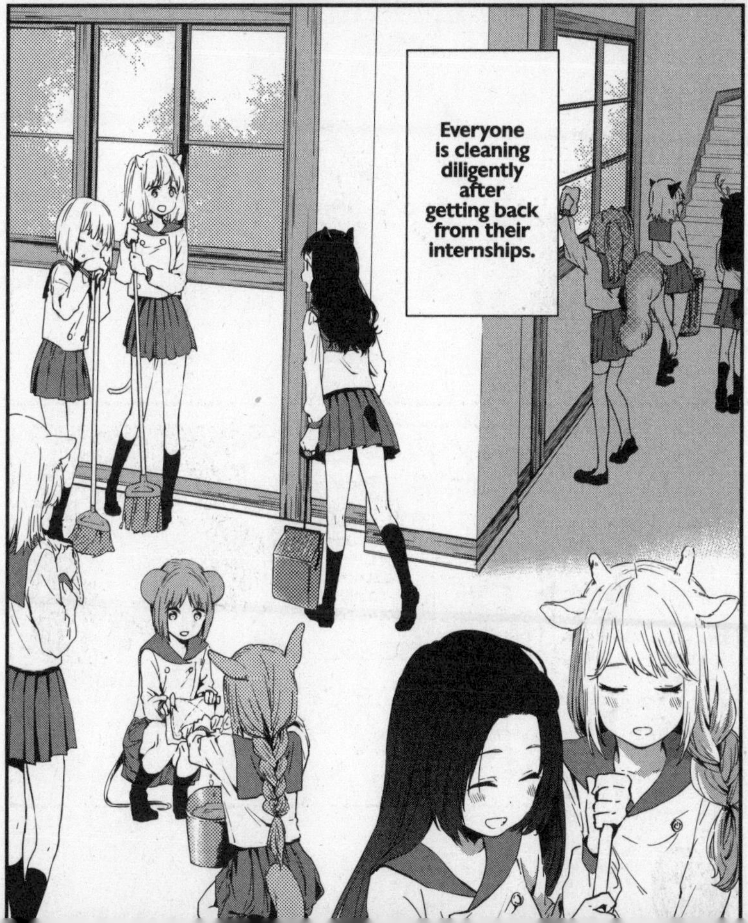
Everyone is cleaning diligently after getting back from their internships.

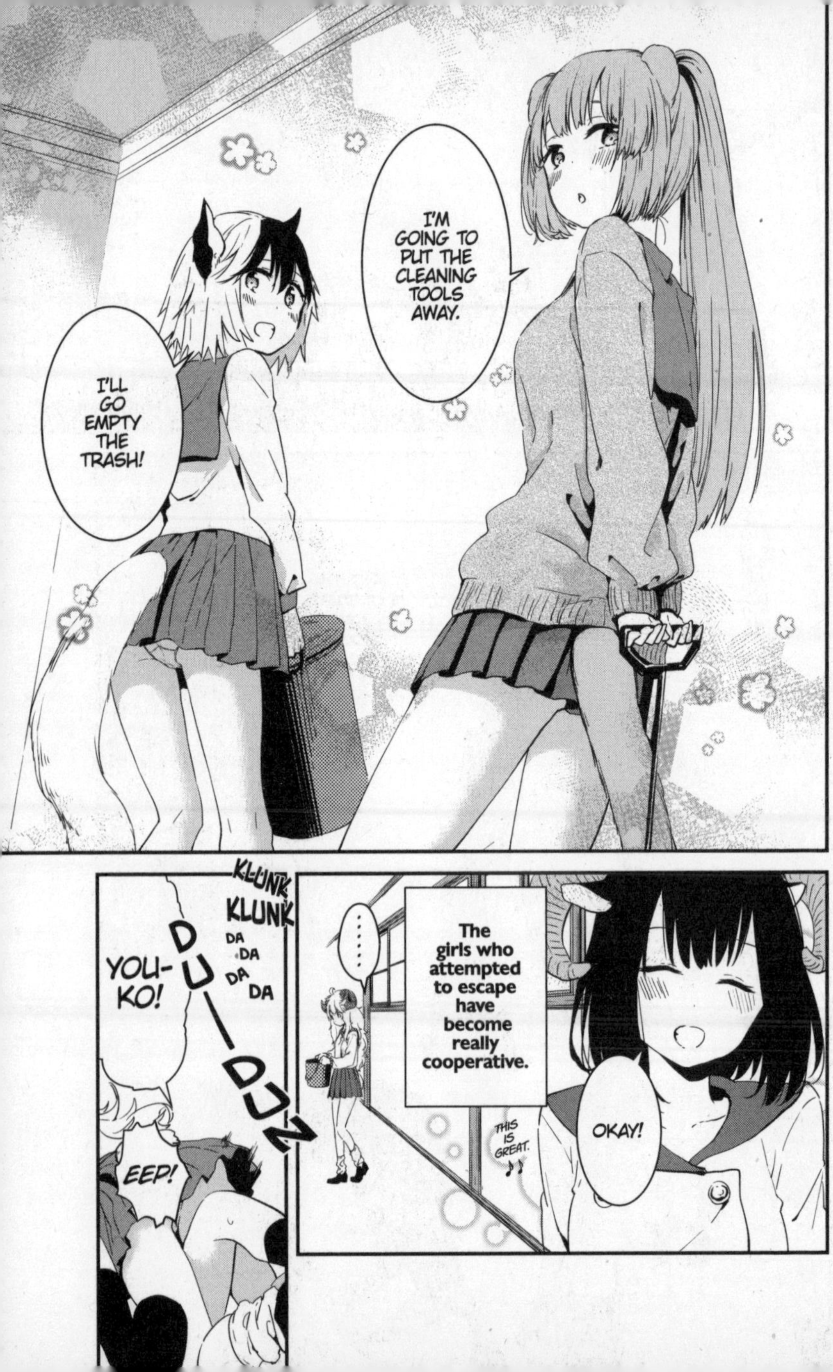
I'M GOING TO PUT THE CLEANING TOOLS AWAY.
I'LL GO EMPTY THE TRASH!
The girls who attempted to escape have become really cooperative.
OKAY!
THIS IS GREAT. ♪♪
......
KLUNK
KLUNK
DA DA DA DA
DU-DUN
YOU-KO!
EEP!

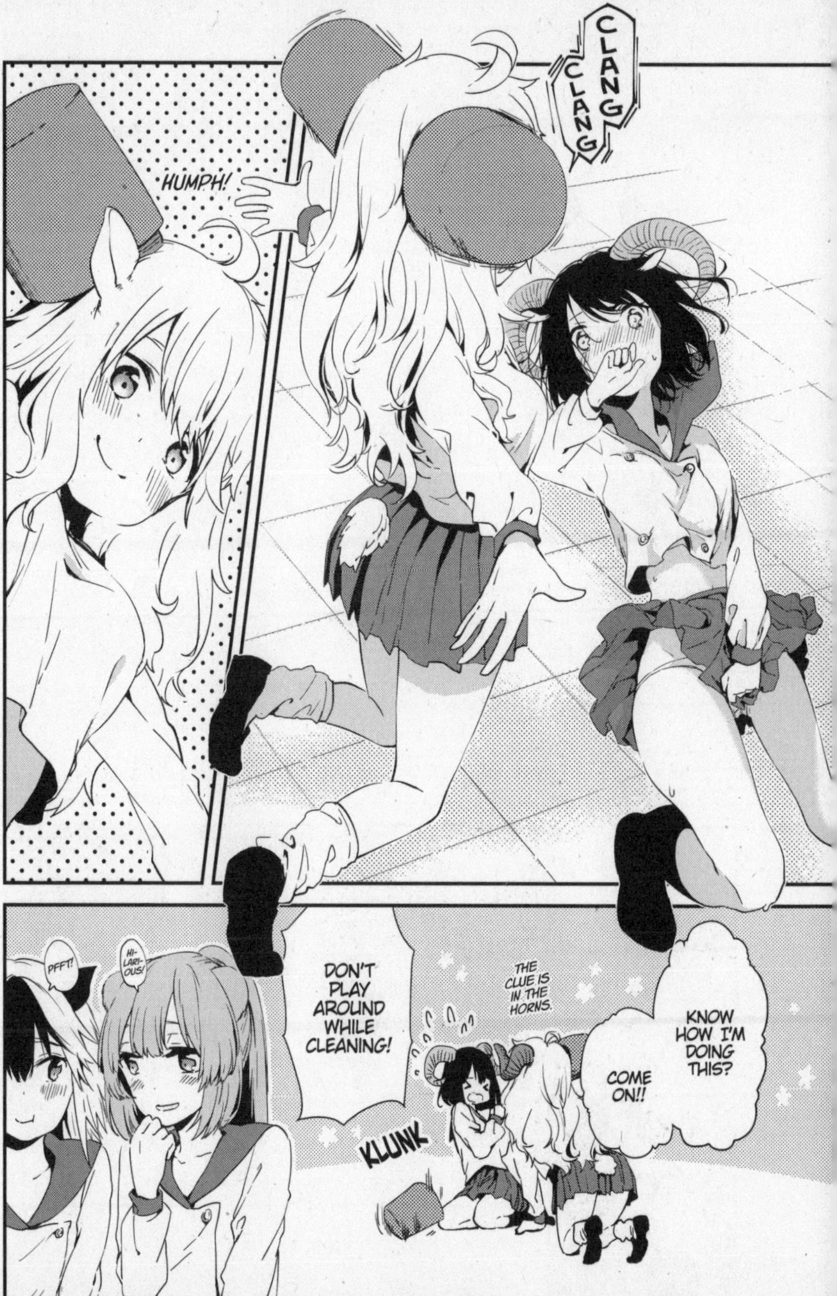
CLANG
CLANG
HUMPH!
KNOW HOW I'M DOING THIS?
COME ON!!
THE CLUE IS IN THE HORNS.
DON'T PLAY AROUND WHILE CLEANING!
KLUNK
HI-LARIOUS!
PFFT!

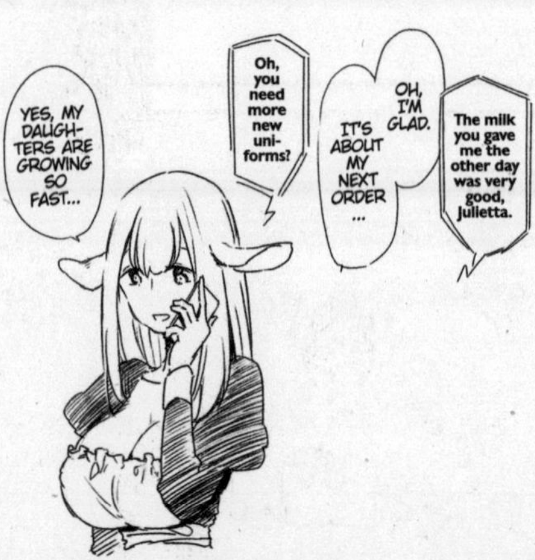
The milk you gave me the other day was very good, Julietta.
OH, I'M GLAD.
IT'S ABOUT MY NEXT ORDER...
Oh, you need more new uniforms?
YES, MY DAUGHTERS ARE GROWING SO FAST...

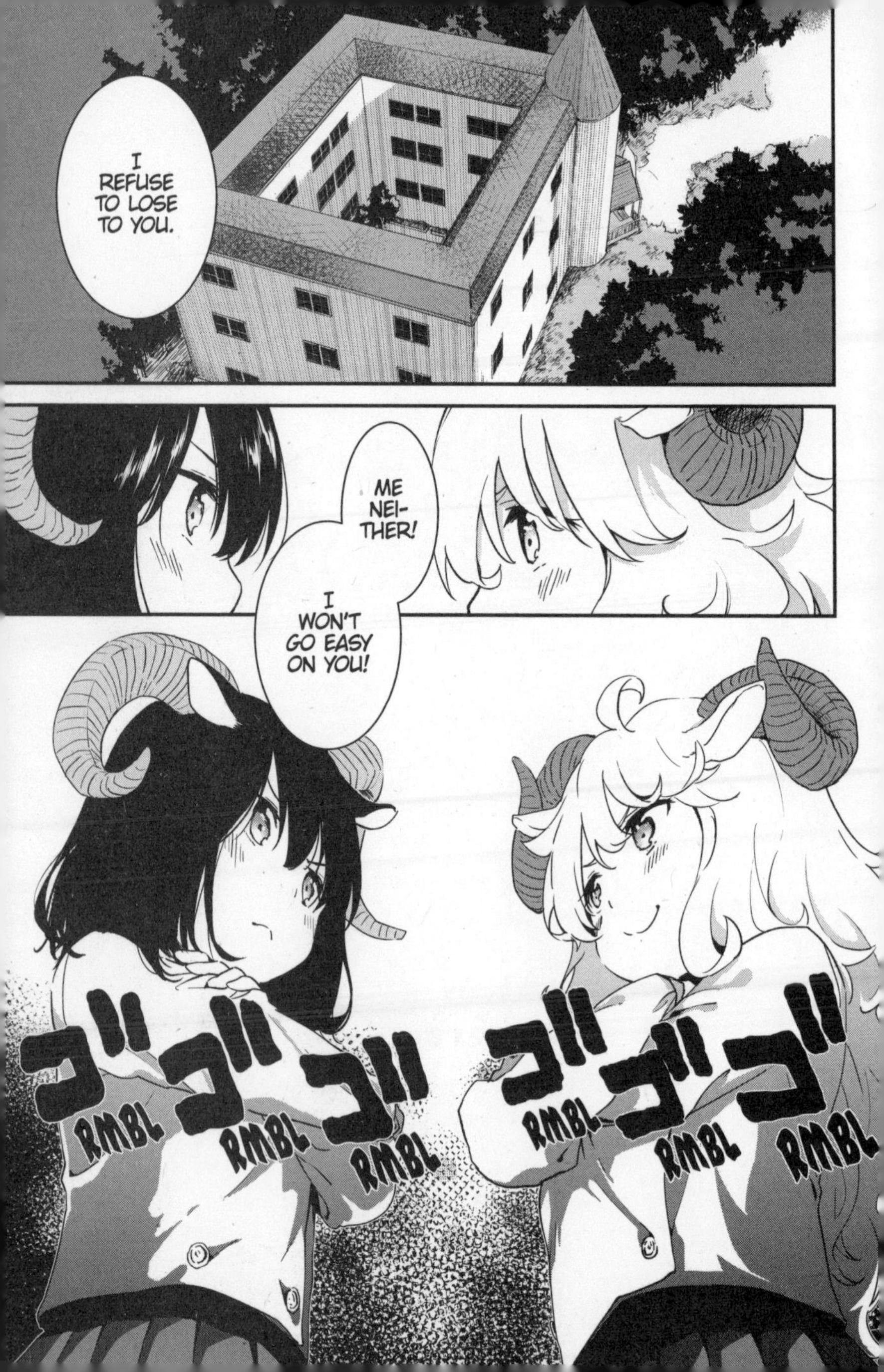
I REFUSE TO LOSE TO YOU.
ME NEI-THER!
I WON'T GO EASY ON YOU!
ゴゴゴ
RMBL RMBL RMBL
ゴゴゴ
RMBL RMBL RMBL

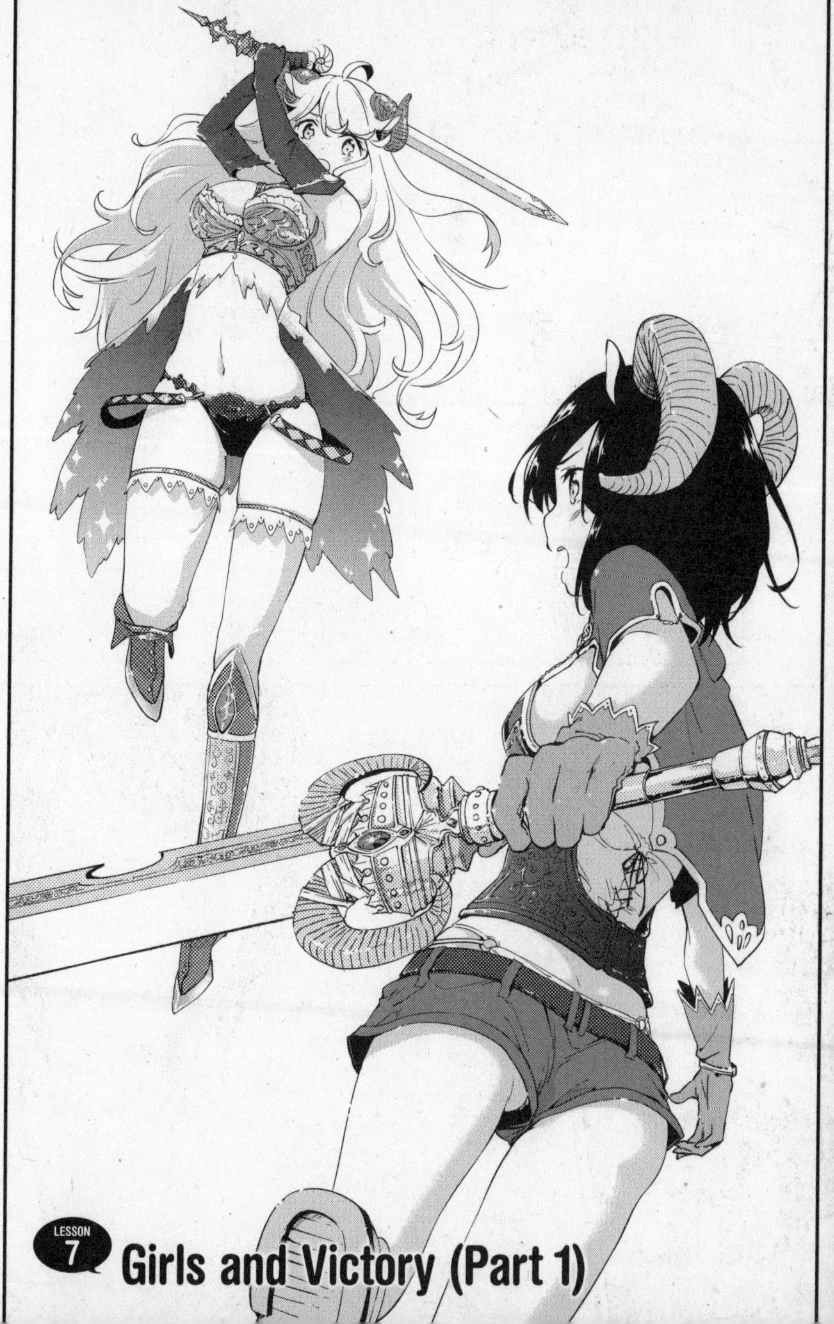

LESSON 7 Girls and Victory (Part 1)

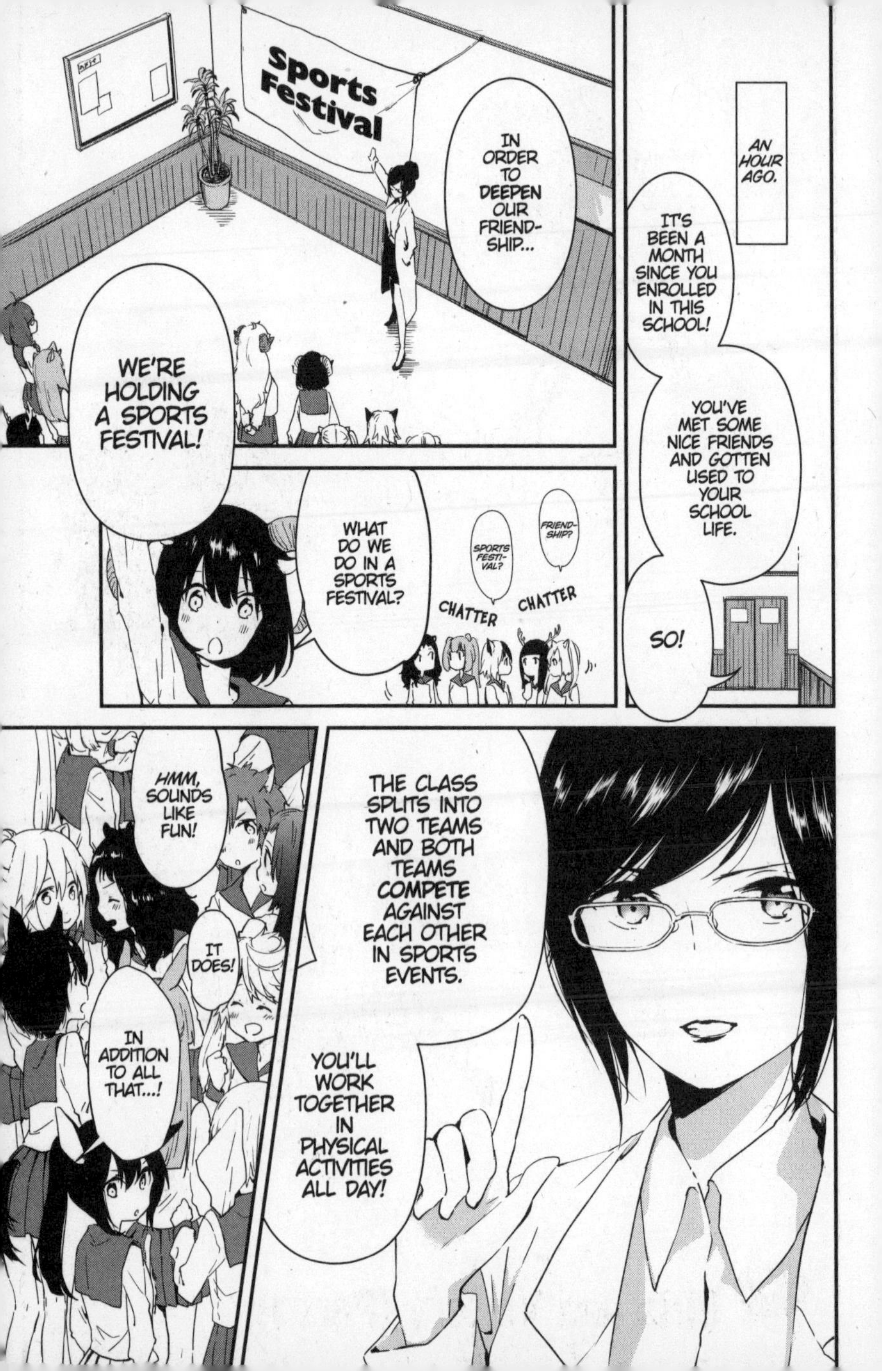
AN HOUR AGO.
IT'S BEEN A MONTH SINCE YOU ENROLLED IN THIS SCHOOL!
YOU'VE MET SOME NICE FRIENDS AND GOTTEN USED TO YOUR SCHOOL LIFE.
SO!
Sports Festival
IN ORDER TO DEEPEN OUR FRIENDSHIP...
WE'RE HOLDING A SPORTS FESTIVAL!
FRIENDSHIP?
SPORTS FESTIVAL?
CHATTER
CHATTER
WHAT DO WE DO IN A SPORTS FESTIVAL?
THE CLASS SPLITS INTO TWO TEAMS AND BOTH TEAMS COMPETE AGAINST EACH OTHER IN SPORTS EVENTS.
YOU'LL WORK TOGETHER IN PHYSICAL ACTIVITIES ALL DAY!
HMM, SOUNDS LIKE FUN!
IT DOES!
IN ADDITION TO ALL THAT...!

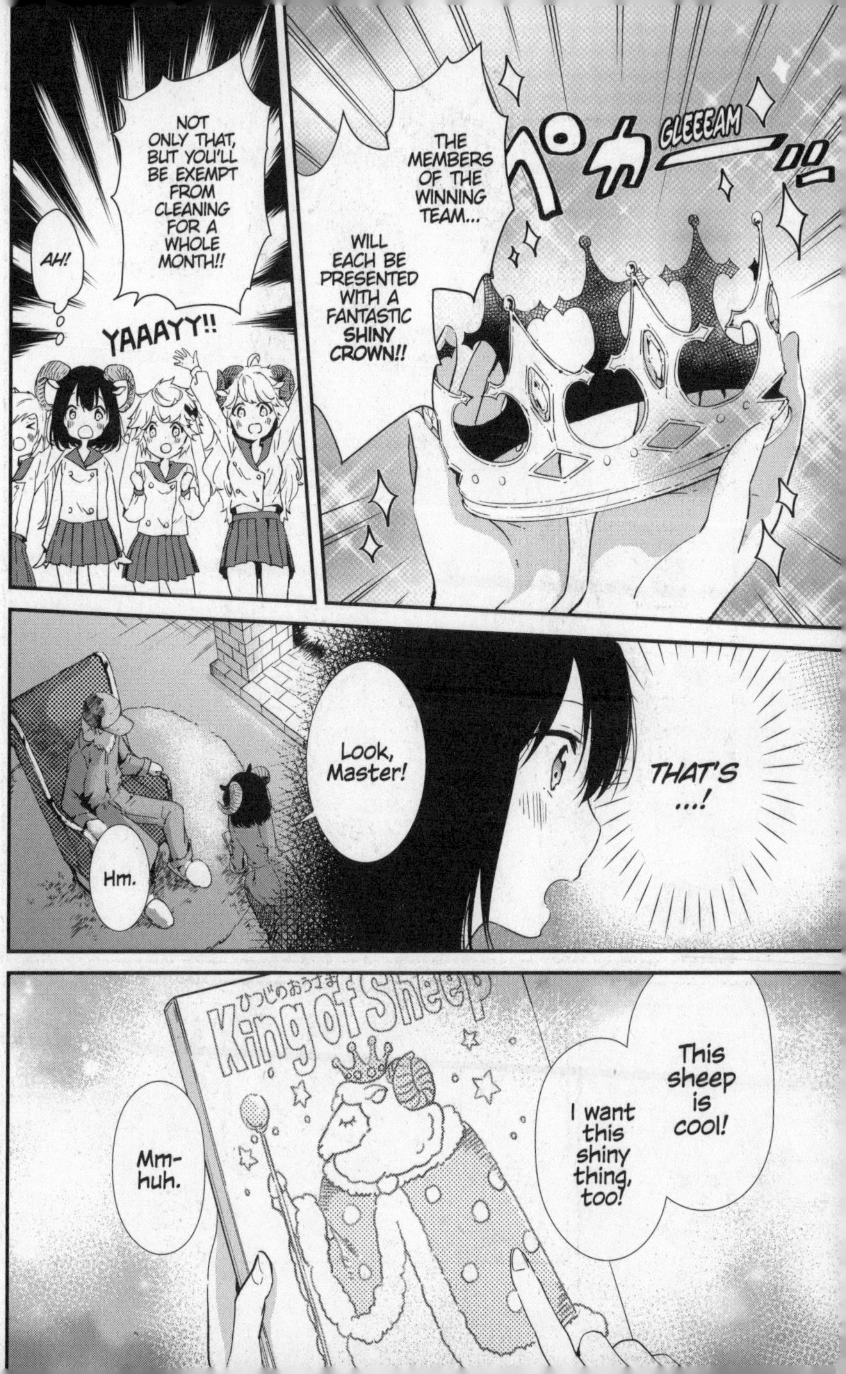
THE MEMBERS OF THE WINNING TEAM...
WILL EACH BE PRESENTED WITH A FANTASTIC SHINY CROWN!!
GLEEEAM
NOT ONLY THAT, BUT YOU'LL BE EXEMPT FROM CLEANING FOR A WHOLE MONTH!!
AH!
YAAAYY!!
THAT'S ...!
Look, Master!
Hm.
This sheep is cool!
I want this shiny thing, too!
Mm-huh.
ひつじのおうさま
King of Sheep

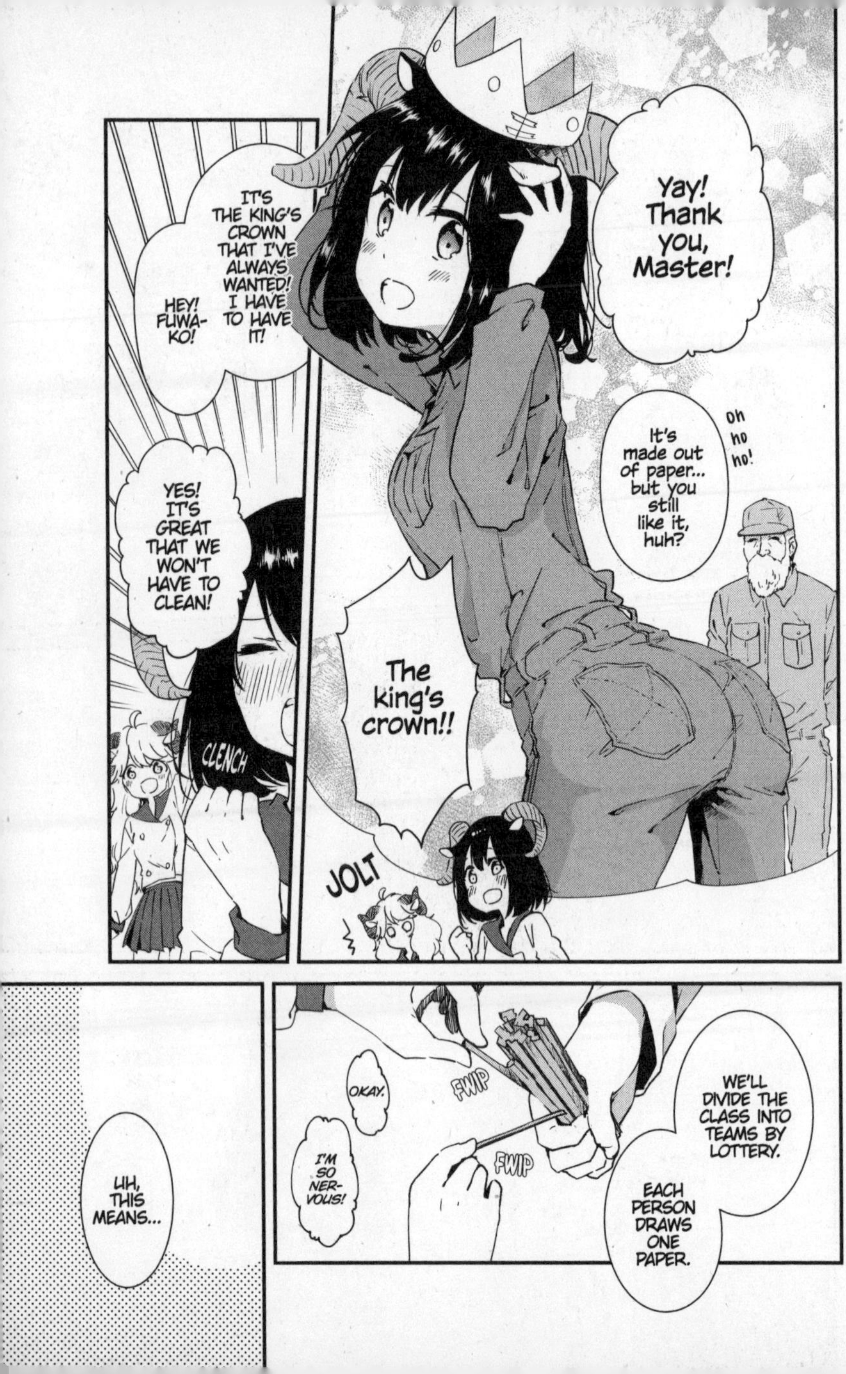
Yay! Thank you, Master!
Oh ho ho!
It's made out of paper... but you still like it, huh?
The king's crown!!
JOLT
IT'S THE KING'S CROWN THAT I'VE ALWAYS WANTED! I HAVE TO HAVE IT!
HEY! FUWAKO!
YES! IT'S GREAT THAT WE WON'T HAVE TO CLEAN!
CLENCH
WE'LL DIVIDE THE CLASS INTO TEAMS BY LOTTERY.
EACH PERSON DRAWS ONE PAPER.
FWIP
OKAY.
FWIP
I'M SO NERVOUS!
UH, THIS MEANS...

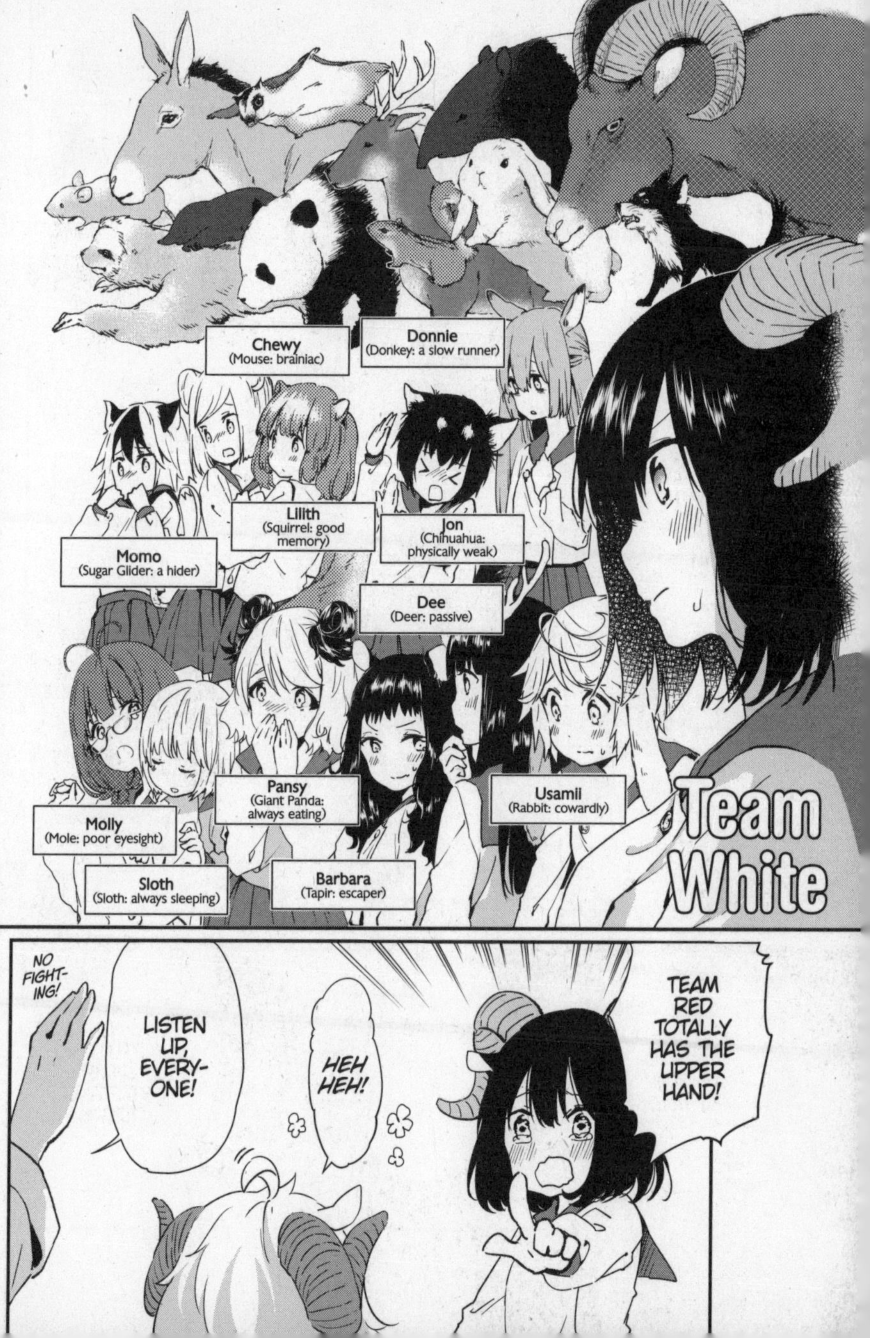
Donnie (Donkey: a slow runner)
Chewy (Mouse: brainiac)
Jon (Chihuahua: physically weak)
Lilith (Squirrel: good memory)
Momo (Sugar Glider: a hider)
Dee (Deer: passive)
Team White
Usamii (Rabbit: cowardly)
Pansy (Giant Panda: always eating)
Molly (Mole: poor eyesight)
Barbara (Tapir: escaper)
Sloth (Sloth: always sleeping)
TEAM RED TOTALLY HAS THE UPPER HAND!
HEH HEH!
LISTEN UP, EVERYONE!
NO FIGHTING!

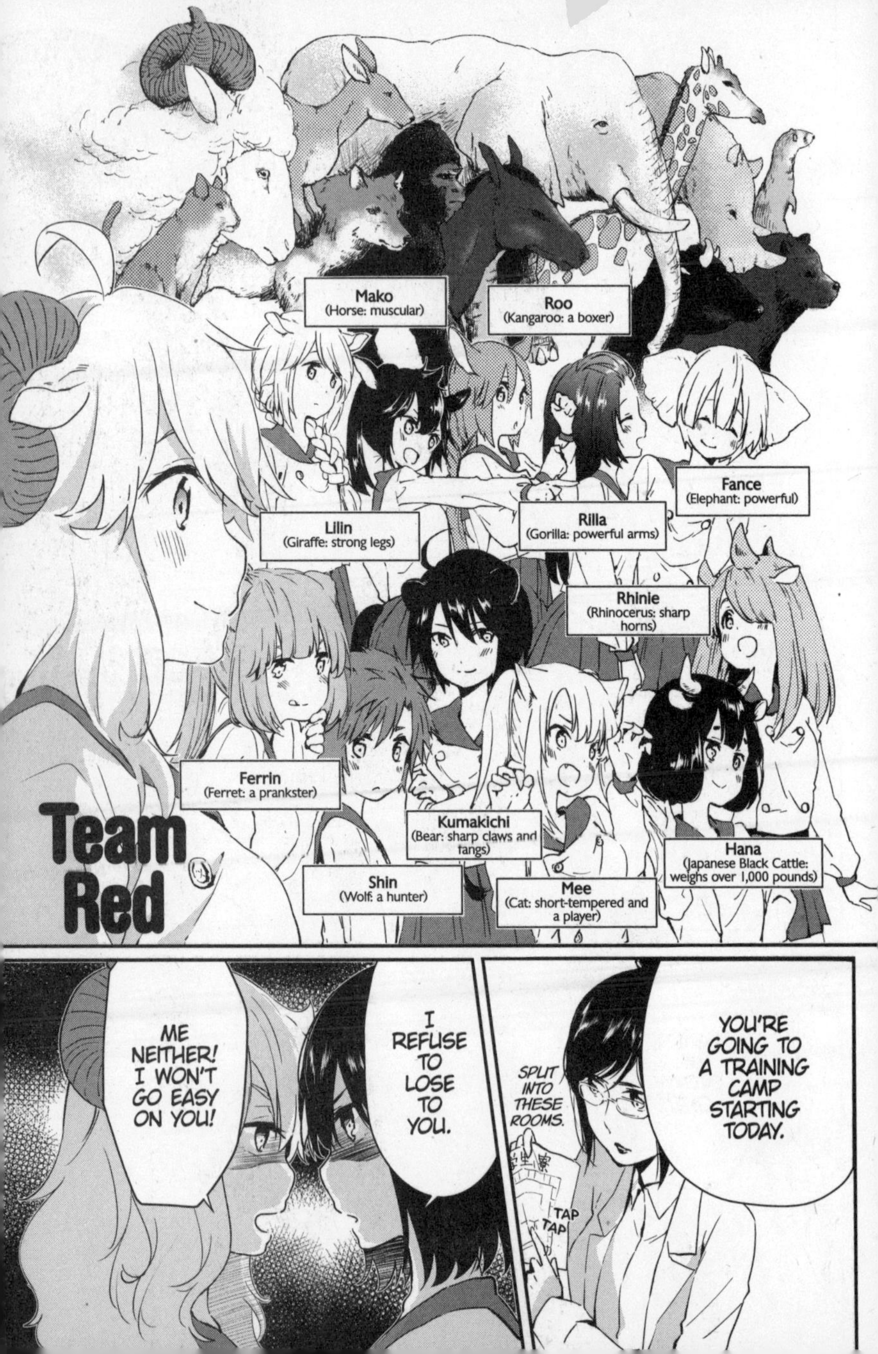
Roo
(Kangaroo: a boxer)
Mako
(Horse: muscular)
Fance
(Elephant: powerful)
Rilla
(Gorilla: powerful arms)
Lilin
(Giraffe: strong legs)
Rhinie
(Rhinocerus: sharp horns)
Hana
(Japanese Black Cattle: weighs over 1,000 pounds)
Mee
(Cat: short-tempered and a player)
Kumakichi
(Bear: sharp claws and fangs)
Shin
(Wolf: a hunter)
Ferrin
(Ferret: a prankster)
Team Red
YOU'RE GOING TO A TRAINING CAMP STARTING TODAY.
SPLIT INTO THESE ROOMS.
TAP TAP
I REFUSE TO LOSE TO YOU.
ME NEITHER! I WON'T GO EASY ON YOU!

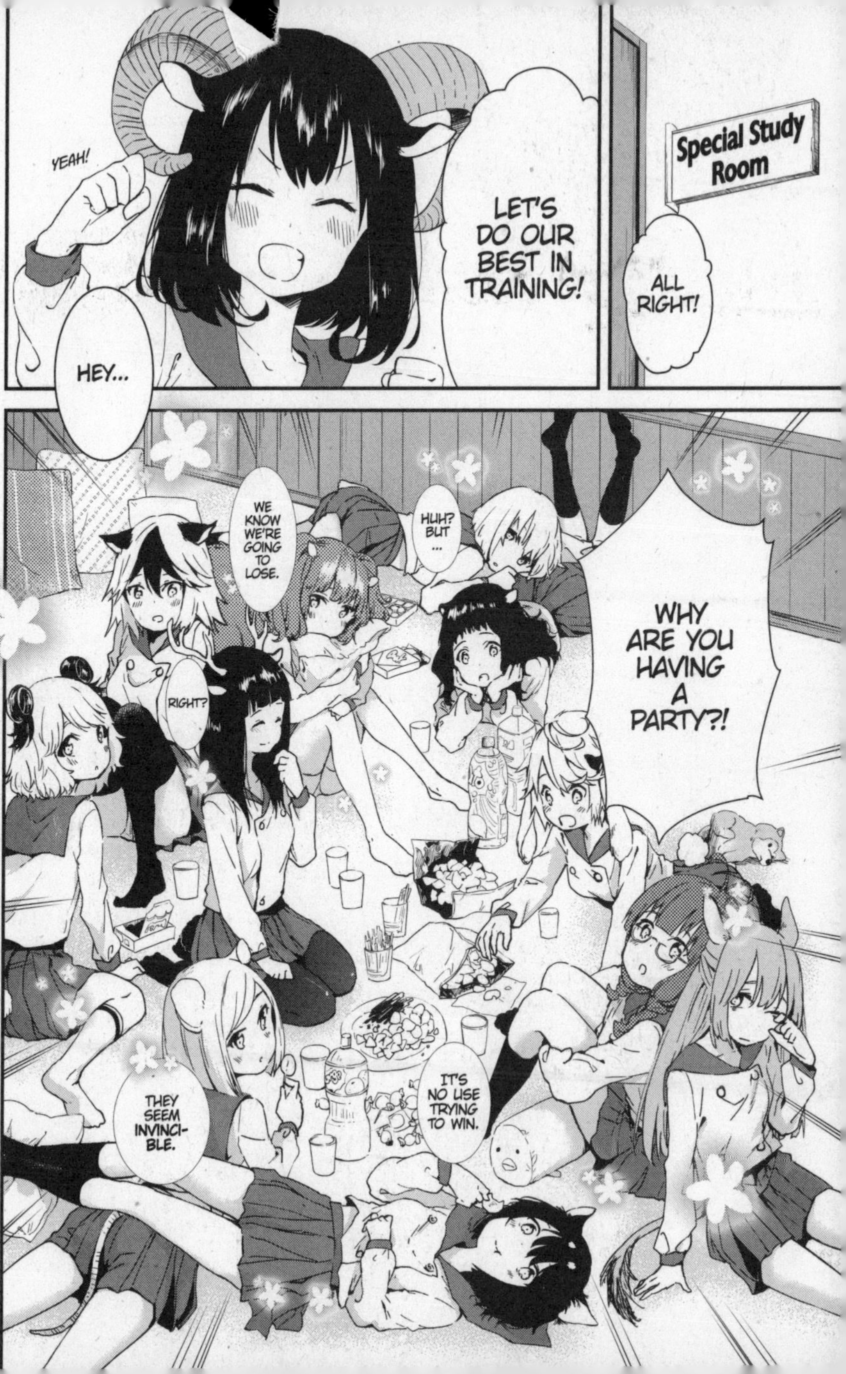
Special Study Room
ALL RIGHT!
LET'S DO OUR BEST IN TRAINING!
YEAH!
HEY...
WHY ARE YOU HAVING A PARTY?!
HUH? BUT ...
WE KNOW WE'RE GOING TO LOSE.
RIGHT?
IT'S NO USE TRYING TO WIN.
THEY SEEM INVINCIBLE.

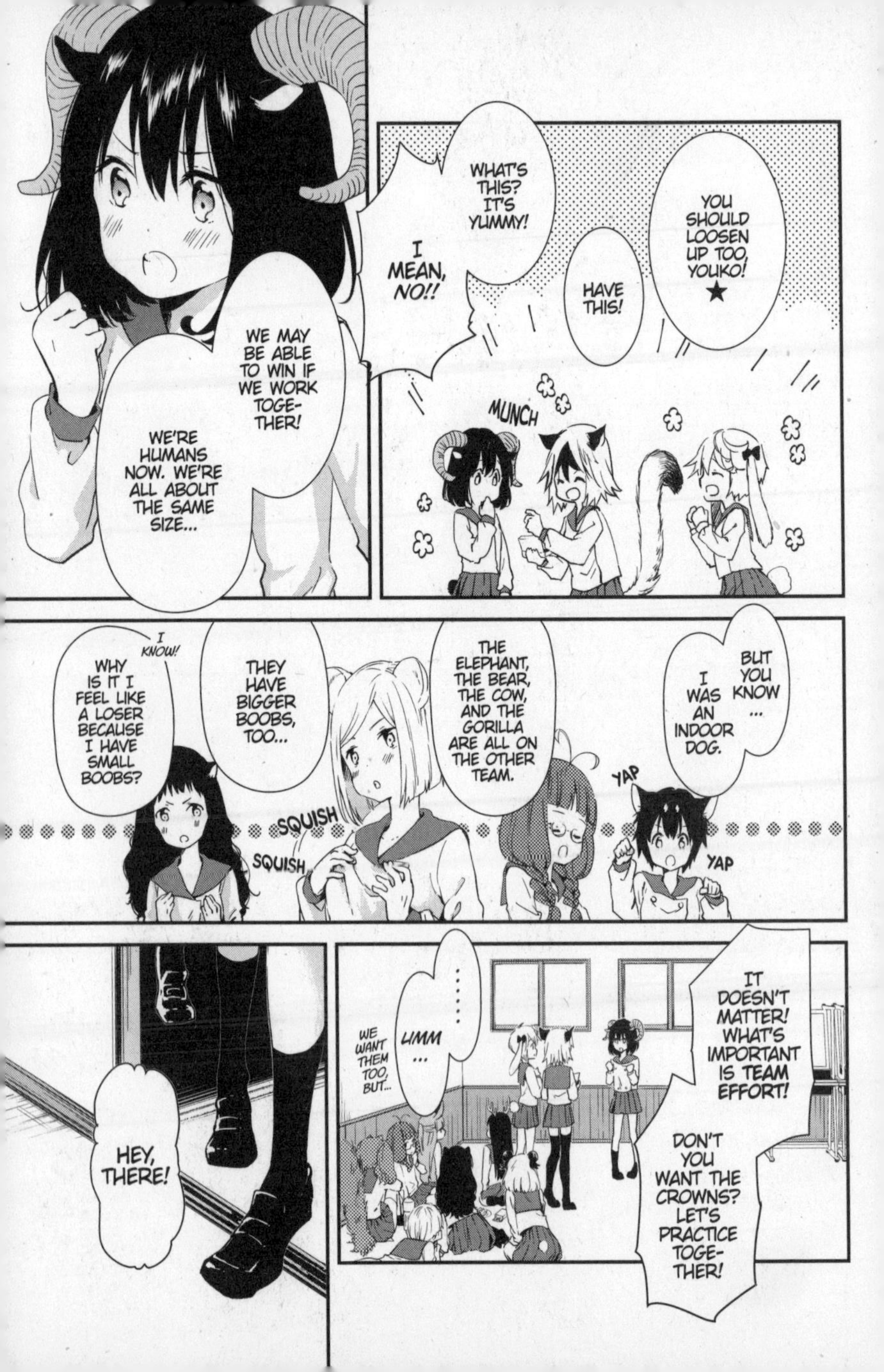
YOU SHOULD LOOSEN UP TOO, YOUKO! ★
HAVE THIS!
WHAT'S THIS? IT'S YUMMY!
I MEAN, NO!!
MUNCH
WE MAY BE ABLE TO WIN IF WE WORK TOGE-THER!
WE'RE HUMANS NOW. WE'RE ALL ABOUT THE SAME SIZE...
BUT YOU KNOW ...
I WAS AN INDOOR DOG.
YAP
YAP
THE ELEPHANT, THE BEAR, THE COW, AND THE GORILLA ARE ALL ON THE OTHER TEAM.
THEY HAVE BIGGER BOOBS, TOO...
SQUISH
SQUISH
I KNOW!
WHY IS IT I FEEL LIKE A LOSER BECAUSE I HAVE SMALL BOOBS?
IT DOESN'T MATTER! WHAT'S IMPORTANT IS TEAM EFFORT!
DON'T YOU WANT THE CROWNS? LET'S PRACTICE TOGE-THER!
......
UMM ...
WE WANT THEM TOO, BUT...
HEY, THERE!

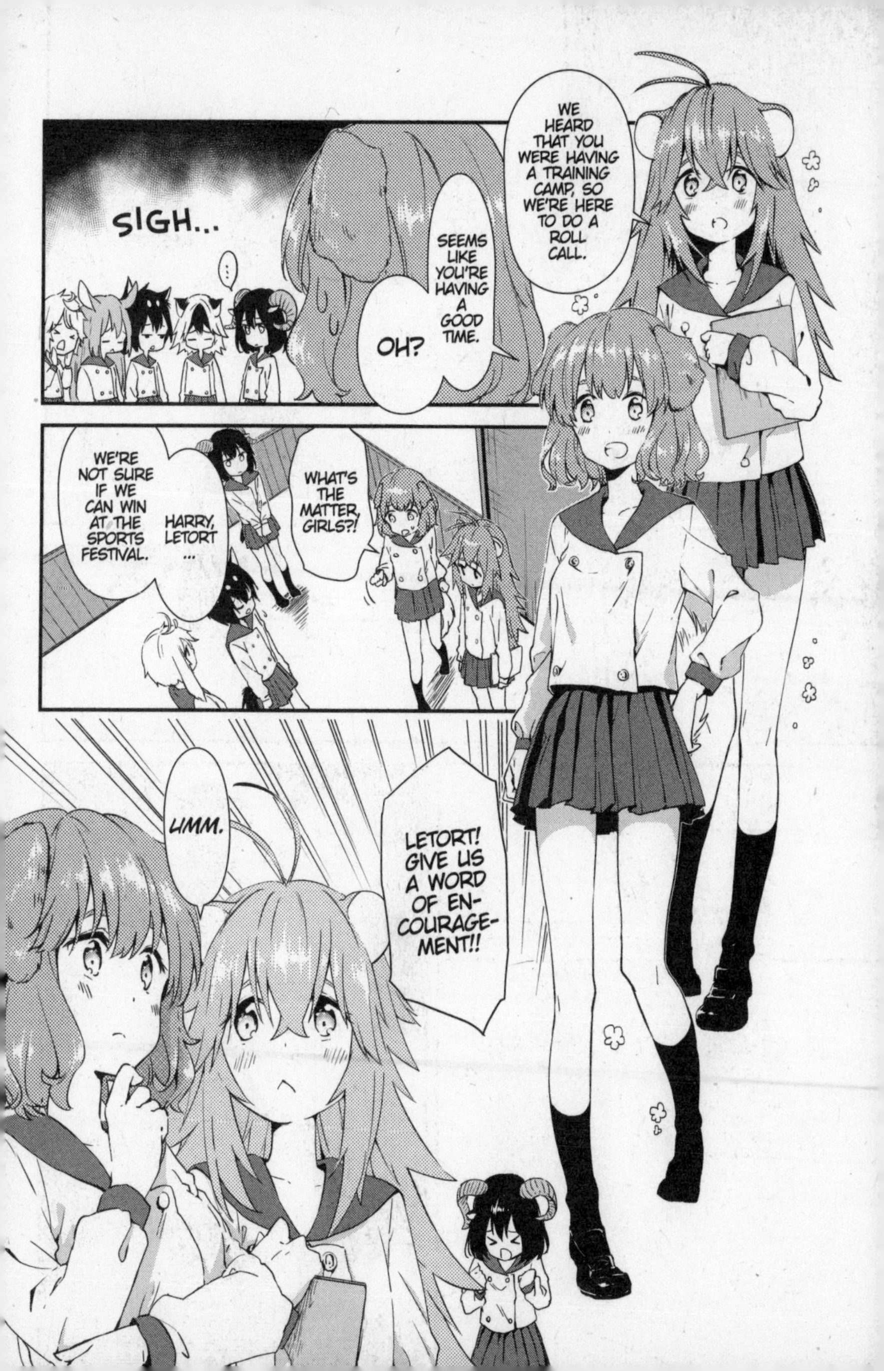
WE HEARD THAT YOU WERE HAVING A TRAINING CAMP, SO WE'RE HERE TO DO A ROLL CALL.
SEEMS LIKE YOU'RE HAVING A GOOD TIME.
OH?
SIGH...
...
WHAT'S THE MATTER, GIRLS?!
HARRY, LETORT ...
WE'RE NOT SURE IF WE CAN WIN AT THE SPORTS FESTIVAL.
LETORT! GIVE US A WORD OF EN-COURAGE-MENT!!
UMM.

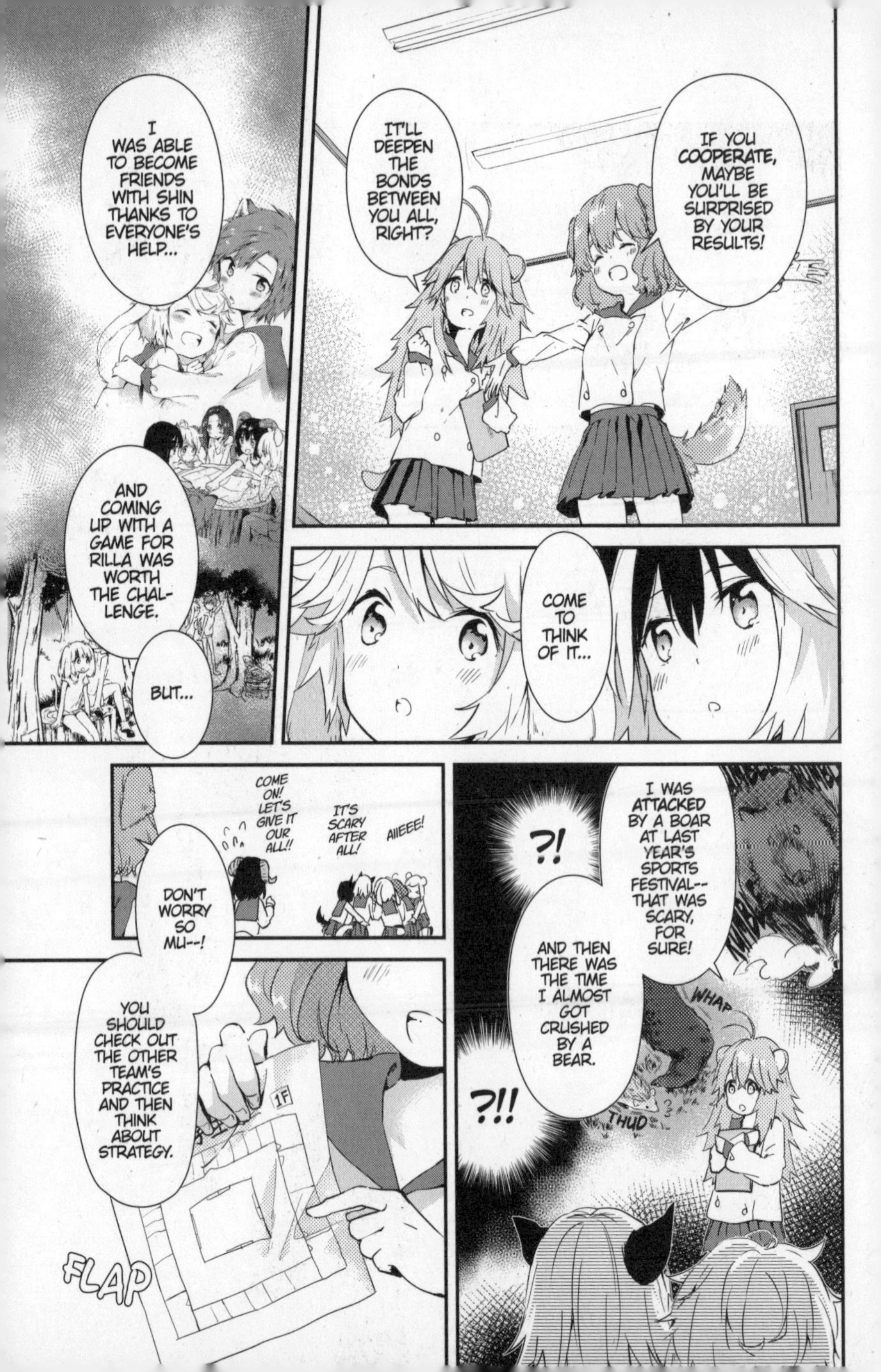
IF YOU COOPERATE, MAYBE YOU'LL BE SURPRISED BY YOUR RESULTS!
IT'LL DEEPEN THE BONDS BETWEEN YOU ALL, RIGHT?
COME TO THINK OF IT...
I WAS ABLE TO BECOME FRIENDS WITH SHIN THANKS TO EVERYONE'S HELP...
AND COMING UP WITH A GAME FOR RILLA WAS WORTH THE CHAL-LENGE.
BUT...
I WAS ATTACKED BY A BOAR AT LAST YEAR'S SPORTS FESTIVAL--THAT WAS SCARY, FOR SURE!
?!
WHAP
AND THEN THERE WAS THE TIME I ALMOST GOT CRUSHED BY A BEAR.
?!!
THUD
COME ON! LET'S GIVE IT OUR ALL!!
IT'S SCARY AFTER ALL!
AIIEEE!
DON'T WORRY SO MU--!
YOU SHOULD CHECK OUT THE OTHER TEAM'S PRACTICE AND THEN THINK ABOUT STRATEGY.
1F
FLAP

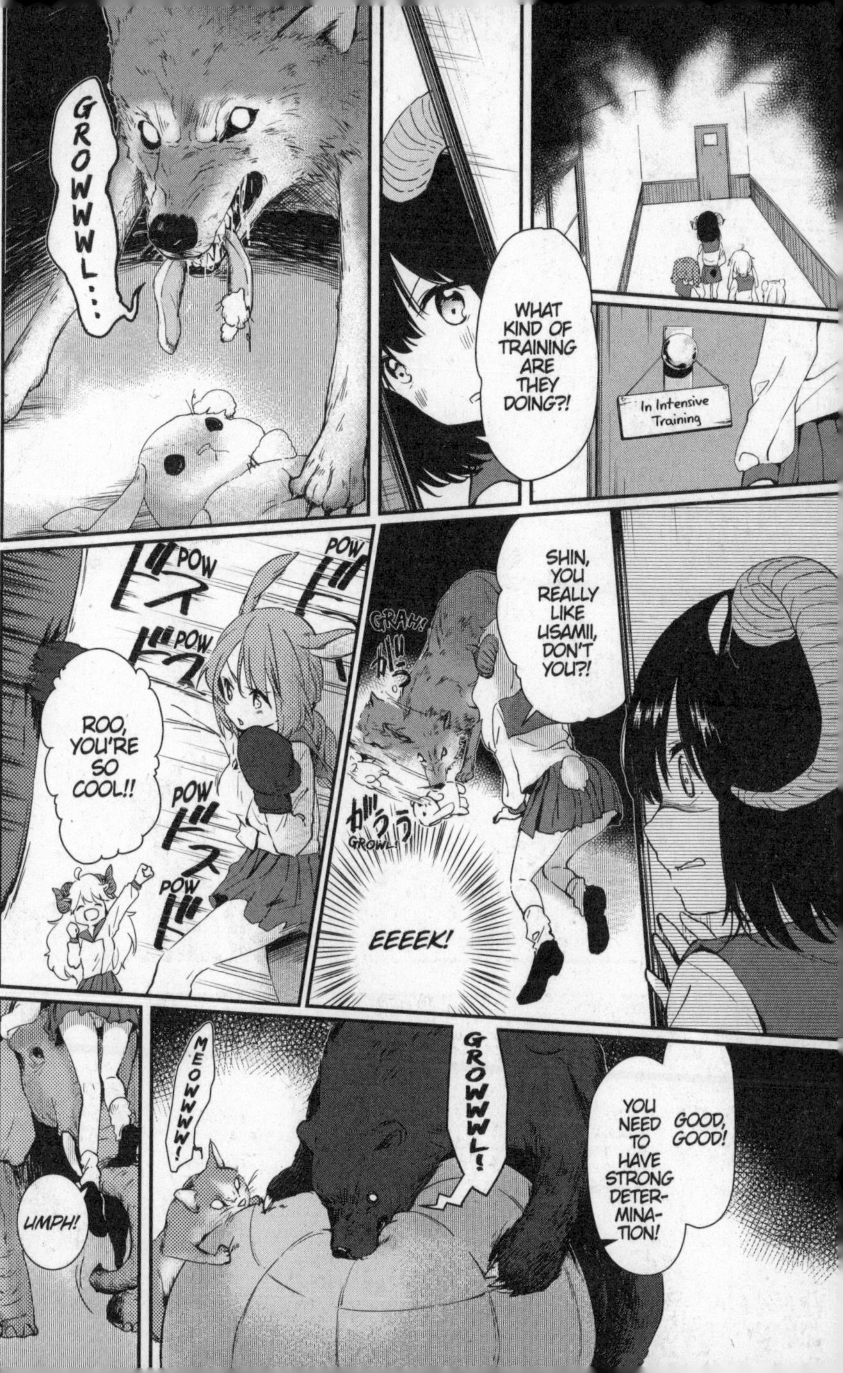
In Intensive Training
WHAT KIND OF TRAINING ARE THEY DOING?!
GROWWWL...
SHIN, YOU REALLY LIKE USAMII, DON'T YOU?!
GRAH!
GROWL!
EEEEK!
POW
POW
POW
ROO, YOU'RE SO COOL!!
POW
POW
GOOD, GOOD!
YOU NEED TO HAVE STRONG DETER-MINA-TION!
GROWWWL!
MEOWWWWW!
UMPH!

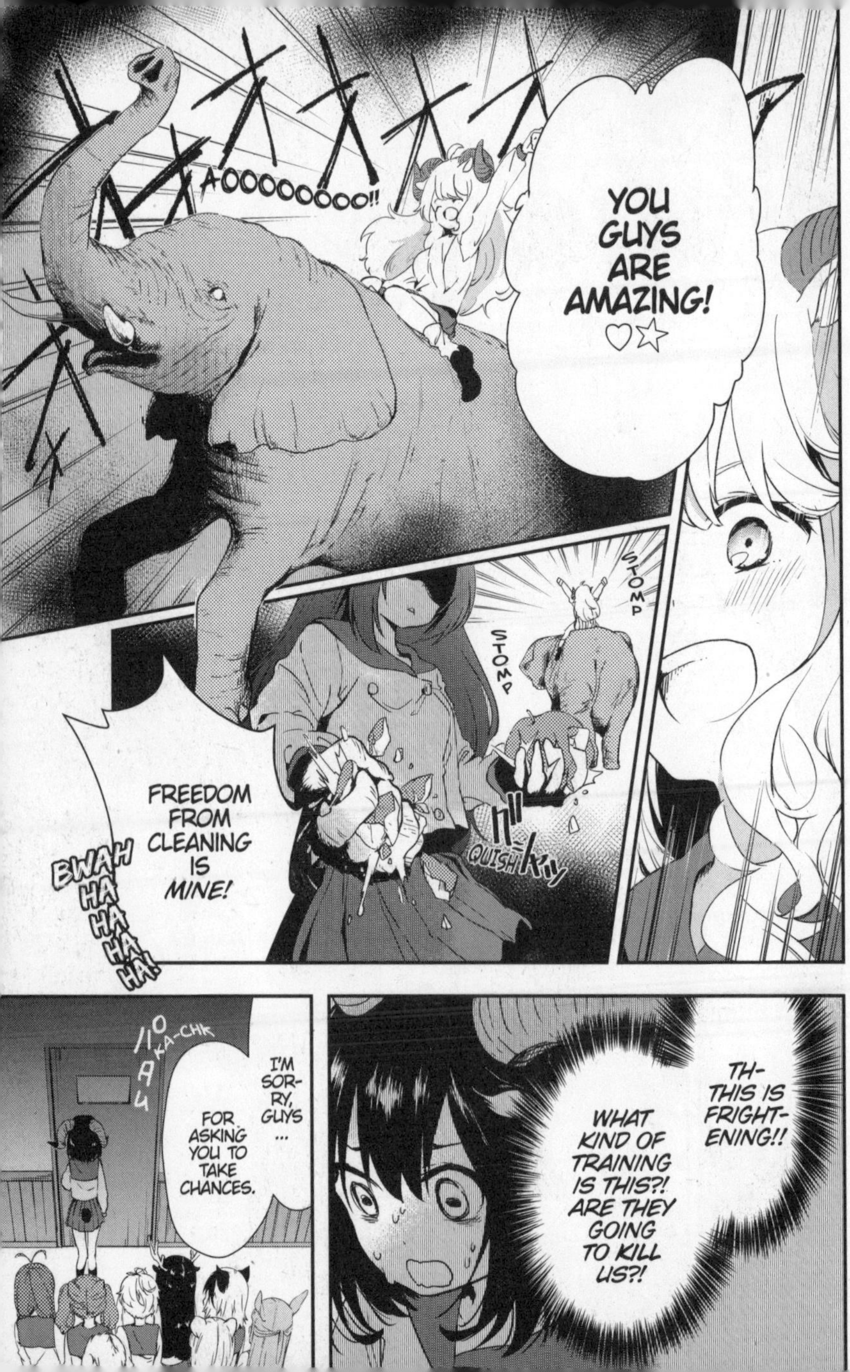
YOU GUYS ARE AMAZING! ♡☆
AOOOOOOOOO!!
STOMP
STOMP
QUISH
FREEDOM FROM CLEANING IS MINE!
BWAH HA HA HA HA HA!
TH- THIS IS FRIGHTENING!!
WHAT KIND OF TRAINING IS THIS?! ARE THEY GOING TO KILL US?!
KA-CHK
I'M SORRY, GUYS...
FOR ASKING YOU TO TAKE CHANCES.

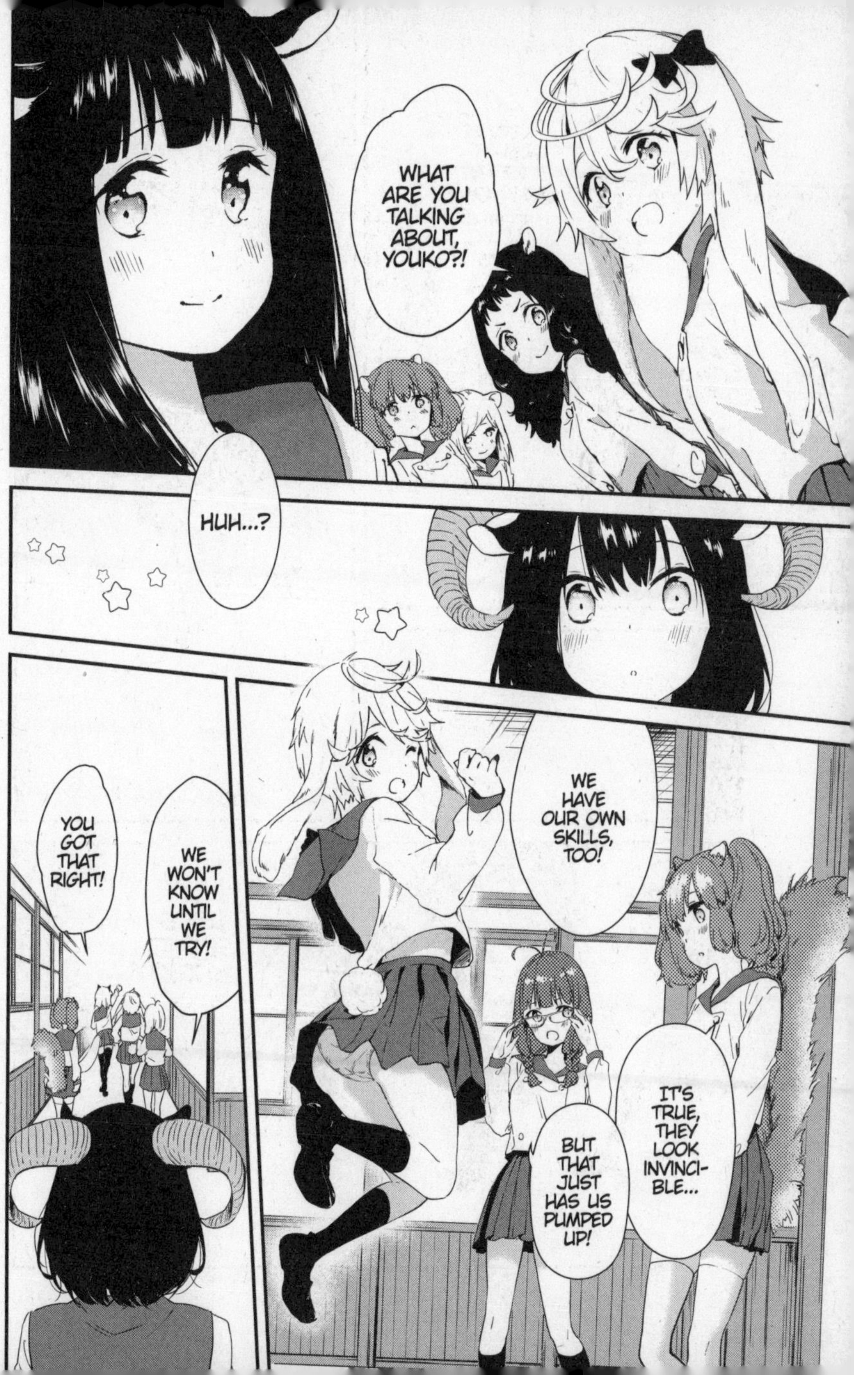
WHAT ARE YOU TALKING ABOUT, YOUKO?!
HUH...?
WE HAVE OUR OWN SKILLS, TOO!
IT'S TRUE, THEY LOOK INVINCIBLE...
BUT THAT JUST HAS US PUMPED UP!
WE WON'T KNOW UNTIL WE TRY!
YOU GOT THAT RIGHT!

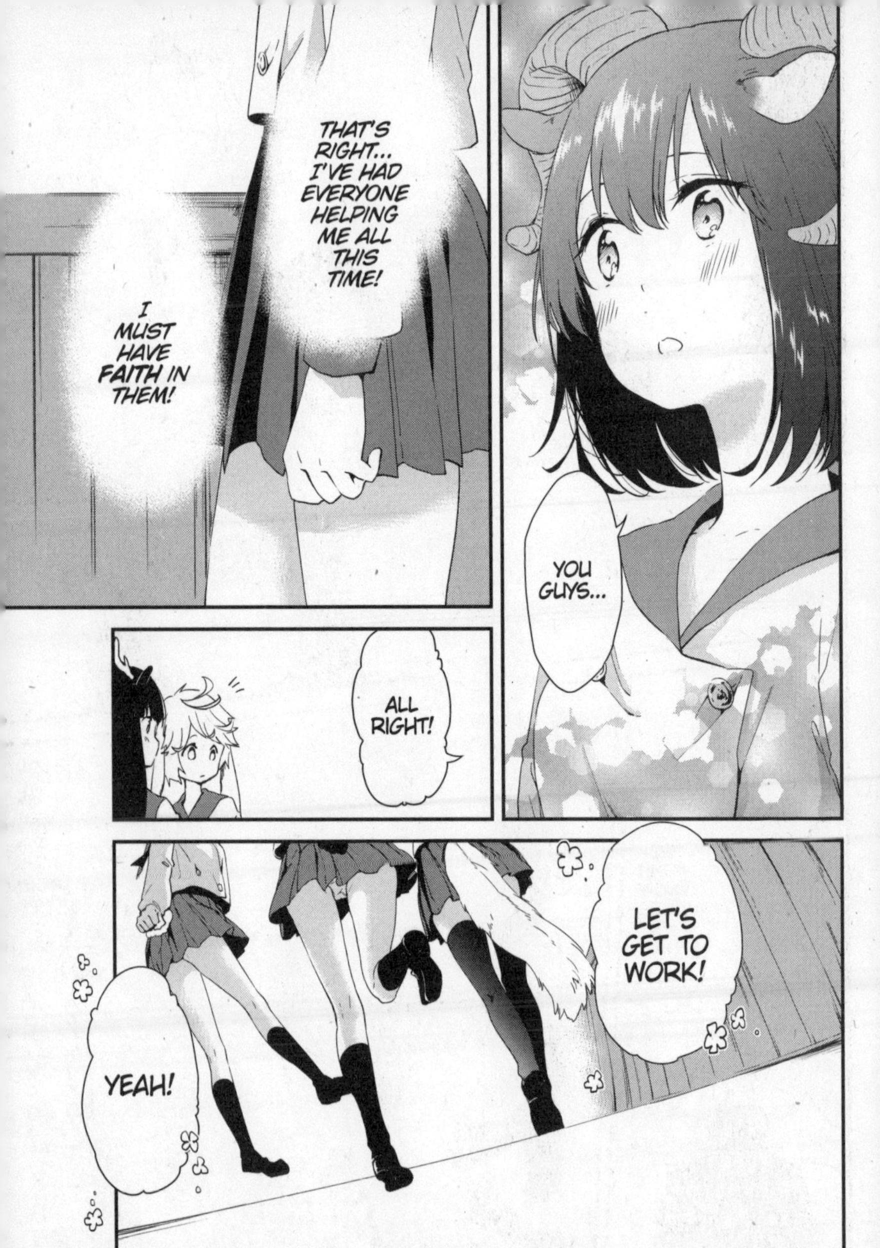
YOU GUYS...
THAT'S RIGHT... I'VE HAD EVERYONE HELPING ME ALL THIS TIME!
I MUST HAVE FAITH IN THEM!
ALL RIGHT!
LET'S GET TO WORK!
YEAH!

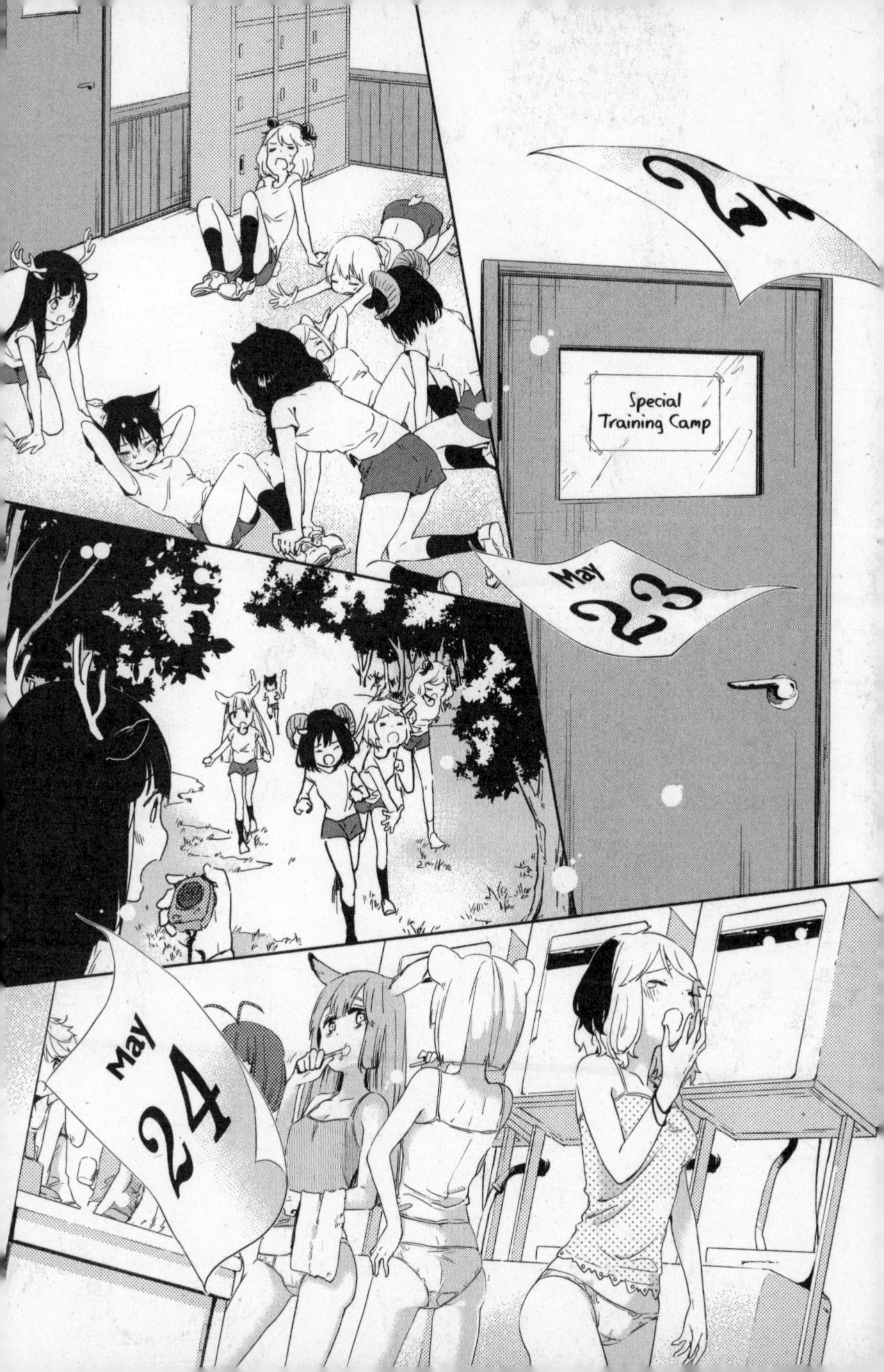
24
Special Training Camp
May
23
May
24

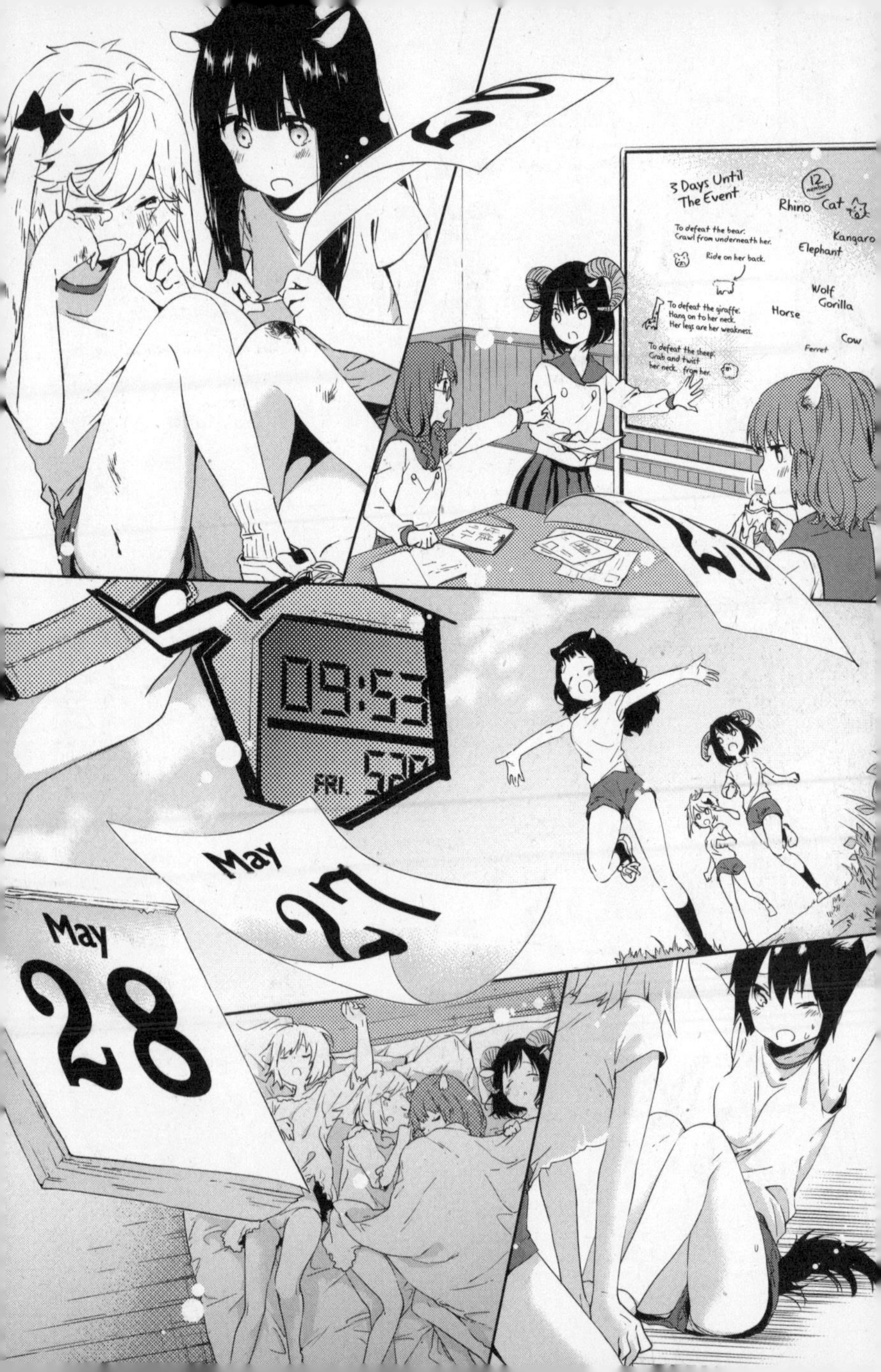
3 Days Until
The Event
12 members
Rhino
Cat
Kangaro
Elephant
Wolf
Gorilla
Horse
Cow
Ferret
To defeat the bear.
Crawl from underneath her.
Ride on her back.
To defeat the giraffe:
Hang on to her neck.
Her legs are her weakness.
To defeat the sheep:
Grab and twist
her neck. from her.
09:53
FRI.
May
27
May
28

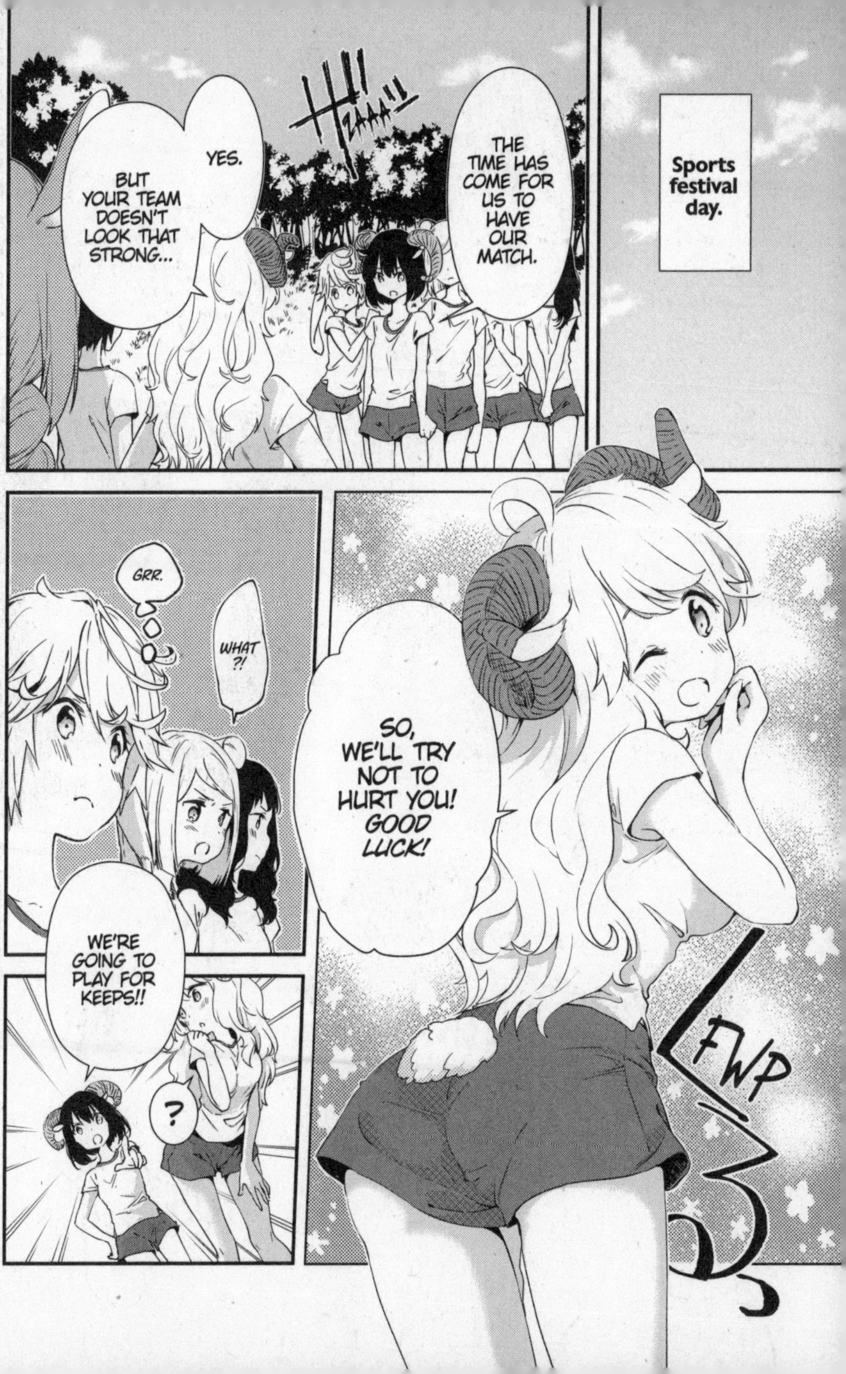

Sports festival day.
THE TIME HAS COME FOR US TO HAVE OUR MATCH.
H!! ZAAA!!
YES.
BUT YOUR TEAM DOESN'T LOOK THAT STRONG...
SO, WE'LL TRY NOT TO HURT YOU! GOOD LUCK!
FWP
WHAT?!
GRR.
WE'RE GOING TO PLAY FOR KEEPS!!
?

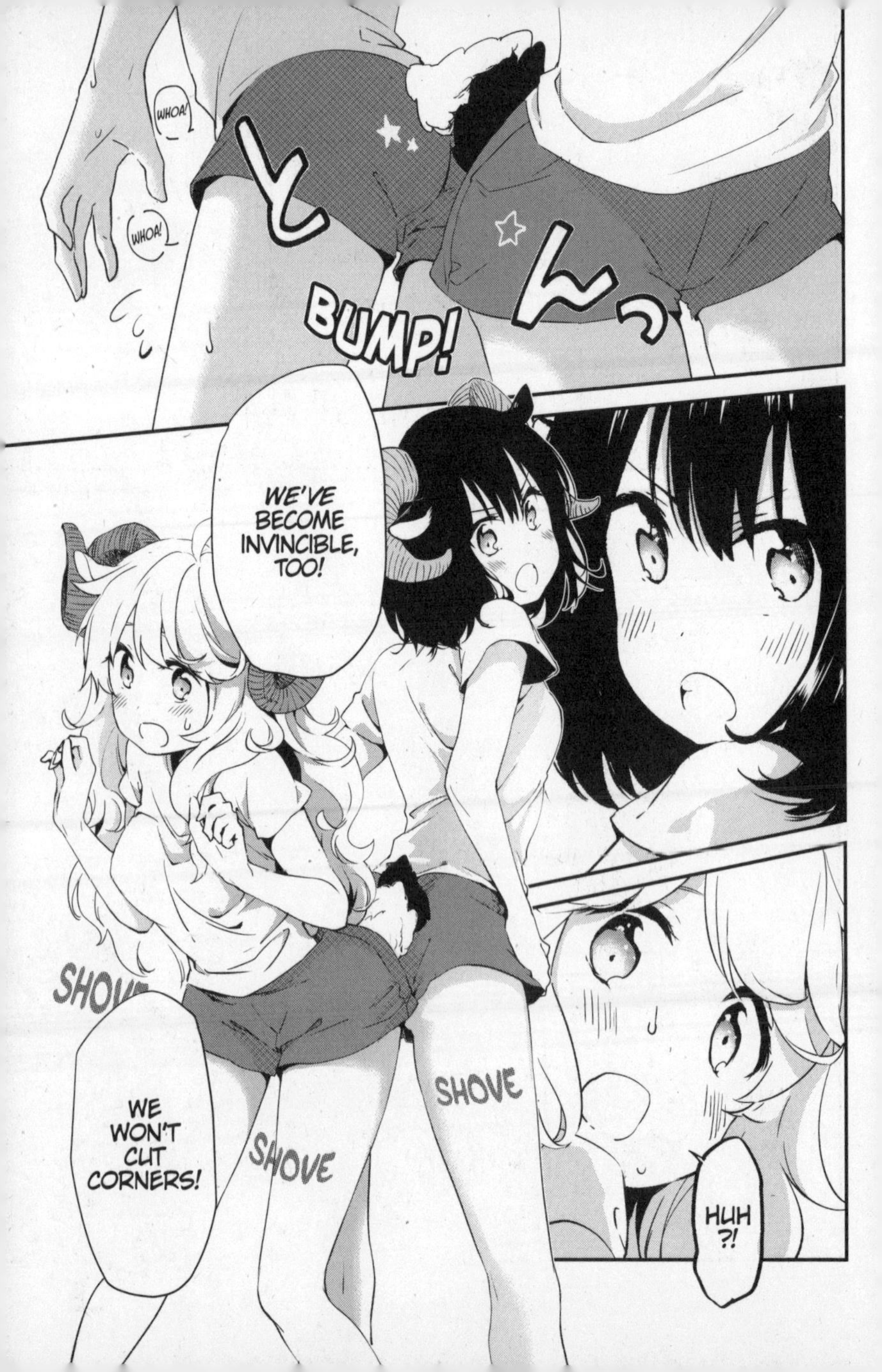
WHOA!
WHOA!
とんっ
BUMP!
HUH ?!
WE'VE BECOME INVINCIBLE, TOO!
SHOVE
SHOVE
SHOVE
WE WON'T CUT CORNERS!

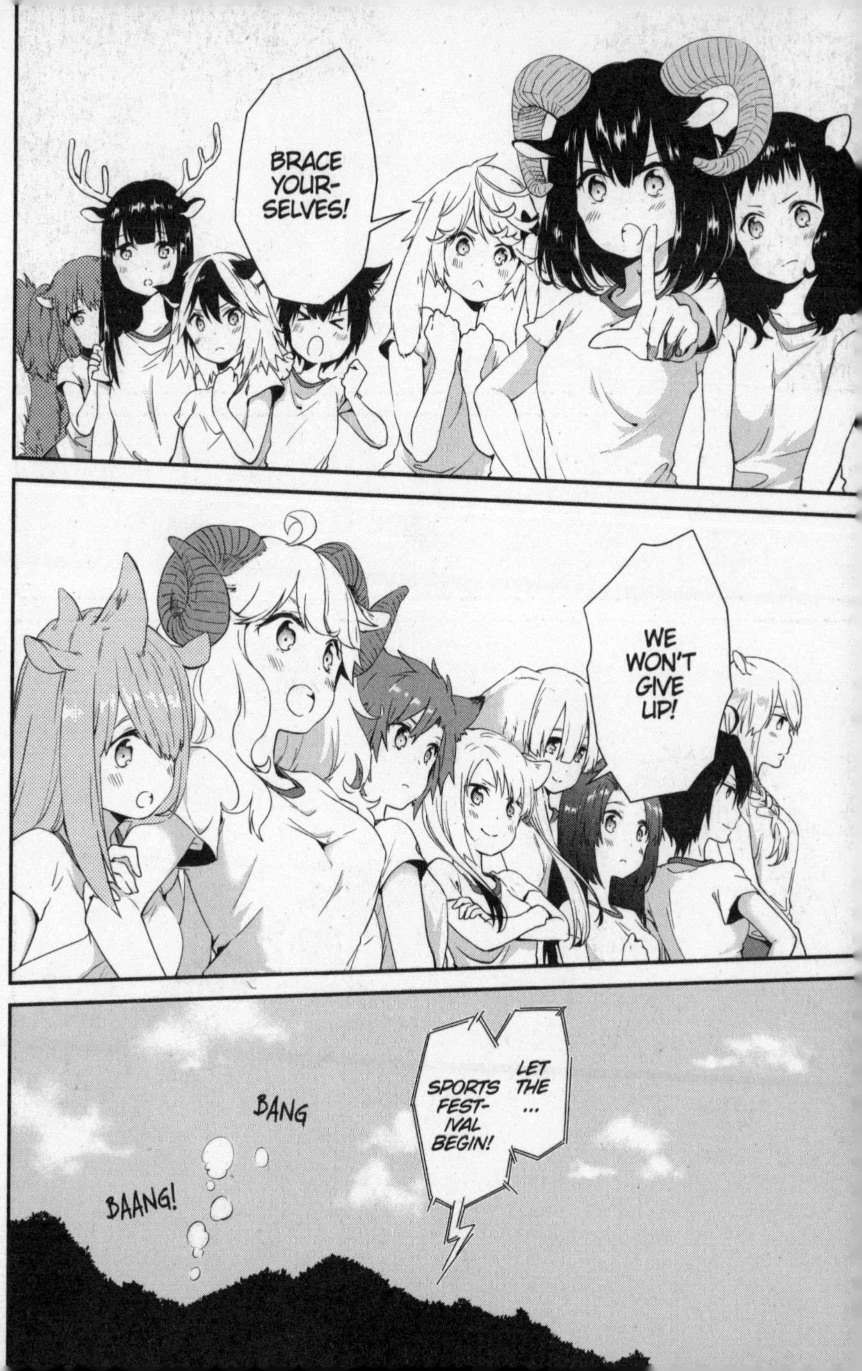
BRACE YOUR-SELVES!
WE WON'T GIVE UP!
LET THE...
SPORTS FEST-IVAL BEGIN!
BANG
BAANG!

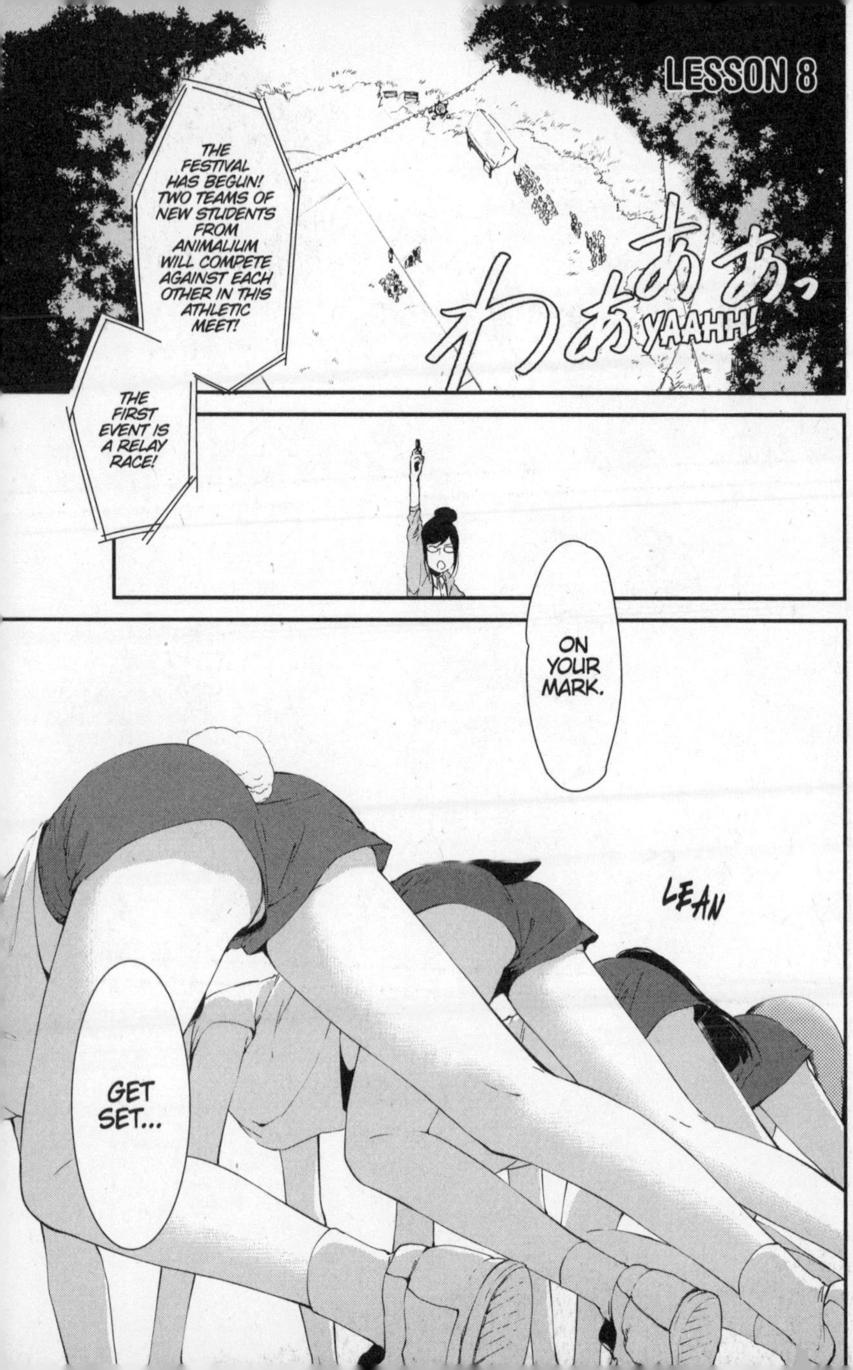
LESSON 8
わあああっ
YAAHH!
THE FESTIVAL HAS BEGUN! TWO TEAMS OF NEW STUDENTS FROM ANIMALIUM WILL COMPETE AGAINST EACH OTHER IN THIS ATHLETIC MEET!
THE FIRST EVENT IS A RELAY RACE!
ON YOUR MARK.
LEAN
GET SET...

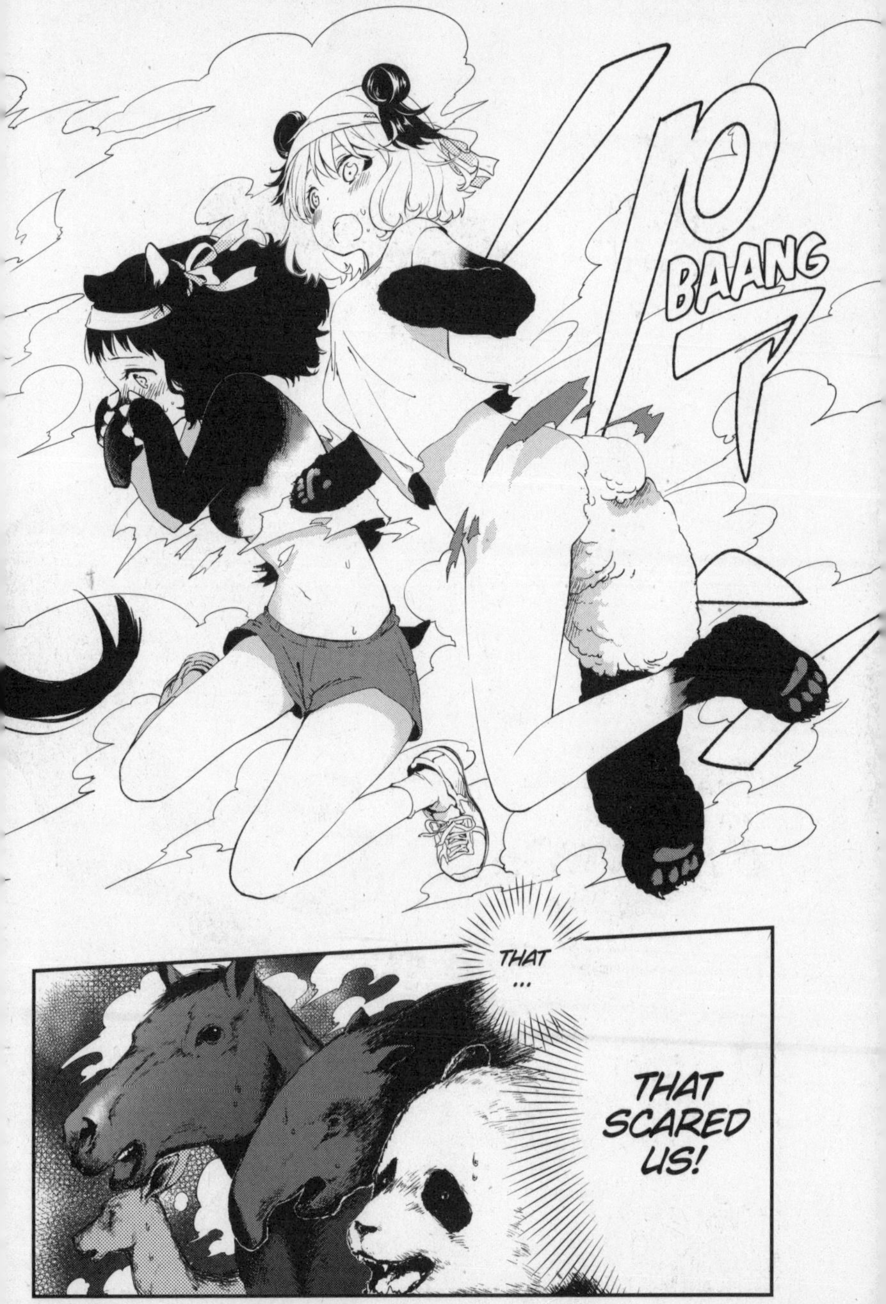
BAANG
THAT ...
THAT SCARED US!

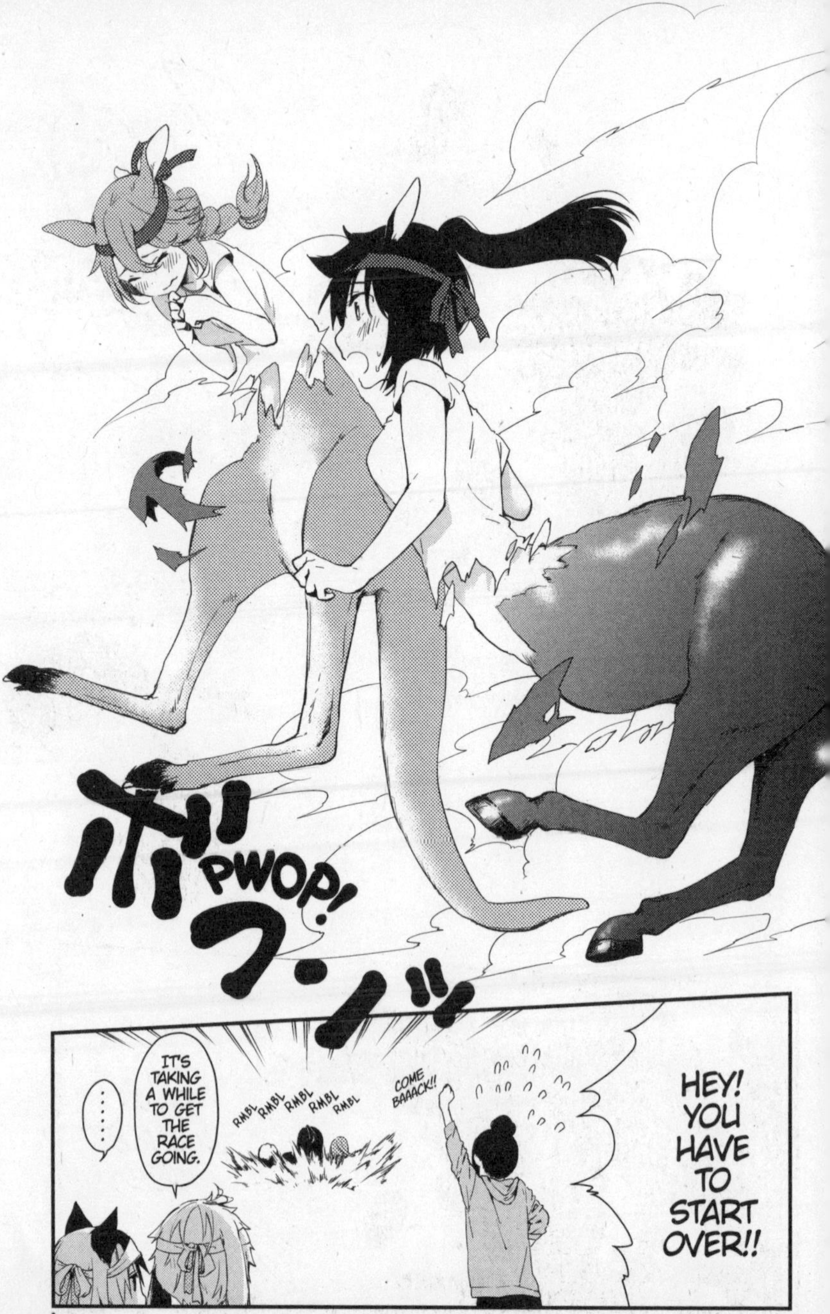
PWOP!
HEY! YOU HAVE TO START OVER!!
COME BAAACK!!
RMBL RMBL RMBL RMBL RMBL
IT'S TAKING A WHILE TO GET THE RACE GOING.
......

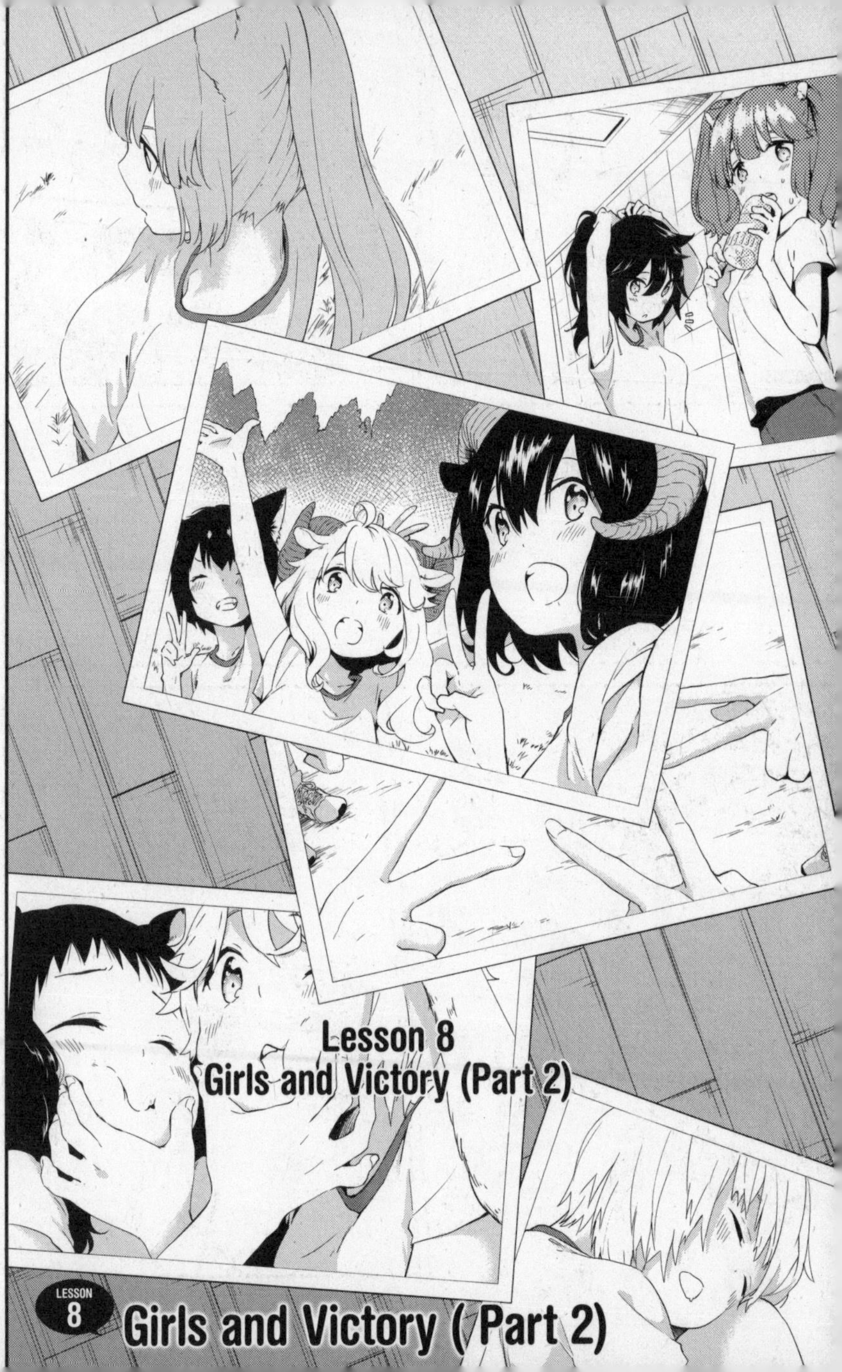
Lesson 8
Girls and Victory (Part 2)
LESSON 8
Girls and Victory (Part 2)

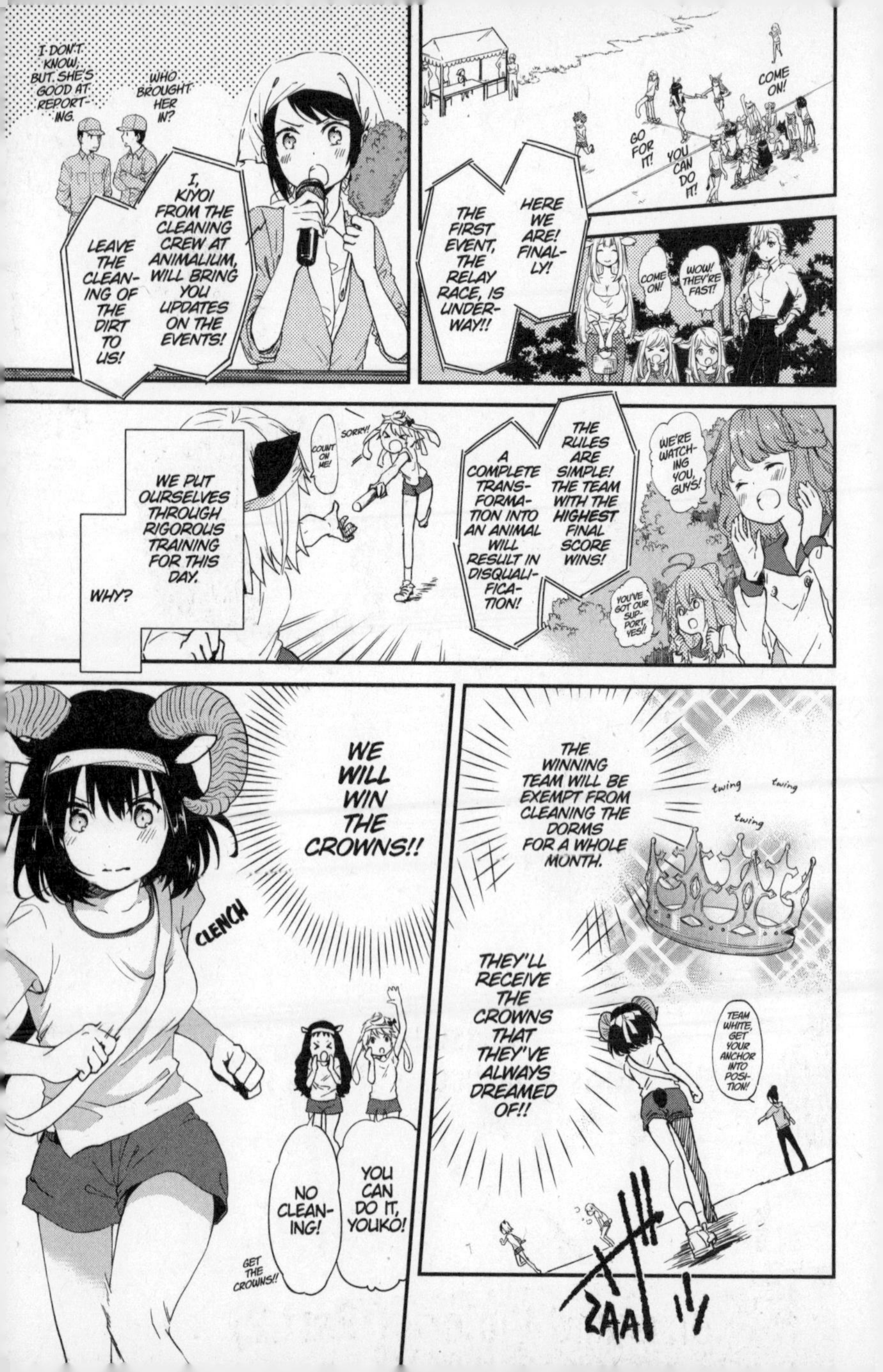
COME ON!
GO FOR IT!
YOU CAN DO IT!
HERE WE ARE! FINALLY!
THE FIRST EVENT, THE RELAY RACE, IS UNDERWAY!!
WOW! THEY'RE FAST!
COME ON!
I, KIYOI FROM THE CLEANING CREW AT ANIMALIUM, WILL BRING YOU UPDATES ON THE EVENTS!
LEAVE THE CLEANING OF THE DIRT TO US!
WHO BROUGHT HER IN?
I DON'T KNOW, BUT SHE'S GOOD AT REPORTING.
THE RULES ARE SIMPLE! THE TEAM WITH THE HIGHEST FINAL SCORE WINS!
WE'RE WATCHING YOU, GUYS!
A COMPLETE TRANSFORMATION INTO AN ANIMAL WILL RESULT IN DISQUALIFICATION!
YOU'VE GOT OUR SUPPORT, YES!!
SORRY!!
COUNT ON ME!
WE PUT OURSELVES THROUGH RIGOROUS TRAINING FOR THIS DAY.
WHY?
THE WINNING TEAM WILL BE EXEMPT FROM CLEANING THE DORMS FOR A WHOLE MONTH.
twing
twing
twing
THEY'LL RECEIVE THE CROWNS THAT THEY'VE ALWAYS DREAMED OF!!
TEAM WHITE, GET YOUR ANCHOR INTO POSITION!
ZAA
WE WILL WIN THE CROWNS!!
CLENCH
YOU CAN DO IT, YOUKO!
NO CLEANING!
GET THE CROWNS!!

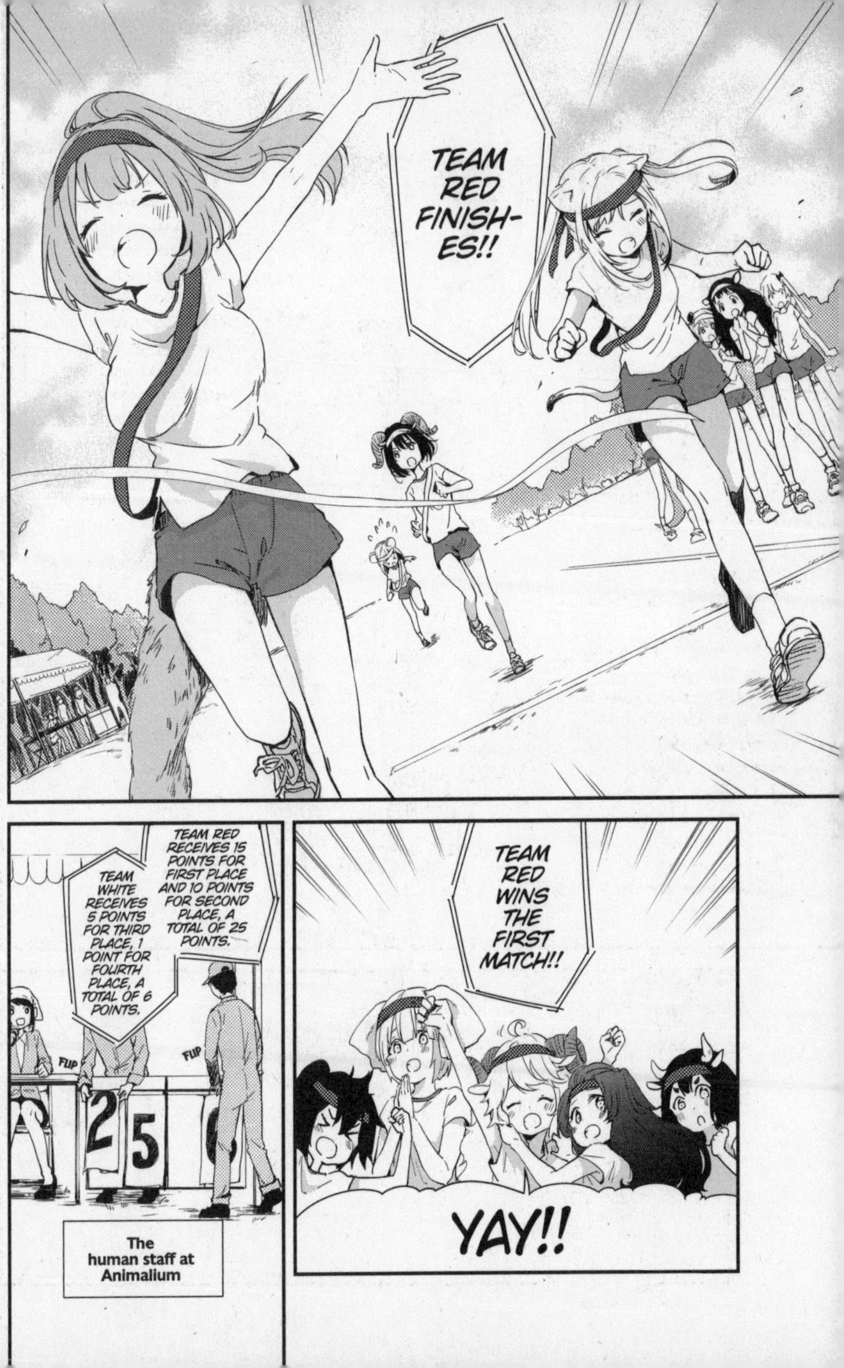
TEAM RED FINISHES!!
TEAM RED WINS THE FIRST MATCH!!
YAY!!
TEAM RED RECEIVES 15 POINTS FOR FIRST PLACE AND 10 POINTS FOR SECOND PLACE, A TOTAL OF 25 POINTS.
TEAM WHITE RECEIVES 5 POINTS FOR THIRD PLACE, 1 POINT FOR FOURTH PLACE, A TOTAL OF 6 POINTS.
FLIP
FLIP
25
The human staff at Animalium

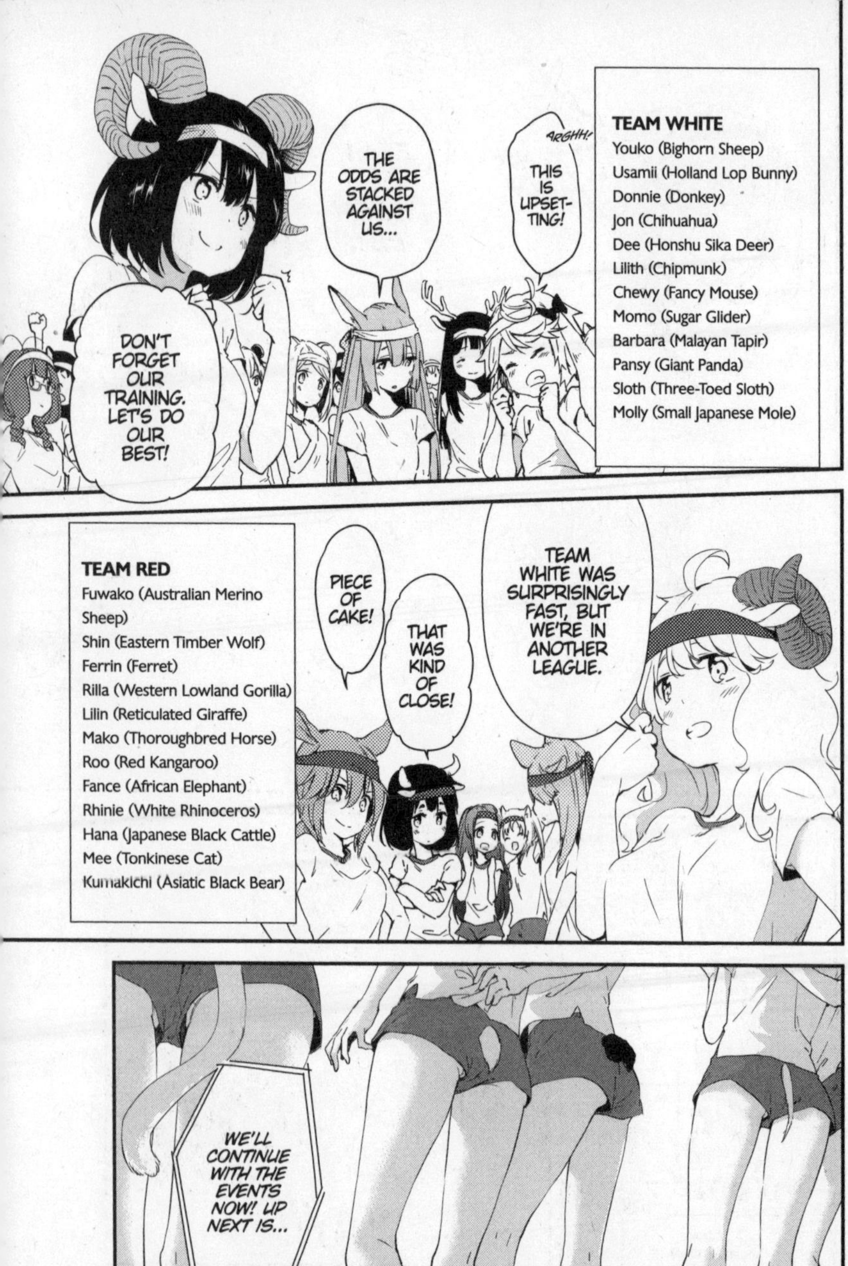
TEAM WHITE
Youko (Bighorn Sheep)
Usamii (Holland Lop Bunny)
Donnie (Donkey)
Jon (Chihuahua)
Dee (Honshu Sika Deer)
Lilith (Chipmunk)
Chewy (Fancy Mouse)
Momo (Sugar Glider)
Barbara (Malayan Tapir)
Pansy (Giant Panda)
Sloth (Three-Toed Sloth)
Molly (Small Japanese Mole)
ARGHH! THIS IS UPSET-TING!
THE ODDS ARE STACKED AGAINST US...
DON'T FORGET OUR TRAINING. LET'S DO OUR BEST!
TEAM WHITE WAS SURPRISINGLY FAST, BUT WE'RE IN ANOTHER LEAGUE.
PIECE OF CAKE!
THAT WAS KIND OF CLOSE!
TEAM RED
Fuwako (Australian Merino Sheep)
Shin (Eastern Timber Wolf)
Ferrin (Ferret)
Rilla (Western Lowland Gorilla)
Lilin (Reticulated Giraffe)
Mako (Thoroughbred Horse)
Roo (Red Kangaroo)
Fance (African Elephant)
Rhinie (White Rhinoceros)
Hana (Japanese Black Cattle)
Mee (Tonkinese Cat)
Kumakichi (Asiatic Black Bear)
WE'LL CONTINUE WITH THE EVENTS NOW! UP NEXT IS...

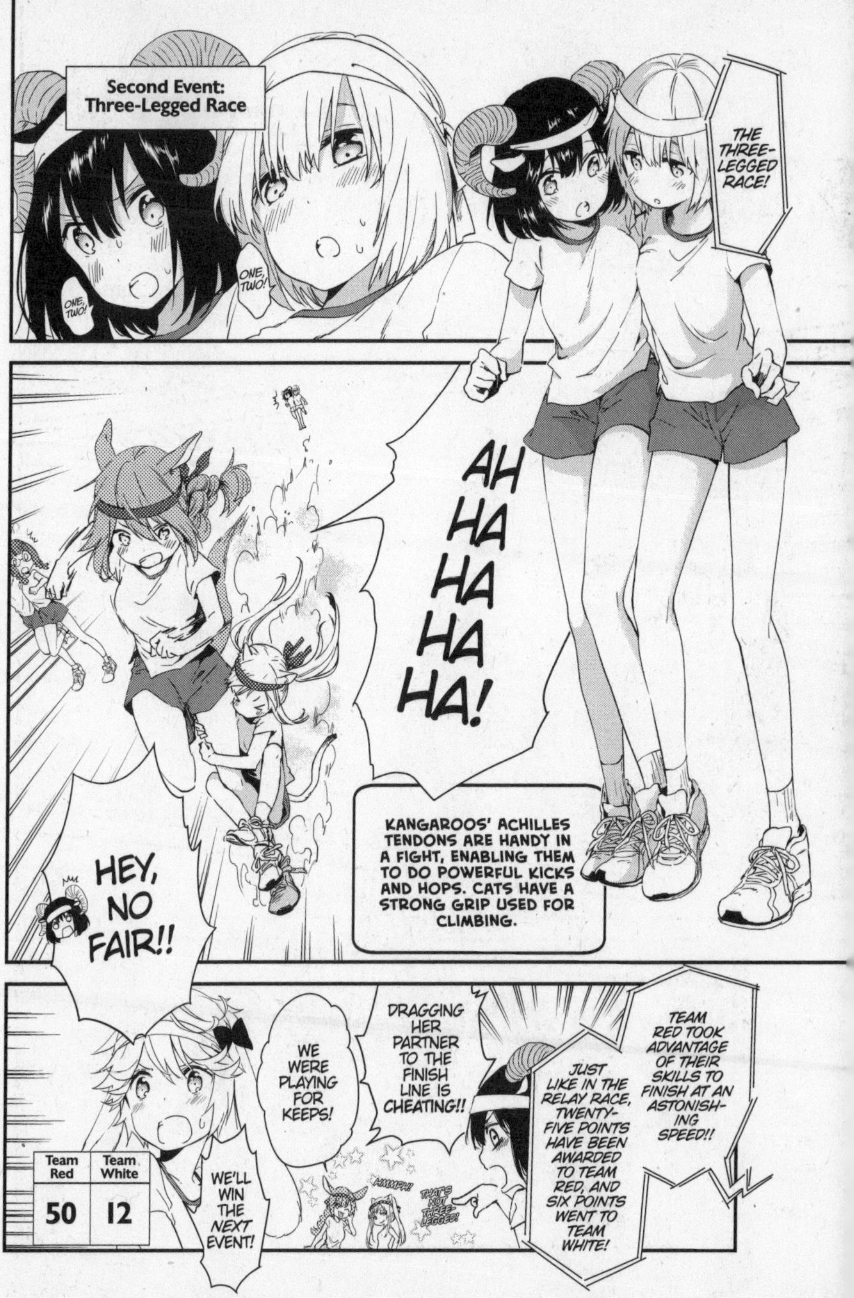
THE THREE-LEGGED RACE!
Second Event: Three-Legged Race
ONE, TWO!
ONE, TWO!
AH HA HA HA HA!
KANGAROOS' ACHILLES TENDONS ARE HANDY IN A FIGHT, ENABLING THEM TO DO POWERFUL KICKS AND HOPS. CATS HAVE A STRONG GRIP USED FOR CLIMBING.
HEY, NO FAIR!!
TEAM RED TOOK ADVANTAGE OF THEIR SKILLS TO FINISH AT AN ASTONISHING SPEED!!
JUST LIKE IN THE RELAY RACE, TWENTY-FIVE POINTS HAVE BEEN AWARDED TO TEAM RED, AND SIX POINTS WENT TO TEAM WHITE!
DRAGGING HER PARTNER TO THE FINISH LINE IS CHEATING!!
WE WERE PLAYING FOR KEEPS!
THAT'S NOT THREE-LEGGED!
HMMPH!
WE'LL WIN THE NEXT EVENT!
Team Red 50
Team White 12

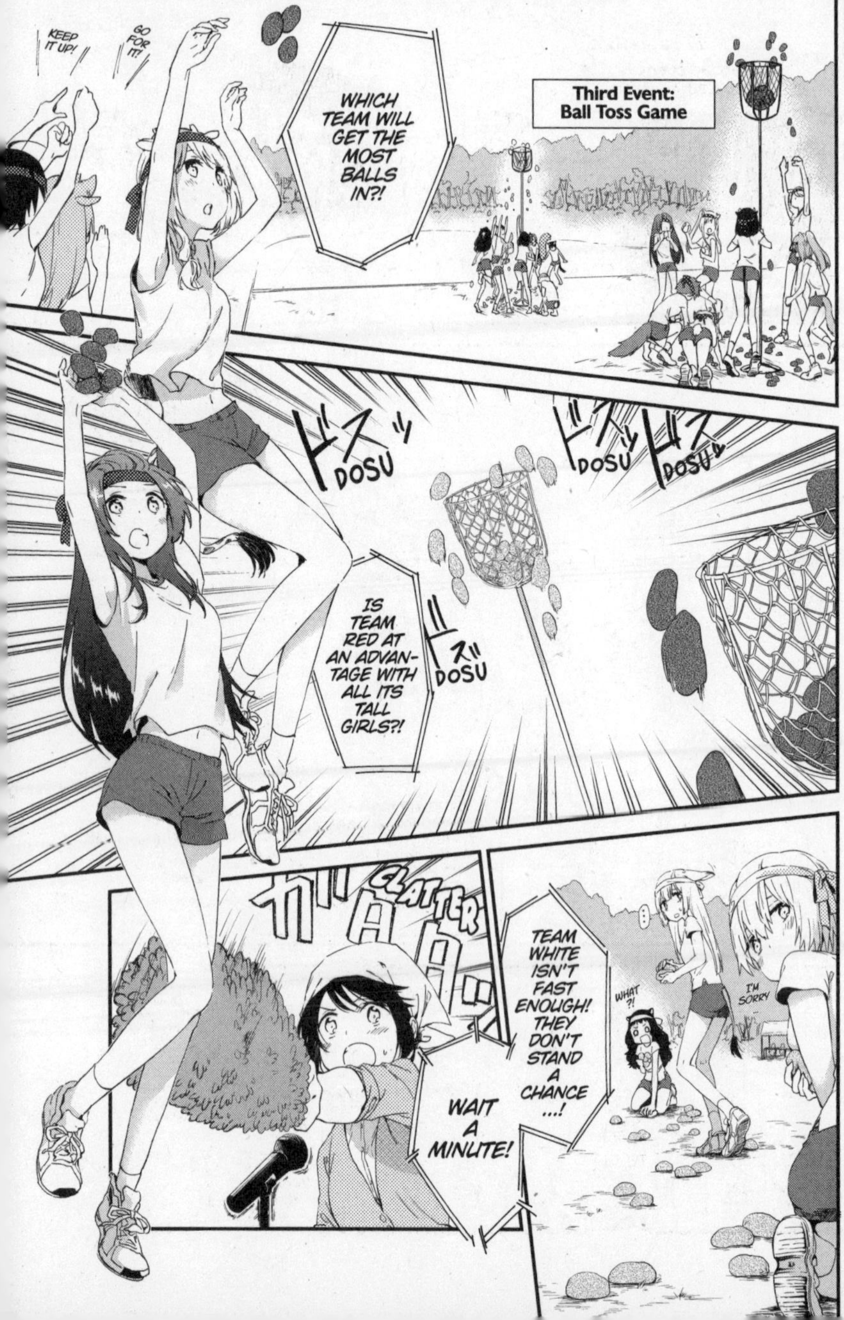
Third Event: Ball Toss Game
WHICH TEAM WILL GET THE MOST BALLS IN?!
GO FOR IT!
KEEP IT UP!
DOSU DOSU
DOSU
IS TEAM RED AT AN ADVANTAGE WITH ALL ITS TALL GIRLS?!
DOSU
I'M SORRY...
...
WHAT?!
TEAM WHITE ISN'T FAST ENOUGH! THEY DON'T STAND A CHANCE...!
WAIT A MINUTE!
CLATTER

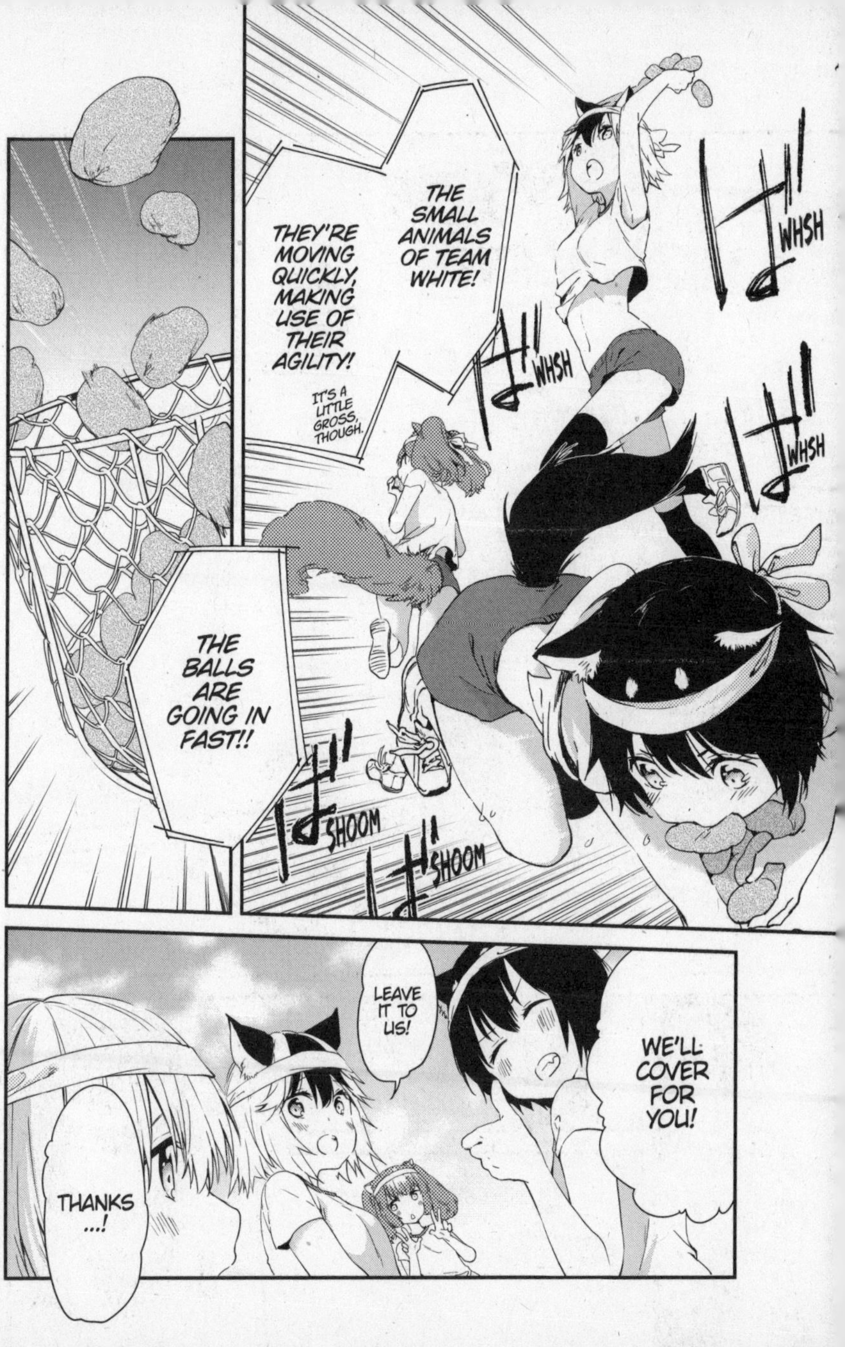
THE SMALL ANIMALS OF TEAM WHITE!
THEY'RE MOVING QUICKLY, MAKING USE OF THEIR AGILITY!
IT'S A LITTLE GROSS, THOUGH.
WHSH
WHSH
WHSH
SHOOM
SHOOM
THE BALLS ARE GOING IN FAST!!
LEAVE IT TO US!
WE'LL COVER FOR YOU!
THANKS ...!

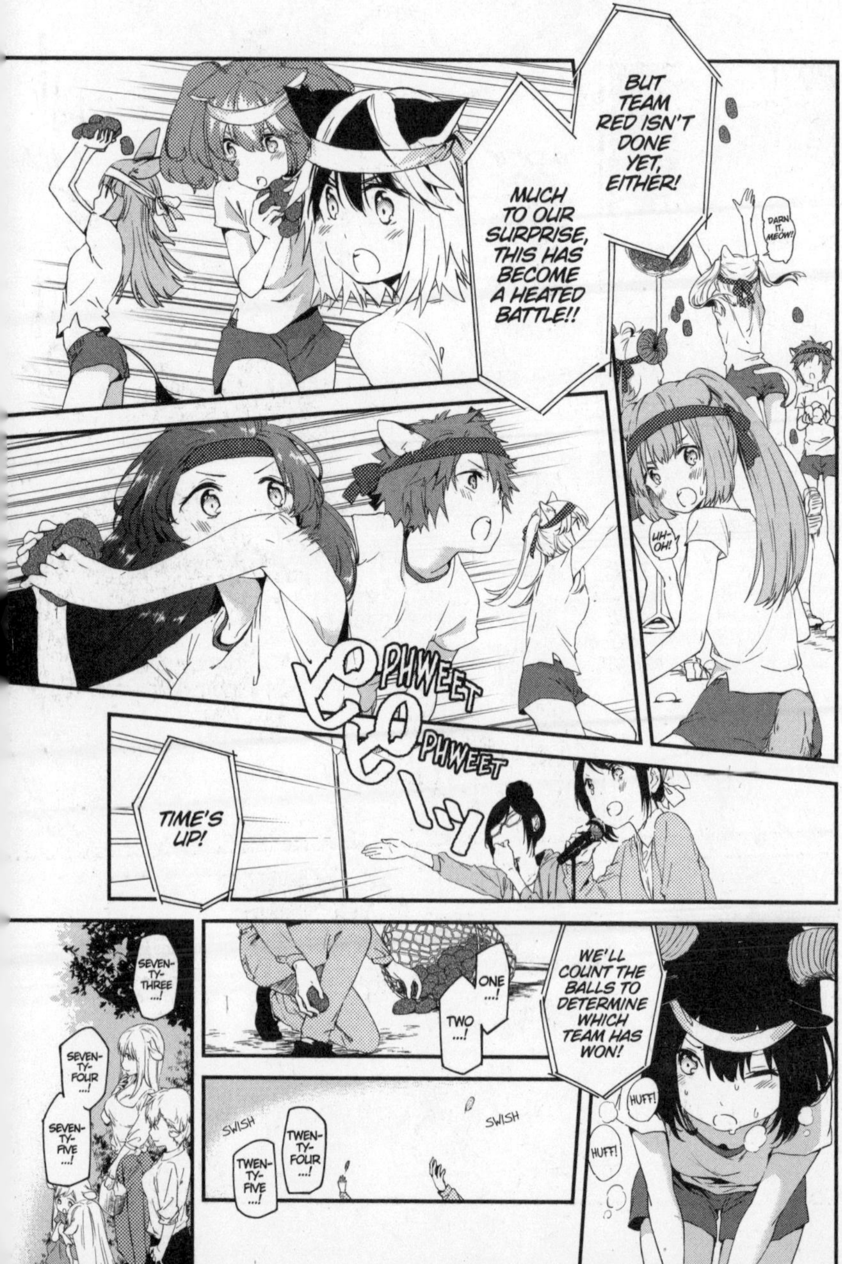
BUT TEAM RED ISN'T DONE YET, EITHER!
MUCH TO OUR SURPRISE, THIS HAS BECOME A HEATED BATTLE!!
DARN IT, MEOW!
UH-OH!
PHWEET
PHWEET
TIME'S UP!
WE'LL COUNT THE BALLS TO DETERMINE WHICH TEAM HAS WON!
HUFF!
HUFF!
ONE ...!
TWO ...!
SWISH
SWISH
TWENTY-FOUR ...!
TWENTY-FIVE ...!
SEVENTY-THREE ...!
SEVENTY-FOUR ...!
SEVENTY-FIVE ...!

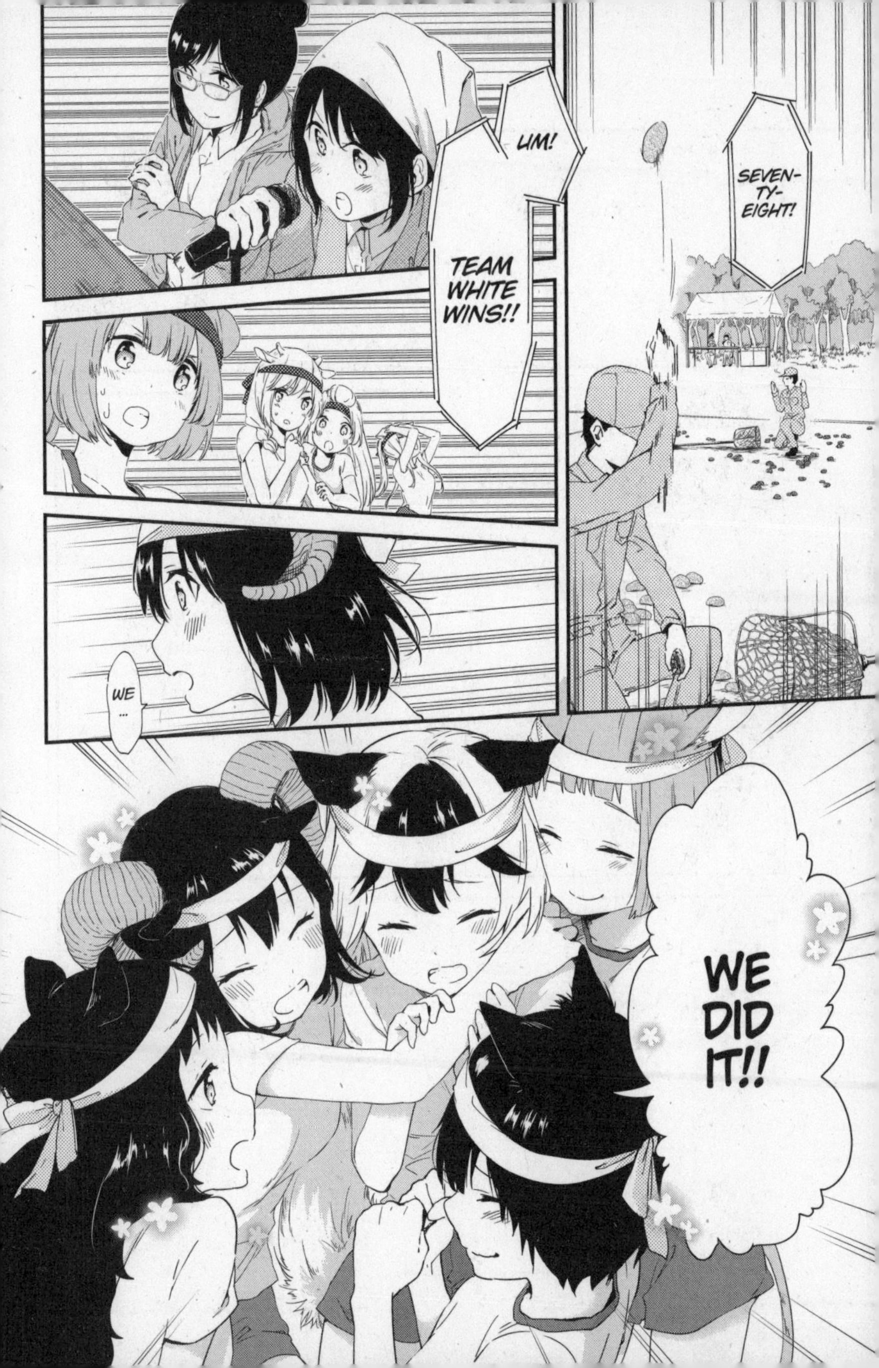
SEVENTY-EIGHT!
UM!
TEAM WHITE WINS!!
WE ...
WE DID IT!!

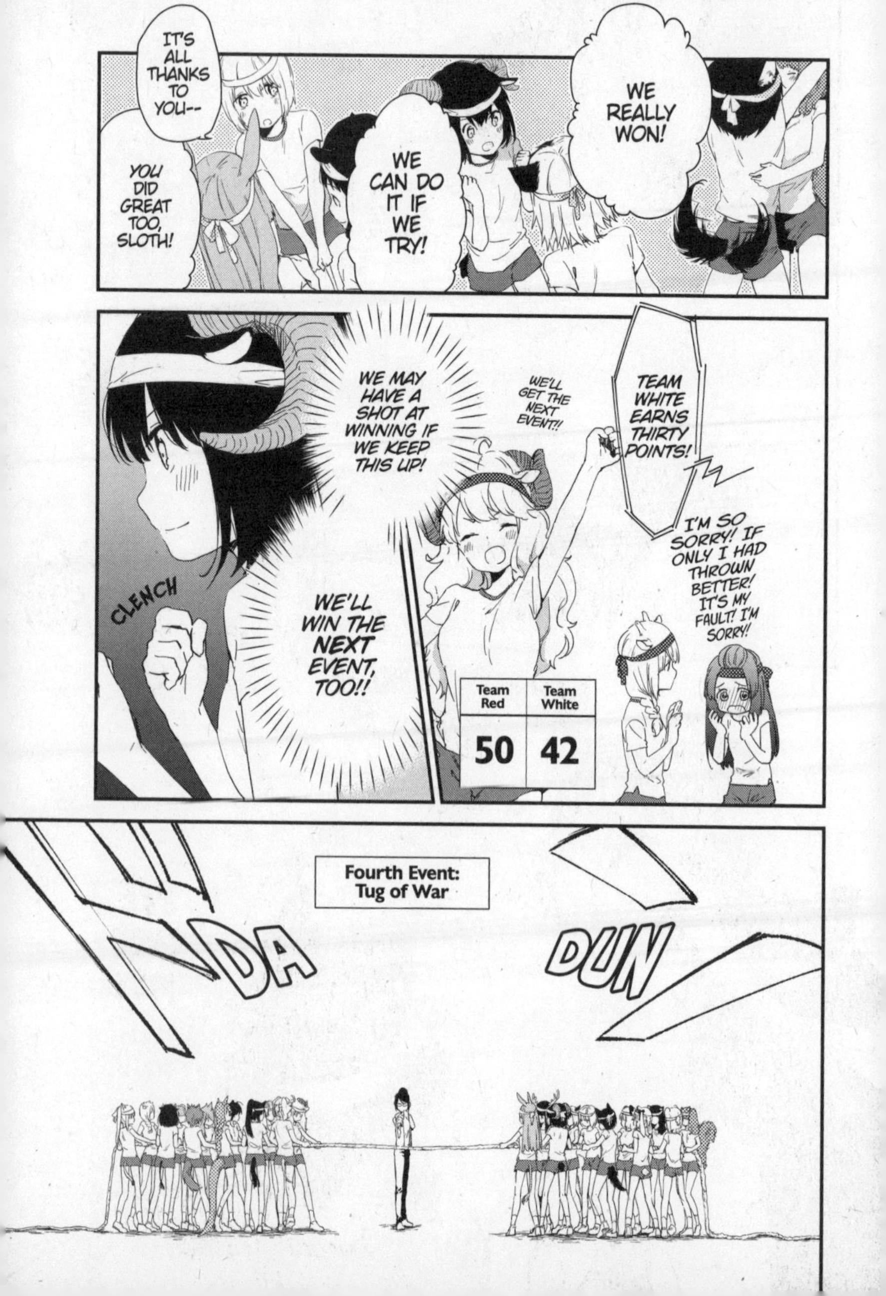
WE REALLY WON!
WE CAN DO IT IF WE TRY!
IT'S ALL THANKS TO YOU--
YOU DID GREAT TOO, SLOTH!
TEAM WHITE EARNS THIRTY POINTS!
WE'LL GET THE NEXT EVENT!!
I'M SO SORRY! IF ONLY I HAD THROWN BETTER! IT'S MY FAULT! I'M SORRY!
Team Red 50
Team White 42
WE MAY HAVE A SHOT AT WINNING IF WE KEEP THIS UP!
WE'LL WIN THE NEXT EVENT, TOO!!
CLENCH
Fourth Event: Tug of War
DA
DUN

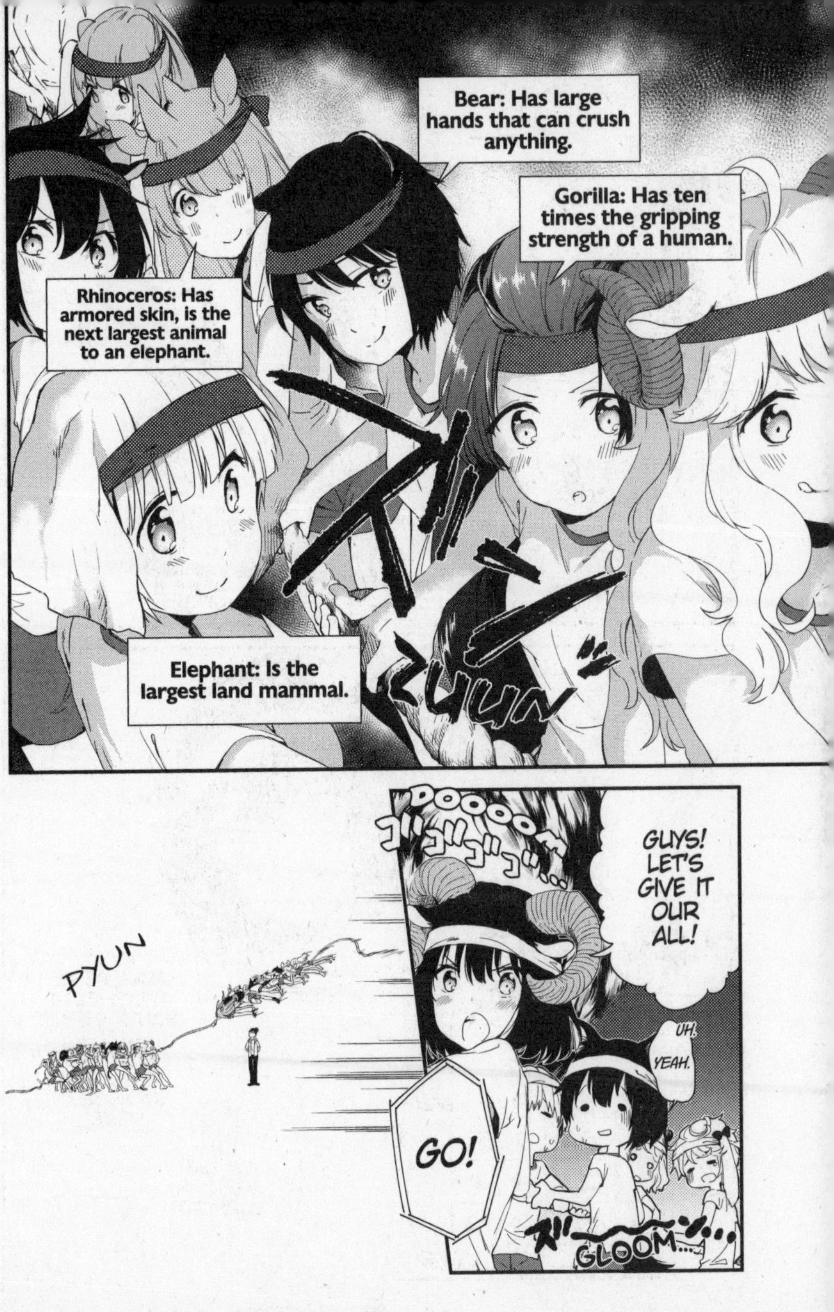
Bear: Has large hands that can crush anything.
Gorilla: Has ten times the gripping strength of a human.
Rhinoceros: Has armored skin, is the next largest animal to an elephant.
Elephant: Is the largest land mammal.
PYUUN
DOOOOOM
GUYS! LET'S GIVE IT OUR ALL!
UH.
YEAH.
GO!
GLOOM...
PYUN

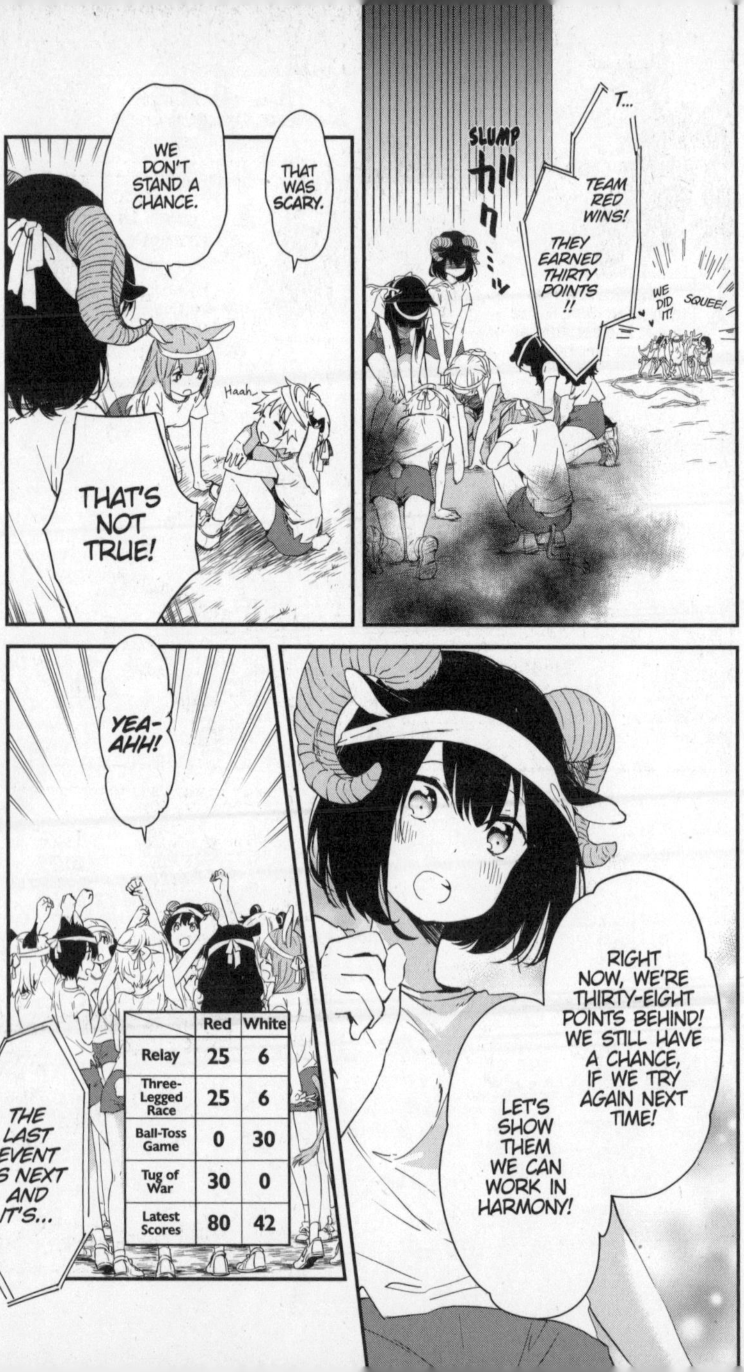
T...
TEAM RED WINS!
THEY EARNED THIRTY POINTS !!
SLUMP
WE DID IT!
SQUEE!
WE DON'T STAND A CHANCE.
THAT WAS SCARY.
Haah...
THAT'S NOT TRUE!
RIGHT NOW, WE'RE THIRTY-EIGHT POINTS BEHIND! WE STILL HAVE A CHANCE, IF WE TRY AGAIN NEXT TIME!
LET'S SHOW THEM WE CAN WORK IN HARMONY!
YEA-AHH!
THE LAST EVENT IS NEXT AND IT'S...

	Red	White
Relay	25	6
Three-Legged Race	25	6
Ball-Toss Game	0	30
Tug of War	30	0
Latest Scores	80	42

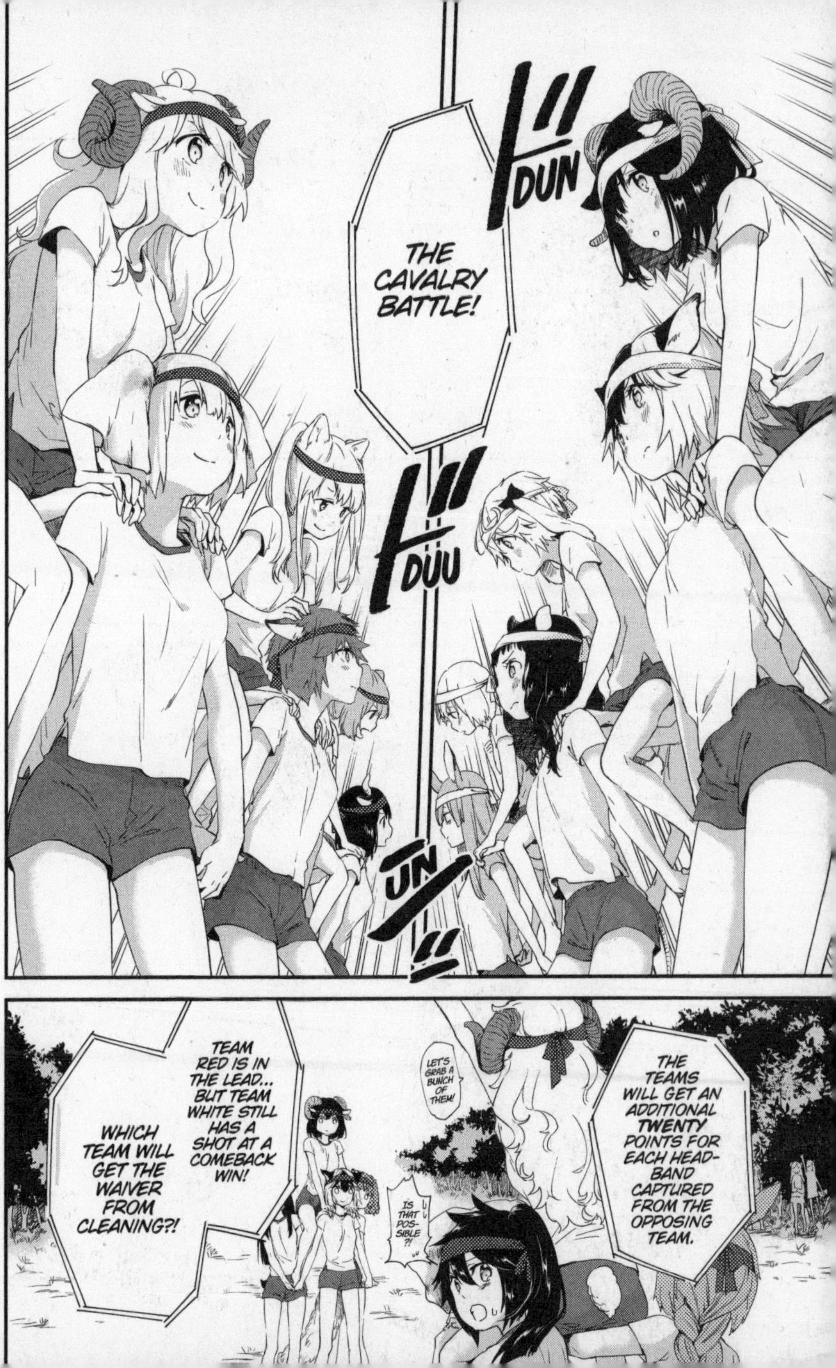
DUN
THE CAVALRY BATTLE!
DUU
UN!!
THE TEAMS WILL GET AN ADDITIONAL TWENTY POINTS FOR EACH HEAD-BAND CAPTURED FROM THE OPPOSING TEAM.
LET'S GRAB A BUNCH OF THEM!
IS THAT POS-SIBLE?!
TEAM RED IS IN THE LEAD... BUT TEAM WHITE STILL HAS A SHOT AT A COMEBACK WIN!
WHICH TEAM WILL GET THE WAIVER FROM CLEANING?!

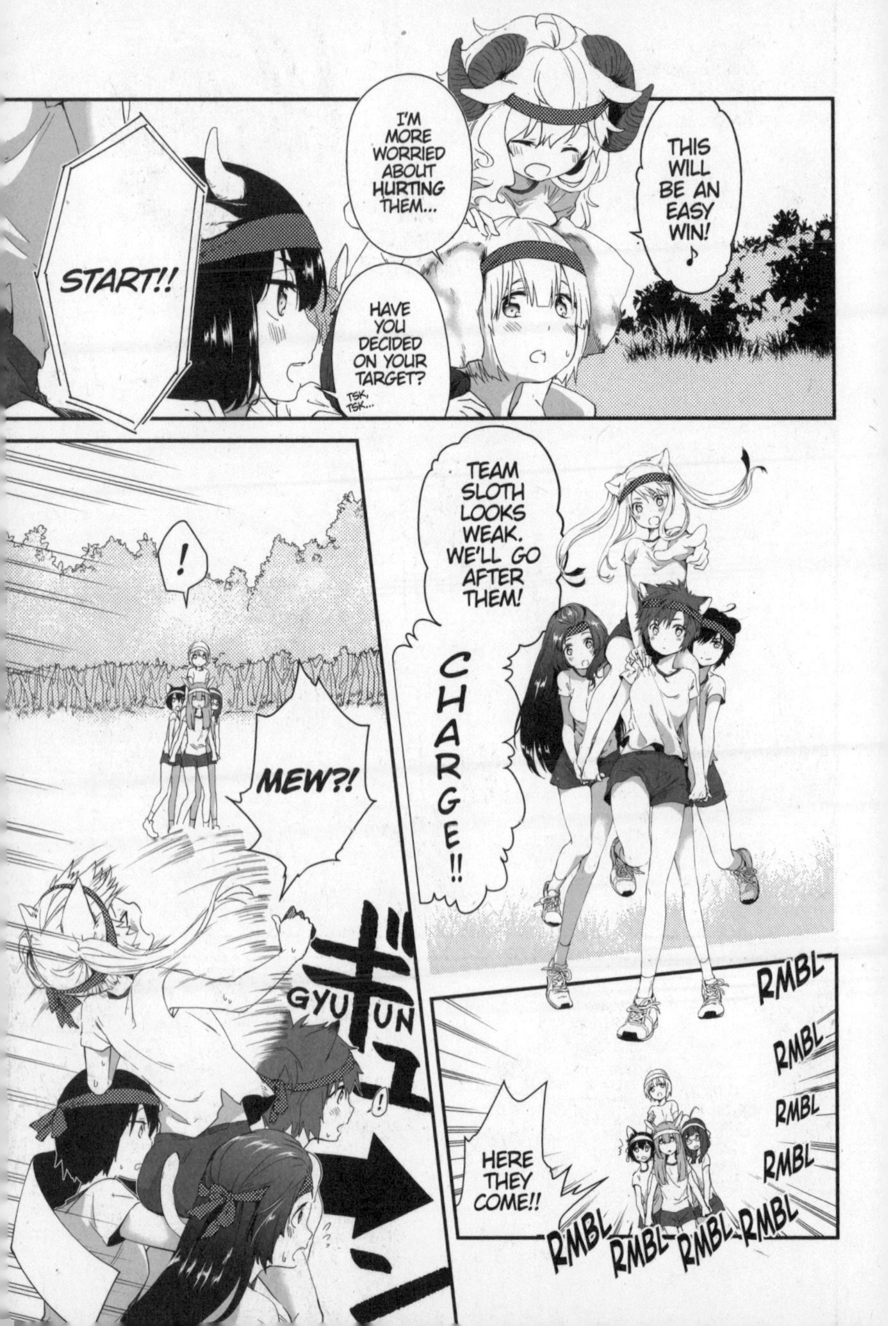
THIS WILL BE AN EASY WIN! ♪
I'M MORE WORRIED ABOUT HURTING THEM...
HAVE YOU DECIDED ON YOUR TARGET?
TSK, TSK...
START!!
TEAM SLOTH LOOKS WEAK. WE'LL GO AFTER THEM!
CHARGE!!
RMBL RMBL RMBL RMBL RMBL RMBL RMBL RMBL
HERE THEY COME!!
!
MEW?!
GYUUN
!

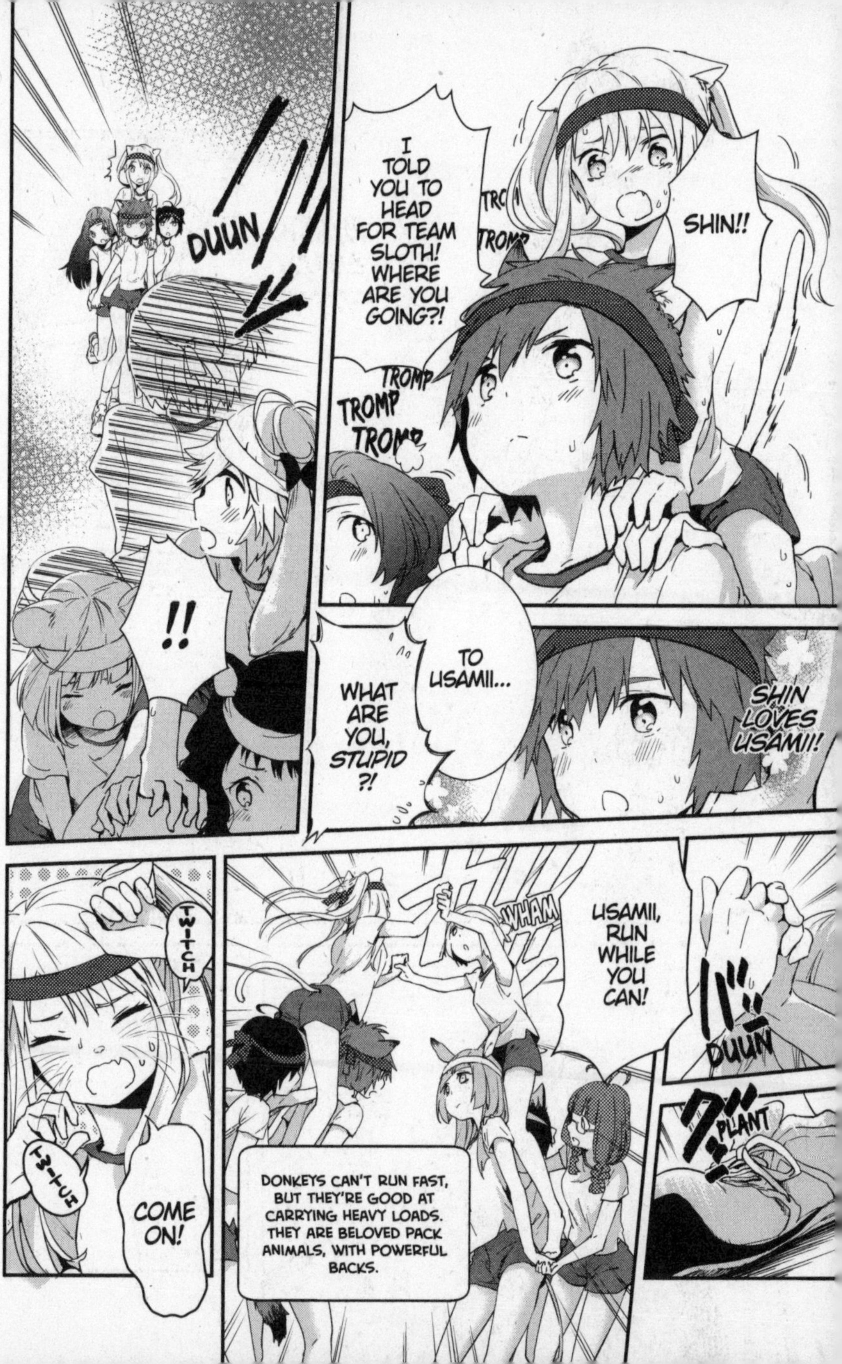
SHIN!!
I TOLD YOU TO HEAD FOR TEAM SLOTH! WHERE ARE YOU GOING?!
TROMP TROMP
TROMP TROMP TROMP
SHIN LOVES USAMII!
TO USAMII...
WHAT ARE YOU, STUPID?!
DUUN
!!
USAMII, RUN WHILE YOU CAN!
DUUN
PLANT
WHAM
DONKEYS CAN'T RUN FAST, BUT THEY'RE GOOD AT CARRYING HEAVY LOADS. THEY ARE BELOVED PACK ANIMALS, WITH POWERFUL BACKS.
TWITCH
COME ON!
TWITCH

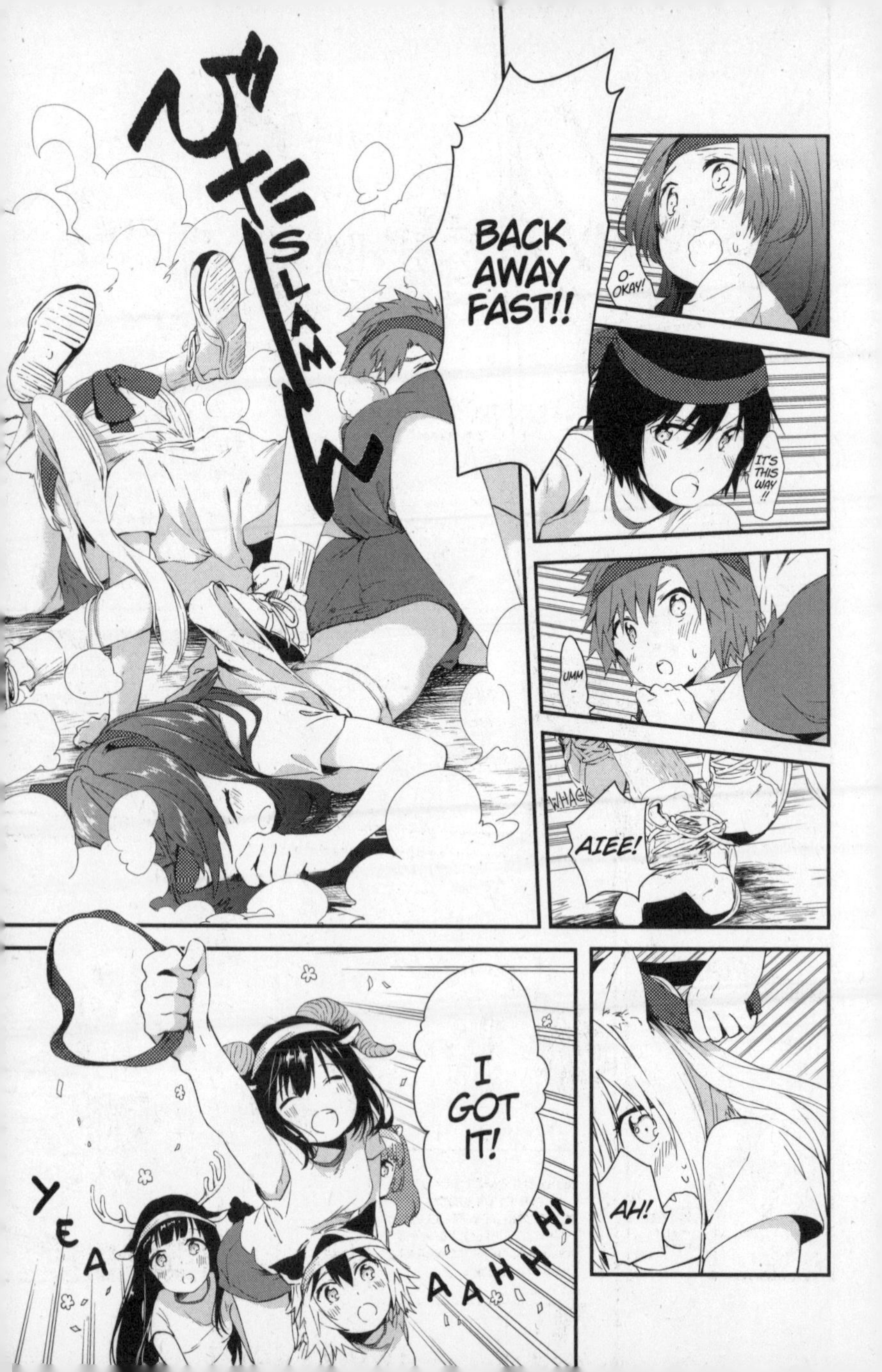
BACK AWAY FAST!!
O-OKAY!
IT'S THIS WAY!!
UMM
WHACK
AIEE!
SLAM
AH!
I GOT IT!
YEAAAHHH!

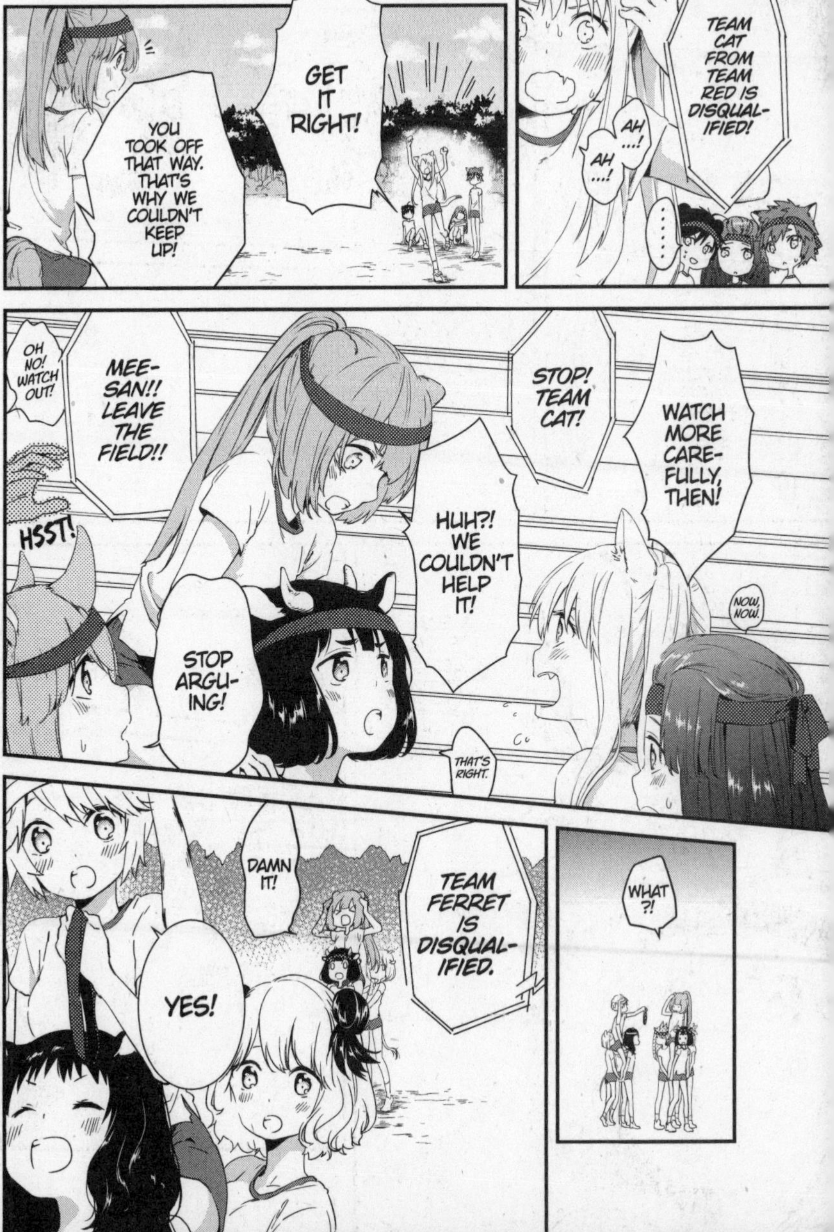
TEAM CAT FROM TEAM RED IS DISQUALIFIED!
AH ...!
AH ...!
......
HEY!
GET IT RIGHT!
YOU TOOK OFF THAT WAY. THAT'S WHY WE COULDN'T KEEP UP!
WATCH MORE CAREFULLY, THEN!
STOP! TEAM CAT!
NOW, NOW.
HUH?! WE COULDN'T HELP IT!
MEE-SAN!! LEAVE THE FIELD!!
OH NO! WATCH OUT!
HSST!
STOP ARGUING!
THAT'S RIGHT.
WHAT ?!
TEAM FERRET IS DISQUALIFIED.
DAMN IT!
YES!

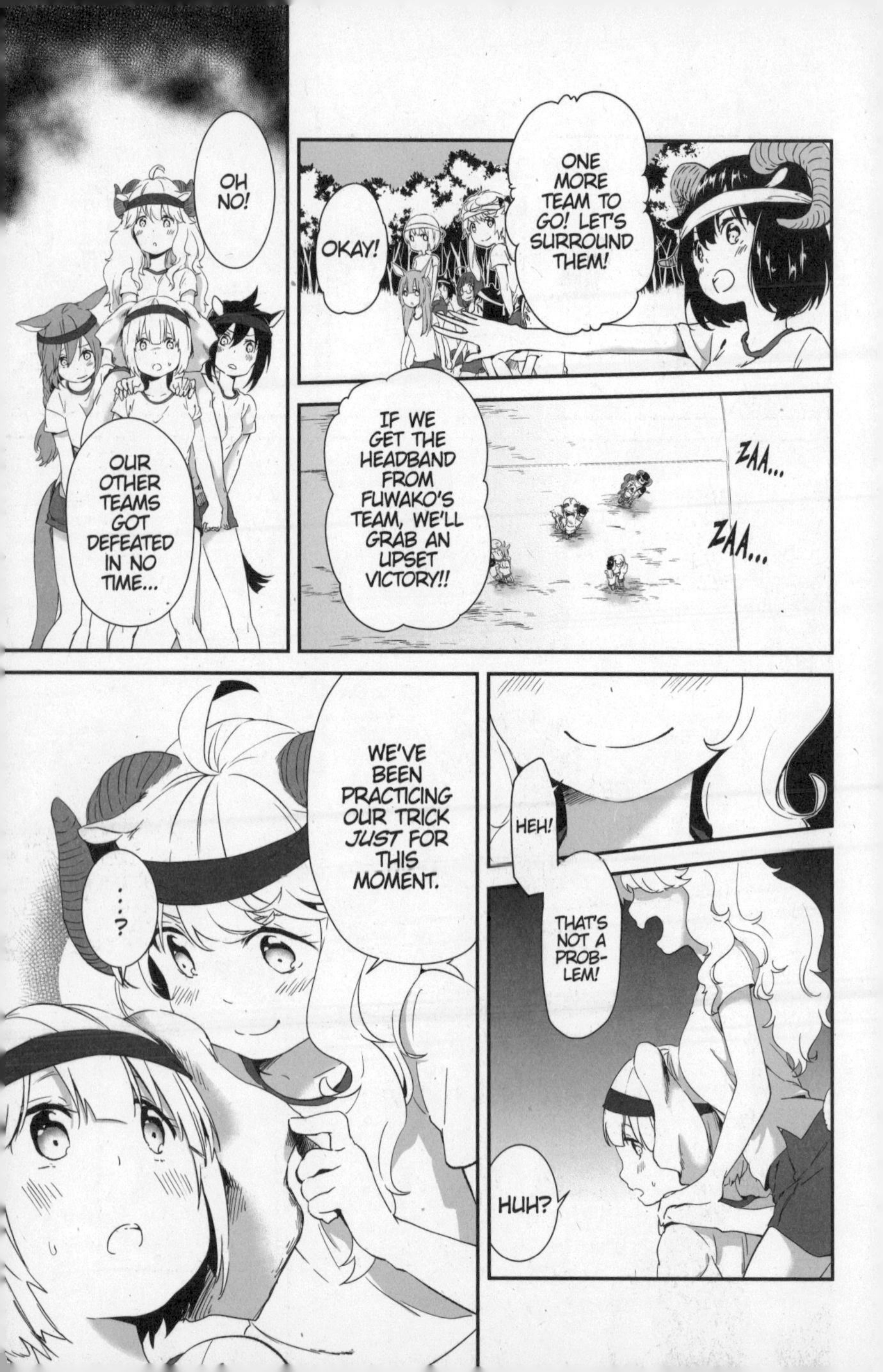
ONE MORE TEAM TO GO! LET'S SURROUND THEM!
OKAY!
ZAA...
ZAA...
IF WE GET THE HEADBAND FROM FUWAKO'S TEAM, WE'LL GRAB AN UPSET VICTORY!!
OH NO!
OUR OTHER TEAMS GOT DEFEATED IN NO TIME...
HEH!
THAT'S NOT A PROB-LEM!
HUH?
WE'VE BEEN PRACTICING OUR TRICK *JUST* FOR THIS MOMENT.
...?

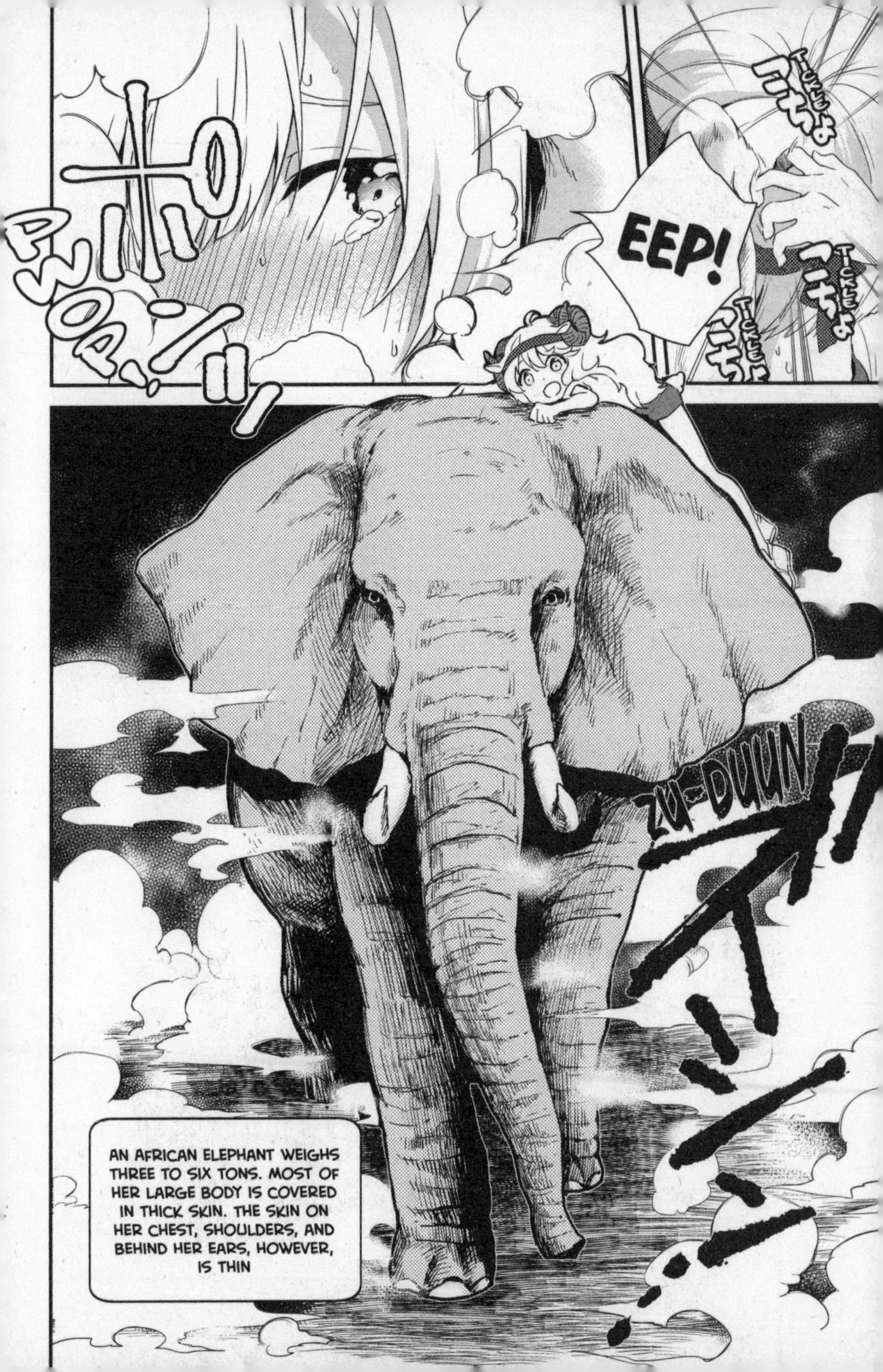
TICKLE こちょ
TICKLE こちょ
TICKLE こちょ
EEP!
ホーン!!
PWOA..!
ZU-DUUN
AN AFRICAN ELEPHANT WEIGHS THREE TO SIX TONS. MOST OF HER LARGE BODY IS COVERED IN THICK SKIN. THE SKIN ON HER CHEST, SHOULDERS, AND BEHIND HER EARS, HOWEVER, IS THIN

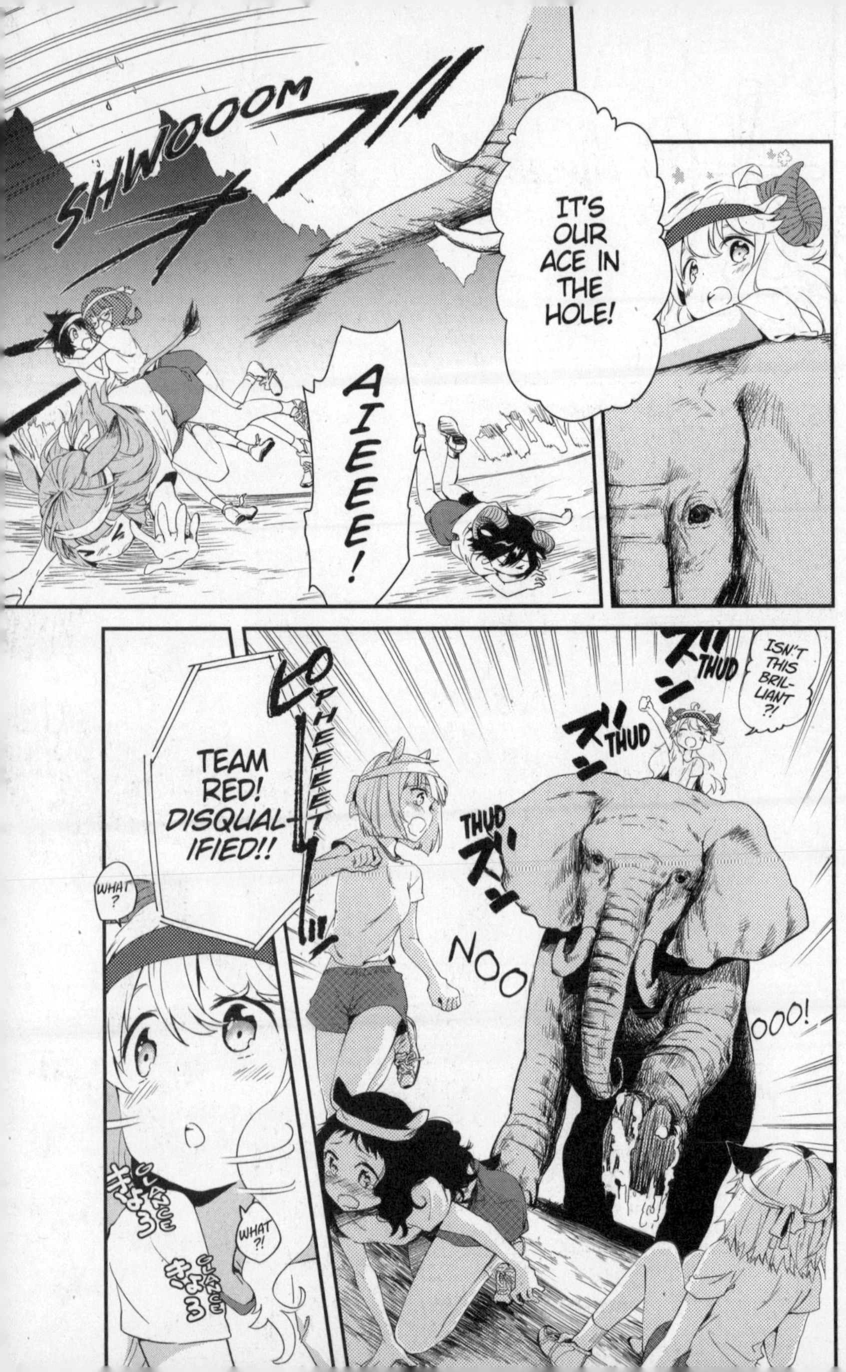
IT'S OUR ACE IN THE HOLE!
SHWOOOM
AIEEE!
THUD
ISN'T THIS BRIL-LIANT?!
THUD
THUD
NOO OOO!
PHEEEEET
TEAM RED! DISQUAL-IFIED!!
WHAT?
WHAT?!
GLANCE
GLANCE

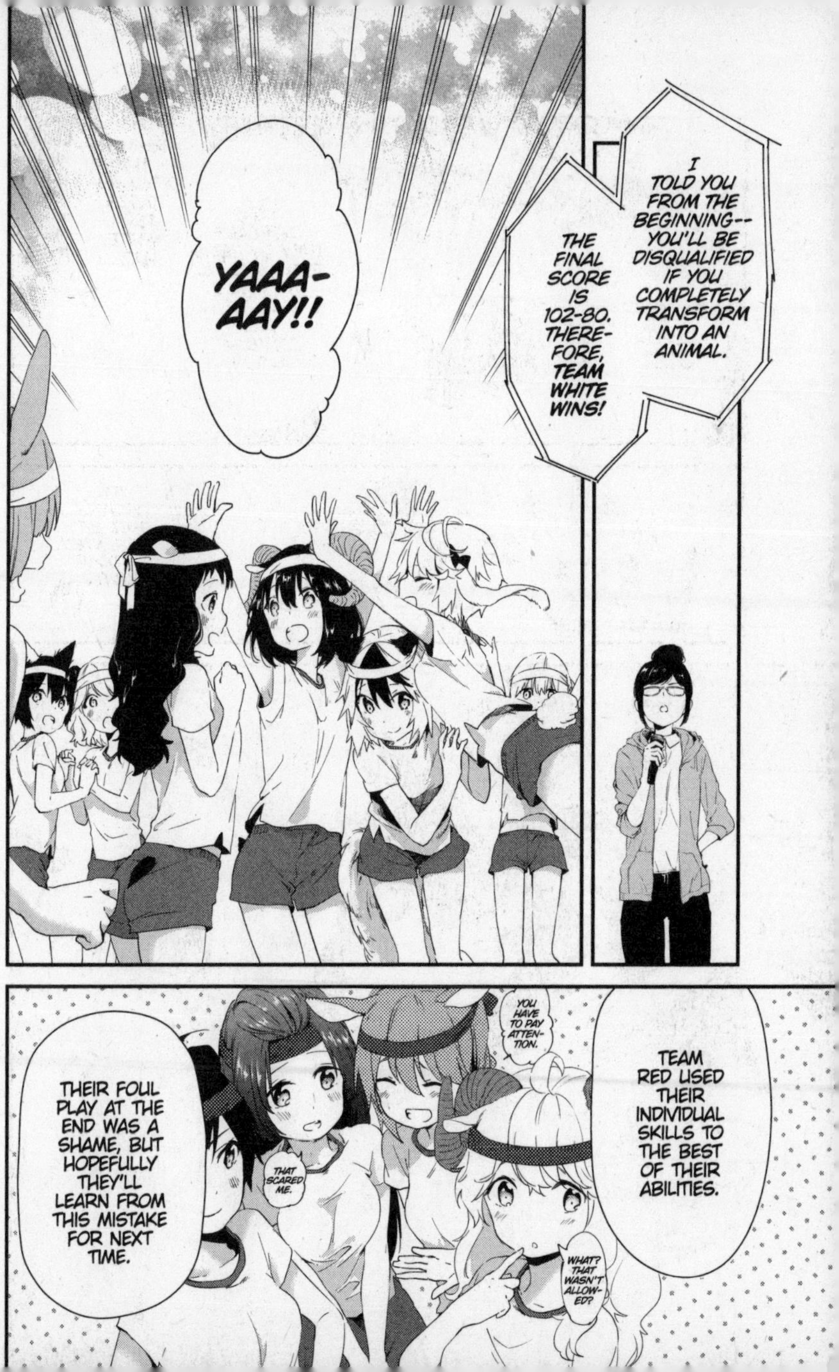
I TOLD YOU FROM THE BEGINNING-- YOU'LL BE DISQUALIFIED IF YOU COMPLETELY TRANSFORM INTO AN ANIMAL.
THE FINAL SCORE IS 102-80. THEREFORE, TEAM WHITE WINS!
YAAAAAY!!
TEAM RED USED THEIR INDIVIDUAL SKILLS TO THE BEST OF THEIR ABILITIES.
YOU HAVE TO PAY ATTENTION.
THEIR FOUL PLAY AT THE END WAS A SHAME, BUT HOPEFULLY THEY'LL LEARN FROM THIS MISTAKE FOR NEXT TIME.
THAT SCARED ME.
WHAT? THAT WASN'T ALLOWED?

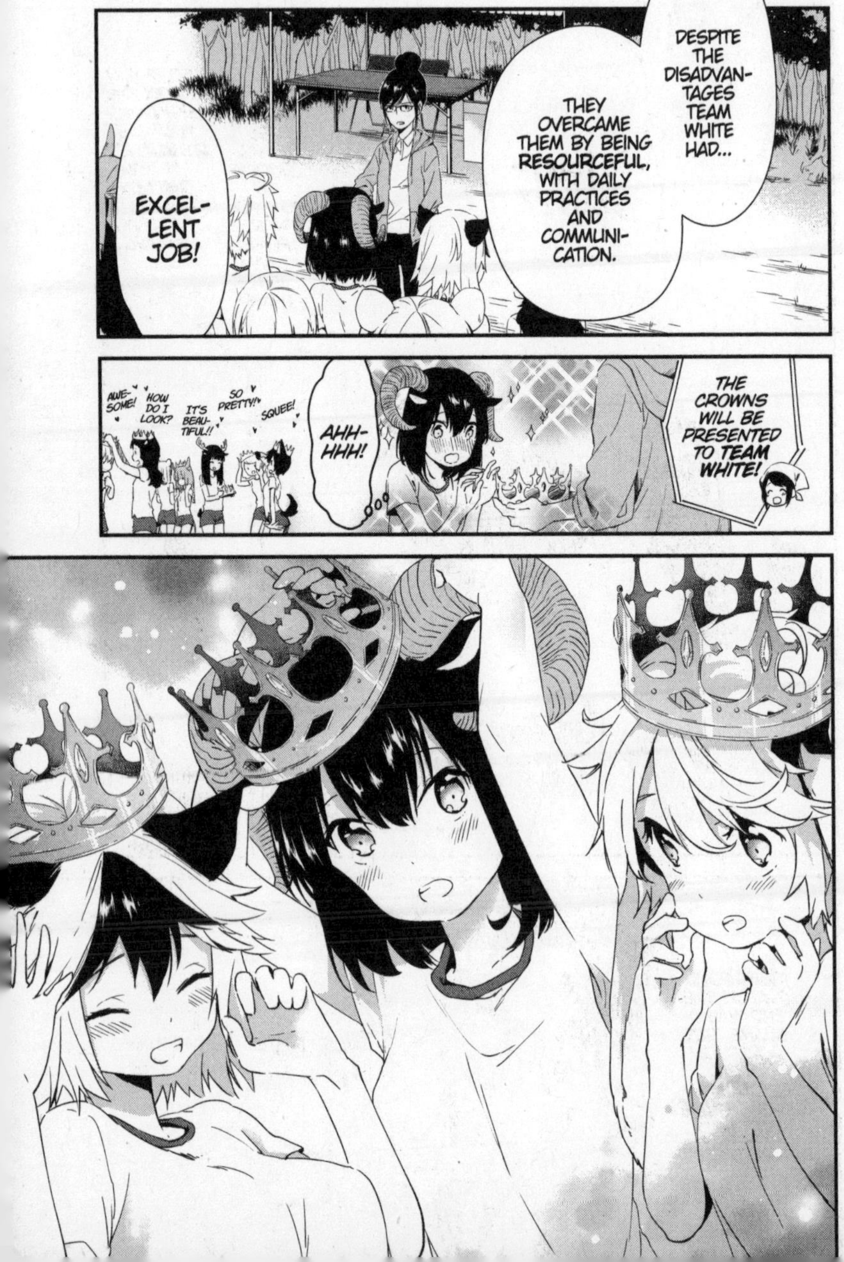
DESPITE THE DISADVANTAGES TEAM WHITE HAD...
THEY OVERCAME THEM BY BEING RESOURCEFUL, WITH DAILY PRACTICES AND COMMUNICATION.
EXCELLENT JOB!
THE CROWNS WILL BE PRESENTED TO TEAM WHITE!
AHHHHH!
SQUEE!
SO PRETTY!
IT'S BEAUTIFUL!!
HOW DO I LOOK?
AWESOME!

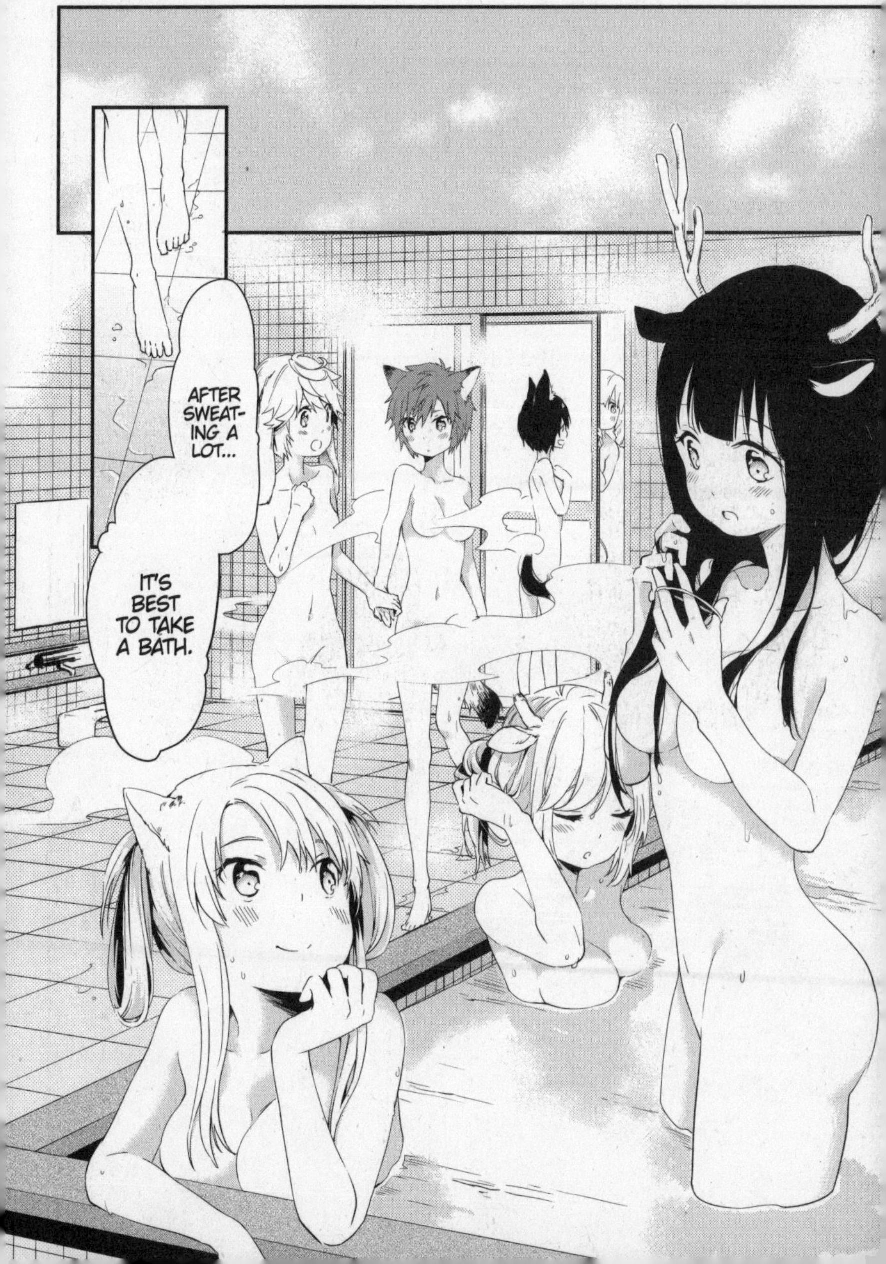
AFTER SWEAT-ING A LOT...
IT'S BEST TO TAKE A BATH.

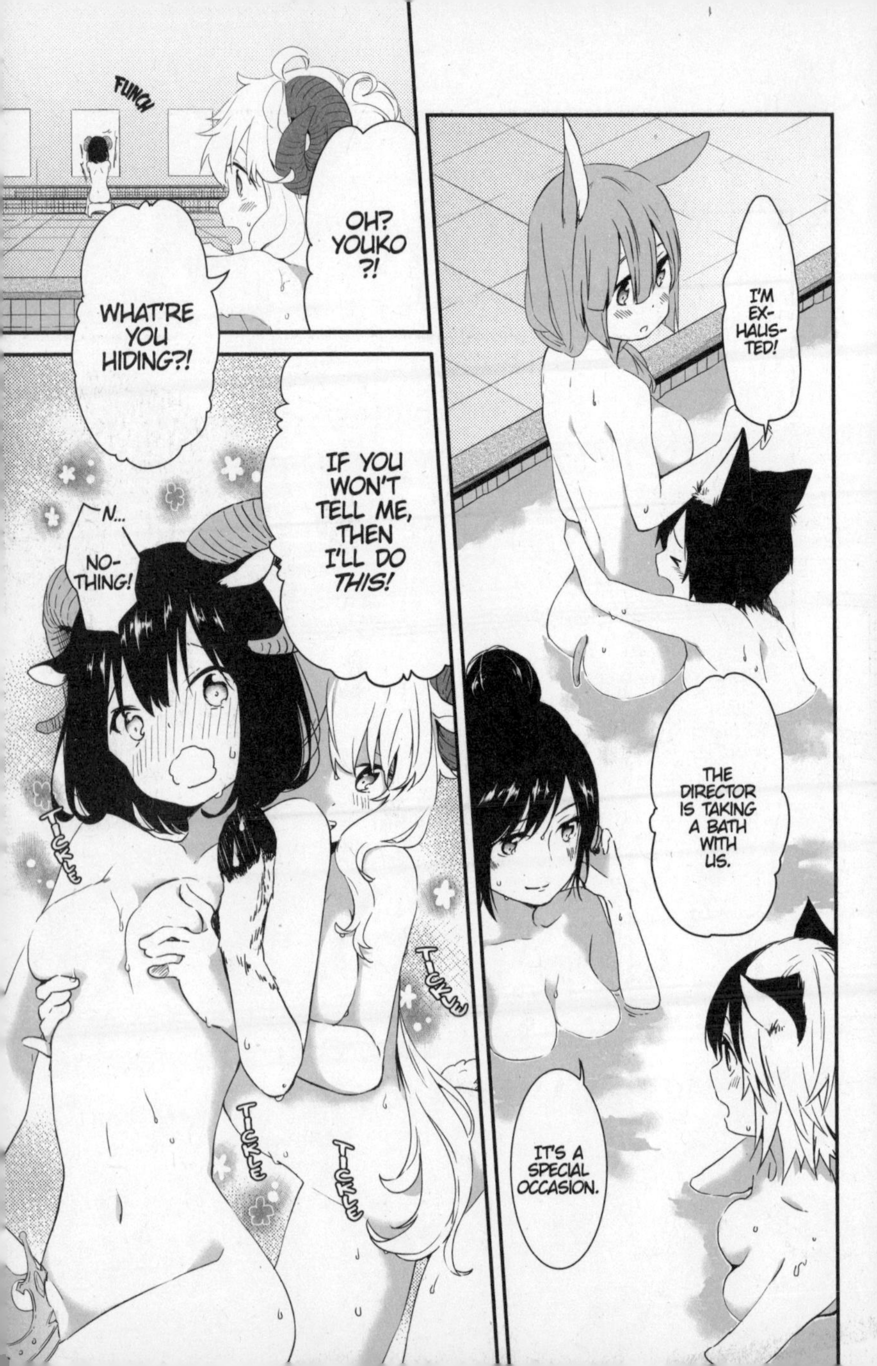
I'M EX-HAUSTED!
THE DIRECTOR IS TAKING A BATH WITH US.
IT'S A SPECIAL OCCASION.
FLINCH
OH? YOUKO?!
WHAT'RE YOU HIDING?!
IF YOU WON'T TELL ME, THEN I'LL DO *THIS!*
N...
NO-THING!
TICKLE
TICKLE
TICKLE
TICKLE

カラーン
KA-KLANG
カラーン
KA-KLANG
AH!
HM?
UM, WELL ...!
AHA HA HA HA!
YOUKO! YOU DON'T NEED TO GIVE YOUR CROWN A BATH!!
EVEN I KNOW THAT!!
YOU DON'T NEED TO REMIND ME!!
HEE HEE...
I GUESS SHE COULDN'T HELP IT...
EEEE!
THEY ALL GET ALONG EVEN AFTER COMPETING AGAINST ONE ANOTHER...
ONCE THEY GRADUATE, THESE GIRLS WILL MAKE GOOD MEDIATORS BETWEEN HUMANS AND ANIMALS.
CAN I SLEEP?
NO!
AHHH!
THE REAL PROBLEM IS THE OTHER CLASS...

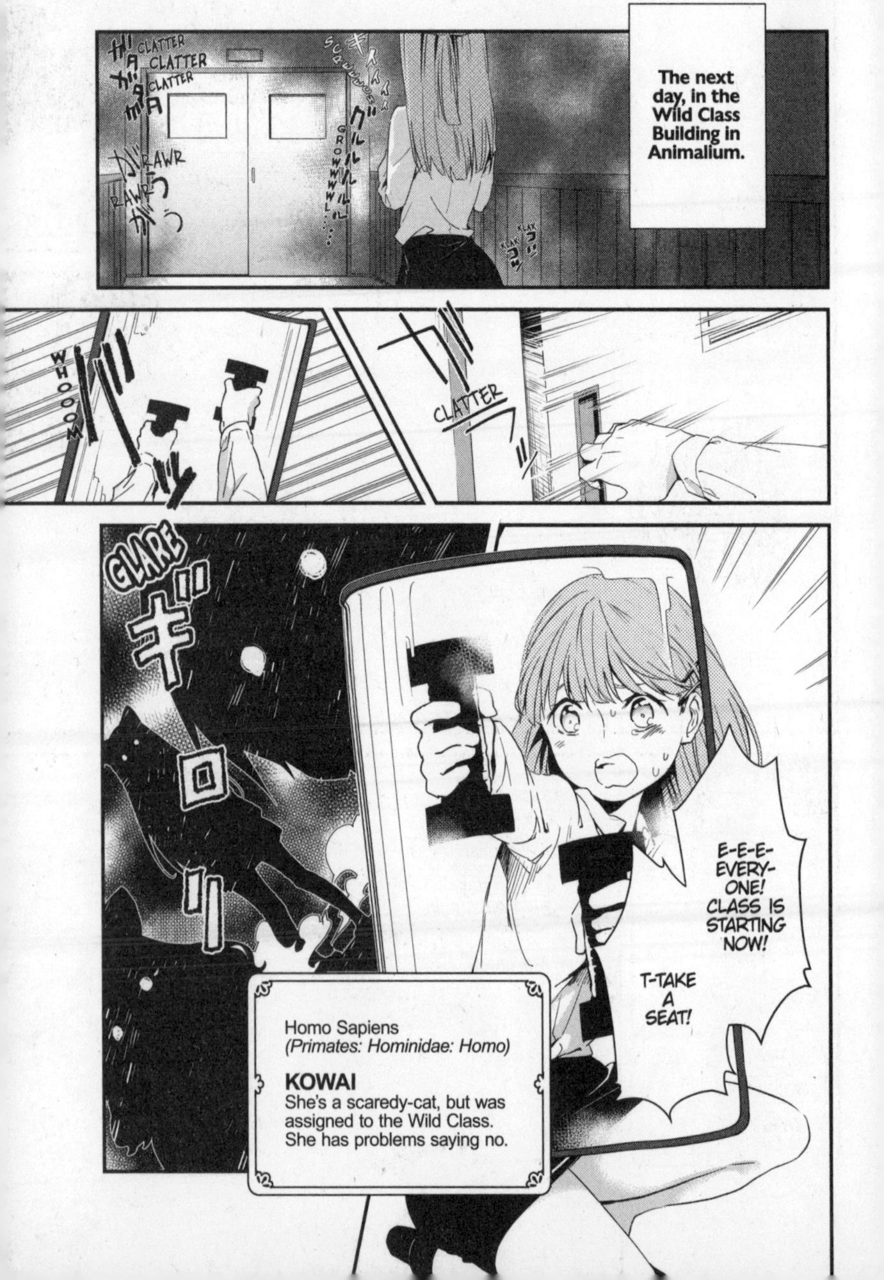

The next day, in the Wild Class Building in Animalium.
KLAK KLAK
GROWWWWL...
SCREEEECH
CLATTER CLATTER CLATTER
RAWR RAWR
CLATTER
WHOOOOM
GLARE
E-E-E-EVERY-ONE! CLASS IS STARTING NOW!
T-TAKE A SEAT!
Homo Sapiens
(Primates: Hominidae: Homo)
KOWAI
She's a scaredy-cat, but was assigned to the Wild Class. She has problems saying no.

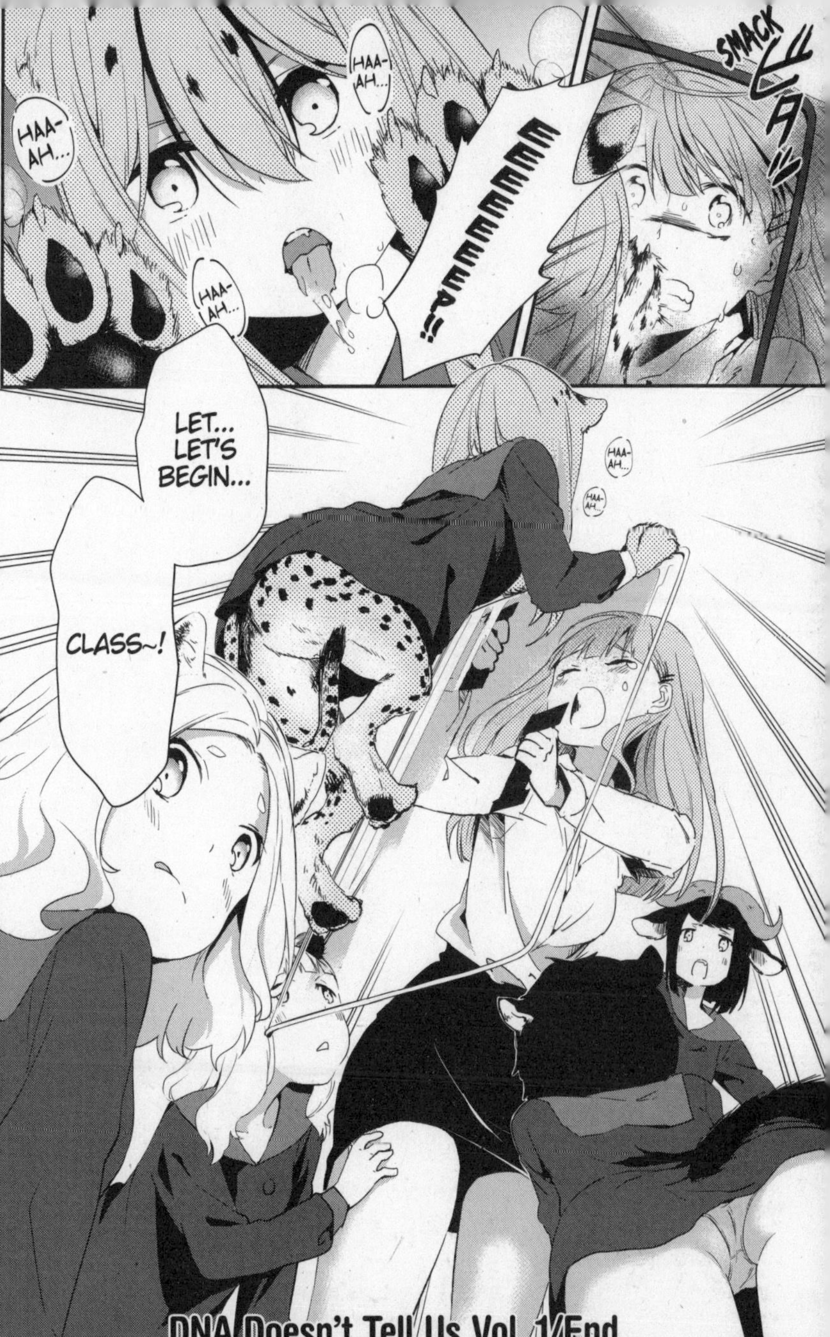

SMACK
ビタッ
EEEEEEEEEEEP!!
HAA-AH...
HAA-AH...
HAA-AH...
HAA-AH...
HAA-AH...
LET... LET'S BEGIN...
CLASS~!

DNA Doesn't Tell Us Vol. 1/End

DNA Doesn't Tell Us

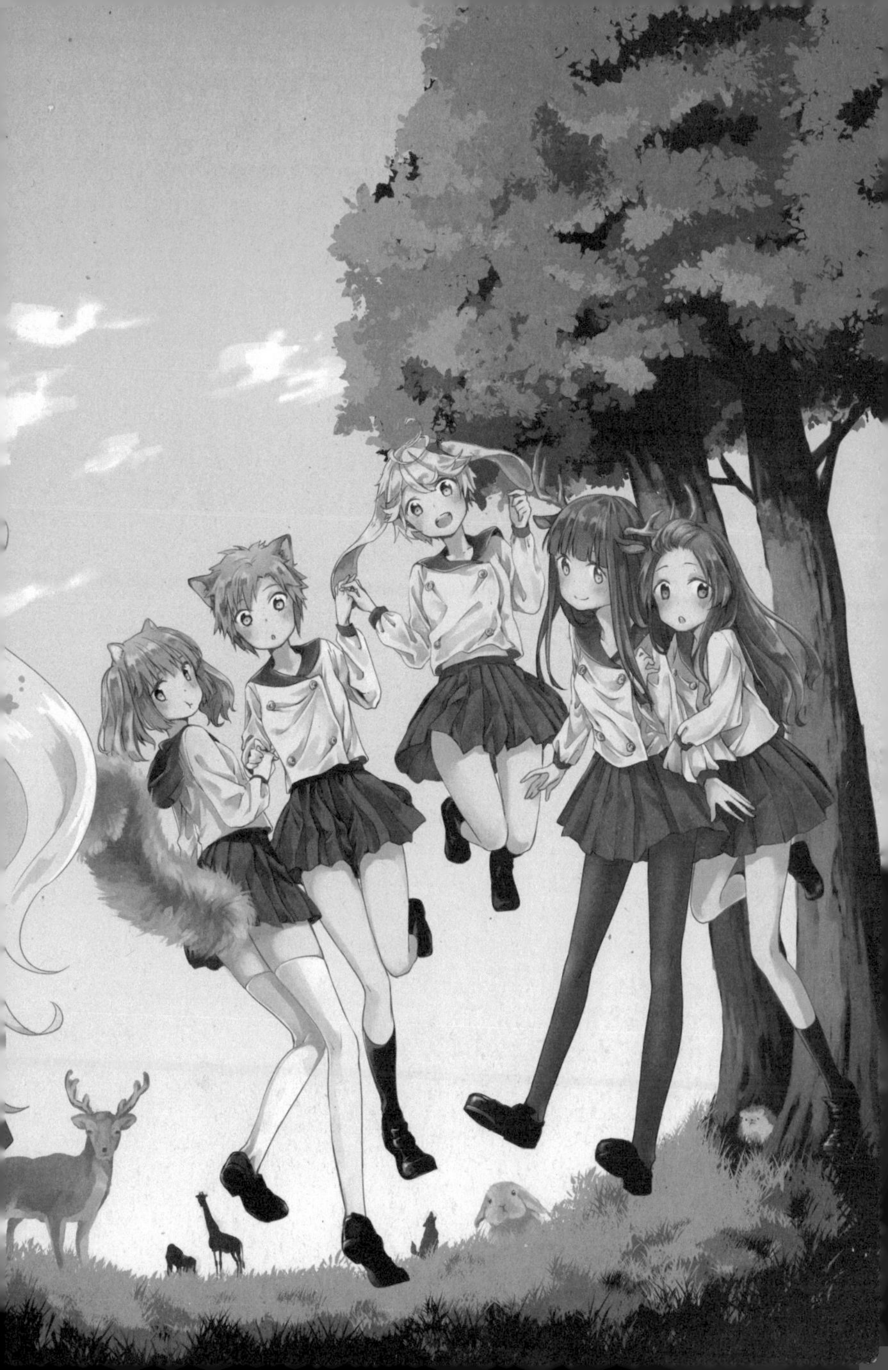

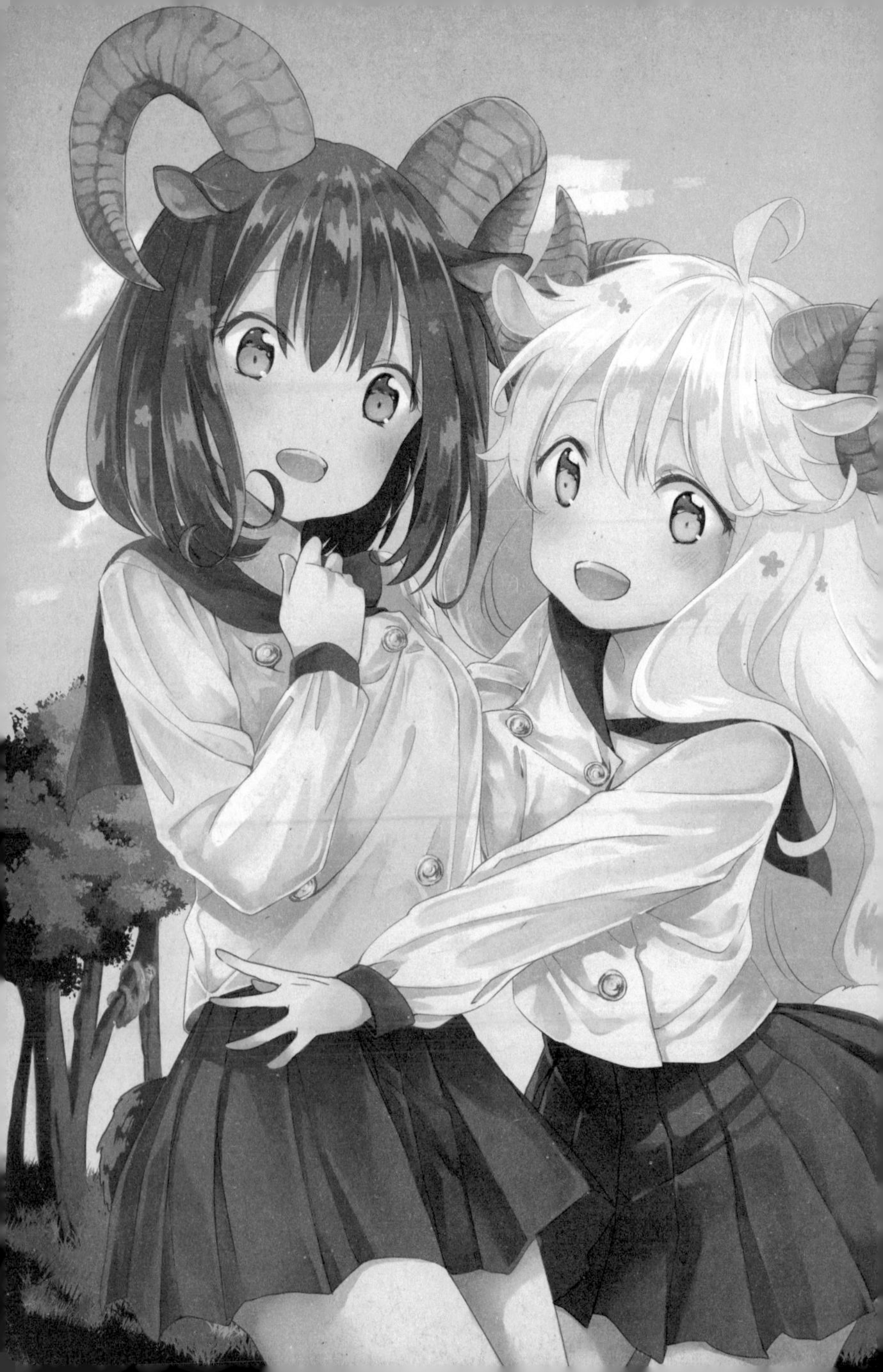

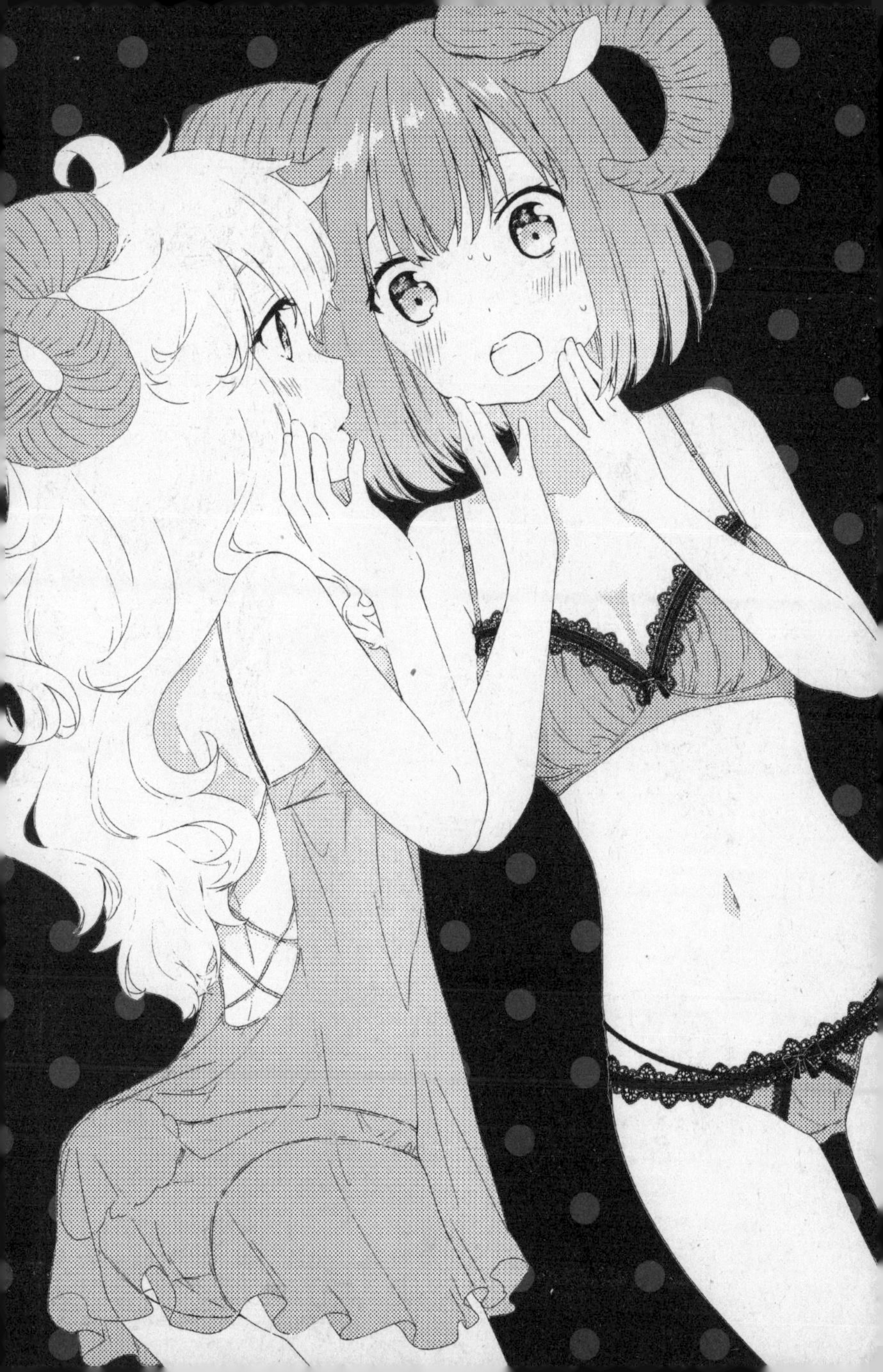